The
Second
Mark

COURAGE, CORRUPTION, AND THE
BATTLE FOR OLYMPIC GOLD

∞

JOY GOODWIN

SIMON & SCHUSTER
New York   London   Toronto   Sydney

SIMON & SCHUSTER
Rockefeller Center
1230 Avenue of the Americas
New York, NY 10020

SIMON & SCHUSTER and colophon are registered trademarks
of Simon & Schuster, Inc.

For information regarding special discounts for bulk purchases,
please contact Simon & Schuster Special Sales at
1-800-456-6798 or business@simonandschuster.com

Designed by Helene Berinsky

Manufactured in the United States of America

1   3   5   7   9   10   8   6   4   2

Library of Congress Cataloging-in-Publication data is available

ISBN 0-7432-4527-X

To Jim and B.

CONTENTS

NOTE ON NAMES, PLACES,
AND PRONUNCIATION

In China, what Americans call the "last name" is actually pronounced first. So the family name (Shen, Zhao, Yao) precedes the given name (Xue, Hongbo, Bin). Yao Bin's surname is Yao; he would therefore be called Mr. Yao or Teacher Yao in formal address.

Xue is pronounced *shoo-way,* but when pronounced quickly it blurs into a one-syllable word. Jie is pronounced *jee-ay,* also blurred into one syllable. Zhao is pronounced like "jowl" without the "l;" Yao is "yowl" without the "l."

Chinese women do not take their husbands' last names; thus Jing Yulan (Ms. Jing) is the mother of Zhao Hongbo, and Lu Manli (Ms. Lu) is the mother of Shen Xue.

Shen Xue is often called "Xiao Xue" (pronounced *shao shoo-way*) by those who know her best. The endearment translates imperfectly as Little Xue, but its true meaning is somewhere between "young," "little," and a simple diminutive.

In Russia husbands, wives, and children typically share a last name, but while the woman's surname has a feminine ending (Tamara Moskvina, Nina Ruchkina), the man's surname has a masculine ending (Igor Moskvin, Sasha Ruchkin). Though Russians often address each other using the patronymic, I have omitted this detail from the book for simplification.

Most Russian first names have a diminutive form, which is used by friends and family: Yelena becomes Lena, Alexander becomes Sasha, and so forth.

Berezhnaya is pronounced *bair-ezh-NIGH-ah*. Sikharulidze is pronounced *seek-har-u-LEED-zah*. Shlyakhov is pronounced *shlee-AH-hoff*.

In Quebec, many women do not take their husband's last name after marriage, so Murielle Bouchard (*moo-ree-ELL boo-SHAR*) is the wife of Jacques Pelletier and the mother of the Pelletier boys.

Pelletier is pronounced *pell-tee-AY*, and Salé is pronounced *sal-AY*, with emphasis on the last syllable. Gauthier is pronounced *go-tee-AY*. Benoît Lavoie is pronounced *ben-WAH la-VWAH*. Paquet is pronounced *pa-KETT*. Sayabec is pronounced *say-BEC*.

Marie-Reine Le Gougne is pronounced *MAH-ree REN le-GOON-ya*. Didier Gailhaguet is pronounced *di-di-AY guy-a-GAY*. Ottavio Cinquanta is pronounced *oh-TAH-vee-o cheen-QUAN-ta*.

St. Petersburg was renamed Leningrad during the Soviet era. It became St. Petersburg again shortly after the collapse of the Soviet Union.

When practical, I have converted figures into American currency, weights, and measures.

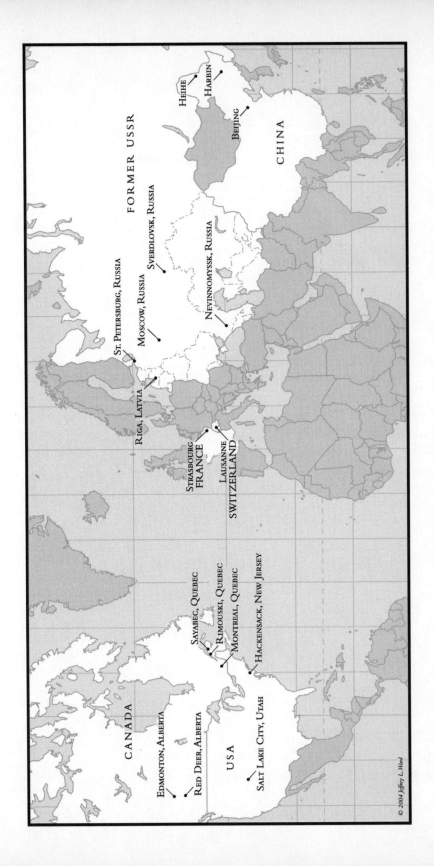

FORMER USSR

HEIHE

HARBIN

BEIJING

CHINA

ST. PETERSBURG, RUSSIA

MOSCOW, RUSSIA

SVERDLOVSK, RUSSIA

NEVINNOMYSSK, RUSSIA

RIGA, LATVIA

STRASBOURG FRANCE

LAUSANNE SWITZERLAND

SAYABEC, QUEBEC

RIMOUSKI, QUEBEC

MONTREAL, QUEBEC

HACKENSACK, NEW JERSEY

CANADA

EDMONTON, ALBERTA

RED DEER, ALBERTA

USA

SALT LAKE CITY, UTAH

© 2004 Jeffrey L. Ward

Prologue

∞

Salt Lake Ice Center
February 11, 2002
8:34 P.M.

*Y*ELENA BEREZHNAYA places one white skate on the ice, bears down on the narrow blade, and surges forward. Before her the freshly made ice stretches out for two hundred feet. The ice is white, very white, bright as snow under a strong sun, but surprisingly there is no glare. From high at the top of the arena, light filters down in a way that warms the long white expanse and suffuses it with a soft glow. Berezhnaya pushes away from the barrier for the six-minute warm-up, and for a few strange seconds she sees no one ahead of her or beside her and experiences the peculiar sensation of skating alone at the Olympics. Then the other skaters come into view. Here are the Chinese pair and the Canadian couple, and here is her partner, Anton Sikharulidze. With two gliding steps she merges seamlessly into the fast-moving queue of skaters circling the perimeter of the rink.

From high up in the stands, the brightly costumed skaters circling below look like a school of tropical fish. The arena itself resembles a giant fishbowl. A four-foot barrier encloses the rink. Normally, the first row of spectators would sit just a few feet behind the rink barrier. But in this rink there is a solid wall rising thirty feet above the ice on three sides. This retaining wall has been painted in soothing marine blues and greens, and for the skater down on the ice the sensation is one of being inside a deep bowl whose sides rise up well above your head. Somewhere in the vast space above you, seventeen thousand people are murmuring, fidgeting. Their sounds of anticipation drift down in one large overhead mass of nervous energy. Up in the stands, packed in shoulder-to-shoulder among the Chevrolet dealers and Coca-Cola executives, are more than twenty of the sport's former champions. They are here primarily because the skaters now on the ice represent the greatest collection of talent ever assembled on a single night in pair skating. The Chinese, the Canadians, and the Russians are generally considered to be three of the six best pairs in the sport's hundred-year history, and that is why, for the past three years, experts have been predicting that this Olympic final will be the greatest pairs competition ever. Every past champion, every great coach wanted to be in the building for this one.

For the moment, however, the world's best pair skaters are pretty much skating forwards and backwards. Within the sport this activity is known as "basic stroking." It is the purest form of skating, and it is the only part of Yelena Berezhnaya's extensive repertoire that she shares with the aristocratic skating enthusiasts who first contested the World Championship on a frozen pond in St. Petersburg in 1896. The simplest movements of skating can be the most difficult to perfect, and few ever achieve absolute mastery over the pure glide. Berezhnaya and Sikharulidze are better at basic stroking than anyone in the world and as good as anyone, ever. Their technique is so singularly exquisite that a few of the former champions up in the stands tonight are looking forward to the first minute of Berezhnaya and Sikharulidze's warm-up more than any other part of the competition. These same past champions will tell you that while they achieved great things in their careers, their one lingering regret is that they could never move over the ice in the way that Berezhnaya and Sikharulidze are moving now.

Berezhnaya comes flying around a corner, generating a sharp gust of wind. She is wearing a striking short dress of dark pink. Berezhnaya is wearing less clothing to compete in the Olympics than most people sleep in, but she's used to it. Her skirt is lightweight, specially designed to flutter in the breeze created by her speed, thus reminding the judges how fast she is. Berezhnaya's face shows no emotion. She is shy, and no matter what dramatic motions she may make with her body, her expression while skating is always slightly distracted. It is a curious sight to see, as if some cord had become disconnected between her body and her face.

Berezhnaya carries herself proudly, with the impeccable posture of a prima ballerina. One can almost make out an invisible line running up her spine, which is always pulled taut. Yet her movement is remarkably easy. While keeping the axis of her body perfectly straight, she sways gently to and fro with each stride, in the way that a tent pinned firmly to earth sways softly in a breeze. She holds her arms like wings, raising them slightly with each stroke of the blade, and she is light, light on her feet. Since Berezhnaya is only carrying around ninety-six pounds, which are distributed through her slim five-foot-one-inch frame in the form of pure muscle, it might seem easy enough for her to be light on her feet, but actually size has nothing to do with it. This point is proven when her partner, Anton Sikharulidze, a six-footer weighing a hundred and seventy pounds, passes her with the same perfect, quiet strokes. Their secret is that they have found the elusive sweet spot of the quarter-inch blade and are pressing it into the ice with every step to generate almost pure speed and almost no resistance. They can cover the length of the ice with half a dozen such perfect strides. The result is that relative to anyone else, they appear to waste very little time just skating around. Their two rivals, the Chinese and the Canadians, can't match the Russians' virtuoso stroking, and though the Chinese are undeniably fast, at times their blades make a telltale scratching sound as they score the ice. To the judge's trained ear, that scraping sound is about as welcome as the sound of a phonograph needle being yanked across a record.

If the Olympic pairs championship were decided on skating forwards and backwards, the Russians would have it in the bag. But twenty minutes hence they will have to make their way through a four-and-a-half-minute program, navigating a minefield of high-risk tricks, any one of which could easily cause a slip. The Russians have never made it through this program in competition without making a mistake, but they will need to tonight. In a competition of this caliber the victory will belong to the team that goes for all the dangerous tricks and hits them all. The program that Berezhnaya and Sikharulidze will attempt tonight would definitely be the most difficult ever attempted in Olympic history, if it weren't for the fact that the Chinese may try an even more difficult program a few minutes later.

All this makes Tamara Moskvina a very nervous woman. Moskvina has coached Berezhnaya and Sikharulidze from the very beginning of their partnership, but she has never been as nervous for them as she is right now. For that matter she has never been this nervous at any competition in her thirty-year coaching career. At this moment Moskvina is standing right up against the rink boards. She is exceedingly tiny, almost elfin, and she has to stand that close because otherwise she can't see over the four-foot-high barrier. Born in Leningrad a few months before the siege in 1941, Moskvina suffered from wartime hardships like everyone else, and she attributes her short stature to a childhood diet of one hundred grams of bread a day. But Moskvina was never one to dwell on misfortunes, and when she took up pair skating, she found a way to turn her height to her advantage. In Moskvina's youth the so-called one-and-a-half situation, in which a tall man is paired with a much shorter woman, was just a glimmer on the horizon of pair skating, and she formed the female half of one of the earliest such Soviet experimental pairs. (In every one of the twenty pairs competing at this Olympics, the woman is almost a foot shorter than her male partner.) Moskvina was not the most naturally talented pair skater of her generation, but she made up for it in drive. She picked up a national title and a European medal on her way to the 1968 Olympics, where she finished a respectable fifth. Then she stopped competing and took on a few skating pupils. And within twenty years Moskvina became probably the greatest pairs coach the sport has ever seen.

Moskvina now fixes her skaters with a piercing gaze. For most of the hundreds of hours each year that she coaches Berezhnaya and Sikharulidze, she is out on the ice on skates, chasing after them, shouting at them to go faster, grabbing hold of an arm or leg and lifting it into place. She is surprisingly spry for a sixty-year-old, and often insists on cutting in to demonstrate a move. Six days a week, three hours a day, her instruments are her body and her voice. But in these last, most nervous moments just before a competition, she believes in using her eyes. "I look at them in their eyes," she says. "I hypnotize. I persuade. I guide them to feel how great they are. I do all my tricks." The main problem at such moments is to calm her skaters down without losing the power of that nervous energy, to harness their adrenaline and let it work for them (anticipation) instead of against them (fear).

In this department, no one in history has more experience than Moskvina. This is the sixth consecutive Olympics at which she has stood beside the rink boards and coached at least one of the top four pairs who comprise the final warm-up group. Over a span of two decades—in Sarajevo, Calgary, Albertville, Lillehammer, Nagano—she has stood almost precisely where she is standing right now, fixing her penetrating gaze on a gold medal contender. Her tricks seem to work. In every case, within the hour, her pair has finished with a brilliant performance and either the gold or silver medal. On two occasions, Moskvina's teams actually won both the gold and silver medals at a single Olympics, a feat that left precisely one bronze medal for the rest of the coaches in the world to fight over. In all, her teams have won three gold and four silver Olympic medals since 1984. If Moskvina's little skating empire constituted a country, it would rank third among nations on the all-time medal count list in Olympic pair skating.

For all her experience, this moment is pressing in on Tamara Moskvina. She is forcing back the overwhelming sensation that though the competition must happen right here, right now, her team is not ready. For the first time in forty years, the top Russian pair is not coming into the Olympics as the gold medal favorite. Berezhnaya and Sikharulidze have not won the World title since 1999. More to the point, they have lost to the Canadians in their past three meetings, including their most recent showdown six weeks ago in Toronto.

All this would be alarming enough, but Moskvina is also struggling to rein in a pair that has always been temperamental and unreliable. In their entire career, Berezhnaya and Sikharulidze have never skated what is called "a clean competition," two programs with no mistakes. They invariably make one or more conspicuous mistakes in either the short or the long program. They are prone to odd mishaps, the kinds of things that don't seem to happen to other couples—they tear a costume in the warm-up, miss their bus, forget the ID badges they need to enter the arena. Earlier this week, Berezhnaya stayed too long in a tanning bed and "came home as red as a pig," in the words of Moskvina, who decidedly was not happy. Pair skating relies on touch, and the sunburn was so painful to the touch that the team could not practice for an entire day. It was a beginner's mistake, a mistake that is almost inconceivable for someone at this level of experience, and yet it was typical of this pair. They are brilliant skaters, but they are inconsistent, and they are unlucky. Moskvina feels it in her bones: They are vulnerable. They could lose.

A loss would be devastating to Moskvina, who has spent her life maintaining the grand tradition of Russian pair skating. A Soviet or Russian team has won the Olympic pairs championship at every Games since 1964, when the legendary Protopopovs first captured the title. Since then, one Russian pair or another has always come through, for ten consecutive Olympics, or Moskvina's entire adult life. Through communism, the fall of communism, the hand-to-mouth transitional years, and the brave new capitalism, Russian pair skating has never wavered. Incredibly, the Russian pairs record is the longest unbroken streak in Olympic history in any sport, summer or winter.

But for the better part of a year now, insiders have been predicting that the dynasty will end tonight. There is a certain bitter irony in the prospect, since for tonight's performance Moskvina has lifted a signature piece from the Protopopovs' repertoire, Massenet's "Meditation" from *Thaïs*. The idea was that the lyrical, elegant music would remind everyone of the unsurpassed beauty of the grand Russian school, and that Berezhnaya and Sikharulidze would join the Protopopovs in history as the latest of the Russian gold medalists. Now it is possible that her team will be reminding everyone of the Protopopovs at the precise moment that they are ending the streak that the Protopopovs began in 1964. Moskvina has done more than any other single person to continue the Russian legacy, but by the end of the night she may find herself at the helm of Russian pair skating at the very moment when the streak comes to an end.

A few feet to Moskvina's left, the Chinese coach, Yao Bin, watches his skaters speed down the ice side by side, a few feet apart. Their motions are perfectly synchronized. As they approach the end of the rink, the two skaters turn, dig a sharp toe pick deep into the ice, and launch themselves into the air. For a second they are flying, a blur of spinning arms and legs. Then they plummet to earth, each landing on the right foot at precisely the same instant. A roar of approval comes from somewhere above their heads.

Yao claps briefly, without noticing that he is doing it. He is completely focused on his strategy. He believes that if his team can land the first throw quadruple jump in history, the judges will be compelled to place them first. Yao has an absolutely ferocious competitive streak that he is constantly honing, like a man who draws a knife back and forth, back and forth through a sharpener. Asked to describe her coach, Shen Xue says only one thing: "Mr. Yao likes to win. He really, really likes to win." Yao believes that Shen and her partner, Zhao Hongbo, can win this title outright, and he does not care that most people feel that he should be happy just to be here coaching a gold medal contender when less than twenty years ago, Chinese pair skating was an international joke.

Yao's path crossed Moskvina's at the 1984 Olympic Games in Sarajevo. Moskvina was there as coach of the eventual gold medalists. Yao and his partner, the first pair skaters ever to represent China, were there to compete. Yao's pair finished dead last, and there was a great yawning gap between them and the team that finished next to last. They were the skating equivalent of the outclassed swimmer who goes through his last two laps alone after the rest of the field has finished. In Sarajevo, the Chinese mainly distinguished themselves by committing amateurish mistakes that had never before been seen in Olympic skating. One Chinese skater competed while wearing a wristwatch. At one of the practices, when a Chinese skater leapt into a flying camel spin, loose coins came flying out of his pockets, astonishing everyone in the rink. The other skaters had to interrupt their Olympic practice to help him pick up his change.

Pair skating was virtually unknown in China in the seventies, when Yao Bin was growing up in the frigid northern city of Harbin, close to the Siberian border. In winter, temperatures often dipped to thirty or forty below zero, and with a little ingenuity the people of Harbin developed a system of flooding the soccer fields in winter to form makeshift skating ponds. In Yao's youth skating in China meant skating outdoors on dull blades in subzero temperatures, and Yao must have really liked to skate. At that time, Chinese Central Television, the main government network, did not broadcast skating, so Yao and a few of his fellow enthusiasts once took the train to the northern border, where they pulled in the Soviet television signal and watched the World Championships. After years of extreme isolation, Sarajevo was a watershed event in Yao's life. For the first time he glimpsed the beauty and magnificence that were possible in his sport. After Sarajevo Yao understood that a difficult movement could be done with infinite ease, so that it floated on the emotion of the music. While he was there he committed thousands of small details to memory. To this day Yao recalls the things he saw in Sarajevo in perfect detail, and with obvious delight: "The unison of the Russians. And the Americans had the high lateral twist lift—amazing! Amazing! And quadruple throw—they did throw quadruple Salchow on practice!"

It is a mark of how far Yao has brought Chinese pair skating that tonight, eighteen years later, his own team is the only team in the world that will even attempt the throw quadruple Salchow. This fearsome jump, the one that impressed him so forcefully in the Olympic practice sessions in 1984, has yet to be landed in competition, and most skaters will not go near it. The risk factor is too high, and the danger too distracting: If you miss the quad, it disrupts the rest of the program, and if you hit it, it disrupts the rest of the program. That Yao was able to teach the most difficult move in skating to a Chinese pair is a miracle almost too large to comprehend. But Yao is no ordinary man.

Everything that has happened or will happen in Chinese pair skating has passed through Yao Bin's grasp; he is the first and last word on the subject. Yao was himself the first—and for a time, the only—male pair skater in China. In the eighteen years since his Olympic debacle, Yao has tended the small fire of his own individual passion, growing his pair skating program little by little, precisely as fast as China's political environment and scant resources would allow. As China slowly opened up in certain ways, remaining shut tight in others, Yao walked the razor's edge, taking care to be on the leading edge of progress but not to leap ahead of the Party. In a nation of 1.3 billion in which few were allowed to pursue individual dreams, Yao persisted. In the 1980s came the first indoor rinks, and by 1996 the Chinese Sport Association had founded a national skating academy in Beijing, subsidized by the government. Yao personally searched the handful of indoor rinks in China, looking for children with extraordinary potential. When he found them, he installed them in a cramped dorm in Beijing, where they lived and breathed skating, eleven months a year.

For Yao's generation, the generation growing up during the hysteria of the Cultural Revolution, the opportunity to study outside of China didn't arrive until the 1990s. As there was literally no preexisting tradition of pair skating in China and he was forbidden to study abroad, Yao realized early on that he would have to teach himself everything. He would have to figure out how to perform and coach the skills of pair skating on his own, from the fundamentals up through the highest-level skills. He did it through hawk-eyed observation at every competition he ever attended, storing all those images in the vaults of his photographic memory and replaying them later. Shen and Zhao were Yao's sixth pair, and by the time he got to them, he had taught himself enough to create a pair that could one day win the World Championship.

Now Yao and his team are taking on Russia and Canada, the two most powerful countries in pair skating. Skating is a national obsession in Canada, where every youngster learns how to skate. Canada, a country with the population of the state of California, has an astonishing three thousand skating rinks. In contrast, since the collapse of the Soviet Union's sports system, the number of rinks still operating in Russia has dropped to about ninety—while at the present time in all of China there are eleven indoor rinks serving a billion people. Yao Bin knows he is fighting incredible odds. He remains the only pairs coach in China, and his four teams are the only four elite pairs in the entire country. So when the Chinese figure skating federation was awarded three Olympic slots, Yao just looked around his rink and tapped three of his four teams to come to Salt Lake City. Already tonight, two of his teams have skated. Remarkably, both of these teams—plus Shen and Zhao, who are yet to skate—will finish in the top ten. But Mr. Yao really, really likes to win, and he is not interested in the top ten. He is gunning for first place.

Shen and Zhao pass by the spot where Yao now stands, rehearsing a sequence of dance steps. For the past two years they have been racing to develop a more Western style of skating in time for this Olympics, and in this sequence, Yao sees the difference. This year, they look into each other's eyes the way the North Americans do; they create emotion through their facial expressions and certain dramatic dance movements. Now the balletic choreography flows through them; it is no longer a layer superimposed on their skating. Now, when they move their arms, one is aware of the fact that they also have wrists, hands, and fingers.

The Chinese skating federation made the surprising decision to hire Western choreographers three years ago, after several instances in which Shen and Zhao lost big competitions because they were said to be lacking in "artistry." The truth was that they had their own artistry, but it was conceived in a traditional Chinese style. They performed to Chinese compositions *(Yellow River Piano Concerto)*, drawing on traditional Chinese opera and Chinese ethnic dance for inspiration. Suffice to say *Yellow River Piano Concerto* looked nothing like *Swan Lake*. The judges, who tend to adore *Swan Lake* regardless of their nationalities, made it abundantly clear that this Chinese style was not going to count as good artistry. And because judges from non-Asian countries absolutely dominate the sport, both in terms of sheer numbers and historical precedent, no one was powerful enough to persuade them otherwise. The Chinese were faced with a stark choice: Copy the West, or go on losing.

This ultimatum generated a minor crisis for a sport federation in China, where a generation ago, any affiliation with bourgeois Western art could land you in trouble. Times have changed, but on the part of the Chinese sport federation there is still a distinct desire to bring Chinese culture to the West rather than bringing more of the West to China. So the skating federation decided to hire Western choreographers for Shen and Zhao, but with the stipulation that the program should have "Chinese characteristics." Thus Shen and Zhao will skate to Puccini's *Turandot* tonight, an Italian opera set in Beijing's Forbidden City. (The Chinese skating federation takes this seriously. Earlier this week, another Chinese pair had to make a last-minute substitution after the federation yanked their intended music—*Seven Years in Tibet*.)

Shen and Zhao's new Western style has given them the possibility of winning. There are two marks to be given tonight: the first for technical merit and the second for artistic presentation. Since Shen and Zhao's Western transformation the judges can no longer use the artistic merit mark to drop the Chinese far below their rivals. But the judges still don't consider the Chinese to be "artistic enough" to beat either the Canadians or the Russians on the second mark, if everyone skates well. To win, the Chinese have to beat their rivals on the first, technical mark. To do that, they have to land the quad.

The quad is so spectacular, so risky, so gutsy that if they can land it, as the last skaters of the evening, the judges cannot deny them the gold. At least, this is Yao's hypothesis. All along, he has felt that he cannot overcome the Western bias of the judges without some kind of miracle, and so he has prepared the miracle of the quad. Thus far in the Olympic practices, they have landed six of them—high, beautiful, unbelievably easy ones. When her partner throws her high into the air for the quad, it's as if Shen has been shot upwards from a trampoline. From the spot on the ice where she takes off to the spot where she lands, she covers *twenty-two feet*. Skaters often "cheat" quadruple jumps, eking out the last revolution as they are landing, but Shen turns so extraordinarily quickly that she finishes the four revolutions still above the ice, with plenty of time to drop down on one foot for a pure landing. For skaters in the building, the sight of Shen landing a quad provokes an involuntary gasp—then a wide smile. Somehow Shen and Zhao's accomplishment seems like a triumph for all skaters everywhere—they have conquered the most difficult move in pair skating, absolutely conquered it.

Trying a new element in pair skating for the first time is both dangerous and intimidating. Belief is key. Yao Bin had believed in the quad early on and because of him, Shen and Zhao had believed in it. Yao had never taught anyone a throw quad Salchow before. But this was true of practically every move he had ever taught them, and at least with the quad, the other coaches in the world had nothing on him. As far as he was aware, only two coaches in the history of pair skating had ever produced a team that could land a quad in practice. Yao was determined to be the third, and he found a strong ally in Shen Xue. Even as a child, Shen Xue was preternaturally tough. Once, when she was six years old, she got new skating boots, and during the first day of practice, the new boots cut her feet badly. But Shen Xue said nothing. It was only when she took off the boots after practice that her parents discovered that her socks were caked with frozen blood.

Years later, this deep-seated toughness was indispensable to her in learning the quad. Shen stands only five foot two and weighs just a hundred pounds. Because of her size she can get amazing height on a throw, but when she falls, there is little meat on her bones to break her fall. When

Shen began to learn the quad, it was understood that she would fall many, many times. She would fall because she couldn't yet complete four revolutions in the air; she would fall because she would come out of the last turn "blind" and not find her footing; she would fall because her partner would throw her with too much or too little force. So every day, Shen bundled up in heavy hip, shoulder, and shin pads and fastened her helmet. "She looked like a spaceman," Zhao says. Forty-three times, Zhao threw her into the air and grimaced as she crashed to the ice. On the forty-fourth try, she landed one.

Six months later, the question of the moment is whether to attempt the quad tonight. The Chinese will skate last. If the Canadians and Russians make at least one mistake each, the Chinese could possibly win the Olympics without the quad. The question has both psychological and physical considerations, and Yao weighed it carefully in the bus on the way to the arena tonight. Then he spoke to the two kids. "I told them that many judges tried to dissuade me from trying this quadruple," Yao says. "The judges said to me, 'Look, if you fall, the whole performance will be damaged by it.' But the kids said to me, 'We've been preparing so long to do this quad. We have paid so much for this move; we've taken so many falls. If we don't do it at the Olympic Games, all that we have paid will go to waste, and maybe we will never have the chance to try it again.' "

That was what Yao wanted to hear, so he told them, "Good. We'll do it. But make two preparations: one is to do the quad, the other is to substitute a triple. The final decision will be based on how you look during the warm-up."

Now Yao is watching the warm-up in a state of agitation. This is a face he rarely wears in public. In practice, he tends to lean against the boards, playing the part of the nonchalant older friend who has just dropped by to give his young friends a little advice. But tonight he is all business. He has always urged Shen and Zhao to try many of their hard elements during the warm-up. He likes them to feel the actual physical sensation of landing everything they will try in their program. It gives confidence, and then they will approach their entire program with a kind of fearless attack. It is in this mood, Yao knows, that any skater skates his best. However, you cannot warm up a quad. You cannot afford the risk. For the past month or so, at home in Beijing, they have been hitting the quad about forty percent of the time—and some of the misses are hard, bruising falls, not what you want just before the most important competition of your life. So they will try only a throw triple Salchow in the warm-up, and if it goes well, they will try the quad in the competition. Yao watches as they tick off the other elements, each one perfect. But he waits—and they wait—for the moment of truth: the throw triple Salchow.

Zhao Hongbo brushes past David Pelletier, and for a moment they look like two forties movie stars passing on a Hollywood back lot. Zhao is wearing a tasseled black prince's costume pulled from the racks of the Metropolitan Opera. Pelletier is wearing a dark gray sweater vest over a lighter gray oxford shirt, and what appears to be a pair of Dockers. To the vast number of people seeing Pelletier for the first time tonight, he will come across as some kind of preppie, but nothing could be farther from the truth. Pelletier, a hockey fanatic, only got into pair skating because he thought it looked like fun to throw girls across the ice. Growing up in rural Quebec, the three Pelletier boys were a rough-and-tumble lot. His two brothers are now in the Canadian army, and if things had gone another way, David Pelletier might well have followed suit. Instead he is circling the Olympic oval dressed as the preppie hero of the American movie *Love Story,* while one of his brothers, who is stationed in Bosnia, watches via a live satellite hookup.

Pelletier glides over to his partner, a girl with a shiny brown ponytail named Jamie Salé, and takes her hand. Something about the gesture suggests a relationship, and it is true that they have their own love story off the ice. They have a charisma that you cannot teach, and when they perform, the spark between them reaches the people in the last row. Their choreographer, Lori Nichol, decided to use this obvious romantic current in her choreography for the *Love Story* program, and the consensus is that she has done so to tremendous effect. Since its debut in the fall of 1999, *Love Story* has received rave reviews. Part of its appeal is its simplicity. As you watch it, it's very easy to see that it is about two college kids flirting, having a snowball fight, falling in love, and suffering a tragedy thereafter. In a common conceit of figure skating routines, Jamie Salé's character (the one played by Ali MacGraw in the movie) develops terminal cancer while executing a throw triple loop, a spiral sequence, and a spinning lift that covers the length of the ice. It is a testament to Nichol's unerring sense of the form in which she works that somehow this does not come off as laughable. The program is far more moving than it has any right to be. It evokes genuine emotion, in the way that a really good Broadway show can be both sentimental and affecting at the same time.

The program is so effective, in fact, that recently Nichol and her pupils decided to scrap their planned Olympic year program and bring back the old *Love Story*. Many inside the Canadians' camp warned that the judges might frown on revisiting a two-year-old program. Their marks could suffer. Nichol also worries about this. So in Salt Lake City she has been getting the word out that such objections are not codified in the rulebook and should play no part in the judging. "Should *The Nutcracker* have only one Christmas?" Nichol asks, as a reporter scribbles away.

Salé and Pelletier are now performing a section of their choreography, performing from the tips of their fingers to the precise expression in their eyes. The music is so ingrained in them that they hear it even when it is not playing, and the effect is a strange one for the people in the stands, to whom the couple appears to be skating to music that the crowd cannot hear. The Canadians are too deep in their own world to notice their coach, Jan Ullmark, as they pass him. Ullmark marvels at their appearance: They look absolutely perfectly trained. No one would ever guess that ten days ago, Salé was lying in bed with the flu, and Pelletier was so freaked out by the pressure that he flat-out refused to come to the Olympics. Now, as they rehearse their routine, it takes a coach's trained eye to zero in on the telltale signs: Salé is even thinner than usual; Pelletier, still nervous, is just the slightest bit up on the toes of his blades. That's what Ullmark sees; everyone else in the arena is under the spell of that incredible charisma. More than anyone else in pair skating now, the Canadians have the actor's capacity for being in character. But while connecting with the audience is the bread and butter of pro skating tours, it does not necessarily move the Olympic judges.

For decades, the so-called North American school has been criticized by European judges for being too show biz, too flashy, too pop. In response, countless North American pairs have tried valiantly to beat the Russians at their own game. They put on elaborate ballet choreography, but it did not suit them, and they struggled under its weight. Nichol's stroke of genius was to go straight into the lion's den, to push the North American style to its limit and, in the process, to reinvent the Canadians' cheesy pop style as popular art. She taught Salé and Pelletier to treat *Love Story* with the same sincere respect that they might treat *Tristan und Isolde*. The result is a piece of great popular entertainment that is hard to resist, even for the most dismissive critic.

Entertaining audiences is what Salé and Pelletier do best; their weakest suit is the dreaded side-by-side triple jumps. The problem is on Salé's side. She can do the jump in her sleep, but she has what she calls "a mental hang-up" about it, and she has a tendency to back off the jump and perform only a double. They lost the 2000 World title because of this weakness, and the next year, when they finally won their World Championship, their one mistake came when Salé watered down a jump. Now they are barreling down the ice, setting up for side-by-side triples at the far end of the rink. Jan Ullmark is glued to the scene. If Salé lands this one, the confidence will be coursing through her veins for the rest of the night. In a split second they are up in the air, whirling, and then abruptly they are back on the ice. To Ullmark's experienced eye, there was something slightly amiss in the blur of limbs, something not quite matched. Pelletier has done a triple jump, and Salé only a double. She skates away from the scene of the crime, looking scared.

It is Ullmark's job now to calm her and cut her off before she starts obsessing over the jump. In the past, Salé has been known to narrow her vision so that the only thing that exists in the entire world is the jump she has just missed. Ullmark knows this well, because he coached Salé as a teenager, and he has watched her go through these motions at dozens of championships, from the regional juniors in a grungy rink in some Canadian backwater to the hallowed ice of the Olympic Games. Now she skates by his place at the boards and looks over at him with wide, unblinking eyes. "You'll do it when the music's on," Ullmark says with a shrug. "You always do it with the music." She nods, and her shoulders relax almost imperceptibly; she looks up at her partner and summons a smile: No problem. She'll do it with the music. And Ullmark can actually see it: She's decided to be confident.

Thirty feet above the skaters' heads, in the front row of the audience, Barbara Wagner and Bob Paul both tensed at the moment that Salé doubled her jump. They know how badly Salé needs that triple, but even more than the triple, she needs to keep a cool head. Wagner and Paul were the last Canadian team to win the Olympic pairs title, way back in 1960. They are here tonight to see if Salé and Pelletier can join them in the record books. It has been a long wait. For years there has been talk of the decline of the once-proud school of Canadian pair skating. One much-quoted theory is that the Canadian free-market system cannot compete with the vast organizational powers of the Russians and the Chinese. In Canada, there is no government scout combing the provincial rinks, matching a talented little girl in Vancouver with a promising boy from Nova Scotia. In Canada, there is no all-encompassing system of training. The Chinese have been with Yao Bin for ten years; the Russians have been with Moskvina for six. But Jan Ullmark has coached Salé and

Pelletier for only nine months—and he's never coached an Olympic contender before.

Nor does the Canadian system pay its athletes to train full-time in the lean years when they are climbing the ranks. The average age of a skater in this warm-up group is twenty-five. Salé and Pelletier are the only two skaters in the group who have ever held a job of any kind. Among other things, Salé spent a few years as a barista at the Second Cup and a hostess at a Joey Tomatoes restaurant. At one point Pelletier was pouring draft beers for hockey fans on the concourse of an arena not unlike the one in which he is now skating. Now that the Canadians have reached a certain level of success, they have a few endorsement deals that pay the bills—in fact, at this very moment their grinning faces are lining the shelves of virtually every Canadian supermarket, duplicated on box after box of Cheerios.

At the halfway point of the six-minute warm-up, all of the couples except the Russians have paired off. Skaters skim past each other, gaining speed for stunning tricks. At center ice, David Pelletier hurls his partner into the air with abandon. She whips through three turns before dropping to the ice on one secure foot. In the cavernous space above them, the crowd applauds. The cost of producing this final, of training these six skaters for twenty years apiece, keeping them in skates and costumes, buying their ice time and their lessons, is somewhere around three million dollars. The bulk of the tab was paid by the Chinese government, the government of the former Soviet Union—and the parents of Jamie Salé and David Pelletier, who are here tonight, almost too nervous to watch.

The Russians' parents are not here, because it is expensive, because they cannot get the time off from work, and, in Berezhnaya's case, because her mother cannot get a visa to come to the United States. Over the past three years, the U.S. consulate has rejected a series of visa requests from Berezhnaya's mother, and her passport has been stamped with the kiss of death, a rejection reading "potential immigrant." Berezhnaya's mother and Sikharulidze's parents are watching at home, at six in the morning, on Russian television. Sikharulidze keeps a cell phone in the pocket of his warm-up suit so he can call his mother when it's over.

In Shen and Zhao's case it is the sheer cost of travel that prevents their parents from watching them skate outside of China; Shen's parents' combined take-home pay before they were laid off by the state was around twenty dollars a month, and now they are unemployed. Right now it is almost lunchtime in China, and soon Chinese Central Television will be broadcasting the Olympic pairs final on a tape delay. Understandably, this knowledge weighs on Shen and Zhao, who do not want to embarrass themselves, their families, and their coach in front of a few hundred million of their countrymen. They sincerely want to bring honor to the country that has given them their entire skating life. In conversation, they will tell you with great earnestness that they embrace their solemn duty to represent China at their highest possible level. Tonight Shen's parents and Zhao's mother will be watching at home; Zhao's father died six years ago. If you ask Zhao about his home, he will tell you that he has lived in skating dormitories for twenty years now, and that "by now it's a strange word to me, this word 'home.' " But in his home tonight his mother will be watching as she always does, and tomorrow she will buy the papers and cut out the articles and paste them in the scrapbook that Zhao's father started so many years ago.

The warm-up is more than half over, and yet Yelena Berezhnaya remains alone, in the center of the ice. She does not seek her partner. Up in the stands, many a spectator wonders why the Russians won't practice together. Is something wrong? Or do they know something the others don't? Berezhnaya is untroubled by any such questions. With an air of absolute calm and control, she remains at center ice while the others circle around her, reeling off tricks. Berezhnaya merely performs a series of fast turns on one foot. For a few seconds, she turns and turns and turns on the ice, on one foot, like a ballerina spinning *en pointe* atop a music box. Then she flings her arms out to stop the motion and balances on that one foot. She stands perfectly upright over the single blade. Her body looks much like a child's spinning top, with her slim leg forming the long wire axis, her torso hugging the axis like the body of the top, and her head resembling the round ball at its crown. The top spins slowly, then fast, then slows to a dead stop. She practices this movement again and again. You will never see her perform these simple turns in any competition, ever. But to the knowing eye, this exercise marks her as a former student of the old Moscow pair skating school. For the rest of her life, the stamp of the Soviet system is on her, as it is on all the great skaters in her country's long, golden history. For back when she was just another little girl dreaming about going to the Olympics, Berezhnaya watched her idol, Yekaterina Gordeyeva, performing these turns in the warm-up on television—just before Gordeyeva won the Olympic gold medal with her partner.

This technique of turning on one foot is an old Russian exercise, a time-honored method of adjusting to the ice, of feeling your spinal column become precisely centered over your skates. Being centered over the narrow blade is crucial for every risky move. When a gymnast performs a back flip on the balance beam, the crowd gasps as she lands precariously on the four-inch surface. When Berezhnaya drops down to earth from a jump, she is landing on a blade that is only a quarter of an inch wide— one-sixteenth of the width of a balance beam. Therefore Berezhnaya wants to warm up until she feels absolutely centered, as though her body has suddenly snapped into place over her skates. She has reached that ideal point now, and unbeknownst to her, she gets a nod of approval from someone now watching her. It is Yekaterina Gordeyeva, the champion whose extraordinary skating inspired Berezhnaya, a young girl from the provincial south, to take up pair skating.

Twenty yards away, Sikharulidze too is warming up simply. All around him, other men throw their partners, land difficult jumps, execute strenuous lifts. Sikharulidze, on the other hand, is doing a series of easy jumps that any third-grader could pull off. Like his partner, he is methodical, unhurried, in his own designated space. But unlike his partner, he looks tense. "It's strange, but you get a feeling," Gordeyeva says. "You know who is more shaky in the pair." Four years ago, at the last Olympics, Gordeyeva caused a stir by floating the opinion that Berezhnaya and Sikharulidze, who at that point had been together for less than two years, were the finest team there. But Gordeyeva also predicted that the Olympic gold would hinge on Sikharulidze's nerves. While everyone else worried about Berezhnaya, who was thought to be fragile, Gordeyeva kept an eye on Sikharulidze. And she was right—it was Sikharulidze who made the mistakes that dropped them to second.

From her spot at the barrier, Moskvina looks out and meets Sikharulidze's eyes. Now, like a jockey applying the whip, she gives him a stern nod, as if to say, *Well, go on, then!* And Sikharulidze responds, building speed and launching into his first real jump. It is, thank God, a perfectly good triple toe. (Fifteen seconds later, at the other end of the rink, Berezhnaya performs her own triple toe, landing it with ease.) Watching Sikharulidze now, as he goes up crooked in the air and barely pulls off a shaky double Axel, Moskvina knows his nerves could cost them this title. But without him, they wouldn't have a chance. If somehow the Russians do extend their dynasty one more time, it will be largely because of Sikharulidze and his ability to dare, to risk, to perform.

In almost every famous pair that has ever lived, the woman has been the center of attention. Male skaters are urged to present their partners beautifully, never overshadowing them, and most men are only too happy to become the blander partner. In the whole long history of pair skating, there have been only a handful of men who could command an audience, who had the opportunity to become leading men. There is a growing consensus that Sikharulidze is on a short list of his sport's great leading men. Over the past four years, cameramen from all over the world have readjusted their formula to accommodate him, and now they know that whereas with most pairs, the center ice camera will shoot close-ups of the woman's face, when Sikharulidze is on, many close-ups belong to him. Directors sometimes resist cutting to this unusual shot, but when they do, they find that Sikharulidze's expression jumps off the screen at them. Sikharulidze feels that this is because he is Russian. "Russians feel deeper anyways than Europeans and Americans," he has said. "We are raised on the grand traditions of theater and the ballet. I'm sure that half the American skaters have never even been to the theater—where do you get the feeling for skating, then? And look at the Chinese. They jump higher than anyone else, but you may as well watch pole vaulting. The people want to see a dance—a reflection of life—emotion, jealousy, ardor." In this department, he feels he has no rivals.

There are those in skating who have accused Sikharulidze of being arrogant, headstrong, temperamental. He possesses all three qualities, but in a leading man, those qualities can work to one's advantage. Moskvina says that he is like a match—when you strike the match, there is a rush of flame, a small explosion. And Moskvina knows that Sikharulidze has a profound capacity for daring, because in 1996, when he was already world junior champion with another partner and heading straight for the top, he gave it all up and cast his lot with Yelena Berezhnaya. At the time, Berezhnaya was lying in a hospital bed, recovering from a horrifying accident in which her former partner's blade had pierced her skull. She had gone through massive brain surgery, and it was not clear whether she would ever recover from the "temporary" paralysis of her right side. There was some brain damage, and no one could say whether she would someday walk normally, let alone skate. Sikharulidze can't really explain it, even now. "I don't know why," he muses, "but suddenly we just thought: Let's skate together." It was Sikharulidze who knelt down to tie Berezhnaya's skates the first time she came back to the ice. Her doctors didn't allow her to bend over yet, still fearful of letting the blood rush to her head.

Like many people who have endured a hard life, Tamara Moskvina scorns easy sentimentality, but this memory cannot help but move her. Berezhnaya's bravery was an awesome thing to behold, almost a terrifying thing to behold under the circumstances. But somehow Sikharulidze's decision was the more unbelievable of the two. Berezhnaya had to go forward, had to try to regain her life. But there was no force pressing on Anton Sikharulidze to skate with an invalid, except possibly the pressure of his own heart. Sikharulidze took a wild gamble. He did it out of compassion and out of a kind of love for Berezhnaya; and probably he also had some far-fetched idea that in the end, the pair they would create would be a surpassingly beautiful one. This last vision Moskvina also shared, and in the years that followed, when there would not be enough money and Moskvina would have to chip in to support the two skaters, she would feel somehow that she could not give up on what the two young people had started. Now, at last, Sikharulidze skates over to his partner and takes her hand.

On his way, Sikharulidze passes the judges' table. Nine pairs of eyes go with him. He completes his movement, and now the judges' heads turn in different directions, separating their attention into nine smaller beams. A casual observer looking down the table would be arrested by the sight of Judge Number Four, a younger woman with striking red hair. She wears her hair long, and it curls extravagantly over the shoulders of her fur-collared coat. Something about that enormous fur collar summons up an image of a rainy Paris street scene, and in fact, this is the French judge. She has the Frenchwoman's knack for dressing and for carrying herself in such a way that wherever she is, the moment seems to be an occasion. Whether she is standing in the mundane lobby of a drab Utah hotel or sitting at a folding table covered with white butcher's paper, an air of sophistication clings to Marie-Reine Le Gougne. In such unfavorable settings she seems to pull away a bit from her environment and become an island of sophistication, as she is right now, sitting at the judges' table in her fur-collared coat, adjusting her stylish eyeglass frames.

Marie-Reine Le Gougne feels the pressure. The tension created by the Olympic Games is already immense, but there is another source of pressure on either side of her. She does not turn to look at the Canadian judge sitting ten feet to her right. Ten feet to her left sits the Chinese judge, and just beyond him is the Russian judge. Tension radiates down the long table, forming a kind of force field between the nine people locked in its grip. For months now, in hotel dining rooms and chauffeured vans and hospitality suites, Le Gougne has heard whispers about who will vote with whom. One expects certain judges to stick together—Canada and America, for example, or Russia and Ukraine. The rumor mill has gone so far as to predict that tonight there will be a five–four split on the panel, and that it will come down to the vote of the French judge. Because the pairs event has no French medal contender, the French judge was perceived all along as a swing vote, someone to be lobbied—and Le Gougne has been lobbied. The pressure radiating down to her from both sides of the table is immense. She does not turn her head, but it is palpable.

But increasingly, a larger tension is mounting—a tension imposed by the noise behind the judges and above their heads, the disembodied voices of the crowd—a tension that increases every time they look at the skaters on the ice or at the Olympic rings displayed on the tall blue wall at one end of the rink. The arrival of a long-imagined Olympic moment is a surreal thing. The big-name athletes are actually here, now, all on the ice at the same time. There are so, so many cameras. One has the feeling of being watched at all times. The pressure is crushing, almost debilitating. At only forty, Le Gougne is one of the youngest judges ever selected for an Olympic post—and this is her second time judging the Olympics. Le Gougne is one of the rising stars of her generation of judges. Already, people in the narrow community that decides such matters are considering her for an important elected office within the International Skating Union. Most of the sport's opinion makers are sitting in the stands behind her now. How she votes tonight could influence her standing with the people who count. If her vote goes against the grain, she could go from front-runner to also-ran in one night. Four of the six minutes of the warm-up are gone. In two minutes it will begin.

The Russians now join the rest of the pairs. They seem to engage an internal lever and activate that sixth sense that all competitive skaters have, a kind of extra awareness that will allow them to stay in their own orbit without colliding with any of the other bodies in motion. Watching the skaters weave in and out, performing spectacular maneuvers only a few yards apart, one is reminded of an air traffic controller guiding dozens of planes safely through limited airspace. It is a remarkable sight. But to these skaters it is old hat. They are used to being on the same ice with each other. This warm-up is only special because it is the Olympics, the long-awaited moment. As the clock ticks down the seconds, the tempo builds. Throws and jumps are happening faster now, everywhere you look. The quality of the movements is exquisite. It is going to be a terrific competition. Now that the moment is upon them, the three teams relish the fight. The best pairs in the world are here, and the best are evenly matched. Victory will require everything a team has. It will be extremely satisfying.

Coming out of a perfectly executed jump, Zhao Hongbo has the transitory feeling of skating in a perfect place, a rink almost out of a dream. The ice feels wonderful. Skaters are sensitive to tiny changes in the ice surface. Let it be too cold and it is hard, crunchy, "hockey ice," and when a woman falls to earth after a throw jump and her blade hits that hard surface, there is a thud and she is jolted. But when ice is just right, her blade sinks in like a warm knife in butter, and she flows away in one smooth motion. This ice is perfect ice. All the skaters have been saying so for a week now. On takeoffs, they say, it has great "spring," meaning that it reacts to the push you give, gives you back the most possible lift to go high and far in the air. On landings this ice is forgiving. It accepts the blade easily but then grabs it firmly; it is not too soft or slippery. For much of his life Zhao has skated on pitted outdoor ponds or chewed-up hockey ice, sometimes practicing at two in the morning because there was no other time available. Even at the academy in Beijing, the arena is dingy, lit by the greenish glare of banks of fluorescent lights. Zhao has never in his life skated in such a perfect place. He feels now that he is ready. If they are to do the throw triple Salchow, let them do it now.

Zhao and his partner build speed, navigating around the moving bodies. As they near the point of takeoff, the other skaters clear the space ahead, like a parting of the waters. Zhao must adjust the timing to make sure that Shen does only three revolutions and not four. For her part, Shen must reduce her efforts by precisely one rotation, no more and no less. It is complicated, but Zhao has no doubts. He feels a surge of confidence. And suddenly Shen is in the air—up, up, impossibly high. The cameramen lurch to keep her in the frame. To the people standing near the barrier it seems that her ankles are level with the top of the rink boards, that she is almost four feet off the ground. It is a joy to watch her fly. Three rotations, which will look like a blur when anyone else does them, seem to unfurl for Shen in a more leisurely way, so that you have time to count each one. She lands moving backwards on one foot, gliding effortlessly, *perfectly,* about twenty feet away from where she took off. Her eyes meet Zhao's, and for the first time, she smiles.

Jamie Salé skates by the Chinese couple, oblivious to them and everything around her. She is in a zone. She will circle the ice once, and then she will try one last time to pull off a good toe jump. The jump has been bothering her, tugging at the edge of her mind throughout the warm-up. It is her one weakness and—as she is painfully aware—it is her team's one weakness. Pelletier does not miss his triple toe, so if anyone is going to make the mistake, it will be Salé. Pelletier has a short fuse, and when Salé missed the triple toe at the Canadian National Championships last month, he lost his temper in front of both the crowd and the TV cameras. He swore, stormed off the ice, and reduced his partner (and live-in girlfriend of two years) to tears. He ended up on the couch that night. Pelletier later apologized, both privately and publicly, but the incident left its mark. Salé is hell-bent on landing her triple toe tonight. She won't try the triple now—she just wants to do one really good double toe so she can leave the ice satisfied. Her mind is absolutely concentrated on the jump. The other skaters have receded, her coach has receded, her partner has receded. She does not hear the crowd. Her ears bring in sound as if she were underwater. Her absorption is so complete that you can actually *see* that she is in her own world. No sign of anyone else's presence crosses her face, interrupts her stride. At one end of the rink, she gains speed for the jump she will attempt at the opposite end, making a half turn so that she will approach the jump moving backwards at top speed. She is five seconds away.

At precisely the same moment the Russians are heading straight for their first—and only—attempt at the throw jump. The throw is their weakest element, and they need two of them tonight to win. They are completely attuned to each other and to the ice. They are moving at almost twenty miles an hour. Berezhnaya feels only her blades against the ice, her palms against his palms. They are five seconds away from takeoff.

The Russians are sweeping down the ice backwards at full speed, heading for the precise spot where they will launch their throw. Salé, with her back to them, is en route to the same end of the rink, aiming for another spot. Both accelerate. And just two seconds before it happens, it is suddenly clear that their two paths will cross. They will collide. The crowd inhales sharply, almost as one body, and in the split second before it happens, Sikharulidze senses someone behind him.

He turns just as Salé crashes into him at full speed. The crowd gasps. Both go down hard; Berezhnaya is flung away by the impact. Sikharulidze leaps to his feet and rushes to Salé's side. She is kneeling on the ice, pressing her hands to one side of her stomach. She does not move. From halfway across the rink, Pelletier sees that she's down and sprints to the spot. Gingerly, he helps her to her feet, and she begins to move slowly forwards, bent over in a crouch, like a runner panting after a punishing race. Sikharulidze rejoins his partner, shaking out his limbs, trying to assess the damage. The atmosphere at ice level is surreal. There is the feeling that comes after a quick reaction to danger—say, swerving to avoid another car—relief mingled with shock. Overhead, a giant video screen shows four replays of the collision in a row. Each time, the crowd cries out at the brute force of the crash. And then, without warning, a disembodied voice says: "Competitors, this warm-up has ended. Please leave the ice."

Tamara Moskvina's stomach clenches up. She hurries her skaters off the ice, desperate to find out if they are hurt. She has eight minutes to get them ready. Suddenly everything is happening too fast. Jamie Salé is still hunched over, obviously shaken. Her partner puts his arm around her. Above them, seventeen thousand people try to catch a glimpse of her face and wonder if the poor girl will even be able to skate. But she too must leave the ice immediately. She disappears through a curtain into the bowels of the arena. The question of whether she will return hangs in the air. And still the competition moves forwards, inexorably, propelled by an unalterable momentum. The first pair of the final group is announced, and they skate to center ice.

PART ONE

The Partners

∞

Pair skating is the skating of two persons . . . who perform their movements in such harmony with each other as to give the impression of *genuine pair skating*.

Note: Attention should be paid to the selection of an appropriate partner.

—*International Skating Union Rule 313*

Chapter One

*E*ACH TIME YELENA BEREZHNAYA FALLS, she hits the ice with the same impact as a cyclist crashing at twenty miles an hour. Berezhnaya has a slight build and not much flesh on it, and the ice is hard as a sidewalk. So on any given day, her knees, hips, shoulders, and even her rib cage are various shades of blue and green. On days when Berezhnaya has a photo shoot, it can take up to an hour for the makeup artist to hide all the bruises on her legs. Still, falling—especially on throw jumps—is just a part of the daily routine of a world-class pair skater. So Berezhnaya gets up quickly, gliding on one foot and shaking the other one until the pain subsides. Then she goes again.

Even for a world champion in pair skating—which Berezhnaya is, twice over—it's easy to fall on a throw jump. A throw jump is not one movement, but a sequence of precise actions and reactions between Berezhnaya and her partner. If any one of these motions is even slightly mistimed, the woman doesn't have a chance of landing the jump. Once her partner heaves her up and across the ice, she's traveling eighteen feet through the air, with her toes as high as three feet off the ground. She has to execute three turns in the air in less than a second—not to mention landing on one foot on a quarter-inch-wide blade and not sliding off that blade when, as they say in skating, ice is a very slippery thing.

Yelena Berezhnaya, who stands five foot one and weighs less than a hundred pounds, is no bigger than your average sixth-grade girl. Watching from the hockey bleachers of a practice rink as her small body crashes to the ice time after time, the typical response is to want to run out and stop her before she really hurts herself. But again, she and her partner come around the bend of the rink, gathering tremendous speed. They sail by, generating a breeze that blows the hair of the coaches in the front row, and he launches her across the ice.

Too hard. She hurtles eighteen feet through the air and comes down precariously on one foot, balancing for a split second. Then her ankle buckles and she's down. That same bruised hip strikes the ice with a thud that echoes through the small rink.

This one knocks the wind out of her, and she sits there for a minute, crushed. Her partner, Anton Sikharulidze, a muscular six-footer, glides over to the spot where she sits and skids to a stop just behind her. With one quick motion, he places his hands under her arms and gently lifts her to her feet. The gesture recalls a mother setting down a toddler. For a couple of easy laps, they simply skate. But inevitably they start circling again. Once more they go by with that startling speed, and he throws her.

It happens in less than a second. She whirls three times in the air and drops down on one strong foot, arms outstretched like wings, the other leg rising high behind her back. At the instant that she lands, she glances across the distance she's just traveled to her partner, and for one brief second she gives him that smiling look that means, in the language of pair skaters, "Oh, you threw me just right!" Then she turns and takes one long stride, and he is already there beside her, his step matched exactly to hers.

∞

To an observer watching from fifty feet away, the sight of Yelena Berezhnaya's slight frame taking some hard knocks is alarming. Seen from up close she is even more of a damsel in distress: wide blue eyes that are never quite happy, cute-as-a-button features that hold themselves aloof in a serious look. Some people say she never smiles; the truth is that she rarely smiles, at least in public, and that her natural expression is a solemn one.

So when Berezhnaya's coach, Tamara Moskvina, cast her as a Chaplin heroine in the team's long program one season, the casting was dead-on. She has that same winsome but forlorn quality, that beauty submerged in pathos. It's easy to picture her walking along the railroad tracks in a black-and-white film, or turning her small chin up to the camera and looking in with big, wistful eyes. Not only is Berezhnaya silent, but, much of the time, she exudes silence, the way the silent movie heroines did at times. You feel about her the way you felt about some of Chaplin's orphans—that if only somehow she would be moved to smile, your own heart would fly to the moon, just like that.

It is surprising, then, to learn that Berezhnaya can most definitely take care of herself. She is a formidable athlete, one of the best in the world in a sport of mind-boggling difficulty, and a green belt in karate besides. Underneath her pixie haircut there is a four-inch scar running along the side of her forehead, where her former partner's skate blade pierced her skull, a grim reminder of what she has already survived. To be precise, she has survived two brain operations in a Latvian hospital and the temporary paralysis of her right side. To this day, when you shake her right hand, her grip is surprisingly feeble for an athlete who uses her right hand to, say, balance her entire body weight above her partner's head, eight feet over the ice. When she got out of the hospital, Berezhnaya had to relearn how to walk and speak. Then, for her third act, she relearned pair skating. She is decidedly not defeated by these events. But like the blind flower girl in *City Lights* or the homeless waif in *Modern Times,* the meanness of life stays close to her, even in moments when she is really happy. When she smiles, it means a great deal.

And so when Berezhnaya played a Chaplin heroine on the ice, there was something very right about the whole thing—particularly the final pose, when she dropped to her knees and threw her arms around one of Sikharulidze's legs and looked out into the distance, waiting for better times. Just as it was resoundingly right when, one day in practice, Moskvina seized upon the idea of having Berezhnaya begin a program by actually stepping up onto her partner's skating boots. Berezhnaya balanced her blades lightly on his toes, wrapped her arms around him, and nestled her forehead in his neck. It was an inspired idea—her blades weightless on his feet, she seemed light as air. And later, when they took the ice before a crowd and Yelena Berezhnaya stepped up lightly, oh, lightly onto her partner's feet—well, anyone could see that here was someone truly delicate and floating: a wraith caught, momentarily, in an embrace.

∞

Yelena Berezhnaya is a lovely girl. Her fine face is paired with a light, strong body, and audiences warm to her whether she smiles or not. Sometimes, when she passes through a backstage hallway, the middle-aged Russian women who invariably congregate there will murmur, "That girl is an angel, an absolute angel. . . ." And when she is flying above her partner's head in a gauzy dress, there are moments when she really does seem to be floating.

Another element of the glorious feeling she inspires is her carriage. On the ice her bearing is purely aristocratic, as if she had gone to a finishing school where the girls practiced walking with stacks of books on their heads. Once, when asked what character she was portraying in a program, she replied in an offhand way, "Oh, you know, something like Natasha Rostova at her first ball." And she really did carry herself like a young countess out of Tolstoy. But this polish was acquired at a later stage of life, courtesy of Tamara Moskvina, for Berezhnaya was not raised in genteel surroundings. She may look like a cross between Natasha Rostova and an angel, but when she does smile, the angel shows her overbite.

Berezhnaya is a girl from the provinces. To get to her hometown from St. Petersburg, you must go to the railway station and take the overnight train to Moscow. Beyond Moscow, it is another thirty hours by the fast train to Berezhnaya's small city of Nevinnomyssk. It is an unimportant city in an unimpressive region known as the Northern Caucasus, the last bit of Russia before Georgia and Chechnya. The region is best known for producing wildflower varieties, mineral spas, and Mikhail Gorbachev. Eight months of the year Nevinnomyssk swelters under a blazing sun, and it is as different in climate as it is in culture from the big cities of Moscow and St. Petersburg. It is easy to see why, as a young girl, Berezhnaya assumed she would never leave Nevinnomyssk.

The Northern Caucasus is both remote and poor, and in Soviet times the entire region had just one ice rink, which happened to be in Nevinnomyssk. Today the rink is a parking garage; it closed down soon after what Russians call "the changes," the chaotic period in the early nineties when the Soviet Union stumbled, teetered, and finally fell. In addition to its now-defunct ice rink, Nevinnomyssk has two chemical plants, a wool factory, and a power plant. Berezhnaya's father works at the power plant, and for thirty years her mother worked as a payroll clerk at the state bureau of construction.

Berezhnaya and her two brothers grew up in a typical Soviet working-class home——one of those ubiquitous two-room apartments with the kitchen in the corridor. At night, Berezhnaya and her two brothers slept in one room, her parents in the other. In such cramped quarters every piece of furniture did double or triple duty: Couches also served as beds, and a single table was used for eating, sewing, doing homework, and everything else. Storage compartments were hidden everywhere. It was a common enough sight during dinner in a Soviet home to see a mother reach underneath the tablecloth, pull out a drawer, and grab an extra spoon. But if she and her family were packed into their apartment like sardines, Berezhnaya hardly noticed, for the same was true of every other family in town.

Berezhnaya has memories of her father letting her ride on the back of his motor scooter and buying her packets of the earliest Soviet bubble gum. He was also "an irrevocable alcoholic," and one day when she was five, Berezhnaya's mother sat her down and explained to her that her father wouldn't be living with them anymore. "I just said, 'Well then, I guess that's the way it's supposed to be,'" she says with a shrug. "It's strange, but back then, I simply took things as they came." After her mother remarried, there was a seven-year stretch when the girl had no contact with her father at all, though he lived in the same city, and this too she accepted quietly.

There was no one to look after Yelena, so she used to tag along to the construction bureau, where she became the adopted daughter of the entire office. She was always tiny for her age; as a baby she struggled to gain weight, and the first time she went skating she had to wear five pairs of socks to fit into the smallest toddler skates. At the construction bureau the secretaries used to allow the nicer stray dogs to drift in and out of the office, so the tiny blonde girl with enormous chiffon bows in her hair would play on the floor with the big dogs while her mother wrote checks and balanced the books. From time to time a sunburned construction worker would duck into the office, pick her up with one hand, and carry her off for a ride on the tractor.

Growing up poor in the sunny south, much of life was spent in outdoor pastimes that cost nothing. Berezhnaya's mother liked to sit out in the courtyard of their five-story apartment block, chatting with the other mothers in the sun. "Well, you know," Berezhnaya says wryly, "there is always that one bench in front of the apartment building, and there my mother loved to go for the neighbors, *the neighbors,* and the endless conversations." The mothers sat in the courtyard and gossiped, and whenever a teenage girl came downstairs in a pair of ripped jeans, the older generation tittered on the bench. The children, too, passed the evenings in the courtyard, staging their own theatricals and trivia contests and talent shows, and it was here in the courtyard that Berezhnaya, who was ordinarily very shy, discovered that she loved to perform.

"Back then," Berezhnaya says, "everyone had some money worries. But I never felt as if I was *limited,* or lacking in something. For instance, if I saw something that I liked in a shop window, my mother would immediately say, 'Oh, I'll make the same for you.'" Everyone's mother sewed, but Berezhnaya's mother was "a true master," who over the years proved her virtuosity by pulling off elaborate skating costumes and even a tiny fur coat. Berezhnaya remembers how one evening, sitting out on the courtyard bench, her mother bet the neighbors that she could make Yelena a certain kind of blouse in one hour. "And indeed," Berezhnaya says triumphantly, "in one hour I came down to the courtyard wearing the new blouse, and looking very well."

In sleepy Nevinnomyssk, children were allowed to roam freely, and Berezhnaya remembers games of Cossacks and Bandits where the Cossacks covered half the city looking for the hidden Bandits. The neighborhood kids delighted in harmless pranks, like stealing green apples out of the collective gardens and eating the evidence. One spring night when Berezhnaya was nine, she participated in a thrilling plot to steal tulips from her neighbor's garden. "We crawled in, my boy buddies and I, in the pitch dark," she recalls. "It was ridiculous, since there were tulips growing everywhere like weeds. But still, we did it!"

Most of all, she loved to be with the other kids. She felt tremendous affection for her classmates and tried to show it the best way a shy girl could. In the kindergarten there was one boy to whom she always gave her meatballs, and she used to make friends by bringing extra sandwiches from home. All week long she yearned for Saturday, the only day when she didn't have a skating practice, because then, "at last, we would all walk home from school together. And off we went, joking and talking, skipping over the puddles. It's quite a distance. If you walk very fast it would take half an hour. But sometimes we would stretch those walks to an hour and a half, just to prolong our pleasure." It was the life she would have chosen without a moment's hesitation, had it been up to her. But as things stood she could live it only on Saturdays. The rest of the time, she was skating.

∞

If skipping through puddles and pinching green apples were high on Berezhnaya's list, figure skating was near the very bottom. She started skating by chance at the age of four, and by the time she was six it was already a chore. "Going to practice was like reporting to work," she says tersely. "I did not like it. I did not like it at all. And it wasn't even that my mother wanted it," she continues, her voice rising. "My mom never went very far into my skating life. No, it was the coaches who insisted that I continue skating. I was just doing what they wanted. Sometimes they would even come to my regular school and yank me out of class and take me to the rink for extra practice."

Deep in the girl's psychology, deeper than any native childish selfishness, was a powerful inertia. Once a plan was set in motion, the little girl would endure anything rather than change the plan. Like every Soviet child, she wore her Young Pioneer jumper to school and sang odes to Lenin, and perhaps the propaganda of being an obedient little worker affected her as well. In any case she took direction exceedingly well. "I didn't want to skate," she insists. "In fact, I wanted to do gymnastics very badly. However, it happened that my mother took me to the skating rink first. And after that, it was simply impossible to change anything. There was not even this *concept* of liking and not liking things. Frankly, I never even asked myself if I would want to change something. To live somewhere else, or to do something different—these ideas were not even in the discussion. You started doing something, and that was it. You couldn't change." So she went—automatically—to the skating rink.

Though Nevinnomyssk was barely on the central office map, the Soviet sports system prided itself on extending its reach into the provinces, and even a distant outpost like Nevinnomyssk offered its best pupils free lessons, ice, and mandatory ballet classes. This early foundation would make all the difference later on, for at an age when children in other countries were staring at their boots, Berezhnaya was learning how to hold her head, her neck, her shoulders. At least that much of the Soviet skating orthodoxy had filtered down to the provinces. The provincial rinks also enforced the Soviet policy that parents are forbidden to come to practices, so right from the start Berezhnaya internalized the principle that one's parents have no right to interfere with the coach. Soviet sports were the state's business: The parents didn't pay, so they had no say. Without her mother at the boards to comfort her when she took a hard fall, Berezhnaya quickly learned to treat practice like a job. By the time she was six, she was a cool professional.

From an early age, it was obvious that Berezhnaya had talent. But more important, she had the steely determination that was so prized by Soviet coaches. She would work until she got it right. "Even as a toddler, she was very insistent," her mother recalls. "If she tried to climb up on a chair and I helped her up, she would immediately get down and climb up again *by herself*." Because Berezhnaya was always the smallest in any group, people often tried to baby her, but this she would not tolerate. Even when she was five years old, she would travel alone to juvenile competitions and carry her own skates in a knapsack on her back. Arriving home from a competition late at night, she would neatly store her knapsack and trophy in their assigned places, and immediately sit down to her homework. Her mother would often find her bent over her books, her stubborn brow furrowed above her sleepy eyes, willing herself to stay awake and catch up with her classmates before morning.

She didn't like skating, but she was good at it, and almost from the beginning she attracted attention. Every coach seemed to need a tiny girl to put into a pair. "Basically, they wanted me to skate pairs since I was six years old," Berezhnaya scoffs. "Six years old, and they wanted to send me to Cheliabinsk. Then, when I was nine, they wanted to send me to Pervouralsk. Well, I was tiny, small-boned. So naturally! I *had* to do pair skating!"

Secretly, Berezhnaya would have liked to try pairs. When she was nine years old she had seen Yekaterina Gordeyeva on television winning the Olympic pairs event, and she had never forgotten it. In the sixteen-year-old Gordeyeva, who was tiny like herself, she discovered for the first time the lightness, the absolute lightness with which a girl could move when her partner lifted her. It was beautiful; it touched something in her soul. When Gordeyeva rose over her partner's head in a lift, she was practically in flight. Sitting in front of the TV set in remote Nevinnomyssk, Berezhnaya, too, wanted to fly—but not if it meant leaving home.

For many years, whenever her coach, Nina Ruchkina, approached her mother about sending Lena to another city to skate, her mother, to her immense relief, flat-out refused to consider the suggestion. But Nina Ruchkina was persistent, and she had a powerful motive: She wanted Berezhnaya to skate pairs with her son, Sasha Ruchkin. Ruchkina lobbied Berezhnaya's mother for years. Berezhnaya says that she finally went to Moscow when she was thirteen because she simply became too exhausted to go on resisting. "When I was thirteen," she says wearily, "they wanted me to skate pairs again. And then we were in some training camp, and one evening, Sasha, Nina's son, came up to me and whispered, 'Lena, would you like to skate in a pair with me?' In a whisper, as if it was so very dramatic. So I whispered back, 'Sasha—*no way*!' And then the next day, Nina Ruchkina was asking me, 'Why did you say no? You always wanted to skate in a pair.' I couldn't tell her that I always wanted to skate in a pair, I just didn't want to skate with Sasha. So I simply said, 'I just don't want to go anywhere. I don't want to skate in a pair at all.' "

But in the end she did skate with Sasha, for there was always that powerful inertia deep within her, that terror of having to contradict. "My coach paired me with her son." Berezhnaya shrugs. "She decided. I didn't want to do it." Her mother, finally persuaded that skating was her daughter's best hope for a career, gave in and agreed to let Ruchkina take her to Moscow. The only person who might have stopped her from leaving was Berezhnaya's father, but Tatyana Berezhnaya lied to him, telling him that Yelena was only going to a training camp. By the time he found out the truth, months later, it was too late to object.

So Berezhnaya packed up her things. "Truly, at that moment, I didn't want to go and live somewhere else," she insists. "It's just that people kept telling me, 'Well, you should just go and try it,' and so the decisions were made for me. I just followed along.

"I was on the train. I didn't understand why I was going to Moscow. What for . . . ? Somehow, someone else decided for me. All I wanted was for them not to take me. You see, I always had bad eyesight. So I was thinking, Well, great. I'll just go and make them all happy, and because of my eyes, I won't be accepted to the pair skating school. And then it will all be over, and I'll go home.

"It was somehow too uncomfortable to change things, to say anything, and I was never thinking that I would remain in Moscow forever. But when they dropped me off in this hotel that was affiliated with the Red Army Club, not far from the bus station, I saw that some kids were really staying there—big boxers and wrestlers. They were staying in this hotel, and they were not going home. And that's when I realized: Oh, my God, where did I end up? What am I doing here?"

∞

Today Yelena Berezhnaya is known the world over as the skater with the most exquisite vocabulary of essential skating skills. Her gliding, her positions, her lines are the ones coaches point to when they lecture about how it should be done. But when the thirteen-year-old Berezhnaya tried out in Moscow for the Red Army Club, the man assigned to her case, Vladimir Zakharov, thought she was a mess. Zakharov watched the tryout feeling glum. This girl was going to be a lot of work. "I could see that we would have to clean up her jump technique, but we could fix it. Her posture and stroking were, in a word, horrible." Zakharov pauses. "On the good side," he says, "she was small."

At some clubs a skater whose good side was being small would have been rejected straightaway, but the Red Army coaches ran their tryouts on the principle that talent was useless if a skater couldn't develop it. "Now, she had problems," Zakharov says, "but—she was a hard worker. So we were watching her closely, to see how well she listened. Does she work hard, and is there progress? Can she bring the talent out? And we saw that she worked incredibly hard. She was extremely desirous, concentrated." It was her desire that sold him. "You see, the great Stanislav Zhuk used to say, 'Here in this club, we want to be the champions. We want to take the medals. We're not interested in the rest,'" Zakharov explains. "And so from the beginning, it was this type of kid that we brought into our school." So Berezhnaya was accepted, and her heart sank. She was staying in Moscow; she was not going home.

In those years the Central Sports Club of the Red Army was the object of many a Soviet child's daydreams. Passing through its high wrought-iron gates, one caught a glimpse of the uniformed soldiers striding over the adjacent military grounds. The soldiers, like the athletes, trained here for the greater glory of Russia, and the grandeur of that mission was reflected in the compound's architecture. Arriving in a splendid courtyard, one stood between two ornate palaces: swimming on the left, gymnastics on the right. Between them, the two palaces were responsible for more than a hundred Olympic medals. Directly in front of them lay the stairs that led to the storied halls of the ice arena, where so many great figure skaters and hockey players had trained. In Berezhnaya's imagination, these steps were the ones ascended every morning by the young Gordeyeva.

What Berezhnaya had never imagined was that Gordeyeva had been miserable here, training under the infamous Colonel Stanislav Zhuk. Zhuk had ruled the club for decades, and the school had been formed in his own image. He was a brilliant technical coach, and his pupils were technically brilliant; he was also, by all accounts, a yeller and an alcoholic of the first order. There was nothing more typical than to walk into the practice rink at ten in the morning and hear him absolutely screaming at some crestfallen girl. "I must say," former student Stanislav Leonovich says, "that Stanislav Zhuk was complex and difficult even by Russian standards. He could even smile at you, but at the same time say something in such a way that it just destroys you." The atmosphere of a Zhuk practice session was highly combustible. "Oh, he was a yeller," Leonovich affirms. "And if that didn't work, well, he would use his hand. But only on the girls. The boys he didn't hit. They were too big for him." At the Red Army Club, where all coaches held actual military posts, Colonel Zhuk's orders had the air of military commands. "If you missed something," Leonovich says, "you didn't say a word. You just went out and did it again."

Zhuk was "rough verbally and physically, too rough on his students," Leonovich admits, "but the times were like that. Everyone, coaches and athletes alike, worked more than they could bear to work. To exceed your limitations was normal then." Every year, the State Sports Committee forced each skater to sign a plan, stating that he or she would earn certain medals at specific international competitions. "You were told, 'You will get third at this competition, first at this one.' And so this kind of system cultivated people such as Zhuk, the people who were tough enough to be able to do whatever they had to do to win those medals. Otherwise, you're being dragged around in all kinds of offices, to explain why you failed."

Zhuk ruled by fear in part because fear got results. Throughout the seventies and eighties, Zhuk's pairs were winning everything in sight. Rodnina and her two partners won ten world championships; Gordeyeva and Grinkov another five. Every year, every competition, the Red Army Club was coming home with medals, and the front office was happy. So if there was attendant ugliness—alcoholic outbursts, girls being struck on the ice or propositioned by a lecherous coach—no one was interested. Besides, who was going to stand up to Zhuk? The other coaches were his military subordinates, and the skaters whose destinies he controlled wouldn't dare oppose him. Most skaters even came to take a perverse pride in their ability to endure the worst Zhuk could dish out. Leonovich remembers that "even outside of the rink, we, his athletes, felt that we were tougher than everyone else. We could handle more, both physically and psychologically, than the others."

By the time Berezhnaya arrived at the Red Army Club Zhuk was no longer at the helm, but there was still a palpable atmosphere of fear in the building, especially for the girls. Berezhnaya was unnerved to see how the boys constantly degraded their partners. "They would yell at the girls, call them names, just to look cool," she says flatly. "The theme, which was passed down from one generation to the next, was that these small, stupid girls were always screwing things up for the boys."

The truth was that Zhuk's training methods were harder on girls by their very nature. It was the girl who had to sprint to keep up with her long-legged partner; she took the falls when a twist was launched higher or a crazy new lift was attempted. It was typical in a new pair for a girl to be fourteen or fifteen and her partner to be nineteen or twenty, and it was easy for a young man to become frustrated with this small girl who was not as skilled as he was. With Zhuk, the head coach, slapping girls in practice, no one much questioned a man's right to vent his anger on the girl who had provoked it.

For the first year Berezhnaya was shielded from the worst of it, because she worked with Zakharov in the junior group, where the pressure was lower and tempers flared less. But Berezhnaya still felt out of place, for the coaches treated her brusquely, and they were merciless in their criticism. Berezhnaya soon realized that "there would be no one mothering us in practice, as our coaches used to do back home."

There was no one mothering her when she got home from practice, either. Berezhnaya arrived in Moscow in the uncertain autumn of 1991. The capital was in turmoil. Republics were seceding from the Soviet Union, the economy was in chaos, Gorbachev's government was hanging by a thread. The girl cared little about politics, but she needed a place to stay. After her first couple of months in Moscow, the sportsmen's hotel lost its government subsidy and announced that it would charge the staggering sum of three thousand rubles a month, an amount greater than most people's monthly salary. Realizing that the kids from Nevinnomyssk were about to be thrown into the street, Zakharov offered them a place in his own cramped apartment, just until their paperwork went through for another dormitory.

That autumn Berezhnaya was lonely and homesick. She used to play with dolls when she thought no one was looking, and in the evenings she passed the time with reading and knitting. She went to practice and to school, kept herself company every night, and every morning at a quarter to eight, her mother telephoned and gave her all the news from the neighborhood bench. These phone calls were precious, but they only sharpened the homesickness; they did not take away the ache. There was never a time when she was not yearning for home.

During that first autumn in Moscow Berezhnaya suffered in another way, for she soon figured out that her childhood coach, Nina Ruchkina, had used her. From the things people said in Moscow, she now realized that she was far more talented than Sasha. And yet when Ruchkina had brought the two of them to Zakharov, she had told him that Berezhnaya refused to skate with anyone but Sasha, and in this way she had used Berezhnaya to get her son into the club. This knowledge gave an extra edge of bitterness to the whole experience of being dragged to Moscow. Now Berezhnaya understood—oh, she understood perfectly!—that in pair skating small, skilled girls were a commodity, to be traded like horses between shrewd Soviet coaches.

The world of a Soviet child athlete could be an extremely grim place at times. You went on doing what the coach told you to do even when you would rather be crying on your mother's shoulder. The fact was that your mother wasn't even allowed in the rink, and in Berezhnaya's case, she was a thousand miles away. But there was always some coach nearby to shout instructions at you and schedule all your waking hours. Berezhnaya buried her child's misery in her own breast and kept her own counsel. Her mother had just suffered a mild heart attack, and this had terrified the girl, who became adamant that her mother should have no worries about her. She was determined to be nothing but cheerful when she spoke to her mother, and it sometimes happened that she was more cheerful on the telephone at a quarter to eight in the morning than she was during the entire day that followed.

Berezhnaya's first winter in Moscow, the winter of 1991–1992, was the hardest the city had known in forty-five years, a winter of bread lines winding around the block and empty shelves in the markets. "My mother, kind soul, used to send me boxes from Nevinnomyssk to Moscow by train, passing things to the conductor with a few rubles, and then I would meet the train," Berezhnaya remembers. "And poor Sasha had to drag all my parcels from the train station back to the place where we were staying. Once she sent a box that weighed nearly fifty pounds. I remember how we dragged that box. It was raining, and the box expanded in the rain and broke open—right when we were almost at the doorstep. Tomatoes and carrots and potatoes spilled in the streets of Moscow, and we were picking them up." Berezhnaya shakes her head at the memory. "Can you imagine," she says. "My mother even used to send me potatoes. She didn't know that even in the worst times, we in Moscow had potatoes, even if we had nothing else."

While the Soviet Union fell to pieces around her, Berezhnaya's small world remained mostly intact. Tanks rolled up to the Russian White House, but Berezhnaya went to the same rink, did the same practices, attended the same middle school. Rubles lost their value overnight, people sold their furniture on the sidewalk and began stockpiling potatoes for a famine—and somehow, somewhere, a bureaucrat had managed to open a new dormitory for Red Army Club sportsmen, and Berezhnaya was living better than she had ever lived in her life. "They fed us very well, and it was totally free of charge," she recalls. "We lived like kings there."

Despite the harsh atmosphere at the Red Army Club, Berezhnaya was improving rapidly, and others were starting to notice. "She was not that student who walks in off the street and blows you away with her talent," Zakharov says. "Oh, no. Now, after I developed her, a lot of people came to me and said, 'Oh, what a girl!' But I can tell you, we worked a lot before people started saying that." Zakharov used to tell Berezhnaya's mother that in Moscow they were turning the ugly duckling from Nevinnomyssk into a swan. That didn't play too well back in Nevinnomyssk, but in Moscow, Berezhnaya rather enjoyed being regarded as an emerging swan.

In the spring and summer of 1992 Berezhnaya was briefly happy in Moscow. At her new dormitory she was the darling of the boys' soccer team, and the soccer players used to escort her back and forth to school under the linden trees. Between the school and the dorm there was a large and lovely park, and stepping out of the park the teenagers would pass through the impressive gates of the Ministry of Defense Central Red Army Sports Club Dormitory. The building itself was a well-proportioned four-story brick house. In its former life it had been a boarding house for children of Stalin's diplomats and spies. Berezhnaya shared a small room with another girl. It had high ceilings, pale blue walls, and large windows overlooking the greenery of the park. Berezhnaya, who was alert to beauty, would sometimes stand at her easel by the window and paint the scene before her, while the sounds of the boys' soccer game drifted up from the yard below.

The teenagers ate their meals together in the dining room, and after homework they would all gather around the one television set to watch a movie. Berezhnaya had always liked to be with the other kids, and this arrangement made her happy: "It was like one family. Good times." The main problem of this period, as she saw it, was that Sasha Ruchkin was all wrong for her, and as long as she was stuck with him she would never progress in pairs. But even this was soon addressed, because Zakharov gave up on Sasha Ruchkin and dismissed him from the school. Sasha, her last link with Nevinnomyssk, got on a train, and Berezhnaya remained in Moscow, more alone than ever. A few months later the coaches assigned her a new partner: Oleg Shlyakhov.

∞

The Bolsheviks called ballet a "hothouse flower." You had to lavish resources upon it to coax it into bloom. Elite figure skating was another hothouse flower, and when the Soviet Union collapsed, the greenhouses and gardeners that produced elite skating nearly collapsed with it. There was almost no money to run the sports system. The new Russia could sponsor only the most established skaters; everyone else was on their own. A girl like Berezhnaya, whose family had no money, needed a state scholarship, but since the changes her scholarship had been eliminated. So when Berezhnaya was assigned to skate with Oleg Shlyakhov, a native of Riga, Latvia, in 1992, the Latvian solution immediately presented itself.

Back in 1991, Latvia had been one of the first upstart republics to declare its independence from the USSR. After the 1992 Olympics, the Latvians started competing under their own flag, and they were looking for athletes to sponsor. For someone like Oleg Shlyakhov, a young pair skater at the Red Army Club, the advantages of such an arrangement were enormous. Latvia, a relatively well-off republic, could afford to foot his training bills, but more important, skating for Latvia was Shlyakhov's ticket to the big time. Skating for Russia, he might rank fourth or fifth in pairs. It could take years for the Russians ahead of him to retire, and in the meantime he could forget about a berth on the World Championship team. But skating for Latvia, which had no other pairs, he was assured of a trip to the World Championships every year. If Berezhnaya joined up with Oleg Shlyakhov and skated for Latvia, she could reap the same benefits—and she wouldn't even have to give up her Russian citizenship.

At the time Oleg Shlyakhov was nineteen, a grown man who shaved and went to bars. Berezhnaya was a fourteen-year-old girl from the provinces. As a rule, a new pair's practices consist almost entirely of mistakes, so Berezhnaya was surprised when Shlyakhov reacted to their mistakes by screaming at her on the ice. During the first few weeks he reduced her to tears almost daily, and one afternoon, in the locker room, one of the older girls took pity on Berezhnaya and told her Shlyakhov's history: He had been through seven partners in three years, and all seven of the girls had quit because he was so abusive. Shlyakhov had the worst temper in the school—and now, Berezhnaya realized with a sick, panicked feeling, she would bear the brunt of it.

The first time Shlyakhov hit Berezhnaya, she was stunned. Zakharov immediately intervened, and she tried to forget the incident. But soon Shlyakhov was hitting her regularly. He hit her in the dressing rooms, in the corridors, even outside the rink. Sometimes Zakharov was there to rein him in; sometimes the fourteen-year-old girl had to face Shlyakhov alone. Her reaction was always the same. "I would close myself," she says. "I wouldn't say anything. I would go inside myself. And I would start fearing everyone." In practice, she was desperate to please him, terrified of making the next mistake, for when Shlyakhov's temper raged out of control, no one in the world could help her. "Even if the coach was there and would yell at him, well, then what?" she demands. "That wouldn't help matters." Who was going to protect her after practice? Some people at the rink felt sorry for Berezhnaya, but no one suggested kicking Shlyakhov out of the school, or finding a new partner for her. Berezhnaya's explanation for why no one tried to help her is chilling. "Because to some degree or another," she says matter-of-factly, "everyone was behaving like that in this school. They all just thought it was supposed to be that way." This was the school that Zhuk had built, where a "small, stupid" girl might skate over to the head coach and be greeted by a slap.

"His aggressiveness—if I tell you about it, you would feel sick. His aggressiveness was in everything," Berezhnaya says. "It was in his attitude on the ice, and I consider it indecent even to talk about it." Asked if she told her mother about what she was suffering, she replies with a harsh laugh, "Of course not." She was persuading herself that she should go on skating to make her mother happy. "I didn't tell her anything about the things that were happening to me. I knew that her health was pretty bad, and that when she watched me on TV, it gave her strength in a way."

She might have complained to someone at the Red Army Club, but at some point, Berezhnaya stopped believing that other people would help her. At the rink, half a dozen adults knew full well that Shlyakhov was beating her. They saw the bruises. They weren't doing anything about it. She felt that she had no one left to confide in. "I was just a small, scared kid," Berezhnaya says. "I was taking everything as it came. So, when everything was going well, that was great. But then when things were going badly, there was nobody teaching you what to do." Another girl might have confided in her mother, but that was the one thing Berezhnaya was determined not to do.

Zakharov will not say exactly what happened, but finally Shlyakhov went too far. According to Zakharov, in their second season as a pair, Shlyakhov did something to Berezhnaya that he could not abide, and Zakharov threw Shlyakhov out of the school. Zakharov shook his head when he saw Berezhnaya following Shlyakhov out the door. "I did want to change Yelena to a different partner," Zakharov says. "But Latvia promised them a lot, and Russia couldn't match that offer, not even close. I couldn't guarantee the funding to keep the girl training. Latvia could." Zakharov shakes his head. "You know, if this had been just a couple years earlier, none of it ever would have happened. If this had been the Soviet Union, we would have just kept her at the Red Army Club and put her with a different partner. But there was no more Soviet Union, no scholarship to give to her. And so she would compete for Latvia, so that she could have the funding, and the chance to go to Worlds."

As she had done all her life, Berezhnaya went on taking everything as it came and relying on herself alone. It is possible that she was afraid of what Shlyakhov would do to her if she quit. She was certainly afraid of being forced to quit skating. High-level sport was the only career she had prepared for; she didn't know how to do anything else. She had seen the rows of wretched people on the street, lined up to sell their furniture, their books, their clothes, desperate for a few rubles. The new Russia was a brutal place for people who had no way of making money. It was out of the question to leave her career. But deepest of all feelings was the old ferocious desire not to disrupt things, not to have to speak up. So she left the Red Army Club, and now she was alone with Shlyakhov.

∞

In ordinary times it would have been difficult for Shlyakhov to find a coach after alienating the head coach of the Red Army Club, but these were no ordinary times. It happened that Mikhail Drey, a well-known Russian coach, had just lost his job with the State Sports Committee after a round of cutbacks. Drey was waiting for a visa to go and coach abroad; in the meantime, he agreed to coach the Latvians, sight unseen, for a fee of one dollar a day.

The times called for people who could work all the angles, and Drey was such a man. He went down to the training camp at Novogorsk, just outside of Moscow. "I didn't tell them that I trained the Latvian pair, because they would have asked for a lot of money," Drey explains. "I told them that I was coaching a Russian girl, and I requested full room and board for her and for myself. Instead, Shlyakhov lived under my name, eating there, spending the nights." Drey, who lived nearby, commuted to the rink.

A few minutes into their first practice, Drey motioned to Berezhnaya to stop what she was doing and come over to the barrier. The girl ignored him, so he motioned again. Still no response. Finally he called out to Shlyakhov, and the two kids skated over.

"What happened?" Drey said to Berezhnaya. "I called you up twice."

Shlyakhov answered for her. "You should shout at her louder," he suggested. "She can't hear, because of the music. And don't bother gesturing to her to come up to you. She can't see anyway."

Drey was surprised. "What do you mean she can't see?"

"Well," Shlyakhov said, "she's minus four. She's nearsighted."

"So how does she skate?"

"Oh, she's used to it."

"What do you mean she's used to it?" Drey roared. "How can she skate pairs if she can't see anything? Get out of here. Go back to Riga right away, and don't come back without contact lenses."

Berezhnaya, who had skated for ten years without being able to see clearly, didn't utter a word. She just followed Shlyakhov off the ice and on to Riga. "In two days they came back," Drey recalls. "She wore contacts. She was happy."

Before he started coaching the pair, Drey had been worried about the girl, because Zakharov had once said to him in passing, "You know, she never skates a free program without falling down at least five times." And it was true, the girl did take a lot of falls. But if you asked Drey, it was hard to say whether she fell because she had bad technique or because she was terrified of her partner, who was a complete monster. As far as Drey was concerned, Shlyakhov was a worthless human being. "I used to tell him," Drey recalls, " 'I hope you realize, you're going to end up somewhere behind a fence. But this girl is going to be great.' "

Whenever there was a blowup on the ice, Drey would take the opportunity to send Shlyakhov "back to his mother in Riga" and work with Berezhnaya alone. For weeks at a time, Drey worked one-on-one with Berezhnaya, remolding her technique, teaching her stability. By the time the 1994 Olympics arrived she was much improved. They were eighth at the Olympics, a very good result for such a young pair, and seventh at the World Championships a month later. After such promising results the Latvian federation agreed to send the pair to London, where Drey was relocating to coach at a new training center. It turned out to be the beginning of a very bad time for Berezhnaya.

Their money did not go far in London, and there were times when

Berezhnaya and Shlyakhov shared a single meal, eating from the same plate. To economize, they moved into a tiny apartment—together. Shlyakhov has called this period the beginning of their romantic relationship, but Berezhnaya has never called it that. For her, the situation was a nightmare. Before, they had always lived in the dorms, chaperoned. Now she could never get away from him, and at night, she faced him behind closed doors.

The situation at the ice rink was horrible. "The minute I turned my back to put on music or attend to another pair, Shlyakhov would kick her or slap her across the face," Drey recalls. The situation was out of control. The British parents who came to watch their kids practice were constantly threatening to call the police and have Shlyakhov arrested. Berezhnaya withdrew into herself, silent and watchful. At times she looked up at Drey with enormous, frightened eyes. He pitied her, but he didn't try to find her another partner.

"Lena never came up to me to say, 'He kicked me,' " Drey recalls. "She never said a word, because she considered herself to be dependent on him. Remember, no one needed her in Russia. She was let go from everywhere in Russia, so she felt that she was dependent on Shlyakhov, on Latvia." Drey sighs. "She was only sixteen," he says. "She was not aware of the greatness of her skating; she did not know at the time that she would become a champion one day. I used to tell her, when she was sad, 'Lenochka, don't worry. Really, you will become great.' " But his words meant little to Berezhnaya. She was in a fog.

At the 1995 World Championships, Berezhnaya and Shlyakhov finished seventh—exactly the same place as the previous year. Shlyakhov was smart enough to know what was wrong. They had the skills, they had the talent, but to the judges, they still looked too—well, Latvian. They had synthesizer music, and they wore cheap costumes that made them look like they were working the pirate ride at an amusement park. The judges weren't going to put them on the podium. What they needed, he felt, was "a kind of pretty packaging that could be presented to the whole world." They needed to arrive perfectly coiffed and costumed, skating to elegant music with delicate choreography. Then the judges would be able to see them not as "the Latvians" but as a classic Russian pair. For this, Shlyakhov insisted, they needed a new coach.

Moscow was out of the question, so Shlyakhov looked to St. Petersburg. He knew the coach he wanted. She had "great experience coaching Olympic champions," and "she knew where, why, and what you had to do so that the pair took first place." He convinced the Latvian federation to pay their way, and in the late spring of 1995, when Berezhnaya was seventeen and he was twenty-one, they packed up yet again and went to St. Petersburg. Shlyakhov said: "I felt the only person who could help us was Tamara Moskvina."

∞

In the Soviet Union only two pair skating schools counted: Moscow and Leningrad. The Moscow school was a highly organized military machine. It was known for athleticism, for big boys hurling small girls into the air higher and farther each year. Its archetypal figure was Irina Rodnina, a tiny fireball who made her long-legged partners chase her around the rink. Rodnina exploded in the air like a cannonball. Her signature music was "Kalinka," a folk-song-turned-back-slapping-bar-song that really got the home crowd going. Rodnina became a prominent Party member, addressed Communist officials backed by a massive portrait of Lenin, and was featured in her own Soviet television special, sitting on her couch next to a pile of thirty gold medals.

Like the city it came from, the Leningrad school felt more aristocratic. It was housed initially in a converted church on Vasilyevsky Island, and later in a glass-walled rink through which skaters could draw inspiration from the spires of St. Petersburg. It was known for its elegant ballets on ice, its languid grace. Its torchbearers were the Protopopovs, a pair of tall, leggy skaters who glided like swans. (Muscovites said, "Slow swans.") Their signature piece was the *Moonlight Sonata,* and when they performed it, a cathedral-like hush filled the arena. The Protopopovs were artsy. They insisted that people call one of their death spirals "the life spiral." They liked to pose for experimental photographs where their bodies were perfectly doubled in untouched, mirrorlike ice. The Protopopovs considered themselves above politics, and later they defected to Switzerland.

The Protopopovs' coach, Igor Moskvin, and his wife, Tamara Moskvina, have led the Leningrad pairs school for almost fifty years. Since 1967, the year it was built to commemorate the fiftieth anniversary of the October Revolution, the Moskvins have coached at the Yubileiny Palace of Sport. Yubileiny has certain idiosyncrasies. It was built as an arena, not a training center, and as a building it is pure Soviet inefficiency: vast space, most of it ill suited to any purpose. Yubileiny has only one rink that is practically useful, but it boasts a concourse and vacant snack booths and a main arena that seats several thousand, which normally sits empty. The only ice at Yubileiny is in the practice rink attached to the main arena.

The Yubileiny practice rink, which has so far produced eleven Olympic champions, is something of a legend. The rink has two walls of floor-to-ceiling glass running down the long sides of the oval. The ice is surrounded on all sides by stacks of chairs and gym mats, making the rink feel like a huge storage closet. Inexplicably, a car is sometimes parked inside the rink, just on the other side of the hockey glass. Because of the two long windowed walls, the sunlight, when there is any, pours through all day long, turning the ice into a giant puddle. In winters past, before the new heating system was put in, those glass walls made the rink feel like a meat locker. In the old days the main refrain of a winter practice session was the sound of one hacking cough answered by another.

Yubileiny feels a little run-down, but it also has the pleasant feeling of a place where it is okay to improvise. Even in Soviet times, there was something unconventional about Yubileiny, something spontaneous. Because Yubileiny is short on facilities but flush with teachers, one can often find a class of eight-year-olds using a handrail on the arena concourse as if it were a ballet barre. Pairs practice lifts in the parking lot, and teachers spread tarps over the dormant rinks to make a floor for the gymnastics class. For years, Yubileiny did not even have showers in the locker rooms. It has no real weight room, and one Olympic pairs champion, Artur Dmitriev, used to bulk up by moving the cases of beer into the Yubileiny café. "I just said to the drivers, 'Look, guys, I have to bump up my muscles. Could I just unload the truck for you?' " Dmitriev recalls. "So we made a deal. I would move the cases, and while I did it they would sit around and smoke. Actually, we got along well. They were quite alcoholic."

Tamara Moskvina, who has taught at Yubileiny for thirty years, is not the type to mind if her skaters spend time with the guys who drive the beer truck. She is herself a rather improvisational type. Moskvina lives by a few maxims, one of which is that life should be as busy as possible. "I live according to Lenin," she says with a wink. "Change of activity is rest." Another of her principles is that people who don't stay busy have only themselves to blame for their problems. On those rare occasions when she returns from a competition feeling jet-lagged, Moskvina knows just what to do. "You think, Wait a second. Make up a plan. Do the laundry, wash the windows, take shoes to the repairman, listen to music for programs, meet the choreographer. And immediately you feel better." Once a Russian reporter dared to ask Moskvina if she ever felt depressed. "It's only when a person doesn't know how to apply himself that so-called psychological dramas occur," she snapped. "And I simply don't have time for that."

Moskvina is always doing at least two things at once. She prefers to do three, and when she can do four, she is at her happiest. Moskvina is ruthless about squeezing the most from every minute, and this tends to make people uncomfortable when they first meet her. The effect is similar to that of being at the airport metal detector and scurrying to unpack a laptop, empty one's pockets, and take off one's shoes while fifty people are waiting. Somehow, Moskvina alone creates as much pressure as those fifty people. Around Moskvina, pupils scramble to lace up their skates; callers race to finish a sentence before she hangs up. In the backstage hallways of an arena you will often see a reporter racing to keep up with her, flipping the pages of a notebook and trying to uncap a pen while Moskvina barks, "Ask! Ask!"

In St. Petersburg, Moskvina lives about twenty minutes away from Yubileiny, but she cannot bear the thought of spending an entire twenty minutes just driving. So while she drives she always packs some wayward pupil or visiting reporter into the passenger seat. While she crisscrosses the canals she will lecture the skater or dispose of the reporter's questions. If her cell phone rings she will pick that up, too. (Before cell phones, in the era of rationing, she used to scan the lines of people waiting for bread or meat and try to figure out if it was worth stopping; in this way she once plowed into a gate.) From time to time, Moskvina will make an illegal U-turn to extricate herself from traffic. Swerving around a couple of horses, she will interrupt her cell phone conversation to yell to the passenger, "Oy, oy, this is traffic! Before, there was one car on the street!" If the traffic does not clear after two minutes, she will mutter, "Hmmm . . . traffic violation. Should I violate or not? *Da, da, da.*" A pause. She pulls a tight U-turn on a bridge. "*Tak.* I violate. Don't judge me severely because otherwise I have to go round, round, round. I hope no police will stop me. Please, please! Okay. Continue." She gets rid of the cell phone call, finishes up with the passenger, and arrives at her destination with two more items crossed off her list.

In the parking lot of Yubileiny she is out the car door in a flash and literally sprinting for the arena. Moskvina recently turned sixty, but not all of her students can keep up with her. It can be a little embarrassing for a world-class skater to be beaten to the door by a sixty-year-old woman in little dress-up flats who is only four foot nine, but it sometimes happens. Within four minutes of entering the rink she has already laced up her skates and put on that same floral-print down jacket she has been putting on for a decade. Then she starts chasing her skaters.

Moskvina's pupils admit that having your coach chase you around the rink does increase your speed. On the other hand, having a pint-sized grandmother underfoot can be a little nerve-racking. "We used to hate it," a former student says. "She was practically pushing us down the ice. And sometimes, when we came out of a lift, we seriously thought we were going to kill her." Moskvina ducks as a leg comes around, sidesteps a skater at the last moment, weaves in and out between teams. She buzzes around like a bee. While she chases, she shouts the most basic of instructions: "No!" or "Hold it, hold it, hold it . . ." or "Strong!" Sometimes she yells, "Perform!"

Moskvina's enthusiasm is the gasoline that makes every engine in the rink run. It must be exhausting to fuel so many people's endeavors, but she doesn't show the strain. Moskvina would have made a great big band singer, getting up the energy for the performance three hundred nights a year, belting it out every single time. For thirty years she has begun every practice with a cheery greeting for everyone—good morning to each skater, *privyet* to the other coaches, *privyet* to the Zamboni driver. Every one of her former students remembers the trill of her voice floating across a seven o'clock practice session: "Good morning, boys and girls!" "It was enough," says one, "to make you want to shake her." Yet if you look at Moskvina as if you want to shake her, she will meet your look with her merry one. She might show off her single Axel jump, just because she can still do it. Often she will play the clown. When that music you have heard a thousand times comes on, she will yell, "Russian restaurant music!" and improvise a silly dance until you have to laugh with her. Or, if you are tired of these tricks, as most of her older students are, she will just wait out your bad temper and speak to you in purely technical terms, so that it's all very professional. Sooner or later, she wears everyone down.

Over the years, many a coach has stood by the boards and called out instructions to a skater, willing the skater to take by osmosis the coach's own positive energy. Moskvina jumped right over the barrier and got in her students' faces. Her pupils had no choice but to respond to her—she was nipping at their heels. During a practice Moskvina is constantly nagging, trying to extract that extra ounce of energy that makes the skater bother to point a toe or stretch a limb another inch. These are the details that make the difference at the top level, and with Moskvina hot on your trail you will probably do them. If she stood behind the boards at seven A.M., chances are you would not.

Moskvina has never been satisfied with any pair, though she has coached several Olympic champions. When she looks at one of her pairs she always sees something else to fix. An arm should be two inches higher here; the unison there is off by a split second. She would like to trim pounds from a girl's frame, curls from the back of her neck, inches from the skirt of a costume, until reality might match the image in her mind's eye. Moskvina is so obsessed with making skaters better that they can begin to feel that she gives them no credit at all for being good, and she might be intolerable if she did not apply the same relentless perfectionism to herself. "I am dieting and exercising like crazy," says Moskvina in one of the many oft-repeated stories about her, "and still my butt is getting bigger!" One of the boys in the locker room calls out, "That's because you are riding so much in the car!" Moskvina mulls this over. A light goes on. "Do you think," she asks, "we can take the driver's seat out of the car?"

For thirty years Moskvina has always had her group at Yubileiny—two, three, or even four pairs that she coached simultaneously. After all, she likes to do three or four things at once. The group approach was not Moskvina's invention; it has been a cornerstone of the Soviet system for decades. The idea was simple: The younger athletes learned from the older ones, preparing to replace them on the podium after they retired; meanwhile the older athletes gained the teaching experience that would help them in their next careers as coaches. A top coach like Moskvina could be shared with maybe four pairs at a maximum, with an assistant coach doing some of the detail work. Over time the group became something like your graduating class—you may not have liked all of them, but you'd known them for years and had been through a lot together.

In Soviet times Moskvina's group was the liveliest and hardest working in Russia. Moskvina could be a stern taskmaster, but there was also something inherently comical about her. "She was so short and funny, always running somewhere, with her scary driving, and she wore those funny clothes. She never wore normal clothes. There was always something wrong, either some crazy style, or else they didn't match," one student remembers. "And she was always coming up with the craziest training methods." One summer Moskvina made her group run through the streets of St. Petersburg in snorkeling masks to increase endurance, and once, at the World Championships, she came running into a practice session with four cotton pads, which she insisted that the skaters keep in their armpits throughout the practice. "Here we are in the World Championships, trying to keep these things under our armpits, and afterwards she seals them up in a bag and sends them to the team doctor," the skater recalls. "Unbelievable." Moskvina was one of the first Soviet citizens to get a home computer, and the rumor at Yubileiny was that she used it to make charts showing the dates of all the girls' periods.

Moskvina might be a comic figure, but she could also be harsh if the occasion demanded it. If a skater repeatedly missed an easy jump, she would impose a fine of ten dollars for every miss. She posted the girls' weights on a bulletin board in the main corridor of Yubileiny, and if that didn't work she would take the rink microphone and announce a girl's weight over the loudspeaker during practice. She put the boys through grueling workouts so they wouldn't have the energy to go to bars at night. "But even when we did go out," one former student complains, "she always found out about our little conspiracies. Next day while we're warming up, she bounds into the room. 'Oh,' she says casually, 'how is that new bar on such-and-such street? How are the drinks?'" He shakes his head. "You know, she never told us, 'Don't go to the bar.' She just showed us that we were totally under her control."

For the first twenty years of her career you would never see Moskvina at rinkside without a notebook. She made practice notes, competition notes, training plans. In her attic in St. Petersburg the old leatherbound notebooks are stacked in a box. Opening one at random, one reads, "Disturbances and Interruptions, 1977–78 Season. Days of missed practice due to illness . . . due to injury. Major injuries." Another says: "What to do in the next thirty days." There is commentary and criticism on every performance. In one section, she has mapped out the programs of her pairs' rivals, minute by minute. Using the notebooks, she eventually devised a system to get an athlete to peak at the most important competitions. For the 2002 Olympics, Moskvina prepared a three-hundred-day plan (three hundred days!) to bring her pairs to peak condition on two nights in Salt Lake City. Every day was linked to the next, and to the next, and each led inexorably to the final, perfect condition: not injured, not tired, not afraid. Her system works. Moskvina's pairs consistently skate better at the Olympics than they do at other competitions, and for this her athletes love her. At the moment that they most want to be great, they are great.

Moskvina holds a doctorate in educational psychology, and in addition to being a coach she fancies herself a kind of life teacher. If a girl is lonely she will find some kind soul to invite her over for dinner. If a boy is lazy she will offer him a ride in the morning, and on the pretense of letting him know that she is leaving her house, she will give him a wake-up call. If a girl lacks self-confidence she will encourage her to take a class at night, and if a boy is getting too big for his britches she will find some excuse to send him to be coached by her husband for a while. Her husband, Igor Moskvin, trained the Protopopovs among others, but she does not send the boy to Igor because he is a great coach. She sends the boy to Igor because Igor is a man in his seventies, and when he gives an order, the boy will be ashamed to contradict him.

Over the years Moskvina has filled drab Yubileiny with colorful personalities from the dance world. She has hired character dancers and repetiteurs from the Kirov to teach choreography in the little ballet room. She found a circus performer to work with the skaters on lifts in the stairwells and the parking lot. Sometimes, when a girl does a new lift just right, the circus performer will give the girl a little kiss on the head and exclaim, "My little bird!" Moskvina's pairs have worked with a modern dance choreographer in his studio above the slightly seamy Troika Restaurant. (At night, the modern dance choreographer makes artistic compositions with scantily clad girls.) Moskvina brings every kind of talented person into contact with her skaters. They give the skaters their own particular genius; they also give them another adult influence in their lives. "For example, our choreographers from the ballet, they give to the boys the proper example," Moskvina explains. "Because in the ballet they teach them to be very attentive to the ladies and this is shown by, like, they can kiss your hand, they support you, they defend, all this stuff."

Because her skaters often cut their formal education short, Moskvina worries that they might neglect the grand tradition of the arts in St. Petersburg. So she will often come to practice with two extra tickets to the ballet or the symphony, always with some pretense of having to cancel at the last minute, and she will beg the skaters not to let the tickets go to waste. Because they can't refuse her, the skaters will go, and because they go, their minds will become more susceptible to art—just as Moskvina, in her wisdom, knew that they would. "I have a lot of tricks," Moskvina says meaningfully. "I can't tell you all my tricks. But depending on the situation, I use them all."

∞

Moskvina was born in Leningrad in 1941, a few days before the siege. As an infant she was evacuated from Leningrad to her mother's native village in the Ural Mountains, near Perm. "And I remember," she says, "that the ration of bread was one piece, just one hundred grams. And that was the only food that people were getting all day. *Yes*. And once, when I was three, my cousin saved this piece of bread. She *hid* it. But I found it and stole it from her and ate it. Why did I do it? I was three."

Moskvina's attitude to life was forged during the war years and during the postwar period of Stalin's purges and camps. In her childhood, people regularly knew extreme hunger. Relatives often disappeared or died. A million people starved to death in the siege of Leningrad *alone,* and altogether twenty million died in what Russians call the Great Patriotic War, fought on their soil, with the bodies of their young men and civilians. There is a cemetery just outside of St. Petersburg for half a million of the dead, and the graves go on and on. Walking through this cemetery one fact of Russian life becomes extremely clear: Back then, everyone knew a lot of people who died.

In Moskvina's mother's family, in the village in the Ural Mountains, there were eighteen children. "Only three remained alive," Moskvina says. When asked what happened to the other fifteen, she replies impatiently, "This I don't know." An uncle "was lost during the war with no traces," and Moskvina's only brother died before she was born. "He was poisoned in the kindergarten. Something was poisoning a lot of children. We don't know what." Her father died when he was forty-seven, "because of—we think—something to do with chemicals in the department of military science, where he worked."

Moskvina's English is excellent, and she has all the words she needs to go into the details if she wanted to. She doesn't want to. If you ask her how exactly her brother died in kindergarten, or what explanation the military officials gave for her father's death, she will say, insistently, "This we don't know." She is not resigned to not knowing; she is still angry—but she is not about to try and find out. To an American, it would be unthinkable that a toddler would die in kindergarten and the parents would not demand an explanation, but this was the Soviet Union, where there was not the same concept of having a right to information. If the authorities wished to tell you the truth, they would, but quite possibly you would never know the truth. And in Moskvina's childhood, when so many millions had died, there was even something unseemly in making too much of your own particular tragedy. So many others had the same grief—or worse.

If Moskvina's family had some good luck it was that her father came home from two wars. He survived World War II and Korea, and in 1948 he brought the family back to Leningrad, where he resumed his studies at the air force academy. There were five of them now, the parents and three little girls, and they all lived in one room in a dormitory for married students on Prospekt Obukhovskoy Oborony. There was a housing shortage in the Soviet cities, and like many families they were stuck with a so-called communal apartment: one of eighteen rooms on a long corridor, with a single toilet at the end that all the families shared. There was a basin in the room for washing, and a kerosene burner for cooking.

The only good thing about the communal apartment was that it was right on the Zhdanavka River, and when the river froze Moskvina's father would take the girls skating. On Sundays their father would walk them over to the Kirov Stadium, where in winter the infield served as a makeshift ice rink. "And *that*," Moskvina declares, "was so good, because it was with the father, it was in the cold winter, it was wind, it was sunshine. So that was great, great feeling."

In one early snapshot Moskvina, only ten years old, leaps above the ice at Kirov Stadium. She is wearing a blue wool skating dress that her mother stitched together from her father's old air force uniforms. Decades later, she scrawled her own caption underneath the picture: "The Masterpiece." "In my group," she explains, "when some small thing is done absolutely perfect, we say it's the masterpiece. This was my first." In the photograph she is wonderfully defiant. As she got better at skating she started trudging over to Kirov Stadium by herself, and not just on Sundays. She hadn't made the team yet and wasn't allowed in the dressing rooms, so she made up her mind to walk to the stadium on the toe picks of her skates. People passing by marveled at this short, determined little girl tiptoeing over two bridges, the railroad tracks, and another bridge before finally reaching the stadium. "Can you imagine that?" she says triumphantly, then answers her own question. "No!" Before long Moskvina made it into the dressing rooms—not because of her middling talent, but because she was the hardest worker in Leningrad.

After the war, figure skating started from scratch in Leningrad. When Moskvina's coach, Igor Moskvin, began skating on a pond in a public garden in 1945, there were exactly five serious skaters in the whole city. Moskvina was of the next generation, but still, Soviet skating—and Soviet sport generally—wasn't even close to being competitive with the West. It was in the postwar years that the Soviet Union began designing a sport system specifically to produce champions. One of the cornerstones of the State Sports Committee's strategy was to send Soviet athletes abroad only if they were judged to have a good chance of winning a medal. Moskvina won the Soviet national title five times, but she was one of those whom the bureaucrats held back for fear that she would embarrass the USSR on the world stage. Four times she was denied the chance to go to the World Championships, and in her fifth year as national champion, she was informed that a fifteen-year-old girl would go to the World Championships in her place. Moskvina was twenty.

There is a photograph from this period of Moskvina standing by the ice, waiting to compete. She is incredibly beautiful and fiery, and it's easy to see how her coach fell in love with her. When she decided to give up on singles skating, Moskvina accepted two proposals from her coach: She would marry him, and she would take up pair skating.

With her second partner, Alexei Mishin, she did wild new stunts that audiences adored. They skated to light French music and catchy gypsy dances. For one exhibition number, they wore the tall stovepipe helmets of marching band leaders. Their style was over the top, a little bizarre, sometimes hilarious. But they pulled it off, and from time to time they had big results. At the 1969 Soviet Championships, they left the crowd in total disbelief by beating both the Protopopovs and Rodnina in a single night. Later that year they won a silver medal at the World Championships, and Moskvina, who was then twenty-eight, decided to try something else.

Shortly after their retirement Moskvina and Mishin were featured in a Soviet propaganda newsreel about sport and higher education. In the film, Moskvina wears a white lab coat and examines a skeleton in a lab. In Igor Moskvin's office, Moskvina and Mishin flip through books, admiring poses from the ballet. Moskvin puts on a record and starts drawing the pattern their skates will make on the ice, while a narrator intones, "They were born in Leningrad, and they live in our city. They are masters of sport, international level, in figure skating. Let's introduce Tamara Moskvina and Alexei Mishin! And now, thanks to the Leningrad Academy of Physical Culture, they are soon to become two of the greatest coaches in the world!"

The strange thing about the propaganda film is that it's all true. The Leningrad Academy of Physical Culture has no equal in the world. For decades, it has consistently produced coaches of a caliber that no other country can dream of matching. Skating coaches in the rest of the world learn coaching on the job. Coaches in the Soviet Union were required to get a five-year degree, studying anatomy, biomechanics, sports medicine, psychology, music, foreign language, and techniques for coaching figure skating. To graduate, you had to write a dissertation and pass an athletic test. Even today in Russia, if you can't do your double jumps up to Axel, forget it—you can't be a coach. Moskvina and Mishin both got their doctorates from the Academy of Physical Culture, and in time each became the greatest coach in the world in their respective disciplines: he in men's singles, she in pairs.

∞

Moskvina was a good Communist, though she had certainly seen her share of the bad side of Soviet life. From her childhood, she knew what it was to live in a communal apartment. Even in the early days of her marriage, she, a five-time national champion, and her husband, the coach of the Olympic champions, lived in an apartment with no bath at all. They bathed once a week at a communal bathhouse. Moskvina knew that a Soviet sports administrator had prevented her from going to five World Championships, and that other bureaucrats had probably ignored the dangerous chemicals that killed her father and her brother. When she traveled with the skating team, there was always that one "team official" whom no one had ever laid eyes on before, the one who was clearly KGB, and in her entire competitive life she had never dared to leave a foreign hotel without asking permission and enlisting a Soviet companion. She knew of skaters who had been caught talking with certain foreigners and were never allowed to leave the country again.

"And yet," she says, "there is this feeling: Every stick has two ends." In her own life, communism had made the difference. She had known skaters from the West, and she knew what their parents paid for them to skate. "So I'm thinking, if my family lived in the United States, did I have the chance to become a skater, a successful skater? A coach, a successful coach? Probably not. Because let's say, military person like my father, can he afford to have three children educated like university education, then figure skating lessons, music lessons for children? I don't think so. And that's why I'm very happy that I was born in the Soviet Union."

In Moskvina's day the national team often toured the Soviet Union, performing in small towns and attending special meetings with workers. These trips affected her profoundly—not as demonstrations of the valor of the worker-hero but as "a very good source of information about life."

The skaters went to factories, farms, and even coal mines, where "they gave us clothes that they put on miners. They installed on our heads those special lamps. Then we went in the very deep mine, how they usually go. We went in the part where they dig the coal with the special electrical equipment. And it was *real work*. So for example my first thoughts were: It was very hard there, they were perspiring, and they were covered with this black dust and coal. It was very, uh, *not nice* atmosphere. What is our life as skaters compared with that? No comparison! We are in very nice atmosphere, with the music, warm ice rink, costume. People applaud us, we travel all around the world. So I need to take my skating more serious, like pay more attention and give more effort. And it gave me the importance of my career, as I'm skating and producing the enjoyment for these people who work hard, who take our competition program as an entertainment."

Even in private Moskvina was a model Soviet citizen. Working with dancers and musicians she must have had ample opportunity to explore the Soviet underground scene, but if you inquire, she will say, "What underground? What? We had no time." She "didn't have time" for reading banned books in samizdat editions, either. She eventually joined the Party "because I thought, Okay, I am a good citizen, and I would like to do everything possible for my country to be good, to develop. So that was honest opinion. And," she continues insistently, "*even* if I was not member of the Party I would *still* be champion of Russia, I would *still* go to international competition. This didn't depend on my decision to join the Party. I got no advantages from it."

Plenty of skaters and coaches never joined the Party, and there were not a few who considered such an action tantamount to making a deal with the devil, but Moskvina was the type who always worked within the system, whatever system it was. Skating mattered more. She has said that "you can be happy in every system. The feeling of this happiness depends on you, on your philosophy." When the Party was in charge, she might have had her quarrels with it, but she joined. When the Party came to an end, she worked within the new system. She started arranging personal meetings with the mayor of St. Petersburg, where she would take a few Olympic champions along with her and beg for free ice at Yubileiny. It worked.

Under perestroika, Moskvina was one of the first people in the Soviet Union to apply for a small-business permit; she used it to sign contracts with her skaters that would guarantee her a percentage of their prize money and professional earnings when they went West, which they all did. When capitalism came she was the first Soviet coach out of the blocks. She had e-mail in 1995 *in Russia*. In the first years of free enterprise Moskvina started a small business producing figure skating tchotchkes— black lacquer boxes painted with figure skating scenes, fake Fabergé eggs, matryoshka dolls. When she stayed in foreign hotels, she would lay velvet cloths over the furniture and the bed and spread out her wares. Then she would invite unsuspecting foreign friends up to her showroom. She took orders at one competition and filled them at the next. For a time, she experimented with a Tamara Moskvina skating school in England, and she got herself a Web site and put up pictures of Yubileiny and all her champions, calling her product "Tamara Moskvina Ice Mansion, Limited." Eventually she came to the United States and made contracts with big ice rinks on favorable terms. And she understood media. After the 1998 Olympics, Russia's gold medalists and their coaches were invited to pose for pictures with Boris Yeltsin. When Moskvina's turn came, she pulled Yeltsin into a dance hold and threw her head back, laughing. It was Moskvina's photo that appeared in all the newspapers the next day.

Moskvina can be charming and is often genuinely kind, but you must never forget that she is also a tactician. Without exception, her former students use the same phrase to sum her up: "Tamara is, like, businessperson." In the 1990s, when the Cup of Russia competition came frequently to St. Petersburg, she decided to organize cocktail parties in her stunning apartment for her foreign associates. Guests murmured above the music in the warm light of antique wall sconces, and Moskvina poured good vodka at a table in an enormous bay window overlooking the Church of the Transfiguration. It was the tourist's dream of the refined St. Petersburg life. The dream came to an end about an hour after the guests arrived, however, when Moskvina ushered them out the door, explaining that she had people coming in shifts, and this shift was over. There was an American shift, and probably a Russian shift, and maybe a few more for particular people who ought to be fêted for particular reasons.

Moskvina is an opportunist. It is one of the essential things about her, and yet she is so transparent about her opportunism that she doesn't come off as conniving. She is an opportunist, and yet the opportunities she has sought have always been for her skaters. Moskvina went on driving her beat-up Lada and wearing those crazy old clothes. To this day, she videotapes practice on a camcorder that dates back to the dawn of technology. She was never trying to get things for herself. It was just that she had an image of a pair in her mind, and she started from her ideal and worked backwards. So if a pair needed ice, or money, or media exposure to get to that exquisite point in her imagination, she would get it for them.

Moskvina has said: "During the practices you don't *see* the program. At competition is where the real performance is. There you see all." It is only in the rapidly passing moment of performance that you have the realization that "you expected somewhere applause, and there is applause," that you see "impulse, electricity between them and the public. Only during the real performance that is *so obvious.*"

Moskvina has always been a busy woman. Her movements are complicated, but her motive has always been simple. She would do whatever was necessary to make certain that at the ultimate moment, when her pair emerged from the backstage tunnel and the arena suddenly opened out over them, when they pushed forwards into the eye of the storm, pressed in on four sides by the inexplicable feeling of ten thousand people watching two—then, at last, in the unfolding moment, she would see the ideal. She would see her mind's creation in the flesh.

∞

Through its window on the West, Russia glimpsed France and pulled in its language, its ballet, its architecture and design. Even in Soviet times, St. Petersburg's better atheists still worshipped at the altar of European culture and grand style. The young Moskvina was steeped in Petersbourg culture, first at a girls' music conservatory and later at the Protopopovs' school of ballet on ice, and as a student she used to find the time to go to the Leningrad State Library and daydream over the ballet books. Ballet was inevitable in St. Petersburg. It was the most complete perfection of form in a city of so many perfections of form. Moskvina came to know and love the quality of a classical line running through a limb, a roofline, a wrought-iron bridge. If you open her kitchen cupboard, you will find it there, too: Moskvina appreciates a Lomonosov teacup.

There is a second box up in Moskvina's attic, containing half a dozen large scrapbooks. The scrapbooks are filled with images Moskvina photocopied at the Leningrad State Library. Each image has been carefully cut out, its edges trimmed, and pasted in a tasteful collage, one collage per page. There are photographs of ballet dancers, folk dancers, modern dancers; of gymnasts and even a few skaters. They are mostly pas de deux; exquisite, highly original poses. Flipping through the pages it is as if someone had compiled all the possible beautiful designs that can be made with one male and one female body.

"Quiet" is not a word one would think of applying to Moskvina; still, she must have her quiet moments like anyone else, and underneath all the living according to Lenin, her attachment to beauty must be profound. Beneath all the layers of commotion beats a quite sensitive heart, but you won't see it in her gestures, which are always a little too efficient, or in her words, which even at their warmest are still a little too composed. You see it in her pairs—at the competition, where the real performance is. There, you see all. You see it when they perform to the strains of Tchaikovsky's "Sentimental Waltz" with a movement pure as the new-fallen snow.

She starts from the image in her mind and works backwards. Simple as that. Other coaches size up their two skaters, see what they have, sigh and make peace with it. Not Moskvina. She constantly challenges, gives chase: The girl can be thinner, the boy can land his triple toe, the stroking can be quieter. Don't tell her they can't. She has never accepted any compromise, and even when things haven't worked out, when the girl hasn't been thinner and the boy isn't landing his triple toe and has taken up cigarettes besides—even then, she hasn't given up. She is constantly measuring the pair against the pair in her mind, asking if they are there yet—and if not, why not?

Her longtime choreographic partner, Alexander Matveyev, a former soloist with the Kirov, says that when they worked together, "Moskvina would create the skeleton of the movement and then I would fill in the design. But I must say that Moskvina herself was capable of doing this part. Many consider her to be only businesslike, rational. They don't understand that she's extremely creative." Matveyev recalls that once, at a training camp outside of Moscow in the early nineties, Moskvina, in a fit of inspiration, woke them all up "just because she had this wonderful idea. And we all went to the ice and stayed there until one in the morning. She was enthralled, and I became captivated by her idea, and then for all of us, this was the instant of creation."

For most of her career, when Moskvina created things in her imagination, she always started with two givens: a certain man and a certain woman. But by 1994 the conditions of her work had changed. She now had all the experience she could need; she had put athletes on the podium at four Olympics in a row. But also the world around her had changed. In the old Soviet system the state's control over skaters made it impossible to "steal" a skater from another coach. But now, while stealing was still frowned upon, there was the possibility of taking one skater out of a pair to form a new team, because athletes suddenly had a say in the matter. An athlete could actually choose to leave a coach, or leave a partner.

Moskvina began to think that she might envision a couple and then go find the skaters to play the parts, for there was a pair in her imagination she had not yet made. It was a couple in the image of Gordeyeva and Grinkov—beautiful long lines, perfect bodies for pair skating, the girl short but small boned and long limbed. They would move gloriously, and they would be beautifully fast. Moskvina would marry the speed of Moscow with the music of St. Petersburg. They would skate the pas de deux, always ballet, always classical, a romantic style. "People," she sighed, "are nostalgic for such a style." She would present them always as a gentleman and his lady, and he should treat her in such a way that "all of the women sitting in the audience would like to be treated by the gentleman, as if they are watching the program and thinking, 'Oh! I wish I will be in her place!'"

She had made two dozen pairs before she came to this one, and she knew now what to look for. She found the girl somewhere in Russia, at a competition. Moskvina, who had some couples in the event, was standing at the boards, watching a practice. There were four or five couples on the ice at once, but suddenly every trained eye in the rink was on Yelena Berezhnaya. This effect will happen now and again—the people who know skating feel it right away, and it's as if the rest of the skaters on the ice are out of focus and the only distinct figure on the rink is one girl, light, light on her feet, and perfectly small, as if her body had been made limb by slender limb for pair skating. So there she was, and by now the people were saying to Zakharov, "Oh, what a girl!" Later, at an international competition in 1994, Moskvina was at the boards again to watch Berezhnaya practice with Shlyakhov. Berezhnaya landed a throw jump, and her free leg rose behind her back, high and beautiful. It was a simple thing, but it was everything. Everything the girl did was stretched and turned out and done with such amplitude that it was glorious to behold. Moskvina turned to the person standing beside her and said, "That's her. That's the girl I want." It was not, however, the boy she wanted.

∞

By the time he was eighteen Anton Sikharulidze was known around Yubileiny as a hotheaded kid with a lot of promise who was basically pissing it all away. He'd been blessed with a perfect build for skating, and he'd had the extraordinary good fortune of being brought up in the Leningrad system from the age of five, which meant that he had marvelous technique. He had an extremely talented partner, a sweet girl named Masha Petrova, and together they had twice won the Junior World Championships. What's more, they had just finished sixth at the 1995 World Championships. These were the kind of results that could lead in a few years' time to the Olympic gold medal; however, it was unlikely that Sikharulidze was going to get there, since currently all of his energies were directed at destroying his team. He spent the better part of his practices shouting at Masha and his coach, Lyudmila Velikova. Sometimes he cursed, sometimes he walked out in the middle of practice.

Of this period, Sikharulidze has said: "Sometimes I lost control. I was acting rashly at times, which I regret now." He has also said, "When I was eighteen years old, why would I want to go to the ice rink? Figure skating is for ladies. My friends were practicing guitar, playing in a band. Why would I go to practice? What for? To see girls?" He thought he might be able to put up with skating if he were in Moskvina's group, but when he asked his partner to go with him she refused, and anyway Moskvina, who was coaching her pairs at the same training sessions where Sikharulidze skated, was wary. "Truthfully speaking, he had examples of bad behavior with his former partner," she says bluntly. "And then, he is little bit egotistical person."

Sikharulidze had "never liked skating, never" and had endured it for two reasons: "because I'm very scared to disappoint my father" and because he enjoyed the attention people paid to him because of it. As a middle school kid he had wowed his peers by going abroad to compete and coming home with foreign bubble gum. As long as he skated, his parents saw to it that he was completely spoiled. His brother and sister did all the chores; they even walked Anton's own dog.

When he was a boy Anton Sikharulidze's fear of disappointing his father was enough to keep him in line, but by the time he was eighteen he didn't give a damn anymore. He had been in the cage too long. He was filled with self-righteous anger—but about what, he could not exactly say. He was sick to death of skating, a sport he had never liked but from which he was now earning some good money, as much as twenty thousand American dollars a year. At eighteen, people still treated him like a boy, but two things had happened that had made him feel he was a man. The authoritarian Soviet sport system that had held him in check all his life had suddenly disappeared, and now he had dollars. So Sikharulidze came roaring into his teenage rebellion. He was looking for something more from life than the monotonous repetition of sport; he craved an opportunity to prove himself outside of an ice rink.

And then suddenly there was Yelena Berezhnaya, warming up one morning at his rink. Like everyone else, Sikharulidze was astonished to see her. As usual, Moskvina had kept her movements secret until the last minute. Sikharulidze knew this girl from competitions, where the rumors about her flew in the hotels. But the rumors were unnecessary, really, since anyone with an ounce of imagination could see for himself what Berezhnaya's life was like. "It was obvious that she was under somebody's influence, and it was also apparent that she was working under strong pressure," Sikharulidze says. "Everybody treated her with sympathy." But to see Yelena Berezhnaya here in St. Petersburg was confusing. Sure, the team was good, and Latvia had money, but why would Moskvina do it? It was not right that Berezhnaya should be here and still be with Shlyakhov. Moskvina didn't tolerate such animal behavior in her school. And yet here Berezhnaya was, and she had an apartment in town with Shlyakhov.

Berezhnaya's situation troubled Sikharulidze deeply. He had a sympathetic imagination and could fill in the details—how she must be treated at home, why she looked so stricken. "At first it was only this feeling of disappointment and pity, because you couldn't help seeing how they did everything, how they lived, how they skated. It was very crude, and I felt sorry. Very sorry." He watched her on the sly at practices, carefully, because Shlyakhov became furious when other men looked at her. She was attractive, of course, but to Sikharulidze the very idea of being attracted to her seemed "not proper," for the girl "was very modest, very shy" and at the same time "very downtrodden and oppressed by her partner. It was a girl who was afraid to contradict. And I would even say a certain female essence was killed in her. It's because she followed him completely, stepped in his footsteps." When she first arrived at Yubileiny, Berezhnaya was afraid to say more than two words in a row. "She was too scared to even tell us good-bye when she was leaving. She used to turn her back to him and wave at us quickly with her hand."

Sikharulidze and the other skaters in his group talked it over, and they decided they would befriend the poor girl. At team parties, the girls would huddle around Berezhnaya so she could be free of Shlyakhov for at least a few hours. Shlyakhov "wouldn't allow her to have any contacts with her girlfriends, to say nothing of men," Sikharulidze recalls, "so we had to be clever." On days off, in the fine summer weather, Berezhnaya's new friends would contrive to sneak her away for an afternoon in the country-side. Sikharulidze watched her solemn little face test out a smile and felt his heart leap. "She started to blossom," he says. "The sparkle appeared in her eyes, a sparkle in her movement, and she started speaking more force-fully. Because now she had all of us around her."

One Saturday, Sikharulidze and two friends stopped by to see what Berezhnaya and Shlyakhov were doing and found Berezhnaya locked in-side their second-story apartment. She confessed that Shlyakhov was in the habit of locking her in when he went away for the weekend. So Sikharulidze and his friends climbed up and carried her out through the window. "Next door was the police department," Sikharulidze says. "And the police came over to us and said, 'Hey, what are you guys doing here?' I said, 'Listen, we don't want to steal anything from this apartment. We just want to take the girl out. Because her stupid boyfriend locked her in the apartment and went somewhere for two days.' "

Moskvina had brought Shlyakhov to Yubileiny on the assumption that she could reform him. "I knew," she admits, "that he had treated the girl very badly, but I thought of myself as a very strong person in psychological influence. I thought, Oh, this will be like great challenge for me, and I could use all my knowledge, all my experience to teach him to work in, as I say, cultural way. Not emotionally, but nicely. And I thought I can do this." She took Shlyakhov to a psychiatrist, counseled him herself, and en-listed her husband and the ballet masters in Shlyakhov's extensive reedu-cation. For a time it seemed to be working. "At the beginning, as usual when you come to the new coach, he behaved nice," Moskvina says. "But then he started to behave as usual. He could kick her, he could shout at her, even hit, hit after her, for no reason. Well, there was reason. Let's say, she fell. Or she was a bit slow. For me it was no reason to hit the girl who was much weaker than him, much younger than him, and well . . . I was shocked. In our school in St. Petersburg nobody hit the girl, nobody shouted. There were some pairs in Russia that we heard that the boys didn't treat girls well, but it was not in our school."

But now there was violence in Moskvina's school, and she didn't know how to stop it. Shlyakhov dominated Berezhnaya in practice. "If I missed a jump, he used to say, 'Do it again, do it again.' And I kept doing it until I was completely crushed," Berezhnaya remembers. But this was the least of her troubles. Sometimes, when Berezhnaya fell on a throw, Shlyakhov would skate right over her and drag his blade dangerously close to her neck, as if to threaten her. And Moskvina would sprint over, yelling, "What's wrong with you? Are you crazy?" Whatever they were doing, Sikharulidze and the other boys on the ice would stiffen. "My reaction," Sikharulidze says darkly, "and not only mine but that of everyone else, was to want to treat him exactly the same way that he was treating her." But Sikharulidze didn't, largely because his own coach used to collar him and tell him "not to get involved, because we were rivals, and somebody might think I was bothering them just to break up the pair."

Shlyakhov by now believed just that—that Sikharulidze was trying to steal his partner. Shlyakhov became jealous and took to spying on Berezhnaya. By the late autumn, Sikharulidze says, Shlyakhov "was doing nothing but spying on her, trying to find out where she was going, who she met with, what she was doing. Twice, he saw us together. And when he came back home to Lena he harassed her. Lena's life became so unbearable at the end that she moved to another place. Some of us would visit her there, and we would stay awake most of the night. And Oleg was always out there in his car under her windows, waiting in a secluded place."

As the months passed, things grew worse. Moskvina began to wonder if the bruises on the girl's body could all be accounted for by skating. Berezhnaya had always been secretive, but now Moskvina broke the silence. Another student in the group remembers that Moskvina became relentless about questioning Berezhnaya about her life at home, if she had her own room, if she was safe. Berezhnaya, Moskvina says, "concealed everything."

But she couldn't conceal what happened on the ice. One of their rinkmates, Yelena Bechke, remembers that "one day they came to the practice and she forgot his pants at home. And she knows that punishment will follow. So he says, 'Okay, let's go home and get them.' And Tamara says, 'No. You go. You drive your car, go home and get the pants, and come back.' 'No,' he says, 'she comes with me.' And Tamara knows that if she goes with him, he's going to beat her up. But the thing is, it was really hard to make Lena stay, because she wanted to go with him. She was too afraid to disobey, you know?" Bechke sighs. "In the end he went alone. But we never knew what happened when they went home after practice. Who knows what he did when we weren't there."

The meaning of Moskvina's interventions was not lost on Berezhnaya. Bechke explains that "when Yelena was in Moscow, skating with Shlyakhov, everybody was hitting the girls. When she got to St. Petersburg she was like, 'Oh, my God! Nobody's getting beat up, it's just me.' And slowly she started seeing that it doesn't have to be violent all the time. It could be just normal—no humiliation. Then she started to stand up to him more."

Moskvina urged Berezhnaya to speak up for herself. "I said to her, don't be a victim," Moskvina recalls. "I teach her, pay no attention to his behavior. Have your own opinion. Say it nicely, in a cultural way. Be strong, equal person. So I also taught her to reject his superiority, not to be afraid of him. At the beginning she didn't, but then she started, slowly." But Moskvina had not anticipated the violence of Shlyakhov's reaction to Berezhnaya's newfound voice. As the fall wore on, Moskvina became truly afraid. "I looked at them skating," she says, "and I thought, Thank God, I wish that nothing will happen. I don't want to go to prison. Because he was not predictable. He could be like a volcano. I was on my toes all the time, fearing something." And still, Moskvina did not send Shlyakhov back to Riga. Everyone at the rink knew that Moskvina would have liked to match Berezhnaya with Sikharulidze to form her ideal pair, but she did not try it yet. Moskvina waited.

One December afternoon, just before the National Championships, Berezhnaya and Shlyakhov were rehearsing their short program with the music. As a courtesy to them, the other pairs stayed near the edges of the rink, and Yelena Bechke was among the skaters who turned her head to watch them. "They started off great," Bechke recalls. "They landed perfect side-by-side triple toe loops. And then they go around the curve and Lena loses her edge and she falls. And the next element is the split double twist, and she's *running,* trying to catch up with him. And he—instead of slowing down, he speeds up. And he's coaxing her, 'Come on, come on, catch up with me.' So she did. They did a perfect twist, he puts her down so nice. And then he punches her right in her face.

"And we were like, *Ohhhhh, my God*—after all the effort she put into catching up to him, and doing the twist—*he punched her in the face?* And she fell down, and she just cried, and cried, and cried. And Tamara's yelling at him, 'What are you doing? You stupid idiot!' " Bechke pauses. "He looked at her so coolly and he said, '*Aww,* shut up. Who are you?' And that's when the older men skaters finally stood up for Tamara. They went right to him and they said, 'You know what? You beat the girl up, and it's terrible, and you are going to pay for it. But if you go against the coach that we love, who we've been with for so many years, you're gonna get really, really hurt.' So they were absolutely clear about it: Don't touch the girl, and never ever try even to say something mean to Tamara."

Moskvina could not go any farther down this path. She confronted

Shlyakhov. "So finally I asked him, 'What's the matter? Why you are so angry with her?' And he confessed that he is afraid of Anton. I asked, 'Why, why you are afraid of him?' And he shouts at me, 'You don't know! I'm telling you that they're in love!' " Shlyakhov told Moskvina he would leave with Berezhnaya for Riga immediately; they would stay there without a coach for the month leading up to the Latvian Championships.

And here again was the rub: They were skating for Latvia. In Soviet times Moskvina had once sent a top skater with a violent temper home to the Ukraine and told him not to come back until he got his behavior under control. But these were different times. Moskvina felt she could not break up the team; they were a foreign team, and Latvia was Berezhnaya's only possibility. Besides—at the moment, the Latvian federation held Berezhnaya's passport.

Moskvina had other worries. If she pushed Shlyakhov too hard— say, broke up his team—how crazed might he become? And then there was another, more disturbing worry: that perhaps Berezhnaya would not agree to leave him. When Berezhnaya's mother is asked the obvious question—why didn't your daughter leave Shlyakhov?—her answer is a chilling one. "You know," she says, "maybe she wouldn't even leave him now. Because they gave her the person, and that's it, she was skating with him."

Berezhnaya herself looks back on these days and does not understand her own actions. She was young—she had just turned eighteen that fall— and she was afraid. And she was passive to her very core. "The fact that his behavior was outrageous is understood by normal people," she says. "He had the eyes of a bull, and if something wasn't going the way he wanted, his eyes would be bloodshot. He was basically sick. He shouldn't have been skating or doing sports at all. Why was I tolerating all that, and why didn't I leave him earlier?" she muses. "I don't know. And yet somehow life was like that. I don't even know. It just happened."

Berezhnaya would not act, so Moskvina acted for her. Moskvina made a plan. She would appease Shlyakhov at first; she would let them go to Riga and train alone there for a month. "Listen," Moskvina told Berezhnaya. "This plan is to let Oleg be relaxed. Because here, Anton is near, they skate at the same rink. In Riga it will be like nice surroundings for Oleg, maybe he will be calmer skating without such a stress every day."

So Berezhnaya was to go to Riga, but she was not to compete at the National Championships under any circumstances. She would come down with the flu—any excuse would do. But she would not compete. Because if she did skate at the Latvian Championships, according to the rules she couldn't skate for Russia the following season. And if Moskvina's plan worked, Berezhnaya was soon going to skate for Russia.

After the Latvian Championships, Berezhnaya was to go to the European Championships, and there the Latvian federation would hand over her passport so she could carry it around for identification. Immediately after the competition, Berezhnaya was to walk out the arena doors, hail a taxi to the airport, and fly directly to St. Petersburg, and that would be the end of Latvia. Moskvina would arrange the plane ticket, and when Berezhnaya reached St. Petersburg, Moskvina would provide the rest—a place to stay and a partner, Anton.

On her last night in St. Petersburg, Berezhnaya stayed up all night talking to Sikharulidze. "I didn't want to leave," she says simply. "I had this strange feeling that something was over—and that something new was just beginning." She would go to Riga, she would follow Moskvina's plan, and when she had her passport in her hands she would go to the airport without looking back. "I would skate with him until the European Championships. I told myself, I will skate there, and then that's it—that's the end."

"She said a lot of things that night," Sikharulidze recalls. "It seems to me now that if I had told her to stay with confidence, she would have stayed, because she was afraid to leave. And besides, she had gotten used to being here; she had gotten used to me, to our group, and she felt she was no longer a stranger here. She wasn't an outsider here like she had been in Riga, where she felt that nobody needed her, and she felt lonely." But still, he didn't ask her to stay. "You see, as she was going anyways, I was trying not to think about bad things that might happen," he says. "But subconsciously I felt that things would be even worse in Riga, because here Tamara and I were near her, and we could help her. But there would be nobody near her in Riga. I felt in my bones that something bad would happen there. But I didn't think it would be that bad."

∞

"We were in Riga," Berezhnaya says. "We were there for the National Championships but we did not skate the long program, because I was sick. After a few days' rest we came to practice and we warmed up, and then we started rehearsing our short program." In perfect unison they glided into the side-by-side camel spins. Both skaters kept one foot on the ice and leaned forward in a spiral position, their back legs outstretched. Each time her head came around, Berezhnaya could briefly glimpse Shlyakhov's skate as it passed by. Then she felt the blow. "I thought: Oh. I guess he hit me in the head. But it wasn't too bad so I continued spinning. And then suddenly I felt that I couldn't stand up anymore. I felt something wet and dripping, and I fell down."

Shlyakhov knew at the moment of impact. "I felt a jolt, that I had hit her. My first thought was: Oh, God, oh, have I hit her eyes? She was lying on the ice. There wasn't any blood yet. I saw that her eyes were okay. From somewhere, there was a cry. I picked her up and carried her to the medical room at the rink, and they started first aid right away." It was then that he noticed the blood. There was a lot of it, all over his hands and clothes. "I saw the amount of blood. I understood that it was very serious."

Shlyakhov climbed into the back of the ambulance with two nurses. Berezhnaya felt so strange. The nurses were asking questions—her name, her address—"but for some reason," she says, "I was unable to talk. Everybody thought that I couldn't talk just because I was spooked. But I was thinking, I feel all right, I just don't know the answers to these questions." At the hospital they stitched her up and wheeled her to the lab for an X ray. "I was sitting there waiting for the X ray. And then I started to feel really, really bad. Very soon the doctor came and told me that they had to operate. And at that point I was in such a state, nothing mattered. I said: Okay, surgery? Fine. Well, I didn't say it, actually, I only nodded my assent.

"They put me under," she says quietly. "Later, when I woke up, I wasn't sure where I was. Then I remembered the operation, and I was so frightened, because I didn't know whether the operation had already happened or if it was about to take place. I was terrified that I would wake up on the operating table. There were people outside my room, and I wanted to ask them: 'Please, has it happened yet?' But I couldn't speak, and nobody knew yet that I was awake. So I waited, and waited, and then finally the doctor came in and asked me how I was, but I couldn't answer him either." She tried for three days before she was finally able to make some pathetic sounds. She lay in the bed in a fog of pain and discomfort; her arms were tied, tubes stuck out from her body everywhere. She could not feel her right side. She was in agony. When Oleg Shlyakhov and his mother showed up, she could not even form words to tell them to get away from her.

Floating in and out of consciousness, she intermittently saw a certain doctor's face. She did not recognize him, but he prowled around the corridor, looking in on her with a frightened expression. "On the fourth day," she recalls, "I was told by a nurse that he was the doctor who did my surgery, and that before me, he'd operated on another girl who died after similar surgery. Nevertheless, he decided to operate on me. And later on, when he realized that I was a figure skater, he became very scared and thought that I wouldn't be able to walk. Like that." Berezhnaya received this news pinned to her bed, unable to talk, utterly alone.

Finally, on the fifth day, her mother came. It was a January afternoon in a northern city, one of those short afternoons that fade into evening at four o'clock at that latitude at that time of year. Berezhnaya lay in a hospital bed, drifting in and out of sleep, and her mother, accompanied by Tamara Moskvina, slipped into the room. Berezhnaya's eyes were closed. Her head was bandaged, hiding the worst. The doctors explained that underneath the bandage was a wide, uneven scar circling the entire crown of her head, where the top of her skull had been removed and then stitched back on. Moskvina felt her heart constrict. "I was scared to death when I saw her," Moskvina says, "because she was lying in the bed like, like dead. Not moving. So pale. Thin like a chicken." Then Berezhnaya opened her eyes and saw her mother, and that rare smile broke across her face. "I was thrilled to see her, thrilled," Berezhnaya says. The memory of the feeling produces the smile again.

Her mother's arrival simplified her situation at a stroke. For more than four years—in Moscow, in Riga, in London, in St. Petersburg—the girl had been missing the touch of home, the simple joy of having her mother at arm's reach. For all that time she had never burdened her mother, but now she could ask for her help. In the last five days, Berezhnaya had suffered through brain surgery in a foreign hospital, the loss of her speech and the use of her entire right side, and the excruciating visits of Oleg Shlyakhov. Her mother's appearance was the balm for all that ache, and at the same time, it trumpeted the arrival of reinforcements. When Moskvina and her mother stood at the foot of the bed, she saw two allies. Immediately, her mother began to defend her against Shlyakhov. "Oleg would come in, and he and his mother would be saying, 'Okay, that's enough lying around in bed, get up and go back to skating,' " Berezhnaya recalls. "And then my mother would say, 'What is it with you people and skating? This girl just had a brain operation and you want her to get up? Absolutely not!' " In her arguments with Shlyakhov, Berezhnaya now had someone more powerful on her side.

Moskvina saw the remedy right away. "She needed human care, as with Oleg she had it very seldom. Very seldom. And after such a tragedy and after her previous relationship with Oleg, she needed human care and kindness, and a little happiness." Whenever she looked at the girl, really looked at her, Moskvina trembled all over. "Why I let them go? Maybe if I was there, it wouldn't have happened. Maybe I didn't take the precautions not to let it happen. It was not my fault, but still I humanly felt that I was to be blamed, that a little kid like this young girl had this problem."

Moskvina was sickened by the distance Berezhnaya's body had traveled in a week. The world-class athlete was a skeleton with fresh red scars all over her head. She could not speak, she could not move her right side. People later asked Moskvina if she could have imagined Berezhnaya skating again. Moskvina finds the question ignorant. "This was brain damage," she says. "We did not speak about skating at all. The question was health and life. When you see such a person you ask about her life, not about skating. This is like as we say a question against humanity. I didn't ask this question."

Oleg Shlyakhov did. He came to the hospital every morning to remind Berezhnaya how many days remained until the European Championships. Berezhnaya's doctors sent him away. The girl wasn't going to be speaking or walking for months, if ever—let alone skating.

At first, Berezhnaya says, she "couldn't think about anything, because everything just hurt." When she felt a little better, she noticed that she could not feel her right arm, and she started poking at it with her good arm just to make sure it was still attached to her body. A doctor came in and said she would have to lie in bed for three weeks without moving, and she began to cry, because she could not imagine lying in that awful bed for so long. "All I wanted," she says, "was to go home and never skate with Oleg anymore." Berezhnaya communicated by writing notes to her mother and to Moskvina. One of her earliest notes said she would never skate with Shlyakhov again. It was Berezhnaya's mother who gave him the news. Moskvina had already gone back to St. Petersburg, and even after everything that had happened, Berezhnaya still couldn't tell him herself.

As her strength improved and she was better able to understand her situation, her spirits sank even lower. "You see," she says, "they didn't give me the mirror. So the first time I saw myself was in the newspaper. A local journalist came to my room in the hospital and took a photograph, and some kind soul brought me an issue of this newspaper. I took one look and

thought: Who is this, some kind of an embryo? And then later they removed the bandages around my head, and they did give me a mirror." She
had tried so hard not to cry, but now she broke down and sobbed. "I fell
into a deep depression."

During those endless hospital days, her mother led her gently through
the alphabet, then through the simplest words, syllable by syllable. All day
long, they did exercises to bring back the feeling on the right side of her
body. Berezhnaya was good at training, and within two weeks much of the
feeling had come back. But her fine-motor skills were still a problem, so
her mother would set tasks before her, like knitting with a certain stitch, or
separating a book of matches.

One afternoon Berezhnaya discovered that she could speak a little
bit—slowly, painfully—and turned to her mother. "It was the first time
she could talk," her mother says quietly. "She said to me, 'Mom, will I
skate?'" Tatyana Berezhnaya shakes her head. "She was lying paralyzed,
and the first question was: Can I skate? Will I be able to skate?" Tatyana
Berezhnaya looked down at her daughter's body, connected to tubes and
ravaged by angry scars. The emaciated body made almost no shape under
the sheet. "What could I say?" she sighs. "I said, 'Yes. Of course you will.'"

∞

Anton Sikharulidze was at a friend's house when Moskvina called him
shortly after midnight. "Hold on to your chair," she told him. "So I sat
down," he recalls, "and she said, 'Lena is in the hospital.'" Sikharulidze
was enraged. "He told me I was stupid," Moskvina recalls. "I was stupid, I
shouldn't have let her go. We all knew something would happen. I should
have told her to stop skating with him, I should have told her not to go to
Riga." Sikharulidze hung up the phone and stayed up all night, deciding
what to do.

Something inside him had snapped. The tension had been building for
a long time—he had needed to change, but he had avoided it, and now this
tragedy had happened. Well, for once he was going to do something. "I decided to leave my partner immediately," he says. "I thought I had to act
somehow. I had to do it at that very moment. Besides, I couldn't just keep
skating with my old partner and visit Lena in Riga at the same time. I was
scheduled to take part in a competition in St. Petersburg a few days later."
He called his partner and told her he was quitting. Then he started packing for Riga.

From Tatyana Berezhnaya, whom he called to check on Lena's

progress, Sikharulidze heard that Shlyakhov might try to stop Yelena from leaving Latvia. Sikharulidze didn't care. "I was going to Riga," Sikharulidze says. "And I would never come back without her. To stop us he would have to kill me." But Sikharulidze didn't want any trouble, so he avoided his figure skating contacts and secretly obtained a visa through friends. When the visa came through, he was on the first train to Riga.

"Why did I rush to the train station?" Sikharulidze muses. "Some kind of internal impulse propelled me forward. And perhaps if I was thirty at the time, and not a teenager, I would have been scared to take such a responsibility upon myself." Some people have said—well, he wanted to get a good skating partner. Sikharulidze shakes his head. "I don't know," he says. "But we were so young. We were just children. And about the partnership, what could I have thought? At that point, it was still unclear whether Lena would be walking, not to speak about skating." No, he went for a simpler reason. It was the same thing that had drawn his attention to her the first time he saw her at Yubileiny. "It all started," he says, "with my wish just to help her."

Sikharulidze made his way to the hospital quietly. He didn't want Shlyakhov to know he was in Riga yet. But when he reached the hospital, it was not Shlyakhov he feared; it was Yelena. "I was so afraid to enter the room," he says. "I went to the intensive care ward, and they said, 'Come in, she's here.' And it was this huge room, maybe twenty beds, and it was not so clean. I looked at all of them, and none of them were her. I'm saying to myself, Where is she? And then I open a door and see that there, in the hallway, there is a cot, and she's lying there, with her head wrapped up in a yellow bandage. And I'll never forget what she looked like at that time. Her arms were just twigs."

Sikharulidze arranged his face in a false smile. Actually he felt like crying. "I couldn't show her my horror," he reasons. "So I smiled and said, 'Lena, *privyet.*' She looked at me and said nothing. So I said again, '*Privyet.*' And then I said to the doctor, 'Maybe she doesn't want to see me.' But the doctor said, 'It's not you. It's just that she can't talk.'"

Lying on the cot, Berezhnaya couldn't speak, couldn't move. The only thing she could do was think. "And the whole time I was thinking, I'm so scary looking, so thin, with a shaved head, barely alive, almost a skeleton," Berezhnaya says. "And yet here is Anton, and he is taking such good, tender care of me." Sikharulidze petted her; he spoke to her cheerfully of her recovery. In a corner, he quietly conferred with her mother, and they decided they would take her from the hospital that very night. They would stay at a hotel near the train station, and the minute that Lena was strong enough, they would go back to St. Petersburg. They would tell Shlyakhov nothing.

"We kept everything secret, because these people are so evil, stupid, and greedy that they could have done anything," Sikharulidze says contemptuously. "When we stayed in the hotel, nobody was to know about it. But suddenly we heard a knock on the door. It was two girls from the rink, so Lena told me I could open the door, but later we found out that Oleg had asked them to come over and try to get out of us when we were leaving. So of course I was nervous. I was sure that Oleg would spy on us."

On the night that they went to the train station, Berezhnaya was trembling. They walked slowly to the platform, the three of them: Berezhnaya, her mother, and Sikharulidze. Sikharulidze held her hand. Unbeknownst to Sikharulidze, Oleg Shlyakhov was on the next track, frantically searching the cars for Berezhnaya. But he never found her. Shlyakhov was searching the wrong train.

"It was on the train that we were sure of ourselves," Sikharulidze recalls. "We ordered food from the restaurant car, and they brought the food to our compartment, and she began eating. She practically didn't eat at all before, and she had lost a lot of weight. But now she began to eat, and she was trying to speak. She was even trying to smile." Sikharulidze's voice grows soft. "It was great," he says simply. "It was enough for me."

The next morning they arrived in St. Petersburg. "I went to the railway station," Moskvina says. "Anton's friend met them with the car. Anton was carrying her from the train to the car in his arms, and she had a big bouquet of flowers in her hands. Her eyes were like shining with— with a happiness. And this was very cold morning, early in the morning. In St. Petersburg it's still dark. Very cold, and she was hardly dressed because she had not many clothes. She was very weak. But she was very happy."

$$\infty$$

In that winter Yelena Berezhnaya was remarkably happy for someone who did not know if she would ever regain her speech or the full use of her body. But she was receiving large doses of the human kindness that she had not felt for five long years. Moskvina arranged for the best doctors. Berezhnaya had no insurance, so Moskvina paid the fees. For a time her mother stayed with her, and when she had to go back to Nevinnomyssk,

Berezhnaya moved in with the Sikharulidze family. Anton's parents had only a two-room apartment, so they squeezed a cot into the room Anton shared with his sister. Moskvina told Anton to get back on the ice immediately, alone. For once, he just followed orders.

The new life was all around her, but there were reminders of the old. Her hair was still painfully short, and she wore hats to hide the scars while she hoped it would grow back. When Anton's mother, who wanted the girl to eat heartily, asked if the cooking was all right, she replied that it was wonderful. In the years with Oleg, she added, she had eaten mostly yogurts, as no one cared if she got meals or not.

Her speech was still slurred, and when she first went back to the rink, Moskvina says, "This was like very sad and emotional moment for our group. Because we had seen her skating with Oleg, full of strength, health, desire to become great skater. And then we saw her like invalid, almost retarded. She could not speak, either she couldn't find word or she couldn't make sound, and this was like very scary."

But people treated her fondly, kindly, and for the first time in years she became a person first, a skater second. Anton listened while she read books aloud to practice her speech. When the girls at the rink found out that she had left most of her belongings in Riga, they gave her some of their clothes. One day a doctor said that she was well enough to try skating again—that perhaps gentle skating might even speed her recovery. So Igor Moskvin found the money to buy new skates for Berezhnaya, and Tamara Moskvina gave Anton a stern lecture.

She said, "Listen, this is a person who had that serious injury. So you should be ready that maybe your pair won't exist. Don't look at her as future partner. You are just trying to help her recover as a human being. If she will skate, then we will talk about the future. If she won't and she won't be healthy, then you just help her to become a little bit more alive and then your pair will not exist. Are you ready for it?" Sikharulidze was ready for it. His friend needed his help. He had been looking for a reason to go on skating. Well, here was a reason.

What must Tamara Moskvina have felt, the first time she saw Berezhnaya just gliding, simply putting one skate in front of the other—merely doing that simple motion she does better than anyone in the world, and holding Sikharulidze's hand for safety? Berezhnaya's body was still thin and malnourished. She looked like a cancer patient, with no hair sticking out from under her stocking cap. Her skull still had a place where it was sickeningly soft; if she touched it gently with her fingers, it would hold the impression. Would she become dizzy? Would she faint? If she fell, would her head hit the ice?

Was it still, at this moment, a question "against humanity" to ask if she would skate—or had it become somehow a question of restoring some of her humanity? For as Sikharulidze would say later on, to skate more was to confirm that she was fine, that she would be whole again; to skate less was to say that she was weak, that she would never be well.

"I was responsible for the life of a child," Moskvina says. "She was eighteen, still a child, and she lived far away from her mother, so I was like a little bit of a mother for her. And then I thought: Let's pretend she's my daughter. She had that injury. She had that operation. Will you teach her?" Moskvina pauses. "No."

But Berezhnaya's own mother had already answered that question, so the two friends stepped onto the ice. Later, after only a month of stroking around, Berezhnaya would astonish Moskvina by reeling off a double jump, and soon after, she would nonchalantly land a triple. Not long afterwards she would do her first spin, a maneuver that is enough to make anyone dizzy, and Moskvina would pray, pray that there would be no sudden cry, no abrupt collapse. There was none. Later still they would do "that dreadful element, the side-by-side spin," and Moskvina would race down the ice toward them, yelling at the top of her lungs: "*Please!* Stay *away* from each other! Stay *far away*!" And they would do the side-by-side spins far apart, with an eerie wide space between them.

In the summer, Sikharulidze would start to lift her above his head on the firm ground. When September came they would do lifts on the ice, and he would drop her too often and sometimes dramatically, and curse himself. And when she would fall Moskvina's heart would hurt, and she would demand of someone: "Why she's so unlucky, as if somehow everything which happens is like against her? I know that, for example, I am very lucky person. And she somehow, so unlucky." (Berezhnaya, still far too thin, in a heap on the ice, rubbing a bruise, and Sikharulidze in the corner, berating himself.) Moskvina would skate over and help her up, ask how she felt, force her to take a rest.

"So we teach her," Moskvina says. "No—not teach. We support her, Anton and I. We support her as people. And she recovers, she moves . . . she fights, fights the unluck of her life." (Berezhnaya up on her feet again, shaking the pain out of the bruised leg, and then beginning again, swaying gently to and fro as she builds speed.) "I think she is afraid, but she goes slowly up—tries, falls, does again. This is really the quality that I admire. I admire, but I don't tell her," Moskvina says. "Very deep in her heart, she must be extremely brave."

There came a time when Sikharulidze found himself afraid to say no to Berezhnaya when she wanted to attempt a dangerous element, for skating, which she had once loathed, now meant normal life. After practice, Berezhnaya went to a speech therapist and practiced tongue twisters; she still spoke Russian slowly, with an American accent. When she called the homes of her friends, their parents would recognize a foreign voice and shout at her, in English: "Hello!" In life she was an object of people's pity. But she had never spoken much on the ice. The ice was the one place where she had some chance of feeling normal. For Berezhnaya, it was simple: the more skating, the more life.

But all these things came later. The first time she stepped on the ice she felt a wave of tenderness. "I felt," she says, "as if I were returning from somewhere very far away." The ice stretched out before her, and sunlight flowed through the old glass walls of Yubileiny. "I knew I wasn't allowed to fall. So I stepped out onto the ice very confidently, and I began to skate."

Chapter Two

ARBIN IS AN OLD CHINESE INDUSTRIAL CITY, a pile of factory smokestacks and five-story apartment buildings plunked down in the middle of an open plain. Harbin is what the Chinese like to call "a very average city, the most average kind of city," home to the usual crowd of workers and teachers and bureaucrats, of old aunts and only children. In the early morning rush hour, armies of bicycle riders weave in and out of the deafening traffic, while over on the sidewalk, a team of men unloads cabbages from the bed of an open truck. Children in matching blue warm-up suits file through the schoolyard gates. At an intersection, on a sunny stretch of sidewalk, an improvised barbershop is open for business. Two men sit in folding chairs; behind them, two women in smocks clip their hair. A third woman sweeps up the clippings. Overhead, smoke streams out of the factories, caking everything in a thin layer of grime and soot: the light blue taxis, the weather-beaten bicycles—even the statue of Chairman Mao in the plaza in front of City Hall.

People born in Harbin tend to stay there for the rest of their days. In the last decade of reforms it's gotten easier to leave the city of one's birth, but it's still extremely difficult to get a *hukuo,* the permit required for moving to a bigger, wealthier city. Unless a person is brilliant at something, he is pretty much stuck in Harbin. At times, Harbin seems curiously provincial, as if a good working-class village with a few factories woke up one morning and suddenly discovered that it had three million residents. The city is a kind of urban backwater—tolerated by its own residents, forgotten by the rest of China, and unknown abroad. China has perhaps a dozen cities like Harbin—sprawling, polluted metropolises of three or four million, insular places where foreigners seldom go. What makes Harbin different is that it is situated in the far, far north of the country, close to the border with Siberia, and that Harbin is extremely—almost unimaginably—cold.

This is how cold Harbin is: It's so cold that even among the hearty northeasterners who make their home in the upper provinces, it is known as Ice City. It's so cold that the ice sculptures carved for the annual festival in November don't melt until March, because for five months solid the mercury never rises above freezing. Ice City's fame has even spread to Hong Kong, where travel agents sell Harbin package trips to wealthy businessmen so they can fulfill their childhood dreams of seeing snow.

Forty below zero is the place on the thermometer where the Fahrenheit and Celsius scales meet, a temperature that most children learn about only in science class but one all too familiar to any eight-year-old Harbiner. At those temperatures the wind is merciless, and the Harbinese, when they can no longer avoid going out, have to bundle themselves up in Russian fur hats, padded pants, and the heaviest coats they can afford. At forty below, water spilled on the ground freezes almost instantly, before your eyes. Actually, everything freezes at forty below: a slice of bread slipped into a pocket for later, car doors, fingers and toes, eyelashes, even noses. To keep their noses from freezing, the people of Harbin cycle around with white masks covering their noses and mouths, or sometimes scarves. The most common present for a Harbinese girl to give her sweetheart is a warm scarf knitted by hand, for him to wear over his nose and mouth on the bike ride home from school. Above their colorful scarves, everybody looks like Santa Claus, eyebrows and lashes completely white with snow.

Within China, northeasterners are known as friendly, good-humored sorts. They speak a Mandarin accented by lilting notes, and it is their Mandarin, with its joking inflections, that is used on popular sitcoms broadcast from Beijing. The people of Harbin are robust types who rise early, work hard, and put away enormous lunches of meat and game dishes. They are famous in China for the size of both their portions and their paunches. During the long winter, most Harbinese seem happiest in the hot pot restaurants, where the steam from the bubbling pots floats above the tables and the beer goes down warm. But there are those brave souls who take a kind of perverse pleasure in stepping outdoors in the minus-twenty-degree air—the people who drive pony carts down the frozen Songhua

River in the dead of winter, and the men who celebrate the ice festival by cutting holes in the river, donning swim trunks, and jumping in.

Ice comes to Ice City in late October, and immediately the skating begins. Skating of the primitive type is almost as old as snowshoeing in these parts, but figure skating has been around for only a century. In 1896 the Trans-Siberian Railroad was extended through Manchuria, making Harbin the terminus of a railway that stretched across Europe to Asia. The railroad brought the Russians, and the Russians brought their skates. At first, people skated on the river; later, they skated on the frozen soccer fields.

Flooding the soccer fields to make cheap ice is still an annual ritual in some of the northeastern cities. One afternoon, not long after the first freeze, the teachers ask each child to bring ten or fifteen ice bricks to the school the next day. All through the afternoon and evening, the children make the bricks, pouring water into their lunch pails, leaving them outside for half an hour to freeze, then running some hot water around the edges to remove the brick. By bedtime, each child has a pile of ice bricks outside the door, and the next morning, each child lugs the pile to the soccer field. The children stack the ice bricks around the perimeter of the rink, shoring them up against banks of dirt, and then the water is turned on, flooding the space inside the borders. By the next morning, the skating rink is open, and with luck it will last until the thaw comes, four or five months later.

Objectively it is coldest in Harbin in January, when the temperature averages twenty below zero. But according to the locals the fall is the coldest time of year, because the central heating hasn't been turned on yet. The brutal wind comes whistling through the cracks in the apartment walls and the cheap windowpanes, and the Harbinese wear the same overcoats indoors and out. They huddle underneath blankets, but the cold still seeps into the bone, and all a person can do is shiver under the covers until morning comes. This goes on for about a month, until the twentieth of November, a day which amounts to a sort of unofficial national holiday, when Beijing gives the nod and the central heating comes on all over China.

Harbin's climate is so extreme that by November, the streets are already slick with layers of ice, and the wind is ferocious down by the banks of the Songhua River. By November, it has already been snowing for a month, and the skies, always gray from pollution, grow even grayer with snow clouds. It's the beginning of the long, dull season, but still, on a peaceful night, when it's very dark, the sight of snow falling can be rather pretty. It was on such a night in November of 1980 that Shen Xue was born in the city hospital in Harbin. Her father, Shen Jie, stood at the window, watching the snow fall. "She was born in the early morning, at about three-thirty. A light snow was falling," he says. "We didn't know what to call her. And after trying several names, we decided to call her Xue"—which means: snow.

∞

Shen Jie is a slim, lanky man. He favors button-down shirts and trousers that billow away from his slender body everywhere except where they are pinned down by his cuffs or cinched in by a belt. When he comes into a room, he shakes everyone's hand and chatters amiably, with a frank look in his big eyes. He is a friendly, good-natured man, and the only complaint some people might have against him is that, even more than a typical Chinese father, he is inclined to go on and on talking about his only child. It is as if his daughter's latest doings were not only his family news but also his career developments, and his hobby, too—which, in fact, they are.

In some ways Shen Jie is typical of a man of his generation, the first born under the red flag of Communist China. His childhood and adolescence were the childhood and adolescence of Mao's young government, and when Chairman Mao's radical policies went horribly wrong, Shen Jie's generation took the brunt of it on the chin. Shen Jie was four when Mao's agricultural "reforms" triggered the worst famine of the century. Like all children of the time, he knew painful hunger, but he was one of the lucky ones who survived the famine. In those years, every pair of eyes was riveted to the hand serving out the portions at mealtimes, and Shen Jie knows what it means to live for three years on gruel made from the grain ration, which was not even good grain but sorghum or even pea dust. Eventually the food returned to the shelves, and things were quiet until he started middle school. Then the Cultural Revolution came. Like everyone else, he stopped studying math and biology. "In those years," he says, "we went to school mainly to study the quotations of Chairman Mao." But by the time Shen Jie finished high school, the tide in China had turned again. Now, in order to get a good job, one needed not Chairman Mao's quotations but the old-fashioned kind of education, which Shen Jie did not have. So at the age of twenty the state assigned him to one of the worst-paying work units in the city, the Harbin electronics store. In 1975, his first year on the job, he was making about a dollar a week.

In all these ways Shen Jie's story is the usual story of a man of his generation, and yet he departed from the script in some ways that are rather surprising. For starters, Shen Jie has always been an ambitious man. This was a rare enough quality in anyone who had come of age in the witch hunt atmosphere of the Cultural Revolution, with neighbors denouncing neighbors in the streets on charges real or invented. Serious consequences invariably followed for the accused, ranging from public humiliation to severe beatings to being "sent down to the countryside" to do hard labor. Not surprisingly, a lot of the men of Shen's generation became cautious yes-men, afraid of offending anyone. People quoted the old Chinese axiom: The gun shoots the bird that sticks its neck out. But somehow Shen Jie had come through the Cultural Revolution still burning with the desire to stand out. He was a bit of a show-off; he knew how to work a room. Just as water inevitably runs downhill, his ambition flowed into whatever was available. In the late seventies what was available was playing sports.

Shen Jie had always liked sports, but sports were banned while he was in school during the Cultural Revolution, which made it impossible to practice them for half a dozen years. By the time he was assigned to work at the electronics store in the late seventies, sports had been officially rehabilitated, and Shen's work unit fielded a variety of teams to compete in a kind of intercity workers' league. Soon he was playing on all of them. Volleyball, soccer, basketball—whatever they had, he led the team. But he was especially good at Ping-Pong.

Ping-Pong is the glamour sport of China, the sport that generates the fan hysteria and the record-breaking crowds. Shen Jie had always prided himself on his table tennis prowess, which he had developed at a young age in the courtyard of his tenement. While the neighborhood mothers were away at their work units, Shen Jie and one of his buddies used to slide the plywood bedboard out from under one family's bed and hustle it down to the courtyard. With the bedboard, a couple of chairs, and some bricks, they could throw together a Ping-Pong table in minutes, and there they held court, showing off for the younger kids until the factory whistle blew. Then they'd grab the bedboard and sprint up the stairs, whisking the frame back under the mattress and slipping out the door just as the unsuspecting mothers were coming up the steps.

For several years Shen Jie represented his work unit at the citywide All Work Unit Table Tennis Tournament, a rollicking affair that drew enormous, enthusiastic crowds. Up in the stands among the thousands of spectators was the woman who would become Shen Jie's wife. Shen Jie had noticed Lu Manli on the sales floor of the electronics store, first of all because she was "really beautiful," second because she knew the prices of more than a thousand pieces of merchandise by heart, which impressed him. For her part, Lu Manli, a lively, warmhearted northeastern girl, liked the Ping-Pong all right, "because it strengthened his body," but she didn't put much stock in sports. She was a romantic, a girl who liked to sing and had played the nurse when her high school put on Peking operas. Lu Manli was more impressed with her future husband's "talent and his honesty—and his calligraphy. His calligraphy was wonderful." She married him in 1979, and Shen Xue was born the next year.

A Harbin reporter who has known the Shens for a long time describes them as "just so average, just such typical people that you would find everywhere in the streets of Harbin," two workers and their one child, rolling down the icy street on the family's only bicycle. There is truth in this description, except that the Shens were even poorer than average. According to the propaganda, all workers in Communist China made the same wages, but as a practical matter everyone knew that the electronics store paid worse than most. It was one of those state-run enterprises that sell goods made in China *for* people in China, goods of such dismal quality that they are forbidden to be exported. The Shens' work unit also lacked apartments, a serious failing in a world where apartments could basically only be gotten from the work unit.

Even by the standards of poor worker families in Harbin, the Shens were badly off. Worker families were accustomed to living in one or two rooms, but the Shens did not even have one room of their own. At the time that Shen Xue was born, they were living in a one-room apartment with Shen Jie's mother in the run-down Daowai district. Lowly Daowai was a rabbit's warren of ancient, ramshackle *hutong* houses and crooked alleyways. It was home to the poorest of the poor: tinkers, peddlers, and the old women who sold Chinese pancakes in the streets. It was also home to dockworkers and shop clerks like the Shens.

The passageway through the Shens' courtyard was dusty and decrepit, littered with the leftover boards and broken tools of many generations. To navigate the narrow passageway at night one needed a candle. Inside the small house the atmosphere was close and stale; a coal stove heated the place in winter, and the walls were plastered over with layers of newspaper. There was no sink, only a tap that fed a basin, and a pitiful kitchen in the corridor. The house was carved into many tiny compartments, and in the Shens' ten-by-sixteen-foot space, three adults and a baby ate, lived, slept, and stored their belongings. At night, a sleeping curtain offered a pathetic amount of privacy.

During the Cultural Revolution, big character posters had glorified the humble worker, and, like everyone else, Shen Jie had believed that the future was bright for workers. But now anyone could see that society was shifting back into its old patterns, and workers were squarely on the bottom again. A cruel trick had been played on his generation. He might have been a cadre—a respected government official—but instead Shen Jie had been put on the shelf in the electronics store at the age of twenty, and there he would remain for life. His wife had no hope of changing her station in life, either. Shen Jie and Lu Manli were barely in their mid-twenties, but already all alternate routes were closed off to them. There was only one person in the whole family who had any prospect at all of a better future, and on that individual's efforts all the unrealized hopes of the entire family depended. It was, of course, Shen Xue.

∞

Shen Xue weighed barely five pounds at birth, and she was always catching cold as an infant. She would wake up crying, flushed with fever, struggling against a hacking baby's cough that broke her mother's heart. Her mother, Lu Manli, blamed herself. "I was young, I didn't know how to take care of her well enough," she says fretfully. "The child was often too cold or too warm, and so she caught cold all the time." Because the baby was always getting over the latest ailment, she played mostly indoors, avoiding the neighborhood kids who played together in the building's courtyard. Because of the one-child policy, if she stayed indoors, she played alone. That suited her just fine. What Little Xue ("Xiao Xue") liked best was to sit quietly on the floor, concentrating on her own projects. There was something almost comical in the scholarly look on her tiny face when she addressed herself to her toys. Even after she learned to talk, Little Xue rarely said a word. "She was a very shy girl, never noisy or naughty," her mother says approvingly. Right from the start, she was the perfect Chinese daughter—quiet, obedient, diligent. Turning the pages of her books over and over, she taught herself to read some Chinese characters before she was three.

Like everyone in Daowai, the Shens were accustomed to using one room for everything. As for clothes, wearing the same faded dark blue or gray uniform day after day was practical, politically correct, and affordable. The women cooked cheap vegetables and grains flavored with morsels of cheap meat or fish, and they washed clothes by hand as they had for centuries. People bathed in cold water from hallway taps they shared with neighbors.

Everyone was poor. Their parents had been poor, their grandparents had been poor, and this generation fully expected to be poor, too. Life had always been hard—if anything, it had been much harder in the past, under the brutal Japanese occupation, or during the civil war or the famine. Children complaining of hunger would be cut off with a smack and a lecture: "If you think you are eating bitterness, just think of what we suffered, of what our parents suffered! Remember the Long March!" If Chairman Mao and his ragtag troops could trek six thousand miles across China to save communism, a child could spend a year studying day and night for an important exam. Life might be hard, but it was certainly harder for peasants than for city folk, certainly harder for the last generation than for this one. Being poor simply meant that you had to know a lot of things just to get by: how to make winter boots with cotton cloth and flour paste, how to hold a place in the queue for cooking oil while simultaneously holding a place in the queue for pork.

In the fifties, people had yearned for just a little more grain. By the sixties, the shelves were again lined with cabbages and watermelons, and people began to dream of owning bicycles, radios, wristwatches. In the seventies, the family usually got the bicycle and maybe even the radio, too. Nobody seems to have found it demoralizing that a Chinese family should have to scrimp and save for three years to buy a transistor radio. Lu Manli, who waited years to get a simple wristwatch, is taken aback by the very idea that she was deprived. "Why," she exclaims, "I already had a wristwatch by the time I was sixteen!" When she was twenty-four she got a transistor radio, and at thirty-two, after six years of penny-pinching, she went with Shen Jie to pick up their first television set.

In such a home—indeed, in such a world—the key thing was to be extraordinarily strict with oneself. Nothing should go to waste. Lu Manli was forever mindful of the older generation, the ones who had eaten the bark from the trees when the grain ran out. "Economizing is a time-honored Chinese tradition, passed down from one generation to the next," she says. "We watched our parents. They never wasted any water. If a grain of rice fell on the floor, they picked it up." Lu Manli, too, picked up the grains of rice. She saved everything. Around the house, she knew how to make things last. She could wash and stitch and press a garment until it looked almost new again. The Shens were experts in mending old shoes, patching bicycle tires, reusing soup bones. In this way they might be able to stretch their salaries and save a little each month toward that elusive second bicycle, or the far-off dream of a washing machine. If you walked into their ten-by-sixteen-foot room at any given moment, you would find that everything they owned was immaculate, in good working condition, and put away in its assigned place. From her vantage point on the freshly scrubbed floor, Little Xue absorbed it all—the frugality, the work ethic, the self-discipline—and in time became the sternest taskmaster of them all.

It began when she was only two years old. "She had a box where she kept all the toys and books," Shen Jie says, "and when she wanted to play or read, she took them out. The first time, we told her to put them back when she was finished with them. Later, she just did it on her own. She was kind of disciplined. And you know"—and now her father is really beaming—"she preserved all the toys and books very well. Even when she was in her teens, they were still like new." Now and then, Shen Jie would take the toys out of the box himself and show them to other parents. None of this was lost on Little Xue, who was already an old hand at reading her mother and father. Before she could walk, she could sense the slightest vibration of her parents' displeasure at fifty paces. She determined early on that she would not provoke it, ever, that nothing mattered except that her parents should never be disappointed in her. "Ever since she was really very young, the child was obedient," her father observes. "Unusually so." She was compliant in everything—so obedient, in fact, that to this day, her parents still don't know if, in the beginning, she really liked skating at all.

It was Shen Jie who took her skating for the first time. It so happened that Shen Xue's kindergarten teacher had come into the electronics shop, and Shen Jie, knowing that the teacher's husband was the head of a prestigious sports school, managed to intercept her. In the course of polite conversation, he mentioned that his daughter, who was sickly, should probably be training at the sports school to improve her health. The teacher agreed to speak to her husband, and the next day Shen Jie showed up at a frozen soccer field to present his daughter to the beginners' skating coach.

Little Xue was a poor specimen: small for her age and weak. The coach hesitated. "But you could see she *really* wanted to try it," the coach recalls. "So I accepted her, thinking, Well, every three months we drop the worst ones, and I can always drop her then." Shen Jie, delighted by his good luck, watched his little girl's every move. Shen Xue said nothing; she just skated.

It was a great day in her father's life. "She was five," Shen Jie recalls. "When I took her to skate, as soon as she got on the ice she could stand up, no problem. She didn't fall down like other kids."

Did she like it?

"I never asked her whether she liked it," he says, considering the idea.

"The child wasn't good at expressing herself," her mother says impatiently. "She wouldn't have said whether she liked it or not. Sometimes she would write in her diary. That was about it."

"She was really obedient," Shen Jie says. "Unusually so. When I said we should go home, she would just follow me."

Shen Xue followed her father back to the sports school the next morning and every morning after that. On his way to work, he would let her off the bicycle at the edge of the soccer field. He would help her tie her skates, then ride off. Little Xue only came up to the coach's knees, but she would skate two hours, rest a bit, then skate another two hours. Little Xue was bundled up in a pink snowsuit and wore literally half her wardrobe underneath, but at twenty or thirty below, she still froze. At intervals she would have to go inside to warm her tiny feet over a heater before gritting her teeth and marching back out to finish a practice. "The kids could endure it, because they were always moving," Shen Jie insists. "Of course we, their parents, worried about them. But what could we do? We couldn't think of the weather, or if the kid was overexercised or not. We had to go to work. So we left the child in the hands of the coach."

At noon Shen Jie would leave work to bring some lunch to Shen Xue. For lunch the Shens could afford about four ounces of dumplings, to be divided between the father and daughter. Shen Xue's tiny fingers would have to thaw before she could even lift the chopsticks, but no matter how cold she was, she would still skate two to four more hours in the afternoon. The last couple of hours were the hardest, and her father tried to get out of work early so he could catch the end of practice. The other parents kidded him about his perfect attendance: *There's Shen Jie again, watching his kid like a hawk.* Other parents, especially workers like Shen Jie, pushed their children hard, and there were many who took it to extremes. But even in a crowd of formidable Chinese parents, Shen Jie was the most intense.

"Many of the coaches used to joke that after I spent one day working in my work unit, then I went to my second job at the sports training school," he chuckles. Shen Xue wasn't laughing. After four grueling hours out in the Siberian winter, she now exerted herself to do better for her father. Just as her strength was failing her, the coach would call for the last break, and the child would look up and see her mother arriving with a bottle of warm milk. Lu Manli, on top of everything else she had to do, redeeming food coupons and cleaning and mending, always took care to know the schedule and to arrive just as the children were stepping off the ice. In any group in Harbin, the Shens could count themselves among the very poorest, and even the bottle of milk bore the stamp of their poverty. Shen Jie felt the other kids' eyes on his daughter. "My wife put the warm milk in a hot water bottle. We didn't have a thermos, like we have now, so she just wrapped this bottle with a towel or some clothes to keep it warm."

While his wife hurried home to cook the dinner, Shen Jie stayed out in the frigid Harbin dusk watching the last hour of practice, stamping his feet to keep them from freezing. As the last light drained from the sky, Little Xue would stumble off the ice. "Skating for a whole day, she looked ragged," Shen Jie says. "By the end of practice, she looked like a small potato, covered in dust and dirt. Every night, my wife had to wash all of our little girl's dirty clothes." Shen Xue would sweat through three or four scarves a day, plus a full layer of inner clothes. After the dishes had been cleared away, Lu Manli would wash the clothes by hand. They had to dry before morning. There were no extra clothes.

The first three months passed, and the coach, Chen Xinping, did not drop Shen Xue from the team after all. "You see, we were training up to eight hours a day," the coach recalls, "and for a five-year-old, it's a lot. I noticed some things about her. At that time, we only had the outdoor rink. It could be very, very cold, even thirty below zero. Shen Xue was very brave, and she wasn't afraid of getting hurt. I realized that Shen Xue was willing to work harder than the other kids. And I thought to myself: This will make her a good athlete."

In those years Chinese sports science was at the level of the stopwatch and the tape measure. The coach gave Shen Xue a running test and a jumping test, measured her limbs, and took a good look at her parents—"their height and their body type. There are no formal regulations for this, but we can judge from our past experience who will be promising physically—even at five years old." Shen Xue was judged promising. Out of forty-six children in the beginner class, she was one of only four to make the first cut.

∞

Shen Jie had brought his daughter to the ice rink with the modest goal of strengthening her weak constitution, for it was believed that six hours a day of vigorous exercise in subzero cold might be good for a five-year-old with chronic bronchitis. But now Shen Jie became convinced that his little girl had the makings of a champion. He was alone in his enthusiasm; certainly none of the coaches agreed with him. Shen Xue puts it bluntly. "When I was young," she says flatly, "nobody said that I skated well." With her scrawny build and hacking cough, she didn't look like a world beater. In Shen Xue's group, the children used to perform a drill where they skated in a single-file line. The first child in the line was the best skater in the group, and this lucky child would lead the drill. If he or she did a waltz jump, the next child would copy it, and the next, and so on down the line. After a few months Shen Jie saw that his daughter was not at the front of the line, and that troubled him.

"It had happened that Shen Xue had missed some practices early on," he explains. "I had to do something at my work unit, so I couldn't take her to the skating lessons for one week. After that, her mother was in the hospital, so we didn't take her to skating lessons that week, either." Shen Jie was tormented by anxiety. What if she were to be cut from the team? Her sports career would be finished. "So I took her to the coach of the city sports team to see if she could make up the work at the special indoor rink. Since we got to know the coach, we were allowed to go there and skate, and in this way, she could catch up. The other kids at the outdoor rink would skate for six hours. My kid would skate for eight hours."

The training started at ten-thirty at night, and sometimes, at around ten o'clock, Little Xue would fall asleep. "Then I would have to wake her up and put clothes on her, and take her to the ice rink," her father remembers. "But the child never complained. When I told her it was time to go, she would just follow me out the door." Little Xue, padded from head to toe in the pink snowsuit, would hop on the bicycle for the long, cold ride to the indoor rink.

Once she got there, she would practice apart from the other children. They were the elite, and she was the interloper, a mere beginner. For a girl who was painfully shy in the first place, being singled out in this way must have been excruciating; however, Little Xue never complained. Alone in one corner of the ice, trying to take up as little space as possible, she would listen patiently as her father repeated the coach's words from earlier in the day. Shen Jie was quite a good athlete himself, and he prided himself on his ability to "tutor her theoretically." For two hours, while the other children in her beginner class slept soundly, her father tutored, and Shen Xue practiced. When the session was over, the kids from the city team would trudge across the parking lot to their team dormitory and up to bed. Shen Jie would lift his daughter up onto the bicycle rack and set off for home.

One night, riding home after midnight in the brutal cold, Shen Jie turned around to discover that Little Xue had passed out in the bicycle rack. In a cold sweat, he pedaled as hard as he could toward the city hospital. By the time they arrived, the little girl had a fever of a hundred and four. She had never said a word.

The child recovered quickly, but the incident terrified Shen Jie. And yet like any Chinese parent, he lived between two terrors: the terror of pushing too much, and the terror of pushing too little. It was dangerous indeed to let a stoical little girl go skating with a fever of a hundred and four, but it was also dangerous to let your child take it easy. For if Shen Xue was resting, her competitor was certainly passing her, taking her future spot on the city sports team. A Chinese child's entire future was often decided before the age of twelve—whether the child would be one of the elite few to go to a sports or music school, or one of the lucky two percent to go to college. In a country of a billion people, parents were determined that their child should have the maximum possibility of getting one of the few coveted places. Let the entire family sacrifice to make it so; after all, the future of the entire family depended on the child rising above the vast undifferentiated mass of workers.

All over Harbin, all over China, small children worked—did real labor in their parents' shops and fields, stayed up until two in the morning bent over textbooks, practiced the piano six hours a day. Children competed with one another from their first day at school. Shen Jie did not want his daughter to grow up to be a shop clerk living in one room in Daowai; he did not want her to know what it felt like to have your life's opportunity taken away from you and be powerless to get it back. Therefore, Shen Xue practiced; therefore, she concentrated and pushed her body to its limit; therefore, she skated up to eight hours a day.

Among the prized possessions of the Shen family is a yellowed old newspaper photograph affixed to the page of a worn scrapbook. It is one of those winter scenes that newspapers the world over publish in the snowy season, a human interest photo from the local pages, and it shows a small girl leading a line of young skaters across a large pond, her arms raised like wings. It is, of course, Shen Xue, promoted to the front of the line, now the best skater in the amateur sports school. But this goal, so cherished only six months earlier, was no longer satisfying to any of the three Shens. Because now they had seen the children of the city sports team, with their identical uniforms and their assigned bunks in the dormitory. These children had shiny new skates; they ate expensive high-calorie meals and wore beautiful costumes. All this the state gave to them, along with the very best coaches. These children traveled to other cities and came home with shiny medals and trophies. Most of all, their future was assured. In exchange for devoting their childhood to China, they were guaranteed a job and a pension after they retired from skating.

All of this remained unspoken at home, but Shen Xue knew how important skating was. Already, the sacrifices had started. "From the day she went to the amateur sports school," Shen Jie says, "her mother did not have one new thread of clothing made for herself in ten years. For our inner clothes, we would wear the very old ones, and for a jacket, we would wear our uniform from the work unit." Old dreams of owning a washing machine or another bicycle had to be delayed so they could buy new skates. The family's efforts became even more concentrated on skating. If the work unit gave them movie tickets, the Shens would give them away to other people, unwilling to miss a single practice. On those rare cases when neither parent could be there, they would send Shen Xue's frail grandparents to keep watch, even in the terrible cold.

"Some of the parents," Shen Jie explains, "could not go on like us. Because in our generation, we missed a lot because of the Cultural Revolution, so some of the parents would prepare for night courses at the university, and some of them wanted to get promoted to cadre. When they were preparing for that, they didn't have time for their children." Shen Jie was a smart, charismatic man who might go far, but he decided instead to focus on his only child. "Her father gave up his career," Lu Manli says matter-of-factly. "If you want your child to be successful, the parents must give up their career."

On snowy afternoons, while her family stood by the ice, stamping their feet and watching her intently, Little Xue, lover of silly cartoons and stuffed animals, would attack the practice like a marine at boot camp. After every hard fall, she would clamber up and try again. From the sidelines, her parents judged her every move. ("Even now," her mother says, "we will all know instantly if Shen Xue makes some small mistake.") One afternoon, the coach was teaching six-year-old Shen Xue the Axel, the one-and-a-half-revolution jump that serves as the dividing line between kiddie skating and serious skating. The coach rigged up a crude jump harness, and Shen Xue landed her first Axel with the help of the harness. After that, the child refused to leave the ice until she landed one on her own. Time after time, she rose into the air, spun, and crashed. It had been dark for half an hour by the time that Shen Xue finally landed her first Axel. Only then would she consent to be taken home.

Her mother watched such scenes with her heart in her throat. Quickly, inexorably, the family had become entwined in a circle of love and guilt, guilt and love. When Shen Xue went into her first competition, the parents gave up any extras for themselves for months so that they could buy her a pretty, flimsy dress and silk stockings. On the day of the competition, it was twenty-nine below zero. Her mother put the dress on her anyway and sent her out onto the frozen soccer field; she still feels guilty about it. "At that time we were so young. We didn't know any better," Lu Manli says, shaking her head. "We just thought: To be a figure skater, she should look beautiful. We put so little clothes on her, and she was really so very cold. She didn't complain. In fact, she performed very well."

When Shen Xue's feet grew, somehow her parents managed to save sixty yuan for a new pair of skates, an amount equivalent to both of their salaries for a month. But the skates were too big and scratched her feet dreadfully. Shen Xue, who felt guilty enough about what the skates had cost, told no one and skated her usual six hours. After practice the socks would not come off; they were glued to her feet with frozen blood. At home she soaked her feet in a basin and painfully peeled the socks from her excoriated feet. Naked, they were a bloody mess of scratches and blisters. But the next day, at her own insistence, Little Xue was on the ice again. "She went on the ice, but she couldn't do the normal skating because of the pain," her father says quietly. "And it went on like this for two weeks." Filled with remorse, her mother put insoles into the boots to cushion the blows, helped the little girl to soak her bloody feet at night. "The reason for the problem was that we had to buy her a pair of skates that were too large for her, and she would have to grow into them," Lu Manli says. "But the skates were too expensive." "It's not like now," her father says earnestly. "Now we can have a pair of skates custom-made for her. But we couldn't afford to do that at that time."

If Shen Xue's six-year-old suffering appears cruel to a Western eye, it was nothing unusual in China, where many parents taught obedience with rough slaps and harsh words. Confucius urged parents to beat their children so that the children would be loyal to them later on, and there is even a Chinese saying that translates roughly as, "Beating your children is love; swearing and cursing shows you care." In the typical Chinese view, the world is a very harsh place, and you must prepare your children to survive in it, to outdistance the competition. The sports schools are full of stories of children passing through a corridor and overhearing the muffled screams of a teammate, shrinking under a parent's blows. And there were stories of parents handing over their children to the coach and saying, in a traditional way, "Treat my child as your own; if you must, discipline the child; deprive him of meals or hit him; do what you think is best . . ."

While some of her teammates ducked blows, Shen Xue disciplined herself. "Shen Xue," says her first coach approvingly, "is that kind of girl that always wants to do everything perfectly." She was the new breed of Chinese athlete, one of the children of worker families who were increasingly prized by the sports system for their complete lack of self-regard. It was in the eighties that track and swimming scouts began traveling to peasant villages to find girls with athletic talent and a history of extreme deprivation. A Chinese sportswriter explains that "kids growing up in that kind of family tend to have these really good personalities for sport— that is, good at eating bitterness." Shen Xue was not an overwhelming natural talent. What she had, and what could be exploited to make her great, was her willingness to work harder, stay on the ice longer, take more falls. She could eat more bitterness.

So Shen Jie kept pushing. "In order to let her skate more, sometimes I would take her to skate at four o'clock in the morning. That's our own decision. The coach had nothing to do with it." Roused from her six-year-old's dreams, Little Xue would climb down from her bed and submit to being dressed. She followed her father out the door into the four o'clock darkness. Father, mother, and daughter climbed onto the bicycle and wove through the streets until they came to a construction site. It was Harbin's second indoor ice rink, and though the building itself was still under construction, the ice, magically, was ready. Shen Jie had discovered this secret ice, and now the family snuck around the back of the building in the early-morning hours and stashed the bicycle in a dark place. Shen Jie tiptoed around, looking for a window that hadn't been installed yet. When he found it, he climbed in through the opening. Lu Manli lifted the child up, and he pulled her through the space where the window would go; Lu Manli was the last one in.

Inside the building it was pitch-black, silent, eerie, bone cold. "In winter," Shen Jie says, "at four o'clock in the morning, it was still dark. So I had to buy candles." Another expense, another sacrifice, another image of Lu Manli standing at the greengrocer's counting out her coins, putting back the turnips and saving the last few pennies for the candles. "What could we do?" her father demands. "We had to buy the candles to give her the light to skate by, so that she could have more time on the ice." Shen Jie and Lu Manli stood on the ice in the paralyzing cold, wearing their old jackets over their work unit uniforms over their ragged underclothes, melting the base of each candle until it stood upright on the rink barrier. And in the one dim corner of flickering light, the child skated. In the cavernous, empty arena, there was only the scraping of her blades against the ice, and, at intervals, the sound of Shen Jie's voice as he tutored her, theoretically. Before sunrise, they blew out the candles. One at a time, they climbed out through the window opening. Then they rode off into the dark gray morning. The sun was rising. Shen Xue leaned her little head against her father's back and clutched his jacket in her tiny fists, fast asleep in the back rack of the bicycle.

∞

In China a lot of jobs are still done the hard way. On a cold October morning in a neighborhood near the Harbin city limits, a group of men struggle down the sidewalk, bearing heavy sacks of cement on their shoulders. Another man pushes an overloaded wheelbarrow, straining to hoist it over the curb. Here, near the outskirts of the city, a donkey cart picks its way through the maze of cars and bicycles. On the sidewalks lining the road, the hawkers have set up their stands and are selling dried shrimps, cellophane noodles, and vegetables just in from the farm, displayed in the cart they rode in on. The abundance of the countryside is laid out on the city sidewalk like a picnic, but the overwhelming feature of this scene is the noise. The noise is equal parts motorcycle engines, blaring horns, braying animals, and the screech of metal on metal at a stand that makes house keys while you wait. Above the general racket, the hawkers scream out slogans to the people passing by.

Zhao Hongbo grew up within a few minutes of the street market. Just off the main drag, a narrow dirt alley curves back towards the twenty-two apartment blocks owned by the Harbin Flax Factory. Zhao Hongbo's mother spent her working life bent over a loom at the flax factory, and as a result the family has lived in these apartments virtually rent-free for more than forty years. By Chinese standards, the Zhaos achieved a good working-class life, and they felt fortunate to have it, since a generation earlier, their families were on the other side of the wall that divides the street vendors' stalls from the factory workers' flats. One grandfather, a peddler, would shoulder his products and walk down the street selling cigarettes and sugar. Another grandfather eked out a living by selling *fentiao,* the cheap, transparent string potatoes eaten by all poor families. By comparison the Zhaos did very well for themselves. During the civil war, Zhao Hongbo's father was an early recruit to the Red Army's performing arts and propaganda troupe. After the war the Party made him a cadre, a member of the bureaucratic class. In his job as a local official he was entitled to greater respect, wages, and privileges than an ordinary worker.

The Zhao family has lived in a few different flax factory apartments over the years, but all of them have been more or less the same: two rooms plus a kitchenette, cracked walls, a bare overhead fluorescent tube for light, and single-paned windows that rattle in the winter winds. The back doors of the apartment blocks give onto a dirt alley, where the workers' skinny children play among the unpenned chickens and geese. The alleyway is bounded on one side by an unbroken row of small, run-down sheds. When Zhao Hongbo was three, he became something of a legend in the flax factory when he managed to scramble up on top of one of the sheds. His triumph was short-lived, because he fell off the roof and wound up at the medical clinic having his leg popped back into its hip socket, but he was unfazed. The neighbors can still picture little Hongbo tearing down the alley, scattering the geese to the winds on his way to the playground to hurl himself off the monkey bars.

From the vantage point of the crude balcony of the Zhaos' fifth-floor apartment, the scene below repeats itself in all directions: identical apartment blocks, alleys, sheds, chickens, children, over and over again, as far as the eye can see. The panorama produces a hint of the profound feeling of anonymity that can creep into Chinese life, the staggering anonymity of being one in a billion. The flax factory compound is but one of the hundreds of compounds controlled by the different work units in Harbin, and at any given time there are thousands of little boys playing in the alleys.

Yet right from the start Zhao Hongbo stood out. He was a surprise, a late-in-life son born to one of the last sets of Chinese parents who were not restricted by China's one-child policy. By the time he came along, his siblings were already seventeen, fourteen, and nine, so the whole household took turns cuddling him. Under the constant glow of so much affection, the child's sunny personality became even sunnier; in one of the two rooms of the family apartment, one could often hear little Hongbo laughing or singing. In a fond mood, his mother describes him as "active, happy, and lively. He loved sports. He was full of activities. He was born that way." In a cross mood, she says, "He was really naughty—really, *really* naughty. He was always hurting himself: arms, legs, everywhere."

Hongbo was a daredevil, hyperactive and basically uncontrollable; he was also adorable. On the playground, the other mothers used to collar him as he went tearing by and pull him onto their laps to hug him. "He was pretty thin and very little, and he looked pretty dark in the skin," his mother recalls, "and in the neighborhood, everybody loved him. They just treated him like a little plaything." On the Zhaos' floor of the apartment building there were fourteen other families, and Hongbo's easy laughter could be heard up and down the corridor as he went door to door, making friends. "Whenever the neighbors saw him come out, they would call to Hongbo, 'Little Rubber Ball, come here!' They laid a hand on Hongbo's head and they would cry, 'Bounce, Rubber Ball, Bounce!' Hongbo would jump and jump, until he exhausted himself."

Some evenings, when the adults came home tired from a day's work, he would summon them for a performance of his own invention, usually jumping and dancing. No matter how tired they were, the neighbors always came to watch Little Rubber Ball put on a show, for it was 1976, the tenth long year of the Cultural Revolution, and this boy was delighted by life at a time when few grown-ups were. For years most people had been going about their lives in a fog of apprehension, hoping they would not be the next ones to be targeted for senseless punishment. And here was a little boy who knew nothing of all that. In fact he had no fear of any kind. In her childhood, his mother had lived through horrors, fleeing her home when the Japanese invaders raided her village, hearing the screams and witnessing the beatings. She had lived through a brutal civil war, one of the worst famines in modern history, and now the Cultural Revolution. So far, little Hongbo had survived falling off the roof of a shed. It was nice to see somebody around with a clean slate.

∞

Zhao Hongbo lived in the family home until he was seven. Then he moved into the Harbin ice sports dormitory a few miles down the road—and never came back. It happened by accident, really. One morning a skating coach came to the flax factory kindergarten, and while he was there, the kids were playing basketball. The flax factory team had just won the city kindergarten championship, mainly because Zhao Hongbo had made the last two shots of the game to put the flax factory on top. For the victory, the school had received a piano; in addition, every player was given a basketball and a sports suit, which were the two best presents any of the kids had ever received. On this particular morning the piano was sitting in the corner and Hongbo was feeling rather good about himself, and as usual he was doing as he liked on the basketball court. He was nimble, with superior coordination and boundless energy. He had extremely quick reactions and good foot speed for his age, such that the other children could seldom get near him, let alone interfere with his shots.

The skating coach plucked him out of the game, wrote down his name and address, and went to pay a call on his parents. The coach put forward a proposition: Hongbo, who did not even know how to lace up a pair of skates, would be accepted right away to the city skating team. The government would pay all his expenses, and he would move into the ice sports dorm immediately. He would come home once a week on Saturday night, returning to the dorm on Sunday afternoon.

Nearly every country has some variant on the sports boarding school, but China alone requires seven-year-olds to live in dormitories within a short bike ride of their homes. Officially, this is because parents cannot be trusted to produce the best results. In the dormitory, children receive the right amount of sleep, arrive on time to every training session, and consume meals that are roughly ten times as expensive—and nutritious—as the meals at home. And families accept the dormitories because they are painfully aware that they cannot provide their children with the high standard of living offered by the dorms.

The Zhaos were fairly well off by Harbin standards, but they were still living in acute poverty, cramming six people into two small rooms. When their four children bedded down in the main room at night, only a few inches separated their cots. Zhao Hongbo remembers that "actually, at that time, because the living conditions were not that good at home, it was considered kind of lucky to go and live in the dorm and have these good meals at the dining hall for sportsmen." But even so, his parents hesitated. After all, the boy was only seven years old. They sent the skating coach away once, twice. And then Jing Yulan and her husband relented, and they handed over their youngest child to the sports school.

In China, accepting what fate brings is as old as Confucius and as contemporary as Mao, and Jing Yulan was well schooled in both. She had always accepted her fate. She submitted to an arranged marriage; she became a weaver at a flax factory because the state assigned her there. Each time she gave birth, she was allotted exactly fifty-eight days maternity leave; each time, on the fifty-ninth day, she reported to work and handed her newborn child over to a nursery attendant. For a time she was assigned to the "dorm for mamas," where she lived with two other mothers and all of their children in a single eight-by-twenty-foot dorm room. For two years she seldom saw her husband, because the authorities sent him away for work. On the rare occasions when he came to Harbin for a two-day visit, he was required to sleep in a nearby workers' dorm.

To Jing Yulan, the idea that the state should tell her husband where to sleep was completely normal. She accepted her fate because she lived under a regime that gave her no choice, really, and when the larger impositions came, she accepted those too. Mrs. Jing, like most Chinese people, still calls the famine by its Party-approved euphemism, "the years of natural disaster." She likely has no idea that the Party's agricultural policies, such as forcing farmers to melt down their scythes, created the famine, or that Mao increased grain exports to the Soviet Union while an estimated thirty million Chinese starved to death. When the famine reached Harbin, she went to pick up her ration coupon book and made due with pitiably small amounts of food for her family. By 1961, cooking at home was no longer permitted, and Jing Yulan and her children were forced to eat from communal pots in the flax factory's kitchen.

When the Cultural Revolution came, and the authorities demanded that she choose one of her children to go to a labor camp in the countryside, Jing Yulan accepted that too. It was 1974, the waning days of the Cultural Revolution, but Party leaders continued to send students to the countryside to "accept retraining from the poor peasants" and purify their Communist spirit. Jing Yulan remembers that "an official came to our family and said: 'Look, you have so many kids—you're going to have to send someone to the countryside. Then, after your child comes back from the countryside, the leaders will consider your child to be much more excellent than all those who did not go.' "

So Jing Yulan sent her oldest son to a camp at the very edge of Siberia, where the laborers cut down trees. Working outside all day in forty-below weather, the high school students lost parts of their ears and toes to frostbite. For six years, they subsisted on a diet of frozen cabbages, leeks, canned meat, and almonds. "The truth is," Jing Yulan says, with some effort, "honestly, I didn't want him to go. But the country was calling on young people to go to the countryside. We were just answering the call."

In China today, *xiangying haozhao,* "answering the call," is one of the few Cultural Revolution slogans still in circulation. "Answering the call" is one of the chief virtues that teachers strive to inculcate in elementary school pupils, and with good reason—for the idea of duty to state before self and family is the foundation on which Communist China is built. Ordinary people must answer the call, period, whether the call is unfair or even irrational. So Jing Yulan sent her oldest son to a labor camp, and within a few months, she could even find it in her heart to be slightly optimistic about it. "The truth is, life was hard in that place. But the funny thing is, everybody came home looking so good," Mrs. Jing says, shaking her head. "Actually, everybody seemed to be gaining weight. I thought: maybe this will be a good opportunity for my son after all." It wasn't. When the Zhaos' oldest son finally came home, he was not considered more excellent. He was considered undereducated, and the state ordered him to spend the rest of his working life in a machinery factory.

∞

In 1980, Mrs. Jing answered the call again and gave her other son to China, this time because China needed him for sports. This time was perhaps different from the others. This time, possibly for the first time in her life, she actually could have refused. People might have thought she was foolhardy, but she wouldn't have been penalized in any way. But after so many years of acquiescing, it had become a way of life. And the boy did love sports very much, and the sports school would guarantee him a decent career. His parents agreed, and Hongbo went to the dormitory. But the singing and the laughter went with him.

To this day, an almost childlike expression comes over Mrs. Jing's lined face when she thinks about her youngest child, the one who left home too young. "When Hongbo was six, one day I gave him a coin," she says. "I told him to buy a popsicle when he feels thirsty. But a few minutes later, when he came up from the street, he brought me a bunch of zucchini and said to me, 'Mom, these zucchini are really inexpensive. They are enough for several meals.' " Ms. Jing finishes this story with a soft chuckle. In her living room, next to the large Soviet-made television set, she keeps just one framed photo. It is a snapshot of a very young Hongbo, standing in the snow looking merry. When asked if she missed him, Jing Yulan snaps, "Of course! How could I not miss him? Whenever I had time, I just couldn't stop myself from going to the school to visit him." But when she got to the sports school, she was reassured. "You know, when the other boys' parents would visit, those boys could not stop crying in their parents' arms. But Zhao Hongbo didn't," she says proudly. "While other kids were crying, he was not paying much attention to his parents. He was not talking too much, he was not bragging, or complaining, or behaving very timidly like some other boys. So we would feel at peace, because he really did like sports, and he was doing fine."

Maybe, but growing up at the sports school seems to have sharpened certain feelings in the young boy, made him a more wistful person. He speaks of Sundays at home in a quiet, reverent way. To Hongbo at that time, Sundays were the part of life that counted. "Every night, in the bunks, I always missed my home, my family. Although I spent most of my time with the kids in the dorm, the time spent with my family was much more precious. I couldn't forget it." He remembers watching his father teach his sisters to play the violin on Sundays. His father had learned to play in the Red Army performing arts troupe, and listening to the violin quickened the boy's own impulses toward beauty. On Sunday afternoons it was his father who took him back to the dorm, and during the week, when he would call home, it was always to his father that he spoke. "I would tell my father that I would like to have some kind of special snack or cookie, and he would buy it for me and bring it while my mother stayed at home, preparing the meals and making the clothes," he recalls. "And when I wasn't treated well by the other kids in the dorm, I would always tell my daddy."

When the team went on training trips to the far north, his father would pack his suitcase for him, nestling small surprises in among the heavy clothes. In the bitterly cold towns on the northern border, the coaches used to break the surface of the lake with hatchets and hand out basins of water to the kids, so they could rewet the surface of the ice and smooth it down. The cold was merciless. When the children had a bathroom break, the coaches would have to help them break open their frozen belt buckles. The ice was extremely rough, and the skaters carried whetting stones and sharpened their blades on the snowy banks during every break. The kids would skate their school figures while belted by the punishing winds, and often Zhao Hongbo would get halfway around a figure eight only to have the wind blow him back in his tracks. As the spring thaw approached, kids sometimes felt the ice give way and found themselves waist deep in water. No one ever drowned, but there were scares.

But whether the training was scary or not, once a child was in the sports school, his parents would never contradict the coach. Mrs. Jing recalls that once she came to visit and found nine-year-old Hongbo in the dormitory, where the coach had sent him to rest after a bad fall. "At that moment," she says, "I thought that maybe the child was homesick. Because Hongbo kept saying, 'Mom, let me go back with you. I can't go back to the ice anyway.'" But Mrs. Jing was unmoved. "I thought, There are rules for the team, and the coach is not around right now. So I said to Hongbo, 'I'll ask your father to come and bring you home so you can have your leg examined. And in the meantime, you can ask for medical leave from the coach.' Hongbo said nothing. But he saw me out, limping, and he went with me for a long walk. I told him to go back to the dorm. He didn't want to. Then he cried. I asked him, 'Why cry? Is it worth it? Aren't you a man? You stay here tonight. I'll send your father to bring you home tomorrow.' Hongbo didn't say a word. He just cried silently. I didn't know what to do, so I said to him, 'Let me see your wound.' So Hongbo lifted his pants. What I saw was an enormous black-and-blue swelling the size of a goose egg at the pelvis." Then his mother sent him back to the dorm, where he stayed that night.

Hongbo had talent, and within three years he had become one of the best skaters in his age group. When he was ten he won the national championship in his age group, and people began to take notice of him. At around the same time, he went to a smaller competition and swept four different championships. The top award for each category was a thermos, so he brought four thermoses home. "He was so happy," his mother recalls. "He gave one to his brother, one to both sisters. Even our neighbors were envious of us. They told me, 'Look at your good boy. He can skate, and he can bring thermoses home. How nice.' And whenever the family drank water, we would remember how excited Hongbo was when he brought those thermoses home." But Hongbo was not a part of such cheerful domestic scenes, except on Sundays. He was at the dorm.

∞

Shen Xue and Zhao Hongbo belong to the third generation of modern Chinese figure skating. Li Yaoming belongs to the first. Leader Li, as he is respectfully called, is a stout, hearty man in his sixties. He ran the Harbin figure skating school for thirty years before officially retiring a few years ago, but he is still the symbolic father of the school. Leader Li is always within shouting distance of the ice, for if he is not at practice, in the dining hall, or in the dorm, he is just around the corner in his apartment building, which is literally next door to the ice sports campus. To get from the door of Li's apartment down the stairwell and across the parking lot to the rink takes three minutes, but after the first minute Leader Li already has a full view of all his facilities, which is the way he likes it.

Li started skating on the frozen lakes on the outskirts of Harbin in the winter of 1948, when he was seven years old. At first he skated on crude blades screwed into the soles of his winter boots, but in 1950 an aunt gave the boy his first real pair of skates. No skates had yet been produced in China, so these were Japanese skates, left behind when the Japanese invading forces were driven from Harbin. Li skated on the flooded infield of the Red Star Stadium with a crowd of Russian émigrés and a handful of Chinese enthusiasts. One of the pioneering Chinese coaches discovered him at Red Star Stadium, and in 1953, when the local authorities opened the first ice sports school in Harbin, Li Yaoming was invited to become one of its first pupils.

The 1953 version of the ice sports school was almost identical to the model still used in Harbin today: academic classes in the morning, training in the afternoon and evening, sleeping overnight in the on-site dorm. Then, as now, coaches were hired and paid by the state; they dined with their pupils, traveled everywhere with the team, and shared night duty in the student dorm. Living expenses for the team were paid by the state, and the sportsmen ate rich meals that no ordinary family could afford. It resembled the current training center in every detail but one: In 1953, no one in Harbin was training for international competition. "The purpose of the sports school was solely to train competitors for the National Championships," Li says. If this seems odd by today's standards, Li has an explanation. "People were simpler then. Our motivation was very simple. We wanted to do well, to help the nation. We just wanted to get better and better at our sport, make the skating more and more perfect. And of course," he adds, "we loved skating a lot."

The first generation did not just love skating a lot. They were obsessed with it. Skating for four or five months in the bitter cold at Red Star Stadium was not enough for them. The team sent scouts to the far north to find the place in China where the ice freezes first. That town turned out to be Heihe, "Black River," a tiny village directly on the border with Siberia. Every September, the team would travel together to Black River, and they would stay until they received reports that the ice back home was solid. They would go back to Harbin until the spring thaw, and then the team would go north again and use every last day of ice on the lakes of Black River.

Conditions were painful enough at Red Star Stadium when the wind blew at forty below, but Black River was even more extreme. The school staff remained behind in Harbin, so each day before breakfast, the skaters grabbed their brooms and shovels and began scraping and smoothing the ice. Desperate to use all the daylight, they would skate the first hours on an empty stomach. At midmorning, a few skaters would chop blocks of ice from a thick section and melt them down for hot water, and each skater would pull out the cakes stowed away in his inner pockets. The cakes emerged soaked in sweat, but the sweat was preferable to the alternative, for a cake left beside the ice turned to stone in minutes.

By late spring the sun came out in Black River, and in the middle of a practice the skaters would suddenly see enormous bubbles rising in the surface of the ice. When the team could no longer skate on the lakes, the boys would be dispatched to find some narrow stretch of the river, where they could skate in the darkness before the sun began to warm up the ice. In spring the coaches always kept a rope with a stick tied to it nearby, and in the fifties the rope and stick saved two lives. "And once," Li recalls, "when we were lining up for the team picture at the end of the season, the ice snapped and everyone fell in together. Luckily, it was very shallow there."

In 1957 the first generation of Harbin skaters experienced a kind of religious revelation in the form of five Czechs who somehow managed to come to Harbin as "scientific technical advisers." Watching a Czech coach and the four world-class skaters was shocking to the Harbinese, for China was so insular in those days that most people had never seen so much as a picture of a foreign skater in a newspaper. The Chinese skaters stared with all their powers of concentration, for in Mao's China, every outside impression was inordinately precious. Every movement, every word was recorded in someone's notebook, for the Harbin skaters knew it could be a long time before they had contact with the outside world again.

As it turned out, it would be twenty years before they saw another foreign skater, for soon after the Czechs' visit, China closed its doors to foreigners. In the summer of 1960 fifteen thousand Soviet advisers left China, and China's expatriate community dwindled to its smallest size in a century. Few Chinese went abroad, and even fewer foreigners were invited inside China. Communication with the outside world was essentially cut off. And in this complete isolation, ordinary Chinese experienced one of the worst famines in human history.

Across China, an estimated thirty million starved to death in three years. But in the Harbin ice sports school, the athletes didn't know it. They received decent rations and went on training, day after day. Harbin, which received urban rations and was located in a region famous for food surpluses, was among the best places in China to ride out the famine. Few people starved to death in Harbin, and since the newspapers were forbidden to mention the gruesome scenes in the countryside, the Harbinese had no idea that millions were dying. Athletes were even more sheltered than normal people; the only sense they got of how bad things were was when they went home once a week to their families and sat down to a thin gruel of whatever cheap grain was currently available. Grain formed at least ninety percent of everyone's diet, but while athletes received forty-two jin (about thirty-eight pounds) a month, schoolchildren received thirty-one jin and housewives only twenty-six jin. For an ordinary person, the meat ration for a month was only half a jin; in contrast, the skaters' monthly meat ration was eight or ten jin. Some of the skaters sent coupons back to their families, realizing that their own meat ration was the equivalent of that of twenty people. The extra coupons were dearly appreciated back home, where families had begun to forage for leaves and dig up roots.

In 1960 skaters understandably felt lucky to be in the sports school, where the food was plentiful and one could even help one's family. But by 1966 the Cultural Revolution had reached Harbin, and the tide had turned. Mao's Cultural Revolution was a mass movement intended to expose and punish anyone who could even tangentially be linked to any kind of bourgeois, counterrevolutionary ideas: descendants of landlords, teachers, intellectuals, former shopkeepers. Sportsmen were on the long list of groups targeted for "thought remolding" by military authorities, which was usually accompanied by punishment in the form of public denunciations, imprisonment, banishment to labor camps, and, in some cases, savage beatings.

In Harbin big character posters denounced sportsmen for their devotion to technical training at the expense of politics and decried the "feudal, bourgeois and revisionist" elements of figure skating, such as the music of *Swan Lake*. Sportsmen, coaches, and sports officials were alleged to have deemphasized the study of Mao's works and been polluted by bourgeois ideas. Among sports, figure skating was a special target, since its Western music, short skirts, and gyrating dance movements were all considered to be unhealthy for young people.

Younger skaters like Li were dealt with more gently, for, according to the orthodoxy of the times, their only crime was to have been misled by their elders. According to one source, many of Li's former coaches were condemned as "dangerous counterrevolutionaries" who had polluted the young. Some coaches were denounced as "reactionary technical authori-

ties," the same criminal category as college professors. Those with "prob-
lematic historical backgrounds," such as descendants of landlords, were
especially punished. There was relatively little violence against coaches in
Harbin, relative to other cities, but the coaches and team officials were humiliated and denounced at regular "struggle sessions," which the young
skaters were required to attend. Sometimes, the young would be called
upon to criticize their former coaches. In a culture where students used the
honorific "Teacher" to address their coaches for life, the act of denouncing
one's teachers broke a powerful taboo.

Chairman Mao's idea was that the polluted young should be sent down
to the countryside to have their thoughts remolded by living among the
peasants. In October 1968 the entire figure skating team was "smashed
and discarded," and its former participants were placed under the supervision of the Management Group of the People's Liberation Army. A formal
order stated that as sports teams had been infiltrated and controlled by bad
people, the athletes must be reeducated and politics must be stressed. In
Harbin, the ice sports school was locked and stood empty, and the skaters were shipped out under army supervision to Chalianhe, Tonghe
County.

Chalianhe was a big farm, a former labor camp for prisoners, and there
the skaters lived in the old, crumbling huts where the prisoners had once
been quartered. Now the huts were filled with skaters, volleyball players,
basketball players, the martial arts team. Mornings at Chalianhe were devoted to studying Chairman Mao's works or propaganda newspapers. Unlike most farms at that time, Chalianhe was mechanized, so in the
afternoon the athletes drove tractors, planted crops, and cut wheat with
sickles and threshed it in enormous combines. (The labor was not particularly hard, and in fact some athletes preferred it to the morning
studies.) Although perfectly good rice and wheat grew in the fields surrounding their mess hall, the athletes ate sorghum and corn flour, because
such a diet was supposed to be better for remolding thoughts. In the
evenings, the coaches and team leaders who were guilty of "historical
blemishes" would be verbally attacked in the struggle sessions. The
coaches did backbreaking labor in the fields, had to undergo military exercises every day, and were kept under tight supervision. They lived apart
from their former pupils, who only saw them during struggle sessions.

The skaters remained at Chalianhe for eight and a half months,
through a long, cold winter. By February, the skaters heard a rumor that
the official order sending sportsmen to the countryside would be reversed,

and by June of 1969, the team was called back to Harbin. But the reprieve was only temporary. Like many of those accused during the Cultural Revolution, the athletes' fate fluctuated, depending on the politics of the moment. "Around the end of 1969, the authorities felt that we were not successfully 'thought-remolded,'" one skater recalls. "So they sent us back to the countryside again, to Feigetu County, to do hard physical labor."

In the spring of 1970 the political winds shifted again, and the team was called back to Harbin to train for a command performance for top-level officials at Capital Stadium in Beijing. It was to be the first indoor skating performance in the nation's history. Overnight, the skaters went from political prisoners to symbols of national pride. Within months of their return from the camps, the skaters went to Beijing, where Chairman Mao's "three armies on ice"—figure skating, speed skating, and hockey— gave thirty-six performances in a single month. The performances were wildly popular with the crowds, since most cultural and artistic life had been banned during the Cultural Revolution. All national leaders except Chairman Mao came to the performances, and after these military-style displays, figure skating was rehabilitated.

The ice sports school was unlocked, and the team settled back into training. But some bunks remained empty. "After 1970, many athletes were not allowed to stay with the sports team," says one of those who survived the housecleaning. "Some did not have good family background; therefore, they were forced to quit. Family backgrounds like landlord, capitalist, parents with historical or current problems. This was not voluntary. Those with problems didn't stay, since the sports team was part of the superstructure." China was still closed to the outside world. The school's mission was simple: Train athletes for internal competition.

Li Yaoming was one of those who labored in the camps for the crime of being an athlete, and during those grim years he did not allow himself to consider his future. "I didn't think about whether I would ever skate again until 1970," he says. "I couldn't. But then the government said that sports are okay again, and I was happy." Li Yaoming was one of the lucky ones. He got to come back to the ice sports school, and he was allowed to become a coach. And so it was all over China, as the hysteria gradually died down throughout the seventies: People returned to what they had been doing before the chaos. A curtain was drawn over this period, and for those who had been allowed to return home, it was not long before the whole experience began to seem surreal, as if it had taken place in an alternate reality. Activities like skating that had briefly been criminalized were now normalized; people who had been purged were rehabilitated; institutions that had been "smashed" were restored. But why they had been smashed, and why they were restored, were mysteries not to be pursued, even within the family circle. In Mao's China, the safest life was to ask no questions.

∞

When Zhao Hongbo was thirteen, Leader Li saw him practicing one afternoon and decided his fate. "I thought: This boy just has to become a pair skater," Li says, rather mystically. "And besides," he adds more prosaically, "we had a slot to fill in a competition and we needed a pair. So, as the team leader, I gave the suggestion to choose Zhao Hongbo for the pair. However, Zhao's father called me and said, 'No way. We don't want to do the pairs.' And he would not be persuaded."

Leader Li chuckles at the memory. "Zhao's father even called Beijing and told them that he didn't want his son becoming a pair skater," he continues merrily. "The authorities in Beijing called me and said, 'Mr. Li, I don't know, maybe you should choose someone else.' So I said to Zhao Hongbo"—and here he slams his fist on the table—" 'Look, if you don't skate pairs, you're going to leave my school. I won't have you on the ice.' " Zhao skated pairs.

When Leader Li became a coach in Harbin in the seventies, China's pair skating tradition was even weaker than its singles skating tradition, which was also the weakest in the world. China had no pairs at all before about 1979, when Leader Li created the nation's first real pair, Luan Bo and Yao Bin. The circumstances were identical to Zhao's case: Leader Li needed a pair for a competition. But in this case, the competition was the 1980 World Championships. China had the chance to enter a pair, and Li was going to enter a pair—never mind that, at this point in his life, he had seen pair skating performed exactly twice. He had seen pairs once in 1977, when the coaches took a special trip to the northern border to watch the World Championships on Soviet television. The second time Li saw pair skating was in 1978, when he was one of four coaches sent to observe at the World Championships in Ottawa, in preparation for China's international figure skating debut in 1980.

To the Chinese, being in Ottawa was like emerging from a time capsule. Forget figure skating—the coaches had never even seen a four-lane highway before. They sat staring at the indoor rink, only the second one they had seen in their lives. They had never seen ice of this quality—so perfectly smooth, with special machines to make it. But it was seeing the world-class skating up close that really astonished the coaches. "We were shocked," Leader Li recalls, shaking his head. "We were absolutely shocked. Because after the Czech coach came to us in 1957, there was a huge void there for many, many years. We stared so hard, our eyes hurt." The coaches bought tape recorders, so they could record their impressions without looking away from the ice. As they watched, they spoke into the tape recorders, noting each element that was performed. For many of the elements the Chinese language had no name, and these they would describe in rapid, unwieldy sentences. They jabbered into the recorders like desperate men. "We treasured every second," Li says. "We didn't even stop to eat."

Armed with his memory, his tape recorder, and a couple of photographs he had cut out of the Ottawa newspapers, Li put together a pair. "In 1979, nobody in China knew how to coach pairs." Li shrugs. "I was the team leader, so I became the pairs coach." He went looking for a tiny girl like the ones he had seen in the pairs competition at the World Championships and found Luan Bo, a twelve-year-old with good basics and a malleable disposition. For her partner, he chose Yao Bin.

Yao Bin, who was twenty, resembled the tall, strong boys who had lifted the tiny girls at the World Championships. But Li really picked Yao Bin because he had a soft spot for the kid. Yao Bin's career was one of the hardest hit by the interruptions of the Cultural Revolution. Yao was nine when the ice sports school closed, and for four of the most critical years of any athlete's development, Yao couldn't skate at all, even in secret. When Li returned from the labor camps, he took pity on Yao, who was now thirteen, and let him train with the senior team. He wasn't sorry. Yao worked harder than any skater he had ever seen, and soon the boy was winning competitions. So Li chose Yao for his experiment in pairs.

For a very talented new pair, a reasonable amount of time to reach the world level is four years. Leader Li's skaters were not especially talented, and they had four months. The newspaper photos were useful—for instance, they showed the girl above the boy's head in an overhead lift position. What the photos didn't tell you was how the girl had gotten up to that position—and how she got back down. "We couldn't do some elements while in motion—only when they were standing," Li admits. "We would just try to do the movements in our own way." They started off by putting a table next to the outdoor rink. Luan Bo, dressed like a hockey player in a helmet and full pads, clambered up on the table in her skates. Standing on the ice, Yao Bin lifted her off the table into the air and tried to hold her there, steady above his head. Once they had that down, they tried to do the lift without the table. But in subzero cold that was a tall order, because you had to take off your gloves for a whole minute to do a real lift. Yao Bin used to stand with his bare hands buried inside his jacket until the last moment. Then he would whip his hands out of the jacket, do the lift, and shove his hands back inside right away.

Wearing her hockey helmet, little Luan Bo went up into the easiest of throw jumps and came crashing down. After each crash she scrambled up and put her hands back under her jacket, to warm them up for the next go. After a day of this, the poor kids were exhausted, and Luan Bo had cried until she ran out of tears. "She was just a little girl, bruised and exhausted, and she was so worried that she wouldn't be able to do it right," Leader Li remembers. "It was really difficult—almost too difficult for anyone." But when they would figure something out, and Luan Bo would eke out her first wobbly landing—"Well, then we were very, very happy. Because you see, we had no idea how to do anything. So when we learned an element, it was really we three who discovered it together. And I would say that the main thread of this time was happiness."

For Luan Bo, the main thread of this time was pain. She took hundreds of hard falls, suffered dozens of concussions, and once, when she hit her head particularly hard, doctors considered brain surgery. But at the end of the four months, Yao Bin and Luan Bo got on a plane and went to Dortmund, Germany, for the 1980 World Championships. There was no budget for the Chinese coaches to go, so they had to leave Leader Li behind.

The two kids had never been out of China before, and they were completely bewildered. When they reported to their first practice, it was literally the first time they had seen an indoor rink in their lives. At first they just stood by the barrier and watched the foreign pairs rehearse their routines. They didn't dare to skate on the same ice with them. By the second practice they had started skating in a small corner of the rink, afraid to venture farther. The ice was so smooth that they glided twice as fast as they did on the choppy ice back home, and they kept bumping into the walls. The Chinese didn't know much about pair skating, but they knew enough to realize that they didn't deserve to be there. The gap between them and the rest of the field was painful. It was as if a beginning skier had shown up for the Olympic slalom.

"In this era we, the coaches and skating people, always said that we should prepare for the international competitions," Li Yaoming recalls.

"We were always repeating that Party slogan that we should be 'breaking out of Asia and advancing on the world.' But in our hearts, we knew that we had a very long way to go." Yao Bin and Luan Bo skated at the World Championships, and the audience laughed at them. It was good-natured laughter, but they laughed all the same, and Yao Bin was annoyed. Luan Bo, a gentle girl with modest hopes, didn't take it too hard, especially when the German reporters consoled her by giving her the "most lovely ice princess" award. "I didn't care that everyone was better than us. I liked being there," she says simply. "I didn't expect anything. I was thirteen years old. I just wanted to learn from them. I thought: It's already an honor just to represent China. It's enough."

But for Yao Bin it was nowhere near enough. He came home from Germany seared by the experience. Yao had been determined before, but now he was almost in physical pain when he thought about the gap between himself and the rest of the world. He had finished fourteenth out of fourteen pairs, but he understood that the level of his pair's performance made them more like the five hundredth best pair in the world. So while he was in Germany, Yao made a precise study of the foreign pairs—their movements, their costumes, their music. He trained himself to record what he saw as if his brain were a videotape machine. He sketched the occasional diagram, but for the most part, he carried the moving pictures around in his head.

In 1980 an American delegation came to Beijing to give a performance and to teach the first seminars since the Czechs. Yao Bin absorbed it all on the spot. In 1981, when the ice sports school was finally able to borrow videotapes from the Soviet Union for a few precious weeks, Leader Li and the others watched the tapes dozens of times, but Yao viewed each tape once and went back to work. He stored all movies in his head, which in his view was the only logical place to keep them, because in this way he could carry them around. Yao Bin's images traveled with him from that luxurious indoor stadium in distant Germany to the soccer fields of Harbin. In early fall they went north with him to Black River, and in the summer they went along to Qingdao, where the team skated on the iced-over cement floor of the Qingdao meat-packing house. To this day, Yao can watch a videotape once and have the entire picture in his head.

His photographic memory was just one of the reasons why Yao Bin was something of a legend around the ice sports school before he was twenty. "With that one," his mother says, "whatever he happens to lay his hand on, he will exhaust all the knowledge of that thing." She should know, because during the Cultural Revolution, he turned her house into a woodshop. Formal sports were banned, so Yao taught himself carpentry in order to make a really fast sled. After the sled he decided to make some furniture, and then a wall of cabinets. Later he made a table and some chairs, and after the ice sports school resumed, Yao Bin used to come home on Sundays with a sack of broken hockey sticks; he found they made good legs for one kind of small stool. In his spare time Yao picked up drawing, which led to designing his own costumes, which in turn led to making his costumes. No one taught him to sew, he just picked it up as he went, and soon he was making costumes for the whole team. Eventually the team moved the sewing machine into Yao's room, and his roommates got used to the sound of the needle humming down the seam as Yao worked the treadle in the evening. One day the accompanist didn't show up to play the piano for the skaters' ballet class. "So Yao Bin just sat down and started to play," says Li, shaking his head. "All of us stopped cold and stared at him. We were incredulous. We didn't even know he could play the piano."

Yao Bin was in a race to catch up with the West. In 1981 Harbin got its first indoor rink, and for the first time, Yao could train without having to stick his hands inside his jacket every thirty seconds. Now Yao could skate every day of the year, and he almost did. He was working frantically to catch up with the Europeans and North Americans.

Not that the West noticed. Each year at the World Championships, Yao Bin and Luan Bo would finish last. But Yao would eye the gap between his own marks and the marks of the next-to-last pair. China was starting to narrow that gap. As a concession to the judges, Yao moved towards more Western costumes and music. A decade after the skating team was sent down to the countryside for its attachment to unhealthy Western music, Yao Bin and Luan Bo skated every day to decadent bourgeois tunes like "Love Is Blue." Each year they ratcheted up the difficulty of their routines, and by their last season, the pair was performing side-by-side double jumps and a throw triple Salchow, a respectable repertoire for a team at the world level.

In 1984 they at last competed in the Olympic Games, and this time Leader Li got to come with them. Again, the Chinese endured the embarrassment of having people point fingers at them and giggle during practice. In the short program Yao dug one skate into the ice and set a pivot for a death spiral. Luan Bo held his hand and dropped down until her body was prone to the ice. With her head resting near his feet, she spun in a circle around him. It was one of the easier moves. All of a sudden, Yao teetered and fell on his backside. The crowd tittered. Again, they finished dead last. Then Yao snapped up his suitcase, boarded a plane for home, and ended his amateur career.

"I didn't really want to be a coach at first," he says. "I wanted to try my hand at other areas, like journalism and photography. I liked things related to art. Some people even suggested that I go into dancing." Leader Li had other ideas. Li wanted to retire from coaching and move into local sports administration, and he wanted Yao Bin to take over as the head pairs coach in Harbin. So Yao moved into a coach's room in the dormitory and started training pairs. Instead of going to a prestigious Beijing university, Yao had to settle for a Harbin night school course in physical culture. On nice afternoons, while the athletes took their afternoon nap, Yao used to climb out the dormitory window onto the roof, carrying his textbooks and a piece of chalk. While the others slept, Yao Bin read his physics and biology texts, making notes on the cement roof with his chalk. Going to night school part-time, it took him three years to graduate, and by the time he finished he had developed a plan for how he could close the gap between China and the West. Now all he needed was a pair.

∞

At moments, Harbin feels like a Soviet city. Walking down the sidewalk, the mass-produced housing blocks suddenly give way to an expanse of grass or a big paved lot. It's as if the topography of the city were a bolt of cloth, and in some places, the fabric is wrinkled and bunched up, whereas in others the fabric is stretched flat. One minute you are peeling off city blocks at a pace of a block every minute, the next you are on the edge of a field that stretches for five or six blocks. The flat stretch of field is pinned down on either side by squat buildings; squinting across the field, you can make out the far edge of the grass, where the city resumes.

Such a field materializes out of the blue in the eighth district of Harbin. In summer, it is a weed-infested soccer field, with rusty goals and bare earth showing through the weeds. In winter, it used to be Shen Xue's ice rink. From the age of five to nine she skated here every day. The soccer field is just across the big parking lot from the city sports school compound, with its exclusive dormitory and indoor rink, so every time Shen Xue glided towards the parking lot she could see the object of her desire. She watched the elite skaters coming and going, on their way from practice to the dining hall to the dorm, and she envied them.

Zhao Hongbo made the city team without lacing up a pair of skates, but it took Shen Xue almost four years of relentless practice to get her bunk in the dorm. Finally, when she was nine, a talent scout recommended her for the city team, and she at last found herself on the other side of the parking lot, among the chosen ones. She was the youngest child in the entire school, and the transition was hard for her. As one of the lowest in the pecking order, her indoor ice sessions were from one to five in the morning, followed by breakfast and elementary school. In her first year her father would come to her dorm in the morning and give her a lift to elementary school on the bicycle. At lunchtime he would pick her up at school and ferry her back to the dining hall. Besides being the youngest, she was also the smallest, and her father can still picture the little girl waiting in line for the hot buffet behind the hockey players and speed skaters. "They towered over her," he remembers. "She barely came up to their waists. So she would crane her little neck to see over the edge of the table to see what kind of food she would like to have, and then she would squeeze over between the hockey players' legs to get the food for herself. When she wanted to get the porridge, the scoop was really long and the bucket was deep, and mostly she would just spill the porridge all over herself."

"It was difficult for her, because she was the youngest at the city sports school," her mother says. "For instance, because she was afraid she would be late for the morning calisthenics, she would go to bed at night with all her warm clothes on. That way, when she woke up in the morning, she could rush out onto the field, and she wouldn't fall behind the others and be criticized by the coach." Determined not to fall behind in school, either, Shen Xue would finish an outdoor skating session, plop down on the snowbank, and open one of her textbooks. "She was a determined girl," her father says proudly. "Even though her schedule was very tightly arranged, from the morning till night, and she only spent half a day to study school subjects, she would always be number three in her class after class examinations."

Though Shen Xue slept in a room with half a dozen other girls, "she didn't have many friends," according to her mother. "She didn't like doing the girly things, because she was being brought up in a certain very strict way by her father." Her father protests that the girls at the sports school "really liked to be around Shen Xue. For example, sometimes I would give her several apples to take to the school, and some of the older girls would cheat her and say, Your apple is not as good as mine. Let's swap. And she would just listen and swap apples with them. She was obedient. And when they jumped rope, the other girls would tell her just to stand there and hold the rope, and even though they jumped twice and she only jumped once, she wouldn't complain. Shen Xue is that kind of girl who wouldn't argue with anybody. And the other girls liked being around her."

"She was shy," her first coach recalls. "She didn't speak much. And if somebody took her toy or her apple, she wouldn't say anything. But on the ice—well, on the ice, she wanted to beat everyone." And for a time, she did beat everyone. She won the Harbin City Championship twice while she was in elementary school. But around the age of twelve, her singles skating career began to plateau. This was a dangerous period for any Chinese child athlete. Bad results in the awkward years of adolescence could lead to being dropped from the team. Shen Jie was worried that Shen Xue was not a good enough jumper for singles, and he began to think of switching his daughter over to pair skating. He started going to pairs competitions and being friendly with the pairs coaches. Then Zhao Hongbo appeared at the rink, skating alone, and the rumor flew that he was looking for a new partner.

By 1992 nineteen-year-old Zhao Hongbo was something of a local hero. With his first partner, he had won the pairs championship at the National Winter Games, a quadrennial competition that was like China's internal Olympics. After that victory Zhao's father had sent Leader Li a whole slew of presents and a note saying, essentially, "You were right," and all was forgiven. At that point the famous Yao Bin had taken the team under his wing and begun grooming them for bigger things. Zhao and his partner had gone on to the 1991 World Junior Championships, where, instead of finishing dead last, they beat out five pairs from Western countries and created a bit of a stir. Yao even took the unprecedented step of taking the pair to Russia to train. They stayed for six months, and while they were there, in the words of Zhao's mother, his first partner "ate too many potatoes and got too fat for pair skating."

Zhao came home and ended his partnership, and he came to the rink to practice by himself while the leaders looked for his next partner. All the girls on the city team stole glances at handsome Zhao Hongbo as he practiced alone; they were more than ready to leap into his arms. But Teacher Yao was taking his time in choosing a replacement. It was rumored that he wanted to find a partner who could one day compete at the World Championships. This generated a lot of excitement, since no Chinese pair had been deemed good enough to be sent to the senior World Championships in the past seven years.

Four girls were being considered, and Shen Xue was not at the top of anyone's list. "Some people," a local reporter recalls, "even thought Yao Bin was out of his mind to consider Shen Xue. After all, since she started skating at the age of five, Shen Xue didn't accomplish much. She had kept silent for these seven years. Why should Yao Bin give her the big chance?" Yao Bin was inclined to agree. "Actually at that time, people were saying, 'Look, Teacher Yao, maybe you should just choose the number one girl from the singles.' And Shen Xue at that time was number four."

But no one had reckoned on Shen Jie. "As soon as we heard the news, that Zhao would change partners, we raised the issue with the leaders, to let them consider it before they had their meetings," Shen Jie explains.

"We also talked about it with Yao Bin," her mother interrupts.

"We went to talk with Yao Bin on our own initiative, and Yao Bin told us, the decision was not his," her father says.

"Her father came to me many times," Yao Bin recalls, with a twinkle in his eye, "and he also asked his friends to persuade me to take her. He even brought me some presents, until finally I said, 'Listen, I appreciate your positive attitude. But I'm going to look more at her quality, just the quality of the girl herself.' "

So Shen Jie put his daughter on display. "We tried our connections to let her skate on the pairs training session," he explains. "And it happened that all of the coaches liked Shen Xue. So they would let her skate on the side of the rink while the pairs were training, and in this way Yao Bin had the opportunity to see her more."

Yao Bin had said that the decision was not his, so Shen Jie also called on Leader Li. Leader Li has a simple philosophy on parents: "If the parents are very cooperative and encourage their children to work hard, then they are welcome. But if the parents are critical—if they say, oh, you shouldn't eat this dorm food, or this dorm is not nice enough for you—then they are not welcome." Shen Jie was a model parent of the first category. He combined the Communist ideal of sacrifice to the state with the traditional ideal of the humble petitioner who arrives bearing gifts. All in all it was quite a successful visit. And after the situation had dragged on for two months, Leader Li called Yao Bin into his office, a dank room on the same stale corridor as the locker rooms, and set him straight.

"I said to Yao Bin, 'Look, with his first partner, Zhao didn't get such great results,' " Li recalls. "So I recommended Shen Xue to him. At first Yao Bin wanted to take a different girl. I said to him, 'No, that girl is uncooperative, and look how tall her parents are. But Shen Xue's got a good character, and her parents are not very tall, and her skills are good.' Yao

Bin said nothing. So I said to him, 'Look, since I'm the leader, you just take her, like I said. And if you make a great achievement, then it's yours; if not, blame me.' So Yao Bin agreed with me, and he took Shen Xue."

Yao Bin took Shen Xue, but he wasn't happy about it. Neither was the rest of Harbin. Everyone was griping about Shen Xue: She could barely land a double Axel, she had never been a champion, she was not pretty enough. Parents came up to Yao and demanded, "How could you choose Shen Xue? When she smiles, her side teeth stick out like a tiger!"

"Can a pretty face grow rice?" Yao snapped, and chose her anyway. But when he got his new pair on the ice, the mismatch between them was blatant. Zhao looked like a dance instructor trying to demonstrate the polka with a girl who had no experience and two left feet. In a single pass down the ice, Zhao would get four strides ahead of Shen Xue.

Shen Xue knew how far behind she was. "At that time, he could do five kinds of different triple jumps, and I could only do one double Axel," Shen Xue says humbly. "And also, in this pair skating, usually the major role is played by the girl. But at that time, I was always kind of hiding behind him." To her, the solution to the problem was clear: "I needed to train more to catch up with him."

Shen Xue had skated extra sessions her whole young life, usually in the middle of the night, so these extra sessions were no problem—especially since Yao Bin would keep her company, if you could call it that. Yao stood at the boards, taciturn and scowling, focusing the whole of his considerable intellect on Shen Xue's lousy triple toe loop. Had there been a superior girl, he would have taken her immediately. But there was only Shen Xue, so Yao figured he would have to use his brain and her work ethic and hope for the best. "Shen Xue wasn't that good, but she was young, and she had a good attitude, so I thought I could improve her," Yao says. Shen Xue did have her good qualities: She had a long neck, she was quiet. And she was obedient—unusually so. "You see," Yao explains, "in a pair, maybe for the girl, her personality shouldn't be too strong, because she has to follow her partner. And Shen Xue is that kind of girl who does whatever you tell her to do."

It was during those hours that they stayed after practice together that Shen Xue gradually won Yao Bin over. She would take the most appalling falls, but she would just dust herself off and go again. If her extra session was over, but she wasn't satisfied yet, she would stay on the ice and keep working. Yao liked the girl. She might be tiny, bruised, soaking wet from sliding all over the ice, but the next time she came around the circle she sailed by him without a trace of self-pity. And when she performed—well, that was actually a lot of fun.

Of her daughter, Lu Manli says, "I think she is a different person on land and on ice. When she is skating on the ice, she can really express her feelings and her imagination. But when she gets off the ice, she's a really quiet girl, a perfect kind of educated, feminine girl who knows just how to behave." Yao Bin liked her better on the ice. When the music was playing, Shen Xue could sometimes flash you a look that was almost vivacious, a look that would never cross her face on land. If there was one thing Yao Bin liked it was personality, and he began to really root for Shen Xue to catch up.

It took her almost three years, but by sheer force of will Shen Xue did catch up with Zhao Hongbo. She made it in time for the 1996 Asian Winter Games, a kind of all-Asia Olympics that had miraculously been assigned to Harbin. Shen Jie wanted to be there more than anything. "Think of it! It was a major international competition at home. She's in her hometown, she's got all the advantages, and we're pretty sure that she's going to win the gold medal," Shen Jie says. "But even for such an exciting event at home, it was still really difficult for us to go and see the competition. Because as her parents, we received no free tickets, and the price of one ticket was fifty yuan. At that time, each of us was earning only sixty yuan a month. But in order to watch my own daughter's competition, I still managed to buy two tickets for a hundred yuan."

On the night that Shen Jie and Lu Manli paid a month's salary to watch Shen Xue beat the rest of Asia, she and Zhao Hongbo skated to the beloved Chinese music of *Yellow River Piano Concerto*. Two months later, the Western European judges were to blast this very program at the World Championships for its "weak artistry," but to Shen Jie, *Yellow River* was poetry he would remember all his life. "I think the reason we loved it so much was the emotional power they expressed in that performance," Shen Jie says. "When they skated, you felt power inside. It's like you can imagine the Yellow River. It's long, it's big, it's flowing, and it is the Chinese national feeling." On the ice, for the first time, his daughter felt her shyness slipping away; she could express her feeling for the music, even in front of a crowd. "That night," Shen Xue says, "I began to enjoy skating, really enjoy it. Because for the first time I was performing."

For Zhao Hongbo the night was bittersweet. His mother watched from the stands, glowing with delight, but his father was not there. He had died a year before of a sudden brain hemorrhage. For a month afterwards,

Hongbo had avoided the ice and considered giving up skating. It was only because his father had entrusted his future to Yao Bin, and because the Asian Games were to be at home in Harbin, that he had postponed quitting. He had decided to compete at the Asian Games in order that his mother could see him skate one last time. And now he was the champion of Asia, and the Chinese federation was sending him to the World Championships. His skating career was not over—in fact, perhaps the real part of his career was only now beginning. He would go to the World Championships, and maybe even the Olympic Games. It was mysterious, it was unbelievable; he could not quite take it in—but Zhao could feel it: The world around him was opening out.

That night, according to their tradition, the three families celebrated together at a restaurant. It was to be the last big party in Harbin for a long time. Not long afterwards, Yao Bin got word from Beijing that a year-round national training center had been approved, and he and his pupils were to relocate immediately. And so Yao Bin left his wife and son behind in Harbin; the Shens said good-bye to their only daughter; the Zhaos gave up their youngest son. They left Harbin, the city of their memories, and went to live in an empty dormitory in Beijing.

Chapter Three

*N*ORTH OF QUEBEC CITY, the highway rolls through the open countryside and the lonely small towns, mile upon mile. After four hours, you come to the place where the Gaspé Peninsula begins. There is wild beauty here—dense old forests, ancient streams where you can fish all day without seeing a soul. The landscape is made out of primary colors: red barns, green pines, white farmhouses, blue rivers. It's a simple place, whose emblems are sawmills and salmon. The Gaspé is so deep in the backcountry, so distant from multiplexes and malls, that it feels like an alternate version of Canada—the rural version, where people think nothing of driving fifteen minutes to get a gallon of milk, or an hour to buy a pair of shoes.

If the Gaspésie, as the French-speaking locals know it, has some of the charm of unspoiled rural life, it also has a number of tired small towns that have seen better days. The factory and sawmill jobs have started to dry up, and lately too many people have to go on welfare during the winter to make ends meet. On the quiet main streets there are vacant storefronts, and the only movie theater for miles around has been boarded up. The teenagers complain that nothing ever happens here; a lot of them go to Quebec City after graduation and never come back.

The Gaspésie has been settled since the 1600s, but at some point it stopped keeping pace with the world to the south of it, and in its heart of hearts it remains a frontier settlement. Many a town still consists of a crossroads, a general store, and a post office. The stables have been replaced by the occasional gas station, but the Sears catalog still does as brisk a business as ever—for if not for the Sears catalog, every lady in town would be wearing the same blouse sold in the one local shop. There are even some old-fashioned traveling professionals, throwbacks to an era when the roving dentist stopped in town for a few days, and the visiting schoolteacher boarded with a local family for the term. Such a journeyman professional is Roland Paquet, figure skating coach, who has been traveling the Gaspé Peninsula for more than twenty years.

Paquet, who is in his mid-forties, is a robust, healthy sort of fellow, full of quiet good cheer. People like him. Wherever he goes in his native city of Rimouski, people call out, "*Salut,* Roland!" and clap him on the back. He is of average height and unremarkable appearance. Paquet does not put on airs, and he has a fine command of the self-deprecating humor of the Québécois. Except for his unusually good disposition, he is a regular guy. He is the kind of coach that parents like—a man who does not take himself too seriously, who believes that sports should be fun.

Paquet didn't plan on becoming a figure skating coach. Until he was seventeen, he had never even taken a skating lesson. He got such a late start that it looked like competitive skating would be out of the question, but Paquet surprised people. He took up pair skating at a time when there were three pairs in the whole province of Quebec, and once, when he was twenty-one, he managed to get himself to the Canadian National Novice Pair Championship. He and his partner finished dead last. His partner promptly quit, and Paquet knew he should quit, too. He said to himself: "I'm too old." He *was* too old, but somehow, whenever the hour for practice rolled around, he kept showing up at the rink. "I'm too old," Paquet said to himself again. "But the trouble is, I love it."

Paquet enrolled at the university in Rimouski in the education department, but he kept on skating. At some point it occurred to him that he might prefer to teach skating than to teach school. At the same time, his own coach happened to be looking for an assistant to help out in the rural towns above Rimouski, up in the Gaspésie. Out there in the sticks, the local rinks could use two or three coaches at every skating session to teach the kids their fundamentals. He could make about eleven dollars an hour to start. Paquet hopped in the car with the other coaches and joined the ranks of the traveling professionals.

∞

The Gaspésie lies seven hundred miles due north of Boston, and the winters are bleak. Roland Paquet has been known to drive his battered car through snow (about twelve feet a winter), ice storms, and full-on blizzards. Occasionally he will get stuck in a blizzard and have to spend the night at the home of one of his students. Paquet spends a lot of his life in his car, and when he doesn't carpool with the other coaches, he listens to music for the kids' competitive programs and maps out the choreography in his head. He buys his CDs in Rimouski, where he lives, because it has the last music store for many, many miles. In winter Paquet leaves his house at six o'clock in the morning and pulls into his driveway after seven at night. On average, he travels eighteen hundred miles a week.

Paquet's route starts in Rimouski and heads north, following the jagged coastline of the peninsula. Up here the road parallels the St. Lawrence, which widens out above Rimouski and smells salty like the sea it is about to join. Paquet passes the fields piled high with snowdrifts, the cow barns overlooking the river, and the farmhouses with their sloping Canadian roofs. He drives past the summer establishments—the *casses-croûtes,* roadside hamburger stands with iced-over picnic tables, and the microscopic vacation cottages, all closed for the winter. At Mont-Joli he leaves the coastline and turns east on the only road there is, Route 132, taking the two-lane highway across the width of the peninsula, into its central valley. This is the real rural Quebec, where the moose have been known to rub their noses against the kitchen window, and Québécois French is still the only language heard anywhere. Along Route 132, every five miles or so, the little towns crop up in the form of a single elegant church spire, for this is Catholic country.

Paquet first came to Sayabec in 1982. He sped along Route 132, dipped down into town, and parked by the big barn of a rink. Then he went in to meet the Club Patinage Artistique de Sayabec. It was the usual scene: a bunch of skating club mothers and their daughters clustered in front of the soda machine, a pack of disgruntled hockey players griping about giving up the ice to the girls. It was a country rink: hockey glass, a penalty box, bleachers, and a donated scoreboard. There were a couple of players' locker rooms plus a big room with a bar that was used for bingo nights. Predictably, it was absolutely freezing. Predictably, someone accosted Paquet at the front door and said, "Here are your kids! Do something with them!" Roland Paquet, who had a knack for getting children to enjoy themselves, whisked the Club Patinage Artistique onto the ice for a group lesson. All in all, Sayabec would have been an entirely typical small town were it not for the Pelletiers.

Both parents were high school teachers. The father was a soft-spoken type with glasses, but an active man; he skied, ran marathons, and coached the peewee hockey team. The mother was one of the founders of the figure skating club—nice woman, a little high-strung. And the three boys—well, they were hell on wheels.

The mother, Murielle, marched into the rink with the three little boys trailing. You could tell by the determined look on her face that she was already under attack from three sides. The boys didn't want to go on the ice; she was hell-bent on getting them there, and Paquet already knew who was going to win. Murielle swept into the rink "like a storm blowing in." Behind her three little tornadoes spun off in all directions. One brother pounced on another and wrestled him to the ground; the smallest one sprinted for the door. "The first time I saw them," Paquet says, laughing and shaking his head at the memory, "I thought: What *is* this?"

In those days Paquet could go to a half dozen rinks and not find three boys in total signed up for figure skating. Now in Sayabec there were three boys on the ice at the same time. Up until now the bulk of Paquet's work was teaching little girls their solos for winter carnival, but with the Pelletier boys, the job became more a matter of making sure nobody was whacking anything with a hockey stick. The brothers were looking for a fight under normal circumstances, but when you trapped them in a confined space against their will, you were really asking for it.

"At the beginning," Paquet recalls, "they didn't like figure skating. They liked hockey. So at lessons they would just chase each other, yelling, around the rink. They would get into fistfights, curse at each other—you know, everything boys do—and naturally, the whole time, Murielle was totally losing it."

When Paquet started coaching, he wasn't looking to make champions. The small community rinks set aside maybe ten hours a week of ice time for figure skating, the lion's share being reserved for hockey, which is a national religion in Canada. In the Gaspésie, figure skating was strictly small time. Few kids had ever competed. Once a year, the local skaters would perform at the winter carnival, a cross between a dance recital and a school play. It was a pageant both of local skating and sewing, and people went as much for the costumes as for the athletic display. If the theme this year was Mrs. Claus's bakeshop, the wooden scenery panels at one end of the ice would be painted to resemble a pâtisserie window filled with cakes and pies. One age group at a time, the children would emerge from behind the panels. The littlest kids would come out dressed as cupcakes, followed by the gingerbread men, and finally the rolling pins would bring down the house. In between the pastry numbers there would be a few featured acts.

Two girls dressed in identical outfits would come out arm in arm and skate in what was called a "similar pair." (There were never enough boys to go around.) Then the emcee, a fellow in a big overcoat and a Russian fur hat, would announce a solo, and a girl who was getting a little long in the tooth would come out in a flimsy chiffon dress and shiver through a pop ballad.

For these and similar glories Paquet trained the youth of the Gaspésie, and he must be forgiven if he didn't see the point in being a drill sergeant. "As a general rule," he explains, "you want to make it look more like a game to achieve something. Keep it fun for the kids."

But the Pelletiers wanted their kids to compete. "The parents took it very seriously. They would do anything for their kid to get ahead. Especially Murielle," Paquet remembers. "Now, if you go to Montreal, you can probably find that type of parent everywhere. But up in these parts, it's not common." The father came to practices on occasion, but "Murielle was definitely the team leader. She would finish teaching school around three o'clock at a town up the road, and by four she would be there, right next to the ice, yelling, 'Come on, David! You can do it!' "

Down on the ice, David Pelletier, age eight, would be slogging away at another stupid practice. Like his brothers, he considered himself a hockey player and *hated* figure skating. He would have given anything to be outside playing street hockey right now. Instead, he and his brothers were suffering sullenly through their first waltz jumps and cross-foot spins, while from the side of the rink, just out of arm's reach, yet another loudmouth kid (in a seemingly endless series of loudmouth kids) jeered at them. The Pelletier brothers knew how to throw a punch, and many a boy who yelled "fairy" during practice found himself shoved up against the lockers an hour later. Still, it did seem harsh that on top of having to take the stupid skating lessons, they had to be harassed for it by the other, normal boys.

Paquet would have been hard-pressed to even keep the boys on the ice were it not for Murielle Bouchard. Whenever Paquet worked, Murielle was there as lion tamer. You could keep David occupied by giving him something new to work on; he was always angling to learn a new trick. But eventually you had to get him to practice the old stuff, and that was no small feat. After David's fifteen-minute private lesson, Paquet would move on to the next kid in the skating club, leaving David to practice on his own. No sooner had Paquet turned his back than he would hear Murielle raise her voice sharply—"*Vas-y*, David! Do it again!" If she was silent, it only meant that she was watching with hawk-eyed concentration. Although she could be pretty loud at times, she could also be very contained. "Sometimes," Paquet recalls, "she was withdrawn. She didn't say a word. But then, the storm always came back."

The storm always had plenty to provoke it. Paquet would be on the ice, showing Mathieu how to do a back crossover, when suddenly out of the corner of his eye he would see David trying to sneak off the ice five minutes early. Instantly a cry from the bleachers rang out across the ice. *"David!"* The boy stopped dead in his tracks. "You stay on," Murielle Bouchard warned. There was a pregnant pause. The boy stamped his foot and scowled up at her. "You stay on," his mother repeated. "There's no way. You finish what you started."

∞

The Pelletier brothers agree that, in the words of the oldest, Martin, "It was our mom who wanted us to do figure skating." Their dad liked anything that would help his sons handle a puck, but his role was secondary. It was Murielle Bouchard's rare intensity that produced—from average talent and the resources of a rural backwater—two excellent skaters and one world champion.

The case of the youngest brother, Mathieu, is illustrative. Mathieu, who says that he was "skating in a diaper," was the least likely boy imaginable to become a figure skater in Canada. He picked fights with boys twice his size and often won; he liked wrestling. Mathieu never liked figure skating, and yet somehow he stayed in it until he was fifteen. He even learned a double Axel, a feat that is nothing short of remarkable for a skater who got most of his coaching in the winters in Sayabec. Yet he achieved nothing comparable in hockey, a sport he actually likes. "My dream was playing hockey," he says. "But that wasn't my mother's dream."

David Pelletier says of his sport: "I didn't choose figure skating. For me, my own opinion, I still don't understand really what a boy can find attractive in figure skating. What, because you get to hang out with girls?" At this point he gets a little riled up. "As a young boy, nobody wants to hang out with girls! You want to be with the other boys! No," he says firmly. "It's like this: You wear funny outfits, and people call you names. Obviously I didn't choose that." He has a simple explanation for why he became a figure skater: "My mom put me in it."

In the first few years, the force of their mother's will was all that kept the boys from quitting. Every Tuesday afternoon, just as the neighborhood street hockey game was getting into full swing, the brothers would glance up and see their mother's car coming down the hill from school and curse their luck. "Countless times," Murielle Bouchard recalls, "I had to go down to the street and grab them out of the hockey game by the skin of their necks and drag them to the rink." On a few occasions Murielle arrived late to a Tuesday practice and found the boys down in the players' room doing nothing—"and at that point," she declares, "I realized I wasn't all that Christian! Because I was so infuriated that I would start cursing."

Even from those innocent days when Mathieu had skated in a diaper, the boys had known instinctively that skating *mattered* to their mom. They could tell by the look on her face when she watched them: so, so serious. She had perfect recall of every detail related to their skating—the schedule, what jumps they were learning, their competition results. She liked to read about figure skating history, and she bought them books about skaters. Between carpooling and cooking and grading papers, she would squeeze in all kinds of skating club fund-raisers: delivering phone books, making Christmas ornaments, serving spaghetti dinners.

In the beginning the boys weren't allowed to quit skating; they had to finish what they'd started. But even when quitting became an option, the brothers were reluctant to take it. Why didn't they quit? They loathed figure skating. On the side of quitting they could line up argument after argument. But there was really only one reason not to quit. Though none of them would ever put it in these words, it seems clear that they went on skating because it made their mother so happy. Quitting would have hurt her. So they saw it through.

Even today, when the brothers talk about figure skating, they are fiercely protective of their mother. "I don't know if she put me into it because that was her dream—I don't think so," David Pelletier says, debating with himself still. "I think she put me into it because it was a good way to expend energy, and there was nothing else to do in Sayabec."

But if you put the question directly to Murielle Bouchard—why did your sons skate?—her answer illuminates the entire tableau. "I've always loved figure skating," she says, smiling. The effort of reining in three wild boys and a bunch of high school kids has built up her stern side, but when she talks about the old days, you can glimpse the fun-loving girl in her. "My dad gave me real figure skates when I was young, with the toe picks in front. It was the only sport I was able to do, anyway. I couldn't play baseball worth a darn. I wasn't too bad at skating, you know? Although we didn't have a club or a coach as such. I was trying to reproduce what I was seeing on TV. I would try the spirals. I was doing all right for myself." Admission to skate cost ten cents, and in those days, "some kids couldn't go because their parents couldn't afford it. Let's say you have five kids—it was fifty cents. And you can buy a lot of food with fifty cents." Murielle, whose father owned a lumber transport company, was allowed to go skating as often as she liked, and felt incredibly lucky.

In Sayabec the Pelletiers live right in town, in the house where Murielle Bouchard was born. It is a modest two-story house, white with blue trim. The village houses are packed close together, the better to take advantage of the snowplow routes, and the town, such as it is, is condensed into a highway minute. From the Pelletiers' back porch you can see all three of the main sights of Sayabec: the church, the school, and the rink.

When Murielle Bouchard was growing up in this house in the fifties, the rink stood exactly where it is today, just on the other side of Route 132, within a long Frisbee toss of the back porch. In her girlhood the rink was the pride of Sayabec. "It was the first indoor rink of the whole Matapédia Valley," Murielle Bouchard recalls. "And the roof was considered a very good thing, because at least it kept the snow and wind out even though it was still only natural ice. As soon as it went above freezing for a day or two, we'd lose the ice, so they left it cold in there. Believe me, you wouldn't be wearing tiny little dresses in that rink."

The girls wouldn't have been wearing tiny little dresses in any case, for in Murielle Bouchard's girlhood, rural Quebec was a deeply conservative, entirely Catholic place. Even in the regular public schools, the girls were taught by nuns and the boys were taught by priests. The ice rink was run on the same principle. "We would go skating three nights a week, because the other three nights were for boys, and we were only allowed to skate with the boys on Sunday afternoons," Murielle says. "In my day, if a boy went to the ice rink, it was with a hockey stick. That's why there weren't many boys who skated on Sunday afternoons, when you weren't allowed to play hockey. A boy only went skating on a Sunday afternoon if he had a crush on a girl."

Murielle Bouchard did not meet her future husband at a Sunday afternoon skate, but in Rimouski, at the regional teachers college. Jacques Pelletier was raised on a small farm in Cap-Chat, another small village an hour farther up the peninsula. Like the Bouchards, his people had been in Quebec for four hundred years. The Pelletiers were in fact the fifth-largest family in all of Quebec, and the Cap-Chat arm of the family tree had produced mostly farmers. Jacques Pelletier had had his fill of raising cows and wheat and wanted another profession. It had just become possible in Quebec for laypeople to teach public school, and Jacques Pelletier was one of the first to enroll at the new teachers college. "We met as students, even though Murielle was staying with the nuns and I was with the fathers," Jacques Pelletier says with a wink. "It happened that there was a shortage of instructors, so for one class the college agreed to put the young men and women together. And that's how we met."

After graduation they took teaching jobs in the same school system, settling near Murielle's family in Sayabec. Sayabec was—and remains— the kind of slow-paced town where, in the summertime, after dinner, you will find a hundred cars in the big dirt parking lot of the local *bar laiterie,* and half the town standing around their cars, eating ice cream and chatting. With just a supermarket, an auto parts store, and a Petro Canada station, the town does not attract visitors. "Of course," Murielle says, "for people who come from a big city, they look at this town and say, 'This place is boring.' But when we were young we had a lot of fun. We had the rink, we still had the movie theater at Amqui, and we had the dance hall. We'd go there. We didn't have a lot of money. We'd just sit there with a soda, you know, and have a good night."

David, the Pelletiers' second child, was a shock to their system. The oldest boy, Martin, had been fairly calm, but right from the start David was uncontrollable. The baby was so hyperactive that he would wake up at midnight and stay awake until five in the morning. His parents took turns staying up all night, arriving exhausted at school the next day. Murielle Bouchard remembers putting "tons of toys in his crib so he would have things to play with. And after he had thrown all of them out of his crib, somebody would have to get out of bed and go toss some toys back in there so he would stop yelling. The only time we actually got some peace was when he got big enough to get out of bed and get his own toys."

Like many hyperactive children, David found himself at the center of an ongoing drama. Every day, no matter how hard he tried, his impulses bumped up against a structured world that simply would not tolerate his energy. When he went waddling down the street in his snowsuit with his little hockey stick, he was the happiest boy alive. But place him under even the simplest constraint and the energy inside him would race to the surface. Even sitting at the dinner table was a battle. His mother would put David by himself on the opposite side of the table from his brothers; still, most meals ended with a plate crashing to the floor.

Murielle Bouchard understood that life was hard for a boy who could never cut loose, and so she used to take the kids out of civilization each year for the months of July and August. Years ago, her father had built a cottage on a nearby wooded lake, a rustic affair where you had to bring in the drinking water. The three brothers spent the short northern summers there by the lake, racing through the woods and learning to windsurf. The boys swam and fished, built secret forts in the woods, and tumbled into the lake at sundown for a bath before supper. It was the one place in their world where they could run wild.

For the rest of the year the only outlet was sports. "That's the main reason why we put the boys in sports, just to let some of that energy out," their father explains. "Otherwise, at home, it was just unbearable. Our idea was to keep them in a structured sport at all times." That had been the original justification for the figure skating: It was just another outlet for all that energy. But soon skating became a much weightier thing, because David started to compete.

∞

Right from the start the Pelletiers took figure skating a lot more seriously than other folks in town. Take, for example, the 1982 Christmas Spectacular of the Club Patinage Artistique de Sayabec. All the other little kids came out in their homemade costumes, dressed as robins and woodpeckers; one robin plunked down on her derriere, and the whole crowd let out a belly laugh. Then David Pelletier appeared. He was only eight, but he looked like he meant business. He stood in the center of the ice, with his chin jutting out and his head held high, waiting for "The Music Box Dancer" to start. And then he did a real solo, choreography from start to finish. He landed a whole bunch of little single jumps and even pulled off a shaky little spiral on one foot. People in the crowd clapped their heavy gloves together and said to one another, *Hey, that kid's pretty good.*

Later in the show, after the Care Bears skated, that same little Pelletier boy came out again, this time with a little girl with a long blonde braid. Clearly he wasn't happy about skating with a girl, but he had a weary, almost professional air about him. He looked over at the little blonde girl as if to say, "Well, we have a job to do," and offered her his hand. A titter came from behind the scenery, where the other kids were waiting for their turn to skate. But you had to hand it to the kid, he handled the whole thing very maturely. He puffed out his little chest, pointed his chin skyward, and waltzed the girl around the rink three times. They took a bow, Santa handed out the presents, and the crowd filed out to the parking lot saying, *You know, that middle Pelletier boy has poise beyond his years.*

Not long after the Christmas Spectacular the Pelletiers started piling into the car on Friday nights and driving south five or six hours so that David could compete on the Quebec juvenile circuit. The same handful of rinks tended to host these things over the years, but whether the scene was Boucherville or Edmundston or Rivière-du-Loup, you could always pick David Pelletier out of a crowd. He was the chubby one in the white outfit with curly hair. In his early years on the circuit he had half a dozen white costumes. Among others, he had a white cowboy suit with fringe and a white soldier's uniform with gold epaulettes. His mother picked out the white fabrics; a lady across the street did the sewing. For a chunky little boy, white seemed an odd choice, but there it was, and soon everyone in the stands knew that the boy in the white outfit was the one from Sayabec, although nobody had any idea where Sayabec was.

At one of the first events there was a crisis in the locker room over his white suit. David, who was only eight, had put on red underpants that morning. Now, under the white pants, the red showed through plain as day. He had to skate his entire routine with the mortifying awareness that the audience could see his red underwear. The boy felt himself the victim of a terrible injustice. How could his mother put him in these white costumes? In the misty rinks where the little kids competed, you couldn't even see the stupid white suits. The Pelletiers sometimes paid up to twenty dollars to get a copy of his routine from the videotape man. But once they got the video home David would be invisible for a good third of his program. Every time he skated into a corner, the white suit vanished in a bank of fog.

Nevertheless, at the next competition, there he was, in white again. "All my friends had cool outfits," he says. "Then I would show up, and she would make me wear this white outfit." *She* was his mother, and *she* was already up in the stands, waiting anxiously. After the first few competitions, Murielle had abandoned the locker room altogether. "I was so nervous, you know? I got nervous whether it was a big competition or a small one. It was just too much for me," she says. "So I would just drop him off with Roland and say, 'Okay. I paid for the lessons. Now you deal with him.'"

Roland Paquet was a good man to have around at such times. He would talk lightly about nothing at all, like a groom soothing a racehorse. David's face was pinched and white; he was always excruciatingly nervous. For some reason the kid felt he had to win at everything, and he got furious with himself whenever he made a mistake. His own insistence on winning made him nervous enough, but there was also the matter of that particular cluster of people sitting a few rows up in the stands. They had invested a lot, too. Just for starters, the whole family had driven five hours last night to get here.

Glancing around the rink at the other competitors, Paquet sighed. The poor kid had more reasons to be nervous than he even realized. The other boys in the group were from the suburbs of big cities. Their rinks were heated. They didn't have to come to practice all but mummified in huge ski jackets and mufflers. Their ice didn't melt down to a puddle in the middle of March. These boys had ice all year long, as much as they needed. David Pelletier had, under the best circumstances, nine hours a week for seven months of the year. Up to this point, the suburban kids had probably logged three times the practice hours of a kid from Sayabec.

But now the announcer intoned "David Pelletier!" A few dozen parents clapped, and the boy skated out of the fog and into a clearing near the center of the ice. These were always the worst ten seconds for him. From the time they called his name to the start of the music, he was in agony. According to his mother, "That's the moment when he'd like to run off the ice. That's when he's saying to himself, 'What the hell am I doing here?' " From her perch in the stands, Murielle Bouchard's experienced eye narrowed in on his knees. There it was: One little white pant leg was trembling.

Paquet saw the pant leg too, but he was more interested in something else. Watching the boy at such moments, it was clear that he was a born performer. He understood exactly how competition was different from practice. Something in his carriage and attitude said, "This, ladies and gentlemen, is a performance." Many a brilliant technical skater has never achieved the quality of *performance,* that ability to convey excitement about what he is about to do. But David Pelletier was born with it. He stood now with his back ramrod straight and his jaw held high. It was actually kind of hilarious, the solemn look on his face and that resolute little chin—clearly it was his own idea of what good posture looked like. He was skating in a dense fog in some tiny rink at eleven o'clock on a Saturday morning. But the kid, God bless him, was treating it like the national championship.

He was skating to a little boy's medley of the mid-eighties: the theme from *Rocky,* an instrumental "For Your Eyes Only," and a rousing finale from *Dallas,* and he was already musical to the tips of his fingers. Where the music called for it, he moved his arms more gently; where the music had spark, he punched every high note. No one had taught him that; up in his part of the world no skater ever took a dance class. He was one of those rare children to whom the musical side of things is just obvious. "It's easy," he shrugs. "You just follow the music. If there's a big moment in the music, you do something big. I mean, how hard is it?" Actually, it was so hard that most kids never figured it out, and it was reason enough for David Pelletier of Sayabec to beat the suburban kids and win his very first medal. And that, as it turned out, changed everything.

∞

"The medals are the thing that motivated David the most," his father says, nodding his head. "That's what made his whole approach change." After he won his first medal, Murielle Bouchard noticed that she didn't have to drag David to practice anymore. His brothers noticed it too. "When he saw that he could get far in figure skating," Mathieu Pelletier says, "that's when he started to like it." He could win at skating, and he dearly loved to win. "What I liked most of all was doing well in a competition," he admits. "I got a big kick out of that. A *big* kick out of that."

"A big kick out of that" is classic Québécois understatement, for when David Pelletier finishes a perfect performance, he may literally roar with triumph on the ice. As an adult, David Pelletier is what people call a great guy: funny, down-to-earth, warmhearted. Anyone would love to watch a hockey game or drink a beer with him. However, few of his familiars would want to play so much as a game of miniature golf against him, for Pelletier is, and always has been, a ferocious competitor.

"He doesn't accept failure," his father warns. "He's a total perfection-ist." His father recalls ice hockey games when David would be on the bench watching as his team made a mistake. "And he would start crying like there was no tomorrow. I'd say to him: 'Listen, there's nothing you could do about it. You weren't even playing!' But still—he was furious! Oh, he was so frustrated. Because he was just too exacting. David couldn't tolerate failure."

If, at the kitchen table, David cleaned up at a board game, he would say, with a grin, "Well, now, Dad, I guess you've still got a thing or two to learn." But if he lost? "*Oh la la,* he was mad," Murielle says. "If he loses, don't go teasing, because then it's all over. If he loses, you'd better not say a word."

David Pelletier hated to lose, a quality that might make him an unpop-ular checkers opponent but had its advantages for an aspiring world champion. He might have applied himself to anything and been extremely successful, but he saw his opening in figure skating. At the 1987 Quebec Games, when he was twelve, he went up against eighteen competitors and won the silver medal. It was the sign he was looking for.

As the medals piled up on his bookcase, the old vaguely embarrassed feeling left him. When the other boys teased him now, he defended not only himself but figure skating. "At some point David started to say to the others, 'You know, by the way, I win medals, which you guys don't do in ice hockey. And the furthest you guys have been with ice hockey is a half-hour bus ride. I go to Montreal with figure skating, and I win medals.' The guys who had teased him before didn't know what to say," Murielle Bouchard recalls. "And then he would look them right in the eye and say, 'Am I still a faggot?' "

Once he stopped resisting the skating lessons, David found a powerful ally in his mother. She would hold conferences with Roland Paquet: What else could he do to improve? Paquet suggested summer skating at Mont-Joli, the nearest place with artificial ice. Murielle agreed and drove the boys an hour each way all summer long. In future summers Paquet suggested a training camp in Toronto, and Murielle found the money to send David there. As long as her boys were progressing in sports, Murielle would find a way to pay whatever it cost. Eventually her entire salary would go to pay for sports, and she would be glad to do it.

As time went by Paquet increasingly found himself in an odd position. After practice, Murielle would sometimes come up to him and tell him he ought to push David harder. To Paquet, it seemed like the boy was already working at his capacity. "I didn't have to motivate David," Paquet says. "The parents were plenty motivating. In fact it worked the other way, where at times I would have to tell the parents, 'Hey, leave the kid alone! Let him skate. Just let him do something on his own!' "

The tension at competitions was increasing, too. David had long ago outdistanced his brothers in terms of skating potential, and his parents' focus was now squarely on him. He wanted more than ever to do well; at the same time the family was investing more and more in his career, and their expectations were rising. "At a certain age," David Pelletier says slowly, "skating well became very, very important. At some point, I guess, it was even more important to my mom than me." If he tanked at a competition, he dreaded the long ride home. "They didn't understand why when I got to competition, I would bomb," he says. "You know, it wasn't easy, now I think of it, to drive six hours in a snowstorm, get a few hours of sleep, and skate against other guys who would get three times as much practice time as me. I got really intimidated. And I would get on the ice and fall about three times, and my parents would get really mad, because—'What's wrong with you?' They didn't understand that if they stopped getting mad at me, it would actually be a relief to me, and then maybe I could actually deal with my own little thing."

At the age of twelve David Pelletier hit a wall. Though he had a whole pile of medals at home, though he had finally slimmed down and gotten rid of the white outfits, somehow his confidence was shot. The pressure had become debilitating. It came from himself—he had to be perfect— and it came from the stands. "There was a period when David wasn't doing too well in skating," his father recalls. "And I wasn't even able to stay in the arena while he was skating. God knows I've seen many parking lots. I just couldn't bring myself to watch." Up in the parents' section, his mother sat alone, stone-faced and silent, always clutching or twisting something in her hands. Down on the ice, the boy knew it was all up to him. Depending on what he did in the next four minutes, the whole family would either be overjoyed—or let down.

"There came a time he could barely step onto the ice for a competition, because he was so nervous," Roland Paquet recalls. "He would get on the ice and go: 'I can't do this.' Now, he could, but—he just didn't believe in himself."

When a skater started freezing up at one competition after another, it was a bad sign. Paquet had seen many kids' careers go down the tubes when they hit adolescence and suddenly lost all confidence. David Pelletier teetered on the precipice, but failure was not an option. "Oh, he got over it all right!" Roland Paquet says cheerfully. "He got over it when he started the pair. For him, it was always easier with someone else on the ice."

∞

The pairs thing was a fluke, really. It was 1988, the Winter Olympics were in Canada, and Jacques Pelletier was glued to the coverage on French-Canadian TV. When the pair skating came on, he hollered to David to come and watch. The Canadian pair was skating, and the girl, Isabelle Brasseur, was from Quebec. She was skating with a six-footer named Lloyd Eisler, and David Pelletier could not believe what he was seeing. This huge guy heaved the tiny girl up into the air, and she went flying so high he couldn't imagine how she would land. Yet she did, and it thrilled him. The boy stared at the screen, mesmerized. Then he turned to his mother and said: "I want to do this."

"Well," she replied, "if you want to skate pairs, you'll have to move away from home."

"Okay," he said immediately. "I'll move."

That was February. By the end of the summer, he was skating pairs in Rimouski. Nobody in Sayabec had ever heard of a thirteen-year-old kid moving an hour away from home to pursue sports. A lot of parents wouldn't have allowed it. A lot of kids wouldn't have considered it. But for David Pelletier it was more than an opportunity. It was a way of declaring independence.

"It was my own decision to do pairs," he says. "It was *not* my parents'. They didn't tell me, 'You're gonna do pairs.' I was the one who said, I want to do this. And that was how I really started to like skating—by doing pairs." He considers a moment. "And that actually saved my career. If I hadn't done pairs, I probably would have quit." The decision had an immediate effect on how he competed. The old pressure was lifted, and the results came. "After the first year in Rimouski," he says, "I don't think I skated badly once in a competition."

To a boy from Sayabec, Rimouski seemed a very big place, and he kept to a few home bases: the rink, a house across the street where he boarded, and his middle school a few blocks away. After spending his whole life in the same small town, suddenly he didn't know anyone. He was the youngest kid by far at the boarding house, which was for students at the junior college in town, and in the evenings he sat alone in his room. He went to school with kids he didn't know and skated with strangers. He had hoped to make friends with the "normal boys" in his class, but that dream was dashed on the first day of school.

"I got to the boarding house on a Sunday night," he recalls. "So—I cry myself to sleep the night before, go to school the next day. I don't know anyone in the class, sit by myself. And the first thing the teacher does is to check our phone number and our address on a list. And she gets to me. 'What's your phone number?' she says. 'I don't know.' I'm thirteen years old, I don't know my phone number, I'm a boy figure skater from Sayabec. How the hell am I going to make friends?"

For a long time he only had friends on the weekends, when he went home. On Friday nights he would take the bus to Sayabec, and five minutes after he was in the front door he would already be wrestling with Mathieu, and the next morning, first thing, they would be out the back door with the hockey sticks. Sunday nights arrived too soon. On the way back, he always cried.

Weeknights, after dinner, his parents called. "Sometimes," his father recalls, "we even raised him over the telephone. We taught him things: math, French. We even fought with him over the telephone. And a couple of times a week after work, we would just have to drive to Rimouski. Maybe we'd stay only twenty or thirty minutes, but by the time we left, he'd be feeling better."

To help the kid out, Paquet used to try to give him a lift to Sayabec one night a week, when he taught skating lessons there. They would ride together down the 132, past all the old familiar things—the raspberry farm, the glowing white cupola of Saint-Moïse—and they would talk things over to pass the time. Paquet would drop him off at home and he would eat dinner at the kitchen table, have a couple of hours of real life. From the Pelletiers' back porch you could see Paquet's headlights go on in the parking lot, and then it would be time to go back. Night came early in winter. Paquet would turn on the brights and pick his way back through the familiar towns. At night you smelled the salt before you saw the shoreline. From his car window David could see the dark river flowing to the sea.

"In Sayabec," David Pelletier observes, "I was really comfortable in my life away from the ice. So I was always trying to spend more time off the ice. But in Rimouski, I was so uncomfortable at school and in my house that I just put myself completely into skating. If there was a skating session at six in the morning, I would go every day, because that was the one comfortable place."

Paquet saw the difference right away. David was learning to skate pairs with a local girl, Julie LaPorte, and it was going very, very well—so well, in fact, that the two kids informed Paquet and their main pairs coach, David Graham, that they were going to win the Canadian Championship. It was highly unlikely that two nobodies from Rimouski were going to win the Canadian title, especially when the two nobodies were skating pairs only three and half hours a week. They had to fit pairs in around a normal school schedule—nobody in Rimouski had ever heard of special schools for elite athletes—and that left them with three and a half hours a week to train together. With that kind of limited schedule, nobody expected much the first year. Their coaches were thrilled that they even qualified for the National Novice Championship.

That year the Nationals were all the way across the country in Saskatoon, and to the Pelletiers there didn't seem to be much point in paying for the whole family to go. Sending the kids and the coaches was already expensive. So David went alone—and won the bronze medal on his first try. "*Oh la la*," Murielle Bouchard says with a laugh. "He was so mad! He marched right up to us and said, 'Mom! Dad! You will never miss Canadian Championships again!' And we never did." The next year, still training only three and a half hours a week, the pair from Rimouski went back to the Novice Nationals. This time, David Pelletier's parents were on hand to see him win the Canadian Championship.

In any skating career, there are just a few precious performances when you are exactly where you should be for your age. The year that he won the Novice Nationals, David Pelletier was perfectly fifteen, and it never crossed his mind that he wouldn't be perfect for his age again for another decade or so. He stepped onto the ice, and the band struck up "The Flight of the Bumblebee," and in the music the bumblebee was zipping all over the place. For a few seconds, the crowd tensed, thinking, *Oh, no—how are they going to keep up the pace?* And then it dawned on the whole audience at the same instant that the two kids were going to do it. They could keep pace with the flight of the bumblebee.

Now the boy and girl were moving as fast as their legs could carry them, and the look on their faces was pure excitement. They were dressed alike in simple homemade outfits, and they looked just right for fifteen: young high schoolers, not old enough to drive or get in much trouble, still kind of innocent. The boy treated the girl like a kid sister, and when they did a section of quick little dance steps, she gave him a look that said, "*I'll* show *you* how it's done!"

Down the ice they flew, and by now the whole crowd was thinking as one mind: *Hang on for dear life! Don't go falling apart at the end!* And sure enough there was danger ahead. They had to pull off a big finish. He had to launch her in a throw Axel, which was one of their hardest moves, and then step right into a side-by-side jump, which was another one of their hardest moves. But they did it all just right and finished with a flourish, and the crowd roared like the crowd at a high school basketball tournament. The two kids stood in the middle, grinning from ear to ear, and took a bow. Suddenly, overcome with happiness, the boy crushed the girl in a spontaneous hug, and the audience clapped even harder.

That year David Pelletier and Julie LaPorte were perfect for their age, and it lasted just a little longer. The next year they moved up to the junior division and won again. It was a good solid show, and a gold medal besides, but it didn't look quite as effortless as the previous year, and their coaches knew what that meant. In the minds of two teenagers who had just won their second Canadians in a row, the next year was sure to be a grand one. They would climb right up the ladder. But a coach knew better. To the coach, each progressive level is a new danger; each time you take a step up the ladder, a majority of kids get brushed off the next rung.

"You can see the traces of talent, of course," Roland Paquet says. "But the question is: Will the talent develop? How will it survive the body's changes during teenage years? I've seen so many girls who were extraordinary when they were young, and when their bodies changed they were done. It's sad. It's an unforgiving sport." For a male pair skater, the question was whether his genes would deliver enough height and strength. David Pelletier got bigger; his shoulders spread wider and his stance became more solid. He started to look more and more like a pair skater. But Julie LaPorte was not going to stand as tall on this step as she had in that perfect year when she kept pace with the flight of the bumblebee. She suffered a few injuries and gained a little weight.

It is a very specific body type that can sustain pair skating up into a woman's twenties, when pairs ripen and become world champions. The sport requires a grown woman to be uncommonly slim. Standing in her socks, the woman ought to come up to the man's chin and have the shape of a preteen—without having to starve herself. Like the vast majority of girls everywhere, this was not the body type that Julie LaPorte had been given.

It was unfortunate, but Roland Paquet remained philosophical. "There comes a time," he says, "when you reach the limits of, for instance, Sayabec. You can still have fun, but you can't build a career there. If you want to push things further, you have to move on. In Rimouski there is a bigger club, more ice, more coaches. In Rimouski we can get you to the provincial scene, the Canadian scene, even. Then the same problem arises again. You reach the limits. It's not possible to train an Olympic skater in Rimouski. If you want to go further, you have to go to Montreal."

At competitions, the elite Montreal coaches began to approach David Pelletier. In Montreal the clubs had ice all day long, and they trained the best pairs in Canada. One day David Pelletier dared to think of skating in Montreal. And one day not long after that he dared to think of skating without Julie. But to say such words out loud—to actually do such things—well, just to contemplate it made his stomach churn.

"I was seventeen," David Pelletier says, shaking his head. "Oh, it was terrible. You can barely swallow. It's a kind of divorce, you know? Roland was my best friend. He was the reason why I was skating. He was the only person who made me enjoy it." Then there was David Graham, his pair coach, who had brought him this far. "And then with Julie," he says, "it was so, so hard. We had just won Nationals! She wasn't expecting me to go. And she was too young to understand, you know? I mean, to this day it's something I regret. But it needed to be done."

There came a day when he knew that he would go to Montreal. He just didn't know how he was going to tell them. It was the hardest thing he'd ever had to do, but he had to do it. For in North America, if a young pair skater wants to reach the top, at some point he will have to fire his coach and his partner. David Pelletier could have done the nice thing and stuck by Julie, but his entire career would have been buried under the weight of that one kind gesture.

"So I sat with my partner," Pelletier says. "I sat down with her, broke her heart, broke my heart." Then he told David Graham. But Roland Paquet—Roland, who had gotten him through the white outfits— Roland, who used to say, "Give the kid a chance to do something on his own!"—Roland, who drove him home one evening a week and brought him back feeling heartened and able to face life—well, he never could bring himself to break the news to Roland Paquet. "He didn't tell me," Paquet says simply. "He told David Graham, and David Graham told me." He pauses. "It was hard."

But it was just as hard on David Pelletier. In the way that young people will avoid thinking about a painful encounter, Pelletier tried hard to push Rimouski from his mind for a time. It was an awful lot to handle for a seventeen-year-old. Besides, he had no choice but to look forward. He was about to take a very big leap. The boy from the countryside was going to Montreal.

∞

Canada has no national training center for figure skating. Although some coaches have been complaining for years that Canada needs one, others argue that the very concept is incompatible with Canadian values. Parents value home too much to let their young kids move away. Canada's free-agent coaches are self-made men and women who value their autonomy too much to be bossed around by bureaucrats. North American skating it-self would suffer if elite skaters were mass produced; for while Soviet-style systems, so the argument goes, churn out robots, capitalism nurtures unique personalities. In other words: Up in Canada we like our haphazard, free-market system, thank you very much.

In Canada skating is dominated by coach-entrepreneurs. The coaches are typically backed by an arena that can offer abundant ice and a wealthy parent base, for no Canadian coach earns a living solely by teaching champions. In the best-case scenario, the coach-entrepreneur succeeds in pulling all the elements together—ice, choreographers, assistant coaches, and talented kids—and manages to produce more contenders than any other rink in Canada. To do this requires an extraordinary effort, and no one rink dominates for long. It's too hard to keep all the elements in place. Coaches quit, skaters move on. But for a brief but glorious stretch, one or two clubs will dominate the Canadian Championships, and every young skater in Canada will dream of training there.

In the mid-eighties, two coach-entrepreneurs came to Boucherville, a suburb of Montreal, to found a skating school. At the time, Montreal seemed an odd choice. Each year at Canadians, skaters compete for their provinces, and each province has its own warm-up jacket, its own team colors, its own hotel. For years at Canadians it was rare to see more than a couple of Quebec jackets passing through a backstage hallway, and no one would have picked Quebec as a good place to start an elite training center. But by the early nineties Boucherville would change all that, and at future Canadian Championships, Quebec would be able to commandeer the biggest hotel.

The story of Boucherville's rise from obscurity to greatness is the story of three people: Eric Gillies, Josée Picard, and a little girl from the Montreal suburbs. Gillies was an ice dancer from English-speaking Ontario; Picard was a singles skater with French flair and a temper to match. Gillies was the technical whiz; Picard was more in the mold of the Russian coach-managers who pull together the whole package: music, costumes, choreography. When Gillies and Picard started they knew almost nothing about pairs. That was where the little girl from Montreal came in. She was a natural at pairs, so every summer the two coaches took the girl and her partner to a training camp at Lake Placid, where they absorbed everything they could from the best pair coaches in North America. As the girl progressed, so did the coaches, and soon the girl was winning the novice championships, the junior championships. The girl was Isabelle Brasseur, and eventually, with Lloyd Eisler, she won the 1993 World Championships.

Isabelle Brasseur was the girl who had been flying across the TV screen in David Pelletier's living room in Sayabec when Jacques Pelletier called to him to come and watch the Olympics. Because of her, he had decided to leave home and become a pair skater. Now, in the summer of 1993, David Pelletier walked into the warm-up room at Boucherville and found himself warming up next to Isabelle Brasseur and Lloyd Eisler, the the newly crowned world champions.

To a kid from Sayabec, the Boucherville atmosphere was unreal. At home he had a few hours of ice a week; here the figure skaters had ice all day. The club employed a specialized jump coach, a choreographer, a ballet teacher, even a seamstress. In Rimouski his pair had been the only one at the rink. There were *two dozen* pair skaters at Boucherville, of which David Pelletier was not the worst but far from the best. The whole thing was on a scale he had never imagined. People even dressed differently— more urban, somehow. David Pelletier went around the rink in a checkered shirt. "That's about the only shirt he ever wore," Josée Picard recalls. "And he *really* looked like the boy from the country, going around in a pair of jeans and his checkered shirt."

To David Pelletier, Montreal was a city of expensive cars and elegant restaurants he could not afford. It was, moreover, an island of icy people who looked at you like you were crazy if you went and rang your neighbor's doorbell to introduce yourself. (He did, and was sent packing.) At Boucherville, there were a lot of transplanted skaters who didn't speak French, including his new partner, so the coaches mainly spoke English. David Pelletier had picked up a smattering of English over the years, much of it from watching cartoons after practice during summer skating schools in Ontario. (One of the first English phrases to roll smoothly off his tongue was "After these messages, we'll be right back.") But it was not his own language, and here again, he was out of his element.

Everything cost more in Montreal—the coaches, the ice, the choreographers. The costs of skating were reaching a staggering new level. He was skating both singles and pairs, so he needed twice the lessons, twice the costumes. (In Rimouski, he had sometimes worn the same outfit for singles and pairs, but clearly that was not an option for someone who trained at Boucherville.) On top of skating, his parents paid his rent, utilities, and food, plus his junior college fees and books. Like many college kids before him, he lived on cereal and spaghetti, and salvaged furniture from the trash. But still, his parents—two schoolteachers in Sayabec—had to come up with twenty thousand a year after taxes to keep him afloat in Montreal. Had he placed in the top two or three at Nationals, he could have gotten a full ride from Sport Canada, the national Olympic training fund. But while he climbed the ranks, the best he could hope for was a couple of thousand here or there from Sport Canada, the Canadian skating association, or the province of Quebec's provincial sports fund. The small grants helped, but they were drops in a very big bucket.

Every year at Boucherville, there were skaters who had to quit for financial reasons. Once Pelletier's roommate paid a visit home and discovered that his sisters had no winter boots and his father couldn't afford a pair of eyeglasses; he quit temporarily. When a family reached that point, the skater either quit or tried to raise money. The Boucherville skaters used to go door-to-door in their hometowns, carrying their medals and photo albums down Main Street, collecting twenty bucks here and ten bucks there. David Pelletier did this too, and when he heard the other skaters talking about raising big sums by putting on annual benefit shows at their home rinks, he asked the world champions, Brasseur and Eisler, to come up to Sayabec to skate in *his* show.

It was not often that the world champion of anything passed through Sayabec, and the whole town came. David Pelletier stepped out onto the ice with his partner and saw every inch of the bleachers packed with people. "There wasn't even space for a mouse to squeeze in," Murielle Bouchard says, with a laugh. "They almost blew the roof off." In a part of the world where many people were out of a job in the winter, the whole town had paid ten dollars apiece to support the local boy and see the world champions. "The people were unbelievably generous," David Pelletier says, shaking his head. "And I remember going over to the bar afterwards, and the lady who owned the bar, she made me bartend, so I would get all the tips. I made an extra thousand there. And the next day we did the breakfast and raised another few thousand. All around we raised about fifteen thousand, and it really helped a lot."

But the harsh truth was that fifteen thousand split with his partner was not enough to pay his skating expenses for even one year. Even with all the support from his parents, there were plenty of times when Pelletier wondered what he would do for grocery money next week. "One time," he recalls, "JoJo Starbuck came to choreograph our program. So we paid her, and I had three dollars left. Well, JoJo stayed at my apartment, and all I had was this little bar of soap for the two of us. And she says, 'Oh, we're out of soap. Can you go out and buy some?'" He pauses. "Now, all I know is, I have three dollars left in my bank account, and I've got a debit card. I don't know if there's a five-dollar minimum for the debit card. So she says to me,

'Do you need money?' I said, 'Oh, no, no. I'll do it.' So I'm walking to the drugstore. I'm thinking, What am I gonna say if I come back with no soap? What story am I going to make up?" He shakes his head at the memory. "Anyhow, it worked. The bar of soap was maybe two dollars, I gave my debit card, and it worked. I came back with the soap. But whoa— that was tight times."

Other skaters struggled with money and had to quit temporarily, but David Pelletier always managed to stay on the ice. To him, it was almost a mystical thing. Just when he had reached the bottom of his bank account, something always came up—either a forgotten check or maybe a phone call with an offer to do a local show for two hundred dollars. Knowing that he was low on funds, Josée Picard used to bring him along as a demonstrator when she taught seminars. "I'd be on the ice maybe seven hours a day, in Newfoundland or wherever it was. It didn't matter where it was. I had to go where I could make money," Pelletier says. "And if it was far away, well, that was even more exciting. I always liked to travel. I'd spend a week away, and I felt like a businessman.

"Nope," he says, shaking his head, "I never thought of quitting. Because for some reason, in my life, every time I was broke, something would always come up."

∞

In those lean years in Montreal, Lloyd Eisler took the guy in the checkered shirt under his wing. Before he was a world champion, Eisler had been, at various times, a housepainter, a cashier, a security guard, a waiter, a lawn service guy, and a technician who retreaded tires. Eisler knew what it felt like to have to work for it. "Dave reminded me of me," Eisler says. "A guy from a normal family. A person with talent, not getting much funding." Pelletier and Eisler lived across the street from one another, and if Eisler stepped out on his balcony and saw Pelletier's light on, he might call him to come over for dinner. Eisler hooked Pelletier up with odd jobs and gave him a place to stay when he needed it. He showed his protégé how to use weights to build the muscle he needed for pair skating, being careful not to get too bulked up and inflexible. And it was Eisler who inspired David Pelletier to pursue the neglected art of pair lifts.

Every pair in the world did lifts, but Brasseur and Eisler had taken it upon themselves to become the greatest lifting team in history. Eisler could raise his tiny partner above his head *with one hand.* Once she was aloft, he would stand under her with that one arm upraised, like a waiter holding a tray over his head, all the while traveling down the ice at fifteen miles an hour. Brasseur and Eisler concocted lifts whose changes of hand-hold and position defied anyone to explain how they were possible. Other pair skaters would watch Eisler and grumble, *How can he do it?* Eisler was putting up lifts that everyone had thought were just too damn dangerous. Because in any lift, the higher the difficulty, the greater the possibility that the speeding airborne girl could come crashing to the ice from a height of eight feet.

The answer to this question was found in Eisler's feet. While Eisler stood like a waiter holding a tray—let us say, a tray on which a dozen crystal champagne glasses are tinkling precariously—he was also moving down the ice at high speed—*and he was turning.* Eisler was turning, moving backwards, and with every step he took he was temporarily balancing the whole shebang over one foot's quarter-inch blade. If, by any chance, that blade skidded or jammed into the ice, Eisler's arm would immediately teeter, and the girl above him, who was balanced on that arm like an acrobat, would fall. Therefore, for a veteran skater, the only place worth looking during a lift was at the man's feet.

Lloyd Eisler became the best in the business with the help of Eric Gillies and Josée Picard. Picard explains that "the feet are something I worked on with all my guys, because *man,* I'm *scared* watching lifts." Eric Gillies, too, was scared watching lifts. Like anyone who had been around pair skating for decades, Gillies had seen a few bad accidents, the kind that give you nightmares. Even at Boucherville, where he trained his pairs with extreme care, there had been a bad one. A junior girl went up in a lift and flew over her partner's shoulder like an airplane, landing on her forehead. Gillies raced over and found her lying on the ice, unconscious. Her head lay in a pool of blood. "The impact peeled the skull from one side to the other, and I had to grab the skin and pull it down over the skull," Gillies says quietly. "And the boy's pacing in a circle on the ice going, 'I killed her! I killed her!' " The ambulance came, the girl survived, but Eric Gillies had a somber respect for lifts. You bet he did.

With a six-footer like Eisler and a tiny girl like Isabelle Brasseur, magnificent lifts were possible, but the height and weight differential also created the potential for horrifying accidents. "I won't skate with him!" Isabelle Brasseur famously declared when first asked to skate with Eisler. "I don't want to end up in a wheelchair!" People laughed, but they laughed nervously. The trouble was that you couldn't make lifts foolproof. One stray sequin on the ice was all it took to cause a stumble and take down a lift. All you could do was drill the boys in lift technique, and this Gillies did. While a pair practiced a lift on the floor, Gillies swatted at their arms and legs to destabilize the lift, forcing the man to adjust in a split second to save the girl. When a pair was ready he spotted the lift on the ice, and often it was Gillies's body that broke a girl's fall. Gillies made the men practice the footwork for the lifts without a partner, holding a glass of water above their heads as they turned. If they didn't want to get wet, they'd better be stable on their feet. Eric Gillies filled up a glass for Eisler, and later, Eisler would fill up a glass for David Pelletier.

But it wasn't technical training alone that made a man smooth on his feet; it was desire. Eisler would spend hours alone, working on his footwork. "You do it until it becomes second nature," Eisler says, "until you don't have to think about your feet anymore, and you can concentrate on one thing: the person you're lifting above your head." Eisler practiced with a hundred-pound bag of potatoes, feeling the weight of the lift. He asked Gillies to poke him in the ribs unexpectedly, and still he turned smoothly, routinely. No ice flew. The ankle held. In the end, Eisler's feet became so quiet that you had to listen hard to hear his blades against the ice.

"When you get to the World Championships," Eisler told Pelletier, "go and watch the guys at the top. Listen to their feet. You'll see they're not that great. You can do better." So David Pelletier would practice his footwork after the rink had emptied out, hour after hour. The world narrowed to three points: his mind, his feet, and the blue hockey line. "I watched Lloyd not making a noise while doing a lift. So I tried to do the same," Pelletier says. "I would be out there on the blue line. Walk-through after walk-through. And I would challenge myself to be as quiet as possible. Always challenge myself to be as quiet as possible, because I got a kick out of it. To put up somebody in the air and not hear a thing in the rink— I always got a big kick out of that."

Eric Gillies was hard at work remaking Pelletier's pairs technique, and if David Pelletier had any say in it, he wanted to be remade in Lloyd Eisler's image. Like Eisler, he pierced his left ear and played in Boucherville's pickup hockey games. Some folks found the friendship between a young greenhorn and a world champion heartwarming, but there were also people in Boucherville who raised their eyebrows and said, "Oh, Lord, not another one . . ." Because for all his many fine qualities, Lloyd Eisler had an explosive temper.

Eisler was famous at Boucherville for the time he kicked the boards. It wasn't so much that he kicked the boards; legions of skaters before him had done that. It was that Eisler jammed his blade so deep in the boards that his foot actually got stuck. He stood there, shaking his leg, trying to pull free, yelling obscenities, while the other skaters laughed until their sides ached. One might well ask what had inspired Lloyd Eisler to kick the boards that hard. The answer was mundane enough: He was mad at himself for missing a double Axel. "Lloyd and David were just alike: They did not *allow* themselves to miss something," Picard says. "They had to be the best, even if they killed themselves."

Whenever an Eisler or a Pelletier raised his voice on the ice, Josée Picard, in her French-accented English, would leap into the fray. "I don't stand for that kind of temper," Picard declares. "I fly off the handle too! I don't care if they're six feet tall. And the girls look up and go, 'Oh, here we go again.' They don't participate." In a group of highly competitive, intense people, tempers flew almost every day. It was not uncommon to walk in and find a guy in a corner berating himself or locked in a shouting match with his partner. Sometimes a girl had had enough, too, and if she got really mad she might rake her fingernails over her partner's arm.

Eric Gillies sees such behavior as regrettable, but he insists that "sport is like that. If you don't have a strong personality, you're probably not going to do well in sport. And that's tough for Canadians to get used to, because in Canada we tend to like the people who are more diplomatic." Gillies says that Canadians like the idea of putting one's whole heart into something, "but they don't accept that once you put your heart into something, it's hard to stay cool."

Gillies believes that under the conditions of extreme training, the human body "focuses in on a single objective and won't take no for an answer. You're just like an animal, and you react aggressively." For Gillies, the lesson is obvious: "You have to control the animal inside and make it work *for* you, so that you get the right result." David Pelletier was a classic case. Whenever he was thwarted from reaching his singular objective, his fury rose so fast that it was easy to believe primal instincts were involved.

It would begin with a trifle. Pelletier would miss a routine jump. "So I know what I've got to do," he says. "What I've got to do is, if I miss, I've got to do ten in a row in practice. And if I can't do ten in a row, then I get mad." Getting mad could mean, variously, cursing, shouting, kicking the ice, and so on. Failure was not an option. Pelletier defends his behavior, saying, "I never had any problem with the fact that I get mad at myself. It's the only way I can get myself to do it. Other people have problems with that, and maybe—I'm not saying my way is the best way. But that's the way I know to be successful. I'm not the kind of person that if I miss something, I'll be laughing about it."

No indeed. Any mistake was enough to push Pelletier into a quiet fury, and a big mistake meant a flare-up. His passionate insistence that everything should be perfect came from his core. It ran so deep one hardly knew how to approach the question of how to stop it. After a time, some people started to turn away from him. "He was not the nicest partner," one of his rinkmates admits. "Some girls thought they wanted to skate with him, but once they saw him live, they were a little afraid. Because he had a very short fuse. He was always landing the stuff, and the partners he had were always missing, and he was getting really frustrated because of that. After all, you cannot get anywhere unless both partners are landing the jumps."

At this point in Pelletier's career, Alison Gaylor was the unlucky girl who was not landing her jumps next to David Pelletier. The team had started off well. In their second year together they had won a silver medal at Canadians, and with it a trip to the 1995 World Championships. But at the World Championships they had made some mistakes and wound up fifteenth. David Pelletier had no interest in being fifteenth. He thought he had what it took to be on the podium, even at the World Championships.

Josée Picard agreed with him. "I knew he could be a world champion," Picard says. "I knew that. He had everything—the personality on the ice, the size, the skating skills. The only thing he had going against him for a long time was his temper. He was very impatient. You see, he never missed—never, ever missed in competition. So if the other person missed—oh, man! He couldn't tolerate that." Picard shakes her head. "Don't get me wrong. He's got lots of charisma. He's a really nice guy," she says. "It's just that nobody can miss."

At the 1996 Canadians, Alison Gaylor missed her jumps, and the pair plummeted to fifth. David Pelletier wanted a new partner, and Josée Picard knew exactly what he was thinking. "Alison was good enough for him up until a point," Picard says with a shrug. "She was good enough to make it to Worlds. But she wasn't good enough to be Olympic champion."

David Pelletier was ridiculously competitive, and for all such people in sports the end goal is never in doubt. He wanted to win the Olympics. And if he was going to win the Olympics, he needed a girl who could land her triple jump next to him. There happened to be such a girl out in Alberta; in fact, she had already been to the Olympics once. She was gorgeous, and she was incredibly sure of herself. For years he had been seeing her in hotel lobbies and shuttle buses at the Canadians, although, being just a hick from

Sayabec in a checkered shirt, he was too shy to talk to her. "She was very popular with everybody. She was *the* skater from the west. She was very outgoing, she was cute, she was a good skater—she had it all. I remember that first national team meeting we had. I was sixteen, she was thirteen, and she was even intimidating *me*. She was a very confident little girl."

In the past she had always been out of his league. But she hadn't had a partner in a couple of years, and she had reached the point where she might want to try out with a guy like him. The Queen of the West, they used to call her, but maybe he could persuade her to come east. Her name was Jamie Salé.

$$\infty$$

To other girls it seemed like everything came awfully easy to Jamie Salé. The first time she entered a skating competition, she won. After that, every time she walked into a rink, she acted like she owned the place. In the dressing room, while the other eight-year-olds rechecked their skate laces and waited nervously for their turn to compete, Jamie Salé would bound in and say cheerfully, "Hi, I'm Jamie. I can do a loop and a flip. What can you do?" Upon hearing the answer, her big brown eyes would widen with a realization. "You know what?" she would say, breaking into an enormous smile. "I'm going to win! I'm gonna beat you, you know?" And she'd skip off in the direction of the ice, while the other girls shot anxious looks at one another.

No one ever looked more self-assured while she waited her turn to skate than Jamie Salé, who used to lean against her coach, rubbing her tummy to "make the butterflies go the right way." If, when her name was called, the announcer happened to say "Jamie Sail"—and this happened from time to time—she would turn in mid-glide and skate right up to the man and holler, "That's Sa-*lay*, mister! Sa-*lay*!" Only after he announced her properly would she go to center ice and strike a pose. Up in the stands, a chorus of little girls whispered "*One, two, three*"—then yelled: "Go Ja-mie!" Then the music started, and Jamie Salé put on a show.

Even when she stood no taller than a yardstick, Jamie Salé could get your attention like *that*. She had you from the first glance of those big brown eyes—right at you, so confident, so alive. And that smile! When she smiled you could count every last perfect white tooth. The smile said *I'm Jamie Salé, and I love this!*—and she did love it, but what she loved was not precisely skating. She loved showing off, and the bigger the audience, the better. Let there be even one spectator at a practice, and every time she passed by that spot in the bleachers, she would flash a smile. Give her a full house, and she would give any Broadway hoofer a run for her money.

Thirty seconds in, she'd have the crowd clapping in time to her music. Her first coach, Debbie Wilson, recalls that "you would get so into watching her program that at the end, you'd kind of scratch your head and say, 'Now, what all did she actually do?'" After the results were posted, her rivals would complain to each other: *It's not fair. Jamie Salé doesn't do the hardest jumps and she still gets higher marks.* And they had a point. Whenever it was close, the judges always gave Jamie Salé the benefit of the doubt, because she was so far ahead of other girls her age in her ability to perform. Other girls telegraphed the next hard jump from thirty yards away. But Jamie Salé got so involved in performing that she actually looked a little annoyed when she had to interrupt her choreography to do a jump, and the instant she landed she would give a little nod of her head, as if to say, "I'm back, folks!"

Jamie Salé was good, and she knew it. When she was only nine, her coach drove her to the Bonnyville Winter Skate, and as they came into town there was a big "Welcome Skaters" banner to greet them. Jamie took one look at the banner and piped up, "Hey, Debbie! Do you think they're gonna have a sign up like that for me when I get to Canadians?" Her mother, Patti Salé, remembers that one summer, during a skating school in Saskatoon, "the team stayed at this RV park that was run by an older gentleman. And Jamie just went right up to him and said, 'Excuse me, sir, would you like my autograph?'"

The maddening thing was that she *did* make it to Canadians a few years later, and before long kids *were* asking for her autograph. Everything went right for Jamie Salé. Photographers liked her, so she was always getting her picture in the paper. As she got older she started going to the big skating banquets, and while the other teenage girls stood around feeling awkward, Jamie Salé would breeze into the room in a killer cocktail dress. It would have been easy to hate her, really, if she hadn't been so incredibly nice.

She had a bubbly personality and that wholehearted Canadian friendliness, and she really was just so *nice* to everybody that you had to like her. She chatted with the Zamboni driver, the sound system technician, the scoreboard operator. Backstage she talked to the cameramen and the flower girls. She was friendly with the senior citizen volunteers, and you would see her nodding her head sympathetically while they told her about their hip replacements and their new grandchildren. If a volunteer looked lost backstage, she would stop the person and ask if she could help. So outgoing was Jamie Salé that "it really bothered me not to talk to the girls in the dressing room at a competition. In the guys' dressing room they're all chitchatting and telling jokes, you know? But the girls are all like this." She demonstrates, slouching down, eyes fixed on the floor. "See? No talking. Like if you said anything, they would think you were psyching them out."

Not talking, even for twenty minutes in the dressing room, was a strain on Jamie Salé, for when she could she chattered nonstop. She talked while she stretched, she talked on the ice, she even talked right after she skated, when she was gulping air in the kiss-and-cry. Everything interested her— what kind of bouquet the champions would get, how her acquaintances had skated earlier. Her curiosity was infinite, and she was known in the press box as the only skater who had ever questioned the reporters. "How can you guys spend so much time on the road, you know?" she'd ask. "Don't you miss home?"

By the time she made it to the seniors at Canadians, people had started calling her the Queen of the West. Whenever someone brought up Jamie Salé, the response was always the same: *Oh, well, Jamie Salé! Of course! Everything goes right for her.* The real story was more complex. "She was definitely a show-off, always wanted to be the center of attention, for sure," says her mother. "Most of the time, she was very, very sure of herself. But if she wasn't, then she would just fake it—like she wasn't gonna let anything daunt her."

The faking it came in handy when she was ten, because that year her parents divorced. She remembers it this way: "My dad took my brother and my mom took me. Not because there were any battles or anything, just because my brother decided he wanted to go with my dad, and I wanted to go with my mom. My mom was always really dedicated to my skating. She almost never went to my brother's stuff. And my dad always went to watch his hockey. My dad never came to watch me."

To the kids at the rink, Jamie Salé was still that little show-off with the Dorothy Hamill haircut. But at home things were changing drastically. "I remember moving out and being excited to actually live in an apartment. Don't ask me why. I thought, *Wow, cool,* we get to stay in those buildings? It was like a hotel," she recalls. "And I remember my mom working *so* hard. I never saw her because she was always working. She never ever told me how much things cost. I remember her telling me later on that there were months when she'd only have like seventy dollars left over, and that's for our spending money. I mean, that's nothing."

Growing up in suburban Red Deer, Alberta, Salé remembers getting teased a lot at school. "I had a real hard time in school because of my skating. I wasn't really a part of a group. I wasn't *popular*." Because her mom couldn't afford to buy her everything the other kids had, she stuck out even more. "I remember I got *one* new outfit for school every year, because we spent all our money on skating. Most kids would go shopping and get like a wardrobe. And I remember being a little bit nervous going to school, because everyone else had new stuff and I was jealous of that."

After the divorce she saw her brother and her father about once a week. "Her brother and her dad lived in town. It wasn't like visitation," Patti Salé says. "But Jamie was really busy. We were on the go a lot, and I was working a lot. We saw them probably every week, just when we could manage it." Gradually Jamie gave up scanning the bleachers for her dad. ("He was never there when I skated bad; he was never there when I skated good.") Now the dinner table was always set for two.

"Oh, absolutely Jamie and I drew closer," Patti Salé says. "We were like two kids raising each other. I mean, I was only twenty-one when I had Jamie. When I got divorced and we were living on our own, her and I, I would've been thirty-one and she was ten. And we basically just . . . we raised each other, we supported each other." Jamie might not have known how much things cost, but she noticed that her mother rarely bought anything for herself. "All her paychecks. She spent all her money on me. You know, she would be really upset some nights, because I think she just felt she didn't have much of a life. She would go to bed and then I would hear her crying, or I would just feel somehow that she was upset." Jamie would knock on the door and come give her mom a hug. "She never wanted to show that to me. But I remember staying with her a lot because she was sad. I always told her, 'The longer you wait, the better he'll be, and you're a beautiful person.' I wrote her letters. I think I was her strength growing up, too—you know? I kept her strong."

"We were like this team," Patti Salé says. "And sometimes Jamie had to show a brave face to the world and be more thoughtful about me, instead of just pushing buttons like some kids do. She knew I was a single mom, this was all happening." Patti Salé chokes up just a little. "And I remember thinking: She's my best friend and in some cases my strongest inspiration to keep me going. 'Cause there were some times it was really hard. I was lonely, I was financially strapped. It was—you know. Some difficult periods there." She sighs, but then a flicker of a memory crosses her face, and she smiles. She has a lovely smile. "But you know I can still see her? Yep. Coming down the ice in that green-and-white dress, doing her little hoedown with that huge smile on her face—*Deep in the hearrrrt . . . of Texas!*"

By the time of the divorce, skating already cost around seven thousand dollars a year, a staggering sum for a single mom in Red Deer. By the age of ten, Jamie had started getting little checks for five hundred dollars from the Alberta sectional skating office, but they still had to go to the relatives to help pay for skating. Her father hardly gave a cent, Patti Salé says, "because he was looking after her brother. I always said, 'You can't squeeze blood from a rock,' and that was that." Patti Salé saved money by doing things herself. She put "a lot of miles on the car, and a lot of miles on the sewing machine." When money got really tight, she gave up her curling club. "But actually," she says, "I don't mind what I gave up, because I'm extremely grateful to skating. The social life I had with skating was as good as anything else I could imagine."

On weekends mother and daughter would drive the four hours to Bonnyville or Lethbridge for a competition. "It would be a hockey rink for sure, and not very nice concessions or anything else to do other than sit and watch the skating. Usually you're staying in motor inns," Patti Salé says. "We always made our fun, though. Like I can remember one competition we took the sewing machine. I wasn't finished sewing Jamie's costume. And a bunch of the mothers had gotten together and instead of getting a bedroom, this one motel had this apartment with a bunch of bedrooms. Must have been for rig guys or something. So three or four of us shared it, and we had the fabric out, and we were cutting and sewing right up until the last minute." Few dads traveled to the little regional competitions, and at an all-night ladies' sewing bee, a divorcée could relax and forget she was single. "We used to do sequining till two, three in the morning," Patti Salé recalls. "Seriously! Oh, we kept ourselves busy! And we would of course have a few drinks. There was plenty of camaraderie. But you had to make your fun in those places because it wasn't like going to your Madison Square Gardens. No, not even close. Not even close."

Competitions were a big deal for Jamie, because at last she had a chance to show off for her mom. "I *loved* having people watch me. *Loved* it," Jamie Salé says. "But my mom never watched my practices." Patti Salé cheerfully admits it. "Oh, I didn't want to watch her practices too much. I was curious, so I might wander in for five minutes, but I didn't stay glued to her." Other girls talked about their moms bribing them to skate, or threatening to quit paying for their lessons if their results didn't improve.

In the car on the way home from practice, Jamie's mom always asked the same ho-hum questions: "How is it? Are you having fun? Did you have a good lesson?"

"She didn't even know what she was watching!" Jamie Salé exclaims. "She didn't know a double toe from a triple flip! She told me once, 'I just liked to watch you skate.' I looked at her and I said, 'Did you not know whether I was going anywhere?' And she just said, 'Oh, I had no idea where you were going.' I mean, my mom got excited about B's! That's like the very first thing in skating, the B's. It's nothing. I won B's, and she was just like"—and here Jamie Salé breaks into the sweet, teary voice of a proud parent—" 'Oh, wow, *wow,* she got a *trophy!*' "

Patti Salé shrugs. "I never knew how long it was going to last. So I was like, okay, there's been some really good stuff, you know?" At competitions Patti Salé would cheer so loud for all the skaters that the other mothers would look at her funny. When it was Jamie's turn, Patti Salé watched especially closely. She saw her daughter's set jaw and the edgy look in her eyes, and she thought: That wasn't there before. She came to believe that "in some strange way the divorce helped to make Jamie a competitor. Sort of like that survival of the fittest thing, right? She just rose above it. And maybe even it was filling a hole, I don't know."

If Jamie skated her best, it was a toss-up who was more excited: the daughter, taking her bows with showbiz flair, or the mother, jumping up and down, clapping and smiling and crying all at the same time. But Jamie didn't always skate well. "There were times when I can remember wanting to cry for her," Patti Salé says. "And when she would come up in the stands I would put my arm around her and let her cry if she needed to cry." But she never let Jamie feel sorry for herself for too long. When the tears had gone on long enough, Patti Salé would hand her a tissue and say briskly, "Well, everything works out in the end, Jamie, so just keep working hard."

Patti Salé knew so little about skating that she really wasn't sure what all the different competitions meant or how good her daughter could become. Into her nonstop stream of chatter, Jamie was constantly inserting phrases like "when I'm at the Olympics" or "when I'm at the World Championships"—always *when,* never *if.* Her mother would look over absently and say, "Mmm-hmm." "Truthfully," Patti Salé remembers, "inside I'm thinking, *probably* won't happen. But you know. You never want to crush the dreams."

Since Patti Salé "knew nothing about skating," she decided to find a good coach and leave all the training decisions in the coach's hands. To some parents, a good coach was the coach who got your kid to Canadians, but that wasn't who Patti Salé was looking for. She wanted a coach who was "compassionate and well-meaning," an adult for whom "ambition was not the first priority." Patti Salé wanted someone "who truly looked after all their little athletes and developed the whole person"—someone, in fact, just like Debbie Wilson.

∞

In North America, there are female skating coaches in leather car coats with long red fingernails, and there are ones who look like off-duty librarians in collared shirts and prim sweaters. Debbie Wilson is more in the mold of a Brownie troop leader. She doesn't look like an athlete; she is rounder and softer than that. There are people in skating who take it all too seriously, but Debbie Wilson doesn't hold with handwringing. And yet neither is she the kind of coach who lets things slide. "I'm one of the stricter ones," she says cheerfully. "I'm still from the old school, that when a person books a fifteen-minute lesson, well, you're gonna get your fifteen minutes."

Years ago Debbie Wilson was working as a secretary in Saskatoon when she got an offer to teach summer skating school. She remembers exactly what she thought at the time: "Well, what do I want to do here? Sit in an office all summer—or skate?" She picked skating. After a few years she moved to Red Deer and started teaching skating there. When she discovered that the local kids didn't have enough ice time, Debbie Wilson took it upon herself to drive them half an hour up the highway to Lacombe, home of Alberta's largest corn maze, where ice was available on Monday nights. As there was no skate shop in Red Deer, she convinced her husband, George, that they should open one. "George," she says fondly, "sharpened all the blades."

Wilson describes herself as a "very structured" coach, and she first noticed Jamie Salé because she was breaking all the rules in the group lessons. "We had this thing where kids took turns being first in a line, and she would always sneak to the front of the line. And with the biggest grin on her face, eh?" Often, when Debbie Wilson turned her back, she would feel a tug on her coattails, and that unmistakable little voice would pipe up, "Watch me, Debbie! Watch me!"

When Jamie was six she was too young to have her own choreo-graphed solo, but she desperately wanted one, so when the other girls' music came on she would improvise her own number, often careening right in front of the poor girl whose solo it was in the first place. Not long afterwards, Jamie did get her own solo, and Debbie Wilson was tickled to discover that this little girl no taller than a table had her own ideas about choreography. "She'd say, 'Debbie, what about this?' And I'd say, 'Hey, that's pretty good. I think we can use that.'" Later, when Jamie started skating her solo in competitions, a curious thing happened. "She'd always throw in a few new things, a little flourish here or there," Wilson recalls. "And I'd think: Oh, *that's* new. Where'd that come from?" Wilson had never seen a kid who was relaxed enough to improvise during a competi-tion, and she started to think she might have something special in Jamie Salé.

In the novice ranks of Canadian skating there is one prize that little girls covet above all others: the divisional team warm-up suit. It is the young skater's first taste of greatness, and by the age of nine Jamie Salé wanted it badly. Moreover, when a skater got the warm-up suit, her coach would automatically get a special divisional jacket. And Jamie became ob-sessed with getting that jacket for Debbie Wilson. "When she was a novice lady all she was worried about was getting that coat," Wilson chuckles. "That was her thing: 'Oh, Deb, I just *gotta* get you that jacket, I *gotta* get you that jacket.' And I remember I had her that competition, because her mom couldn't come. We were sharing a bed, and I tell you, she was very aggressive in her sleep. Finally I just pushed her on the floor so I could get some sleep." Wilson shakes her head. "Anyway, she did win that year. She got her suit and so did I. And that was pretty good at that time, from the little town of Red Deer, to get that jacket."

By the time Jamie was twelve Debbie Wilson could see that she was outgrowing Red Deer's skating program, and Wilson, for one, was ready to see her test her wings. Edmonton lay two hours up the highway, and there the private Royal Glenora Club was training world champions. At a competition Wilson bumped into the Royal Glenora's pair coach and told him, "I have this little girl who would probably do okay in pairs." Wilson went home and told Jamie to write a letter to the coach, asking him to teach her, and before long it was all settled. The Red Deer Club helped pay her entrance fee to the Royal Glenora, the coaches found her a partner, and Patti Salé agreed to drive her up to Edmonton three times a week, two hours each way.

Jamie Salé was comfortable in small-time Canadian skating, and at first she resisted leaving her familiar world behind. "She was upset that first summer that she couldn't come with us to skating school, because she had to stay at the Royal Glenora and do pairs," Wilson says. "And I remember I said to her, 'Well, come on, Jamie! This is the start of your new career. You never know.' " Wilson grins. "And look what happened."

∞

There are at least two distinct worlds within Canadian figure skating. One is the local community rink, a small-time place with limited hours for figure skating and mother hen types like Debbie Wilson. Its roots are in the popular movement to build memorial rinks in every town in Canada after World War II. Almost all of Canada lies north of Michigan, and the small towns rely on their rinks to get them through the long winters. Everyone skates; there is no such thing as a pair of rental skates in Canada. The importance of the community rinks in Canada can be understood by the fact that one appears on the five-dollar bill, accompanied by the following Roch Carrier quotation: "The winters of my childhood were long, long seasons. We lived in three places: the school, the church, and the skating rink. But our real life was on the skating rink."

The other world, at the extreme opposite end of the Canadian spectrum, is the world of the aristocratic private clubs. Figure skating was introduced into Canada as a pastime of the leisured classes, and it was initially practiced in elegant rinks at members-only clubs. Upstairs at the club, dinner was served with silver and linen tablecloths, and a strict dress code was enforced. Skating's aristocratic beginnings continued to influence the sport long after it spread to the masses; as late as 1969, judges at the Canadian Championships still wore tuxedos. By the nineties, although the country club influence had lessened, it was still felt in elite skating, for the truth is that Canada's private clubs possess those two qualities so needed by elite coaches to do their work: ample ice and wealthy parents.

When Jamie Salé left Red Deer for the Royal Glenora Club, she crossed over from the community rink to the country club. The Royal Glenora, a one-time British cricket club, is located on a stretch of prime real estate down along the riverbank in Edmonton. It has lush grounds and an alpine-style summer terrace overlooking the tennis courts, where waiters serve cool drinks. With its thick carpets and good scotch and grand pianos, the Glenora has an upper-class air, and in the early years of its existence it is doubtful that Jamie Salé, the daughter of an interior decorator, would have been admitted as a member. But the Glenora had become less British and more Canadian-egalitarian over the years, and by the time Salé arrived in 1989 it felt less like a bastion of elitism and more like a very nice upper-middle-class swim club. Its functional cafeteria was always humming, while the elegant lounges had fewer and fewer habitués. Now, in the parking lot, Hondas and Volkswagens rubbed shoulders with the BMWs, and while doctors and lawyers were prominent members, there were plenty of other families who could afford the one-time initiation fee of two thousand dollars.

In figure skating the Royal Glenora's golden era began in 1979, when the board hired a Swedish coach to transform the club's recreational skating program into a competitive one. What this meant in practical terms was that one day a bunch of kids went home to their parents and said, "This crazy foreign guy locked us in the rink."

The crazy foreign guy was Jan Ullmark, and he had some credentials. In the sixties, Ullmark had twice been the Swedish champion. He had studied with the great Hans Gerschwiler in London and Davos, and with the great Gustave Lussi in Lake Placid. Ullmark had brought a couple of his Olympic-caliber Swedish skaters over with him to the Royal Glenora, and nobody at the Glenora had ever seen skaters who worked that hard. Kids at the Glenora were accustomed to skating for maybe an hour, then sitting by the pool and tanning for the rest of the day.

Ullmark had no patience with that, so he locked the rink doors so kids couldn't sneak out to the pool. Even to go to the bathroom, the kids had to ask the crazy foreign guy to unlock the door. Ullmark wanted them on the ice twice a day and sometimes more, and he wanted them to stretch and take dance classes and lift weights. He even changed the ice rink. "When I first arrived," Ullmark says, very serious, "the rink corners were *square*. So right away I said, 'If this is gonna be successful, we have to get an ice machine and round these corners.' " The club took his advice. Later, the club also hired more coaches like Ullmark—coaches who wanted to train competitive skaters. Within five years, the Royal Glenora had become a competitive club with a serious atmosphere, and Ullmark no longer had to lock the doors.

The Royal Glenora routinely sent a dozen or so of its skaters to the Canadian Championships, where they were known for being marvelously musical. This, too, was a reflection on the Swedish coach, who was a real music aficionado. At competitions, Ullmark still gets annoyed when coaches don't know their music. "Someone said to me, 'The blues should be sexy,' " he says, incredulous. "I said, 'The blues is a funeral march!' And some people want the tango to be what they call 'sexy.' Well, a true tango is the desperate dance of the poor people living in the slums of Argentina. Not what you'd call a happy, sexy little dance." Ullmark sighs. "My wife says, 'Oh, Jan, you know too much.' But I say, 'Come on! Let's *use* the music.' "

At the Royal Glenora, Ullmark originated the annual musical on ice, where skaters had to lip-sync the lyrics of big shows like *Phantom of the Opera* or *Starlight Express*. Ullmark directed this extravaganza every spring, and he treated it like a serious off-Broadway show. When Jamie Salé first came to the Glenora, she tucked her hair under a little cap and smeared a greasepaint mustache over her lip to play Gavroche in Ullmark's *Les Misérables*. No one was exempt from the annual show; Kurt Browning, then the world champion, played Jean Valjean. To some coaches, it seemed like Ullmark spent an awful lot of time on showbiz, but his approach paid off. In any competition, the Royal Glenora's skaters always ranked near the top in terms of theatrical ability.

For competitive skating, Ullmark was kind of a weird guy. He had the ability to train people for world-class results, but he didn't mind teaching a kid with no talent how to do an Axel, either. "I've never taught skating to teach a world champion," Ullmark says with a shrug. "I teach skating because I find it a challenge to get people to learn things." His colleagues at the Glenora had trained a couple of world champions, but Ullmark never gravitated towards that line of work. He didn't comb the Canadian Championships looking for raw talent that he could groom for Worlds. He just taught the kids from Edmonton or from down the road—kids like Jamie Salé.

Debbie Wilson had sent Salé to the Royal Glenora's pairs coach, David Howe, but since she was at the club anyway, Ullmark was giving her singles lessons. Patti Salé drove her four hours round-trip, every Tuesday and Thursday evening, and on Friday nights they drove up and stayed with relatives for the weekend. Ullmark was impressed by the mother's persistence, and he responded right away to the daughter's ability to perform to music. What Ullmark thought he could give the girl was better technique—and the work habits she needed to unlock her talent. (He was, after all, the guy who had locked the kids in the rink.) Already, he could see that the club's atmosphere was having a good influence on Jamie's work ethic. Two world champions, Kurt Browning and Kristi Yama-guchi, were training on the same ice with her, and by observing them she could see how far she had to go to catch up.

Jamie Salé had a gift for pairs, anyone could see that, and her results were good right away. Her very first year in juniors, it looked like she was going to win Canadians—until her partner dropped her out of a lift right in front of the judges' table. The crowd gasped, the judges' pencils went flying; somebody screamed. But Salé got right up and finished the program. She limped off the ice and collected her silver medal, and she was only annoyed because she had to wait a whole year to come back and win the junior pairs. When she was fifteen, her mother agreed to move with her to Edmonton, so she could train at the club every day. Patti Salé took a job in hospitality at the Royal Glenora, and from what she heard around the club, Jamie was improving rapidly. With hard work and some good luck, by the time the '94 Canadian Nationals came to Edmonton, Jamie and her partner could possibly make the top three—and qualify for the '94 Olympic team.

On the night of the Olympic trials, Patti Salé sat in the stands in Edmonton surrounded by hometown people. Some moms hated to see their daughters take up pair skating, but Patti Salé always told people, "I love to watch her fly." For six years, Patti Salé had spent all her paychecks on skating, and now she had uprooted her life to move to Edmonton for skating. But she remained very low-key. "My mom never made me feel bad about it," Jamie Salé says. "She never said, 'Hey, this is costing a lot, and you better smarten up,' or 'You better start winning.'" Now, as Patti Salé waited for her daughter to step out on the ice, she repeated the things she always told herself before an important competition: You never know how long each phase is going to last. If it ends here tonight, that'll be all right. There've been lots of good things already.

Jamie skated early in the evening and made few mistakes, and she had to wait half an hour to find out if she had made the Olympic team. But when the good news finally came across the scoreboard, there was only one person she wanted. "Where's my mom?" she wailed. The cameras found her wandering around backstage, mascara running down her cheeks, clutching a tissue and asking everyone, anyone if they had seen her mother. "Where's my mom?" she cried. "I want my mom!" It was a raw cry, and suddenly she seemed much younger than her sixteen years. And then finally she found her, and without a word, she collapsed in her mother's arms. Patti Salé hugged her close and smiled through her own tears. They *were* a team, and the team had done very, very well tonight. But the tears were not entirely happy. For all its joy, the moment touched a sadness that ran very deep, for they had been through a lot together.

∞

When Jamie Salé made the Olympic team she was only sixteen, and as the youngest athlete on the whole Canadian team, she got more than her share of press coverage. At the Olympic ice hall, while the top contenders skated around looking tense and guarded, she was the pretty Canadian flashing a huge smile as she sailed by the judges' table. She was, as the cliché went, just thrilled to be there, but Jamie Salé could animate a cliché with the full force of her lively personality. She liked greeting card sentiments; she had various inspirational sayings that rolled off her tongue with complete sincerity. "I always tell everyone, Dream big!" she said, or, "Everything happens for a reason." Jamie Salé had once called her mother at work and held the handset up to a boom box playing "Wind Beneath My Wings." She was corny, but she meant it. And after all, wasn't her own charmed life a testament to the powers of a good attitude?

The cameras loved her, for she embodied (very prettily) the ideal of the innocent, starry-eyed Olympian. It played well: the girl from the Canadian prairies who says "aboot" instead of "about" and jumps up and down every time she gets a complimentary Olympic T-shirt. On the night of the Olympic finals, she and her partner made endearing beginners' mistakes. She seemed to briefly lose track of what she was doing and went down in a fall that got her lilac dress all wet. But she got up smiling and kept up the wattage to the end. Near the finish she and her partner got a little behind the music and had to scramble into their last pose after the music ended. But Jamie Salé came off the ice glowing. Waiting for her marks, she leaned her rosy cheek against her partner's shoulder, and the words started tumbling out. "Oh, it feels so good to be done!" She gasped for air, then rambled on like the irrepressible teenager she was. "Just wish I hadn't missed that double Axel!" she said, wrinkling her nose. "That was a good star lift, though! Hi, Mom, hi, Dad, hi, Jan—I miss you!" Over her head, her partner grinned, as if to say *Yes folks, even when she can't breathe, she can still talk a blue streak*.

To that small portion of the skating world that noticed her, Salé seemed to possess that rarest of commodities—real innocence. Jamie Salé's enormous smile contrasted sharply with, say, the look in Yelena Berezhnaya's eyes as she sat on that same Olympic bench with Oleg Shlyakhov, waiting for her scores. Berezhnaya looked older than her years, and wary, in a way that made adults squirm. Jamie Salé looked as if she'd never had a bad night's sleep. With that shiny ponytail she looked like a cheerleader who had picked up skating as an extracurricular and who would probably be named homecoming queen in the fall. She had that unmistakable Canadian friendliness, and when she skated it came rushing forward to meet the audience. She gave you the feeling that she'd like to climb up into the stands and shake every last hand.

There were a few born pair skaters in the field at those Olympics, and Jamie Salé was clearly one of them. Her sixteen-year-old body would develop in the right way, so that she would be muscular but not chunky. Already, she was a lovely spinner, and she had that innate sense of how to stretch the body in the air over a lift. She used all the notes in the music, even when the choreographer forgot to tell her to; if she came to a flourish in the music and was left without a corresponding gesture, she would toss her head back or snap a wrist at the crucial moment. And she was a good competitor, too. At the Olympics she'd skated better than in practice. She was the type of skater who leaps a level in performance as soon as you put a crowd in the building, and that is a nice quality for any coach to have in reserve.

It wasn't surprising that Salé dropped her partner after the Olympics. He wasn't as strong a skater as she was, and clearly this girl was headed straight to the top. What was surprising was that she ended up sitting out of pair skating for two whole seasons. Only in North America could a talent like Jamie Salé have gone without a partner in the prime of her career. In any socialist sports system she would have been paired with the best boy available and immediately sent to the top coaches. But in the North American free market, pairs are not made at the top but negotiated at the bottom. It was up to Jamie Salé to find her own partner, and male figure skaters were rare in Canada. She was too accomplished to go to a regional mix-and-match, and much too good to go looking for a partner on an Internet site. After all, she was Jamie Salé! Any partner good enough for her would definitely be skating at Canadians and she would see him there— just as soon as she qualified for Canadians in ladies' singles.

And then something inconceivable happened. In 1996 she didn't even *qualify* for Canadians. "I had come fifth the year before, so I thought—you know, I'm Jamie Salé, I'm just gonna keep doing well, I don't *have* to work hard. So I slacked off, and the next year I didn't make it to Nationals. And then I was like, How dare they do that to *me*? Like I had this thing, like I thought I could ride on my name."

How was she going to pick out a new partner if she wasn't even going to Canadians? To make matters worse, the 1996 World Championships were to be held in Edmonton in a few months time. The one time in her life that Worlds would be in her own city, and she didn't even have a partner!

There was, however, one possibility. At Canadians, Ullmark's wife had noticed a guy named David Pelletier. Pelletier had been as high as second in pairs at Canadians, but now his partner was struggling. He might be open to trying out with someone new. With his skills and his spark, he'd be good enough to skate with Jamie. So right after Canadian Nationals, Jan Ullmark called the Canadian federation about putting together a tryout.

"I phoned the federation," Ullmark says, "and I said, 'Look, these two should be together.' And the lady from the federation said: 'Oh, *we* can't do *that*! You can't just *decide* that.' And I said, 'But that's our problem in Canada. See, that's how they do it in Russia. They see a kid from Moscow and the partner is from Irkutsk, and they put them together, because they're interested in the results. You guys are also interested in the results, but at the same time, the method to get to those results is not allowed.'" Ullmark didn't get anywhere. So Jamie Salé called David Pelletier herself, and they agreed to try out together in Boucherville before Worlds.

Jamie Salé was almost too excited to sit still on the plane to Montreal. But as soon as she got to the rink she sensed that something was very, very wrong. "The tryout wasn't organized at all. Dave had no car, so I was getting driven around by this other lady. I went to the rink, and the coach wasn't even there." Jamie Salé realized with a pang that not everyone in Boucherville wanted her there. And then she looked up into the stands and did a double take. There was Alison Gaylor, Pelletier's partner, leaning on a friend's shoulder and sobbing. "It was bizarre. I'm thinking: What's the story? Is this really over? And I felt really awkward—like, three's a crowd." Jamie Salé put on a brave face and went out to skate, but it was hard to concentrate with David Pelletier's partner watching her every move. "Alison would even come on the ice when Dave and I were supposed to be trying out. She was coaching another team or something. And I was like: This is *weird*. I said to Dave, 'Why is she here?' And he goes, 'Well, she has a right. I can't make her go. I can't tell her what to do.'"

The whole thing was deteriorating into a bad soap opera. Jamie Salé was wounded. "I remember sitting in the dressing room thinking: I was told I was coming here for a tryout, and it was going to be professional. I thought Josée Picard always wanted me to be at her school. Then I get here and she's not even showing up?" Eric Gillies and Lloyd Eisler were there to help with the tryout, but things never even got going, really, because on the first day they made the mistake of trying throws. Jamie Salé hadn't done a throw in two years, and fifteen minutes into it, she pulled the hamstring muscle of her landing leg. With an injury like that, jumping was all but impossible.

On the second day Jamie Salé was supposed to prove that she had her double Axel and her triple toe, so she gritted her teeth and tried to jump on her injured leg. Every time she fell, every time she got up and brushed the ice chips from her legs, she felt the eyes of Boucherville on her. Everyone knew Dave Pelletier wasn't going to choose a partner who couldn't land her jumps. "It was," Salé says bluntly, "the worst experience I've ever had in skating."

She was demoralized when she left Boucherville, but still she allowed herself to hope. The jumps hadn't worked, but everything else—lifts, stroking, spins—had been right on. There was a natural match in their timing and body rhythms, a match so uncanny that there were many moments when each looked at the other in amazement: *Did that really happen?* So when she got back to Edmonton, Jamie Salé still thought there was a good chance David Pelletier would say yes. In the meantime, she got a job at the World Championships in Edmonton, hostessing in a corporate box, and waited for Pelletier to call.

She had thought that he was going to come to Edmonton to watch the Worlds. "And then I called him and he's like, 'Well, I'm not sure if I can come now, because I have to do some ice shows with Alison to make some money.' And then I never heard, never heard, never heard. I kept calling him, and he wouldn't call me back." Salé went to work in a skybox at the Edmonton Coliseum, explaining skating to people in suits. And still she waited for Pelletier's call.

"Finally I got a hold of him, and he's like, 'Uh, *well,* I was just uh . . . ' " She shakes her head. "So I said, 'Dave! If you don't want to skate with me, that's fine. But at least have the decency to call me and tell me.' And he's like, 'I'm sorry, you're right. I was just scared to tell you. And I feel bad.' And I said, 'That's fine. You make your choices, I make mine.' " Salé hung up the phone. "And that was it. I was really sad. And I just thought, Well, that's it. That's *it.*"

From the VIP box, Jamie Salé, corporate hostess, watched the pairs she had competed against two years ago at the Olympics. Was it over already? Most of these girls were not as good as she was. They couldn't perform for an audience like she could. Not even close. But there was no getting around that one bitter fact of a pair skater's life: Your fate does not depend only on you. You have to have the luck of getting the right partner.

She knew the stories. A great pair skater who was a clockwise jumper and never found her match. A fabulous Canadian girl who came along at a time when there was no decent Canadian boy to skate with, and that was the end of her career. Boys who stayed with the wrong partners because they had fallen in love with them—or out of loyalty to a coach. There were so many ways for it to go wrong. And then there was her own case. Right now in all of Canada there was just one great partner for her, and he had just turned her down—not for some great opportunity, but to skate another season with a girl with whom he had just finished fifth at Canadians.

Jamie Salé was eighteen years old. She hadn't even qualified for Canadians in singles, and she didn't have a partner for pairs. There were people who hinted that it might be time to give up her childhood hobby and get on with her life. All spring, her mind churned through scenarios. "Then, finally," she says, "I just went, You know what? Screw everyone. I'm gonna make it in singles." If there wasn't a partner for her right now, she would have to make it on her own. "Look," she says honestly, "deep down, I knew I could never be world champion in singles. I knew pair skating was what I really loved, what I was born to do. But what was I going to do? I said to myself, I *can't* just quit! I've got to try *something.*"

PART TWO

The Arena

Chapter Four

AFTER THE ACCIDENT Berezhnaya skated differently. With Shlyakhov she had been timid and a little robotic, but now she performed with the sure command of a dancer. She held her head proudly on her neck; her light hands undulated like the hands of a ballerina. When she rose above her partner's head in a lift, she now seemed slightly pleased to be on display. She was learning to show off a little. To Moskvina she didn't show off enough, and at practice she chased her around the ice shouting, "Smile! Show more!" But Matveyev, the old choreographer, stood at the barrier and yelled, "Don't bother her! At the competition, she will do beautifully."

Berezhnaya came back to the ice painfully thin, and though her hair had grown in enough to cover the scars, it was short and dark red. To people who had known her when her hair was long and blonde, that close-cropped head was a sharp reminder of the accident. But once she started to skate, people forgot everything else, because she was simply so very good.

Moskvina had taken her innate lightness and developed it further. Now Berezhnaya raised one leg high behind her back and held it to a count of two, three, even four. The leg seemed weightless, as though if she didn't pin it to the ice it would naturally float up behind her. The truth was that holding that position made her muscles ache. But when Berezhnaya came back to the ice she spared herself no pain and no exhaustion. She skated at a grueling speed. She fell hard time after time, collected bruises on a body that had no pillows of flesh to break a fall. But Berezhnaya refused nothing.

There were a few things, still, that Moskvina forbade. The side-by-side camel spins stayed far apart in practice, and it was still too early to work on the dangerous triple twist. The lifts remained basic, for in the process of relearning them Sikharulidze had dropped her more times than anyone cared to count. She always got up quickly, saying she was fine, and she never hesitated when it was time to try the same lift again. Actually, it was Sikharulidze whose nerves were strained to the breaking point.

He was terrified of lifting Berezhnaya now. "Before every lift, I said to myself, Okay, one fall, and that's it," Sikharulidze says seriously. "A fall can happen to anybody. You just trip over something on the ice—that's a fall. And I told myself: One more fall, and it's finished for sure. Not for skating—I mean, for *her.*" With his former partner, he had never lain awake nights worrying about dropping her. Rarely, a lift came down, but it was never serious. "Okay, we'd have a fall. She'd stand up, and it's okay. And you never really understand that you have somebody's life in your hand. But here you understand: It's her life in your hand."

Anton Sikharulidze knew better than anyone the condition of the girl he was now lifting. Berezhnaya slept in the same room with him and his sister. "At that time, her head was even soft, because they opened the whole thing. It's soft, like you can touch it and it leaves an impression. That's why I'm understanding, a fall would finish her. It's very strange feelings that I must hide inside. Maybe even Tamara and Lena don't know about this, but every practice was like competition, just, *ohhh,* so nervous."

After practice, on the subway or walking down the sidewalk, his mind was racing. "At first, I said, 'You need to be a man here. If you started something, let's finish this.' And another feeling said, 'Okay. She already can talk, she's already okay. Why we need always skating? Why? Maybe I can do some other job.'" But whenever he even tried to bring up the subject with Tamara Moskvina, she cut him off. "You can do it, all right?" she snapped. "Why are you even thinking about this?"

Maybe so, maybe Tamara was right, but to him, it was still unnatural. He grew pale, tired looking. "And Tamara always asked me, 'You have a lot of power, you're not a small guy. Why you're always so tired?'" He shakes his head. "Because everything's very, very emotional! That's why I'm tired. Not from physical things, but from my head."

One day Berezhnaya slipped out of his grip, and her head smacked the ice with a sickening thud. Immediately she got up, saying she was fine, but Moskvina knew better than to trust her. "Yelena is very secretive," Moskvina warns. "She never tells you what bothers her. I am like *guessing.*" She turned out to be fine that time, but Moskvina never stopped studying that blank face, looking for the slightest flicker of pain.

Any day now she might come down with a terrible headache or a bad case of vertigo, and that would be the end of skating. Her speech was still slurred, so one had to assume that the brain was not fully recovered. It was disturbing to shake her right hand and feel how weakly it pressed your own. "All the time," Sikharulidze says, "I'm understanding that the doctor can say, even tomorrow, 'Stop it. It's getting worse. No more.'" The 1998 Olympics were a year and a half away. They should be ready *then*.

So in the fall of 1997, just four months after they started training in earnest, Berezhnaya and Sikharulidze entered a competition in Paris. It was ridiculously soon for so new a pair to be out among the best pairs in the world, but the old choreographer Matveyev was right. In the competition they did do beautifully. Moskvina glanced around the rink at the faces watching her new pair, and those faces, filled with a special degree of pleasure, confirmed what she had hoped. Four months in, it was already obvious: They were going to be one of the great pairs. Already, the beautiful lines were visible, and the awe-inspiring speed across the ice was there; already anyone could see that here were two souls who felt the orchestra behind them.

There were still weaknesses to fix before the Olympics. Berezhnaya had those knobby-kneed legs of old, and on the throws her legs sometimes collapsed like the wobbly legs of a foal. But somehow even her falls were not so crushing anymore. When she had taken spills with Shlyakhov, he had raced ahead without her, forcing her to muscle the ice like a speed skater to catch up. But now if she fell, Sikharulidze was waiting.

They finished third in Paris and won a little bit of prize money, which Berezhnaya sorely needed. She could finally afford to move out of the Sikharulidzes' and into her own tiny apartment. Moskvina collected extra spoons and chipped plates from all her friends, and in this way Berezhnaya filled her few cupboards. At the housewarming, friends pooled their money to buy her a small television set. People were kind, and this touched her. Once, a visiting American friend bought her a sweater; she cried.

By that autumn she was no longer Anton's girlfriend. He still treated her with special affection, but off the ice they saw each other less and less. She knew he did his share of carousing in nightclubs, and this must have bothered her, but she kept her own counsel. In the evenings now he went out to bars with his friends in their fancy foreign cars, while she mostly stayed in. Sometimes she invited her girlfriends from the rink to her new apartment to drink tea and watch movies, and these evenings made her happy.

Berezhnaya felt her former life, with all its cruelty and loneliness, receding into the past. To wake up in her own apartment each morning and put the kettle on, to be able to skate, to walk down the corridor of Yubileiny and be greeted by the ballet mistress and Matveyev and the friendly man from the circus who taught lifts—well, this was a good life. In fine weather, she and Anton practiced lifts in the parking lot. Across the street a cathedral, sky blue with white filigree, reposed in the sun. After practice one could sit with friends in the café on the steps of Yubileiny and drink a coffee in the sun for a few rubles. During this period, whenever anyone asked how she was feeling, Berezhnaya invariably replied, "Now everything's new, it's the new life, and I'm very, very happy." But how long the new life would last, no one could say.

∞

The ice sports campus for the Chinese national team lies in a northern district of Beijing, near the zoo. By any standards the campus is impressive, but by Chinese standards it is positively deluxe, and it astonished Shen Xue and Zhao Hongbo when they first arrived there from Harbin. Here were two heated arenas, one for practice and one for competition, plus a speed-skating oval, dormitories, two cafeterias, and a gymnasium. Everything an athlete or coach could need was tucked inside these buildings: weight room, ballet studio, medical room, state sports committee offices. There was even a small five-story hotel on the campus, so that when competitions were held at the big arena, the foreign athletes could stay within the compound.

By 1996, the Chinese government had relaxed its grip on most people's daily lives, but the sports teams were still run very much on the old model. The sportsmen lived in old-style worker dormitories. The state sport officials' office was right next to the practice rink, the better to supervise the coaches and athletes. The family unit had been fully replaced by the work unit. The athlete-workers slept in dorm beds in double rooms and bathed in a big shower room. There was no privacy. Skaters wore team uniforms, ate their meals in a cafeteria. And they lived apart from their families, the better to conserve their energy for their work.

When Yao Bin moved to Beijing full-time in 1996, he was assigned a spartan room with a single bed in the dormitory, next door to his athletes and his assistant coach. His wife and son remained in Harbin; he saw them a few times a year. "What can I do?" Yao said when a reporter asked about the separation. "No matter if it's the coach or the athletes, we don't have time to go home. When my wife and I got married, I went back to Harbin under the pretext of participating in a competition. The team gave me a leave of several days. So I married my wife, and afterwards I went back to the team. In the second year my son was born. But when I carried my son, I didn't seem to know him. Of course, he didn't like me, but he scratched at me and kept on crying."

Shen Xue and Zhao Hongbo saw their parents once or twice a year in Harbin, once in Beijing. Team rules prohibited dating. The campus was separated from the surrounding neighborhood by high walls, and the gates were locked every night at ten o'clock. To leave the campus at any time, athletes needed special permission from the coach, and they had to go out in groups. On the whole the skaters lived in a military atmosphere of self-sacrifice and discipline. The core pleasures of life were excluded in order to narrow everyone's focus to a single objective: bringing glory to China at international competitions.

In 1996, when Chinese sports officials summoned Yao Bin and his athletes to Beijing, the 1998 Olympics were less than two years away. The goal for the team was summed up by the familiar sports propaganda slogan painted on the entryway to the athletes' dormitory: "Break out of Asia and advance on the world." The propaganda might have been the same, but compared to earlier generations of Chinese athletes, Shen and Zhao spent almost no time on political education. There was a classroom on the second floor of the dormitory, but it was no longer used for self-criticism sessions. Occasionally there was a very dull team meeting, something about team rules, or how to behave abroad. But mostly the classroom sat empty. The skaters stored their big suitcases there. Eventually, they moved in a Ping-Pong table.

While the campus hummed with the efficiency of the state sports machine marching steadily towards Olympic targets, the surrounding neighborhood teemed with ordinary chaotic Chinese life. On the eight-lane highway just outside the gates, the grimy buses passed by, each with a hundred faces squished against the windows. A massive pedestrian bridge spanned the highway, and there a shabby man with missing teeth sold puppies. The outside world spilled in through the gates every morning, when the street sellers pushed a few carts onto the edge of campus. Decked out in their national team jackets, the skaters walked the two hundred yards from the dorm to the practice rink and caught a whiff of hot coals, sweet buns, meat on a stick. But no skater ever slapped a coin on the counter and ordered a hot doughnut. The skaters weighed in three times a week, and if Yao Bin's girls gained even a quarter pound, he punished them.

Only once had Shen Xue failed one of Yao's weigh-ins. During one of her parents' rare visits to Beijing she had drunk two bottles of Coca-Cola, and she found herself half a pound overweight on the day of the weigh-in. Automatically she received the standard punishment: For three days she had to stop eating with the team and go to a separate cafeteria where the sports administrators ate. "Normally athletes try to avoid being noticed by the leaders," Shen Xue explains. "But when you go to the other cafeteria, all of the leaders take their meals there. When they see an athlete there, they will ask, 'Well, what? Are you overweight?' It's nothing less than a press conference."

Humiliated in front of the leaders, Shen Xue could hardly swallow her food, and she quickly dropped the weight. From that day on she never went over her allotted hundred pounds again. Her discipline was more ferocious than her hunger. Sometimes a skater's mother came to the dorm in the afternoon with a bag of roasted corn, or a dish of meat or fish cooked at home. But when the skaters shared the dish, Shen Xue took only enough to be polite. Whenever she reached for the tongs on the athletes' buffet, no matter how her stomach ached, she measured out her food precisely. The most conspicuous object in her room was a scale.

Shen Xue's life in the years before the 1998 Olympics was divided into two parts. The first and largest part was training. Every morning, in the hallway of the dormitory, Teacher Yao posted a detailed schedule, with times for skating, off-ice training, rest, meals, showers, and bedtimes. Shen Xue did everything on the schedule perfectly. The second part of her life, which was very small, could be considered her private life, although there was really no privacy in the athletes' work unit. In this part of her life there were the brief phone calls to her parents, not more than ten minutes, and the life in the dorm apart from skating. When they had a free hour or two, Shen Xue and the other skaters played card games while they listened to the radio. On nice days, skaters went apple picking or fishing in a nearby park. The boys climbed trees. To a Western eye, the teenagers' pastimes seemed old-fashioned and made them appear younger than their years. Shen Xue collected dolls and stuffed toys well into her twenties. She amused herself by making paper birds and reading innocent romantic novels. For his part, Zhao Hongbo liked stories of Chinese warriors.

Sometimes, at night, the boys would tiptoe past the coach's closed door, sneak past the dorm sentry, and climb over the wall to go play arcade games until two in the morning.

When Shen Xue had a day off she sometimes went window-shopping with her teammates. They would gaze all day long in the shop windows, but Shen Xue bought nothing. Although the leaders gave her pocket money, she spent little on herself. She wore national team practice clothes or complimentary shirts given out at competitions. All of her makeup had been given to her by other people. For many years, the coach cut her hair. Even in her private life, she was strict with herself.

In Shen Xue's regimented life there were just a few deep desires, and one of the deepest was to please Yao Bin. He spent more time with her than with his own son; he lay awake nights creating new programs in his head, devising new treatments for her aches and pains. She worked hard for him not because he was her boss, although he was. She worked as hard as she could because if she disappointed him, after all he had done for her, she would be deeply, deeply ashamed. Everyone had heard about Yao Bin's own career, about the German fans who laughed at him at his first World Championships, and how he had fallen clumsily on a simple death spiral in the Olympic Games. Twenty years later, Yao still couldn't laugh it off. Hearing the stories irritated him to the point that he could lose his temper. Yao had never forgotten for one minute that he was in a race to catch up with the West.

It was a cornerstone of Yao's philosophy that his teams should be "completely made in China, from the manufacture of the parts to the design and assembly." He never allowed Shen and Zhao to go to foreign coaches or choreographers, although judges and officials constantly advised him to do so. "They're no joint venture," he bragged to the Chinese press. "They are genuinely made in China." He stuck to Chinese music and costumes, did all the choreography himself. Most important, he gave them his own radical new Chinese pair skating technique.

Yao had ripped the standard pair elements apart and looked for ways to get more height, more distance, a bigger thrill. He created such a powerful launch into the triple twist that Shen Xue appeared to be shot into the air twice as high as other girls. For the two years leading up to the Olympics, Yao drilled Shen and Zhao in these high-risk moves, until they could perform them with ease. And Yao noticed something: Now, at competitions, the rest of the coaches would stop to watch Shen and Zhao. One day in 1998, a Czech pair accidentally cut in front of Shen and Zhao during practice, and afterwards their coach came up to Yao Bin to apologize. With a start, Yao realized that this had never happened to him in his entire life. "There is a saying: A weak country does not deserve diplomacy," he told his wife on the phone. "I guess now they don't think we're so weak."

In the weeks before the Olympics, Yao walked across campus to the sports committee offices to deal with the political side of things. The pre-Olympic season had been a good one for Shen and Zhao, so the authorities were considering revising the Olympic target from top ten to top six. At the most recent World Championships, Shen and Zhao had been only eleventh. So Yao went to a meeting and discussed the matter, "and after calm analysis," he remembers, "we agreed that breaking into the top six was not impossible—just extremely hard." Yao agreed to the placement, and now it was official: Shen and Zhao had promised the Chinese government that they would be in the top six. Yao walked out of the administration building, turned his collar up against the cold, and lit another cigarette. For the thousandth time, he crossed the campus by the same tree-lined path, covered those same two hundred yards between the rink and the entrance to the dorm. Break out of Asia and advance on the world.

∞

They were in Nagano for the 1998 Olympic final, and now it was time. Standing at the edge of the Olympic ice, Yelena Berezhnaya looked up into Anton Sikharulidze's face. He looked terrified. Her own face was flushed; her wide eyes anxious. Above them, ten thousand people cheered the announcement of their names. Now. With a snap of the elbow Sikharulidze offered his hand, and Berezhnaya dropped her palm into his; both squeezed hard. From this moment they were bound together. Whatever their past differences, now they swiftly closed ranks: two united in the critical moment against everyone, everything else.

On all sides was the din of the crowd. Skating forwards, hand in hand, they put ice between themselves and the wall of noise. They came to a stop at center ice, and the roar dwindled to nothing. Now. Standing tall in his coat with tails, Sikharulidze stretched one arm down towards his partner and placed a hand at the nape of her neck. Berezhnaya, looking elegant in a long-sleeved dress, arched her back, and let her close-cropped blond head fall gently into his waiting palm. They froze in a pose of extreme beauty, breathed deeply, and counted. Two seconds to music. One. Two.

An orchestra played moody Russian music, full of suspense and dramatic violins. They took command in a matter of seconds. After the first two strides they were flying. Earlier pairs had had awkward moments, dumpy costumes, but this pair wore tailored wine-colored clothes, and everything about them was polished to a high gloss. They strode proudly, they moved crisply. And within ten seconds, the crowd as one snapped to attention, realizing that this pair was the class of the field. Quickly the two bodies went up into side-by-side triple jumps, and a split second later they landed in absolute unison, punctuated by a burst of loud applause.

Standing at the barrier on tiptoe, Tamara Moskvina gave a curt nod. For nineteen months she had raced against the calendar. She had used all her powers to get them ready *now,* for this Olympics. No one had thought she could do it in less than two years. "Even the pie needs time to be cooked," Moskvina philosophized. "But"—and here the wink—"you can put it in the microwave." She had accelerated the process, and here they were, skating for a gold medal at the Olympics, fresh off victories at the two biggest Olympic tune-up events. No judge could resist such technical prowess combined with that gorgeous romantic style. Only one element was still not ready: the triple twist. Now the twist was fifteen seconds away.

The triple twist had plagued Berezhnaya and Sikharulidze for a year now. Berezhnaya had never mastered it before the accident, and now she had even more problems with it. The main difficulty was in the timing, for Berezhnaya had Moscow technique on the twist, whereas Sikharulidze had St. Petersburg technique. In the process of merging the two, Berezhnaya had banged him in the head with her elbow on several occasions. The two separate techniques were deeply ingrained, and even now the twist failed more often than not. For the twist, they needed some luck.

Now they sped backwards, setting up for the twist. Moskvina would know in the air. Up went Berezhnaya, high over his head, and for a split second, she delayed. Moskvina's pulse shot up. *She waited too long!* Berezhnaya yanked her arms in to her chest and began to spin, but she didn't have enough time. One, two—she hit the ice still turning, and Sikharulidze had to grab hold of her waist and somehow manage to keep them both on their feet.

Now Moskvina recalculated. Three good pairs were yet to skate, including one of her own. But Lena and Anton could still win, even with that mistake, if they made it through the rest of the program clean. Moskvina tensed as they went into the double Axels, but both were steady. She tensed at the first throw, but Berezhnaya made it easily. The only remaining danger was the second throw.

It looked dicey in the air, and as Berezhnaya came down, her free foot actually clipped the landing skate. Berezhnaya swerved for a split second and righted herself by pure luck. Moskvina exhaled. And after that the rest of the program was easy, just playing to the crowd. We'll have to wait for the marks, Moskvina thought, but even with the mistake on the twist, it will probably be enough for first.

They were skating beautifully now. All of it was moving the judges: the arched backs and pointed toes, the exquisite shapes created by their bodies, the flow generated by each perfect stroke of the blade. On pure skating no one in the event could compete with them. The other pairs were world class, but Berezhnaya and Sikharulidze were in a class with the legends: Gordeyeva and Grinkov, the Protopopovs. Berezhnaya went up over Sikharulidze's head in the final lift and came down smoothly. Five seconds to the end of the program. Her foot touched the ice, he clasped one arm around her waist. The lift was over—

Suddenly they were sprawled in a heap on the ice. Moskvina registered the shock while they scrambled into position just as the music died. A fall? Berezhnaya's shoulders drooped; she looked stricken. *So close, so close! Five seconds away!* And in that split second their fate was sealed: another four years.

∞

On the morning of the 1998 Olympic final, Yao Bin awoke feeling jittery. Tonight the two kids would be the thirteenth pair to skate. The Westerners said thirteen was a bad omen. The kids had also been the thirteenth pair to skate in the short program, where Shen Xue had lost control of an important spin; consequently they were now sitting in eighth place. Although Yao didn't believe in the foreigners' omens, he felt uneasy. But when he mentioned his feeling to the Chinese team doctor, the doctor flew at him. "Teacher Yao, get hold of yourself! You don't want Shen Xue and Zhao Hongbo to hear you!"

Maybe it was just the Olympics that made him uneasy. He made the kids take an earlier bus than planned. On the bus ride to the arena, he tried to calm himself by looking out at the city lights, but he couldn't relax. He would rather the competition start immediately. He told himself: "We have thought of everything, done everything." And yet he couldn't stop himself from doing things that he never did. He checked over the kids' skates, gave Zhao Hongbo a bunch of long-winded advice. But in the midst of his lecture, he looked up at the two young people and stopped in mid-sentence. *After all,* he thought, *it's all up to them when the music starts.*

Backstage, Yao realized he was hovering, so he tried to leave the kids alone. In his mind he went over the scenario again. The teams skated in reverse order of their placement in the short program. The best pairs were in the last group; Shen and Zhao were in the second-best group and would go out next to last tonight. Within each group the draw was random, and Shen and Zhao had drawn the first spot in their group. That meant that the Chinese would have to skate a knockout performance, so the judges couldn't forget about them. Then three more couples would skate, each one of whom could conceivably beat them, and Yao would have to sit backstage and watch to see how many pegs his team would be knocked down. All the Chinese team officials would be at the arena tonight. They didn't expect a medal, but they were coming to see a breakthrough. No Chinese team had ever finished higher than dead last at the Olympics. Tonight's official target: top six.

When Yao finally stepped out into the bright arena, behind his team, he was worried that the Olympic atmosphere might overwhelm the two kids. But when he looked at them, they met his gaze, excited but eager. He liked the way they looked, especially Shen Xue. She was smiling a certain smile that she only smiled on the ice and only in a certain very good mood, and he liked that very much. They were ready.

It was a performance entirely made in China. Yao had designed the costumes, black with white edges. The music, "Mount Olympus," was the kind of half step above Muzak to be found everywhere in China. The choreography also came from Yao Bin. The Western television commentators took one look at the program and said, "If only they could get some decent music and some choreography . . ." Over at the judges' table, the predominantly Western judges knew from the first few bars of "Mount Olympus" that they were going to have to dock this pair on the second mark. That music was obnoxious. But everyone in the building was in complete cross-cultural agreement on one crucial point: Yao Bin's made-in-China pair skating technique was mind-blowing.

That night the Chinese launched nothing less than a revolution in pair skating, and every coach in the building knew it. In the past coaches and judges had tacitly agreed that one successful throw jump was as good as another. No need to add risk by sending the girl higher and farther. But Yao had shown the crowd the maximum height and distance, and never again would they be satisfied with average. Shen Xue launched into the air on the twist as if shot out of a cannon. On throws, Zhao heaved her so hard that his feet came off the ice. Yao didn't care. Let Zhao's feet come off the ice—no one would be looking *there*! The whole world was staring at Shen, who was hurtling twenty-two feet through the air with the control of an expert gymnast. When she dropped to earth easily on one foot, smiling from ear to ear, she actually *gained speed* and flew away from him— *whoosh*. The audience went crazy. And now the other coaches realized that Yao had them by the throat, because in a sport where people usually got ahead for subtle reasons, Yao was hitting people over the head with his improvements. Every throw, every lift was a challenge. Get out the yard-stick, he seemed to be saying. Go ahead. Measure the distance, the height. We're objectively better. And the audience backed him up. Any man on the street could tell the difference between a Chinese throw and an ordinary one.

The official government strategy called for perfection, and Shen Xue and Zhao Hongbo delivered it. Even Yao was pleased. The three of them sat in the kiss-and-cry and watched their good marks come up, and then Yao had to wait. By the time he reached the backstage TV monitor, the American pair had finished skating, and Yao saw from the marks that Shen and Zhao had beaten the Americans. Then the third Russian team skated their routine, and somehow Shen and Zhao beat them too. Top six! The French team finished, and Yao Bin was scanning their marks when behind him the team doctor shouted, "We placed fifth!" and slapped Zhao Hongbo on the back.

All around him the leaders were celebrating, but Yao Bin stayed glued to the TV set. He was the type of hypercompetitive man who, as soon as the goal is reached, is already hungry for more. Yao waited. Maybe they could beat a pair in the final group, pull up to fourth. Someone from the team went to fetch the special bottle of vodka, but Yao still watched as he always watched everything, filing images in the vault between his ears. He was really very pleased with fifth place. But next year, he intended to be first.

So Yao watched all the pairs, especially the Russians. He watched closely, and when he saw Berezhnaya and Sikharulidze fall down and finish with only the silver, he knew the whole future. This pair, then, would be their main rival. For the next four years they would battle this couple. And to win the next Olympics, Yao had to beat Moskvina.

∞

The Salt Lake Ice Center. A high retaining wall separates the spectators from the competitors. *(Jerzy Bukajlo)*

After they collide with one minute remaining in the Olympic warm-up, Anton Sikharulidze helps Jamie Salé to her feet. David Pelletier and Yelena Berezhnaya look on. *(Dave Black)*

Yelena Berezhnaya at around
the time she started skating.
(All photos this page courtesy of
Yelena Berezhnaya)

The Soviet sports system's reach extended to remote
Nevinnomyssk, where Berezhnaya grew up studying
ballet.

From left to right: Oleg Shlyakhov,
Tamara Moskvina, Alexander Matveyev,
and Yelena Berezhnaya pose for a photo
at Yubileiny in the fall of 1995, a few
months before the accident.

A publicity photo of Berezhnaya and Shlyakhov
taken in the fall of 1995.

Tamara Moskvina in her twenties, about to compete. *(Courtesy of Tamara Moskvina)*

"The Masterpiece." Tamara Moskvina, age ten, in a dress made from her father's army surplus. *(Courtesy of Tamara Moskvina)*

A page from one of Moskvina's scrapbooks. *(Courtesy of Tamara Moskvina)*

Moskvina speaks to workers during a sportsmen's tour of the Soviet Union in the mid-eighties. *(Courtesy of Lydia Kissilova)*

Timeless scenes from Yubileiny Palace of Sport in St. Petersburg. From top: Approaching Yubileiny; skaters practice ballet on an arena concourse; mothers steal looks through the holes in the painted-over windows beneath a sign forbidding them to watch; coaches train their skaters on whatever is available—in this case, the outside stairs; a pair of world champions practice on the windowed rink; and Moskvina scrutinizes every detail. *(Andrey Chepakin)*

Yelena Berezhnaya with Anton Sikharulidze shortly after her return to St. Petersburg. A hat conceals her scars. *(Courtesy of the Sikharulidze family)*

Moskvina chases her skaters. *(Andrey Chepakin)*

Berezhnaya and Sikharulidze perform the beloved Chaplin program at the 2001 World Championships. *(Dave Black)*

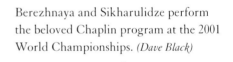

Anton Sikharulidze receives stitches for a gash in his arm just a few months before the 2002 Olympics. *(Andrey Chepakin)*

Shen Xue, age six, ready to go to skating practice. *(Courtesy of the Shen family)*

Shen Xue, Shen Jie, and Lu Manli in their one-room apartment in the Daowai district, circa 1982. *(Courtesy of the Shen family)*

Zhao Hongbo in front of the flax factory apartments, shortly after he left home to live in the ice sports dormitory. *(Courtesy of Jing Yulan)*

The courtyard of the Shens' former apartment in Daowai. *(Graham Maunder)*

Zhao Hongbo, age nine, in his family's apartment with some of his medals. *(Courtesy of Jing Yulan)*

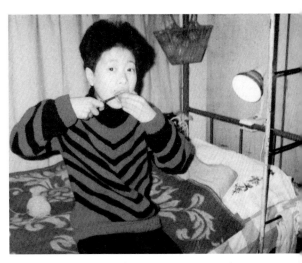

Shen Xue, age ten, on her bunk in the Harbin ice sports dormitory. *(Courtesy of the Shen family)*

Early in their partnership, Shen Xue, fourteen, and Zhao Hongbo, nineteen, practice a lift. *(Courtesy of Jing Yulan)*

Zhao, Shen, and Yao Bin in the kiss-and-cry at one of their first competitions, during Yao's "made in China" period. *(Courtesy of Jing Yulan)*

The first generation of Chinese figure skaters make their own ice; attempt a primitive form of pair skating; and pose for a team photo on the ice in Black River City. *(All photos this page courtesy of Li Yaoming)*

In the seventies, skaters practice ballet in front of a portrait of Chairman Mao.

Luan Bo and Yao Bin on the ice in the early eighties, and posing for an official portrait with Li Yaoming at the 1984 Olympics.

Practice at the national training center in Beijing: Coach Yao gives advice; Shen and Zhao rehearse *Turandot*. *(Yin Nan)*

Zhao Hongbo enters the dorm in Beijing. The characters read: "Break out of Asia and advance on the world." *(Yin Nan)*

In Shen Xue's dorm room, though "it's not time to speak of romance," Shen and Zhao share a warm hug. *(Courtesy of the Shen family)*

David Pelletier, figure skater and hockey player, on the ice in Sayabec. *(Courtesy of the Pelletier family)*

Jamie Salé with her mother, Patti, at around the time of her parents' divorce. *(Courtesy of Patti Salé)*

Jamie Salé starts skating pairs with Jason Turner at the age of twelve. *(Courtesy of Patti Salé)*

In the mid-nineties, David Pelletier and Alison Gaylor put on a show in Sayabec to raise money for training expenses. *(Courtesy of the Pelletier family)*

Salé and Pelletier in the kiss-and-cry with coach Richard Gauthier at Skate America in 1999. *(Courtesy of the Pelletier family)*

In front of 16,000 roaring Canadian fans, Salé and Pelletier finish their long program at the 2001 World Championships in Vancouver. *(Dave Black)*

At the 2002 Olympics, Berezhnaya and Sikharulidze perform a spiral of their own invention. *(Dave Black)*

The final pose of the program entitled "The Eternal Kiss." *(AP/Wide World Photos)*

Berezhnaya and Sikharulidze await their marks in the Olympic kiss-and-cry. *(AP/Wide World Photos)*

Salé and Pelletier skate their *Love Story* program at the 2002 Olympics. *(AP/Wide World Photos)*

After finishing their program, Salé and Pelletier embrace on the ice. *(Dave Black)*

With Jan Ullmark and David Pelletier in the Olympic kiss-and-cry, Jamie Salé reacts to the second mark. *(AP/Wide World Photos)*

A triple twist, Chinese-style, in front of the Olympic rings. *(Christophe Guibbaud/Agence Vandystadt)*

Shen Xue's quad is perfect in the air. *(Jerzy Bukajlo)*

On the night of the Olympic final, Marie-Reine Le Gougne leaves the judges' stand. *(Jerzy Bukajlo)*

The first medal ceremony: Berezhnaya and Sikharulidze (left) and Salé and Pelletier stand on the podium while the Russian anthem plays. *(Dave Black)*

The double gold medal ceremony, one week later. *(AP/Wide World Photos)*

In Sayabec, the arena has been renamed.
(*Author's collection*)

Shen and Zhao perform the *Turandot* program
at the 2003 World Championships. (*AP/Wide
World Photos*)

Yelena Berezhnaya and Anton Sikharulidze
receive a hero's welcome in the airport upon
their return to St. Petersburg. (*Andrey Chepakin*)

David Pelletier didn't make the '98 Olympic team, because in order to qualify, you had to finish in the top two at Canadians, and he and Alison Gaylor finished sixth. This brought his record at Canadians over the past three years to fifth, sixth, and sixth. Three years ago he had been second in Canada, and if things had gone according to plan, 1998 should have been his Olympic year. Instead he had to watch people he had once beaten fight for Olympic team berths, while he sat back in sixth place.

Pelletier was twenty-four years old. His parents were still sinking a minimum of a thousand a month into his skating, and that bothered him. He wasn't a kid anymore, and when you were routinely finishing sixth in Canada, how long could you really expect your parents to humor your belief that you were world champion material? Pelletier had a part-time job at the Molson Centre, filling orders for hot dogs and beers and running them to skyboxes. Sometimes he worked security detail at fashion shows in Montreal. He was a grown man, and he was getting married in the summer. "It's time to do something with my life," he told himself. "It's time to make a living. And if I can't find a partner that can help me get to where I want, then let's call it quits, and that's it."

He'd seen Jamie Salé at Canadians—who hadn't? She'd made a comeback in singles, after not qualifying for Canadians for two years in a row. She wasn't in top shape, and she had competed wearing those telltale black leggings that alert every judge to the fact that a girl is trying to conceal a few extra pounds. But she skated a clean short program with all the old flair, and when the music stopped Jamie Salé was actually crying on the ice. She was only fifth in the short program—*fifth*—and she was so thrilled that she cried, right in front of everybody. There were people there that day who hadn't seen her in three years, people who had always thought she was a little cocky, but even they stood and applauded and yelled, "Good for you, Jamie!"—because anyone could see she was trying so hard. And everyone knew the hand she'd been dealt. She was born to skate pairs, but she'd never found the right partner.

Sure, there'd been offers over the past four years, but she and Jan Ullmark had decided long ago that she wasn't going to skate with just anybody. She'd already been to the Olympics and finished twelfth. Why do that again? She wanted a partner who was good enough to win.

So she waited for a partner, and while she waited she skated part-time, gained a few pounds, and got a string of jobs. For a time she hostessed at Joey Tomatoes, and later she worked as a barista at the Second Cup. For three years, she competed solo in the little qualifying competitions that lead like stepping-stones to Canadians. "I can remember going to regionals and sectionals, and everyone's going, 'Oh, *you're* still skating? *Oh,* I thought you quit,' " she says. "And then it was almost embarrassing. Like, I'd step on the ice and I thought: Oh, everyone's looking at me, thinking this is a joke."

But she stuck with it, for Jamie Salé had a strong ego, and if that rubbed some people the wrong way, it also kept her going at times when more realistic people would have given up their expensive childhood hobby and gone off to community college. She might be a part-time barista, a twenty-year-old singles skater who hadn't been to Canadians in almost three years. She might be out of shape, sluggish, and desperate for a partner. But she was still, after all, Jamie Salé, and by sheer force of will she got herself to the 1998 Canadians in ladies' singles, where David Pelletier had seen her again, crying on the ice.

In her heart of hearts, she had only gotten herself to Canadians because she was still hoping that someone would see her there and ask her for a pair tryout. But no one did, and so she was back in Edmonton, making lattes at the Second Cup, when someone called and said, "Did you hear? Dave Pelletier's getting married, and he's quitting."

Jamie Salé felt it in her gut. *Oh, God! My last chance!* There might have been times in the last two years where she'd sworn that she'd never go chasing after David Pelletier again. But now she was scared. So she called him, and if Jamie Salé talked a lot ordinarily, she talked even more when she was nervous. She remembers that she began by saying, "Uh, Dave, are you interested? Because our first tryout was so good, and I don't know, maybe you have other plans—"

"No!" he cut in. "No, I want to."

On the other end of the line, David Pelletier was feeling just as desperate. For some time now he had been wanting to get away from Boucherville, where he knew his temper was only getting worse. "He just wanted to get away and start fresh," Eric Gillies recalls. "The situation was to the point where it was bothering his spirit." Now Pelletier might have a chance to skate with Jamie Salé—but he knew that if he was going to make that happen, he was going to need help.

He needed a coach. But there was only one other elite pair coach in Montreal—Richard Gauthier—and Gauthier had already said he didn't want to coach Pelletier. Gauthier was known as a New Age kind of guy: He asked skaters to listen to motivational tapes; he was always talking about relationships. In his free time, he liked to play music and design stained glass. He spoke about the mind-body connection, preached against negative energy. Gauthier had heard about Pelletier's temper, and he wanted no part of it.

But David Pelletier, strangely enough, wanted Gauthier. "I knew of Richard," he says, "and I knew how he ran his school. But I also knew that's what I needed. I needed somebody to control me, somebody who would not let me do this kind of stuff."

So Pelletier called Gauthier and asked him to reconsider. Gauthier agreed to take him, but only if Pelletier could meet his conditions. "In my school," Gauthier told him, in no uncertain terms, "I want people to be happy. So if you come and train in my school, you're going to be in *my* environment, and you're going to have to go by my rules. If you get to the point where you kick the ice and swear, if you can't control yourself, then you leave the ice and come back next session. And on the next session, if you're still like that, then you leave the building and don't come back until the next day. Because there's no point. You're wasting your time, you're wasting my time, and you're wasting everyone else's time bringing this negative energy in the building. And I won't allow it."

David Pelletier agreed to Gauthier's terms, so they moved on to details. "I asked him if he planned to skate with the same partner," Gauthier recalls. Pelletier said no. "So I said, 'Well, the only one I see in Canada you can skate with is Jamie Salé.' But he said, 'I don't know if she'll want to move here.' Then he explained to me what happened at the last tryout, how she was treated."

Gauthier knew something about people, and when he called Jamie Salé he began by telling her that the tryout would be in Edmonton. "The last time, you came here," he said, "and I think it's Dave's turn to go to Edmonton." That sounded right to her. They could try out at her rink, with Jan Ullmark there too. Salé agreed, and David Pelletier and Richard Gauthier got on a plane for Edmonton.

The first time they skated together, in Boucherville, they had been two kids, excited just to be trying out. But now the situation was serious. Salé and Pelletier might think that they had untapped potential, but to most of the world she was somebody who worked in a coffee shop, and he was the guy who sold you a hot dog at a hockey game. So now this tryout was to settle the question one way or the other. Let it prove that they had been right to stick with it, that each truly *was* capable of greatness, given the right partner—or let it prove the exact opposite, that they had been two average skaters with an inflated sense of their own brilliance. And in that case, let them both get on with it and stop spending their parents' money hanging around ice rinks with a bunch of kids.

David Pelletier put his blade to the ice and experienced a feeling he had never had before. It was the feeling that the whole world lay before him, and all he had to do was to reach. Each time they tried a new element, it simply happened. Every time he reached for her hand, it was exactly where he expected it to be. "It was perfect," Richard Gauthier says, shaking his head with wonder. "The first time around the rink, the timing was perfect. That *never* happens. Usually it takes a whole year just to get the timing. But they had it that first day."

"We did everything," Pelletier says simply. "And everything was easy. We did the double Axel side by side better than anyone else in Canada at that time. I felt really strongly about it. For the first time in my career I was landing triple toe side by side with a girl. We did the throws. We did the lifts easily. Even though she didn't skate pairs for four years, her positions in the lifts came back, like riding a bike. I just knew."

"I thought it would be good," Jamie Salé says, "but then when we skated, it was so *damn* good." Gauthier and Pelletier went back to Montreal in high spirits, and in no time at all the phone rang in Edmonton. "I remember getting off the phone," Jamie Salé says, with one of her biggest smiles, "and being like, *Oh, my God,* he said yes! And I remember thinking, My dream is coming true. And it just flashes by you, right like that."

"She got the call from David, and she was going to do it," Patti Salé recalls. "We were so excited for her." It was going to cost at least twenty thousand dollars for Jamie to skate for one year in Montreal, but Patti Salé would find a way. "She had never lived away from home before. And I remember I took her to the airport and all she had was a couple of bags and her skates. But she was just—man, no problem! Because it was exciting to be doing what she loved to do. After four years, she had a partner again."

∞

In 1991, when Zhao Hongbo was seventeen and still skating with his first partner, he had gone with Yao Bin to Russia. This was before Yao's made-in-China period, back in the days when Yao went to the trouble of applying to go to Sverdlovsk on a six-month technical exchange. By 1991, Zhao had already been to the Junior World Championships, where he had seen world-class skaters. "But when we went to Russia," he says, "our eyes were really opened. Because at that time, China was not that good in pair skating, and it was the first time for me to see the Russian pairs up close."

After a few months in Sverdlovsk, Zhao and his partner had the chance to go to St. Petersburg and take part in the Cup of Russia. "We finished next to the last out of nine pairs," Zhao remembers. "And after my skate I went up into the stands and watched the Russian pairs. They were the best in the world: Mishketunov and Dmitriev, Shishkova and Naumov. After they finished, I was the first person to stand up and applaud." At this point in his story, Zhao leans forward on his elbows and says, with passion, "It was the turning point for me. From that day on, I began to have a clear picture of pair skating. I began to really like it. You see, those performances in St. Petersburg were kind of a shock to me. Their music, their movement, their steps—all were in such harmony. I had never seen such a beautiful performance."

Eight years later, in 1999, Zhao went to St. Petersburg again, this time with Shen Xue, to compete in the prestigious Grand Prix Final. In the year since the Olympics, many pairs had retired, and Shen and Zhao had rapidly risen to become one of the top two pairs in the world. The other was Berezhnaya and Sikharulidze. Now, just a few weeks before the 1999 World Championships, the Chinese came to the Russians' home city to try to beat Berezhnaya and Sikharulidze for the first time.

On the first day of the competition, Zhao walked into the same arena he had entered in 1991. He climbed up to the very seat in the stands from which he had watched the Russians perform, and sat down. "I had a different feeling," Zhao recalls. "Eight years before, we were there just to learn and to watch. Actually, eight years earlier I didn't think I would vie for the world championship with the Russians. I didn't give it a thought that I would be on the same level with them. And yet this time, we were there to compete."

And after the short program Zhao found himself leading, because in the short program the Russians had fallen apart. Berezhnaya looked totally out of it. She made weird, almost disturbing mistakes, like stopping in the middle of the side-by-side spin for no apparent reason. For a moment it looked as if she might not continue, but she pulled herself together enough to finish the program. Her eyes looked glassed over, as if she might be feverish. She said she was fine, but backstage, people whispered, *Is she really all right in the head?*

So the Chinese took the short program, but it would be a lot harder to beat the Russians in the long. Since finishing second at the Olympics, Berezhnaya and Sikharulidze had won every event they entered, including the 1998 World Championships. Nevertheless Yao thought his pair had a chance, because in the year since the Olympics, he had taken a half step towards the Western judges. All the assembly was still done in China, but these days he was using a few foreign-made parts. Shen and Zhao were skating to the soundtrack from the animated movie *Mulan,* a traditional Chinese story by way of Disney. It was Western music with Chinese characteristics, and it allowed Yao Bin to satisfy the judges while sticking to his principles. The *Mulan* program had all the difficulty of the year before, but now the moves were sharper, crisper; it was satisfying to see how the two skaters now polished off every move before moving on to the next one. The music gave the program more emotion, and there was a fresh, spontaneous feeling in their performance that boosted their second mark considerably. They were never going to look like ballet dancers, but they no longer looked unaware of ballet's existence. They had good stretch and pointed toes and matched lines, and they looked like a typical North American team with enough dance to get by. Shen and Zhao skated first, and it was one of their best nights. They did everything, had just a few bobbles, and got high marks. Now it was up to the Russians.

On Berezhnaya's first jump she landed but kept on turning in circles on the ice, getting completely out of sync with her partner. Then she delayed the twist too long and hit the ice with her feet before he could catch her. Later she stepped out of the landing of her double Axel and got behind the music again. She fell on a throw jump, smacking the ice hard, and then she nearly dropped out of an overhead lift, and the whole crowd gasped. On the last lift, she really did lose her balance and slid over Sikharulidze's head. She landed safely on her feet, but it could have been a disaster. She finished the program with that same glassy-eyed look on her face, and she was probably lucky to get through it without a major incident, for she was clearly in no condition to skate. And again people whispered, *Is she really all right?* Backstage, Berezhnaya shrugged and said she had the flu.

After all that, the judges had no choice but to put the Chinese first. It was the biggest win in the history of Chinese pair skating, but Yao didn't give his skaters a moment to celebrate. As soon as they were backstage, Yao started complaining. "On the first double Axel, Hongbo bent his back a little, and on the second pass he only did a single Axel," Yao snapped. "We don't want to be 'pretty good.' We want to be world champions."

Yao strode out to the ice to wait for the medal ceremony. He loaded his camera and thought gloomily that *he* would have to furnish photos to the Chinese press, who hadn't even bothered to come. Out of the corner of his eye he saw Tamara Moskvina approaching, and he remembered, with some bitterness, how she had spoken to him at another competition a year ago. That time, his pair had lost to her students, and Moskvina had said to him, laughing, "Congratulations on the future world champions! My hands start to tremble when I see you." Yao had laughed politely, but he could tell she wasn't scared of his pair one bit, and that really pissed him off. Now, as Moskvina approached, Yao grinned and thought, *Well, well. Now our positions have been reversed.* And this time when Moskvina shook his hand, he could tell that behind her put-on smile, she was really afraid.

∞

Three weeks later the two pairs met at the 1999 World Championships in Helsinki, Finland. This time, the Russians went first. They stepped forwards, looking like two ballet dancers dressed for the pas de deux. Except for the ballerina's bare legs, their pale green costumes matched, which laid another layer of emphasis on their brilliant unison. They glided out from the barrier, matching every angle of the blade, every bend of the knee. Their blades made identical tracings in the ice. They were like two people with the same footprint.

At center ice Berezhnaya faced Sikharulidze. He embraced her and boosted her up lightly, so that her blades stood on the tops of his skates. She, in turn, leaned her cheek into his neck and clasped him around the waist. The impossibly light girl stood resting her blades on her partner's feet. The romance was palpable. But when the music began it cut against easy sentimentality. It was a moody, sad melody; a soprano sang an aria without words, and as it resounded through the arena her voice was haunting, even a little harsh. After hours of folk songs and action movie soundtracks, Glière's *Concerto for Soprano* seemed to rearrange the molecules of air in the building. This was what Moskvina, at her best, could do. She could bring the atmosphere of the ballet to the arena, transform this sheet of ice surrounded by advertising billboards into a theater. And she was doing it now.

In the first two years Moskvina had been racing to give them elements, but now she was giving them the programs she had dreamed of making. She had known this music for many years, but she had been waiting for a classical pair to perform it. Now Moskvina had taken the perfectly matched bodies and given them something rare in pair skating: asymmetrical movement. This pair could skate in unison easily, easily; but they relied little on shadow skating. Berezhnaya struck one elegant pose; Sikharulidze another, yet they blended in a kind of mysterious harmony.

It was the pas de deux adapted to the ice, and its beauty made the earlier pairs' side-by-side skating look a little gimmicky. It was as if, after a series of clever brother-sister tap dance acts, two ballet dancers had now appeared.

Their movement was pure and light. Berezhnaya leaned into a spread eagle, back exquisitely arched, and reached one arm out to steady herself against Sikharulidze's body while he stretched in a perfect spiral. Every woman in the building sighed. *The masterpiece.* And just when the music seemed to become hopeful again and even inspiring, it shifted again, and the sadness came back strongly. And when it ended, the delicate girl was again standing on top of the man's skates, in his embrace, in the strangely moving pose in which they had begun.

At the beginning of the program Berezhnaya had fallen hard on a double Axel, and this of course detracted from both the technical mark and the overall impression. But still, the overall impression was strong stuff. On the second mark they got 5.9's across the board. There was no way the Chinese would get 5.9's on the second mark, but they might manage some 5.8's and sneak into first place on the strength of their first marks for technical merit. The Chinese could still win, but only if they were extraordinary.

That night Shen and Zhao were as sure-footed as they had ever been in their lives. Each time they jumped, they landed with conviction. That night the ice felt like a giant magnet pulling their blades safely home. There was no grand design, no theme to their program, no theater. But here were two young people at the height of their physical powers, well trained and confident, delighted by what they were able to do. They gave you the feeling of watching a champion gymnast, the satisfaction that came from seeing the element explode into the air and come down with perfect placement. Something so difficult now looked beautifully easy. That night the Chinese did everything as well as they could do it. The Finns were stomping their feet, and Shen Xue smiled so wide you could see her tiger teeth poking out sideways from her gums. Zhao Hongbo completely forgot himself. He pumped his fist and leaned over and kissed Shen Xue on the forehead. Even Yao Bin cracked a smile. They had done all they could do. Now it was in the judges' hands.

The contrast was stark. The Chinese, in garish costumes with huge purple polka dots, represented pure sport. When Shen Xue unleashed three turns high above the ice and came down on the solid leg of a gymnast, she was one of the most extraordinary athletes in the history of pair skating, period. But when Berezhnaya and Sikharulidze passed by the judges' table, hitting a gorgeous spiral position, they were among the greatest artists the sport had ever seen.

Now each judge faced the same question: whether to rank the Chinese first or second. How a judge allocated the first and second marks was ultimately unimportant; what counted was how each judge ranked the teams on the combined total of the two marks. To beat the Russians, the Chinese had to rank first on a majority of the judges' cards. To get a combined score higher than the Russians, the Chinese had to ace the first mark and hope for the best on the second. The first set of marks would tell Yao whether they were even in contention, for if Shen and Zhao didn't beat the Russians on the first mark, they didn't stand a chance.

Now the first set of marks went up, and the Chinese, with a string of 5.9's, beat the Russians easily on technical merit. But when Yao Bin saw the second mark drop, he knew. A few seconds later the scoreboard posted the overall standings: The Russians in first, by a vote of seven judges to two. At the same instant, the arena erupted in boos. The Finns wanted the Chinese. They were stamping, whistling, heckling the judges. The crowd loved Yao's Chinese technique, but the judges preferred the ballet.

Yao Bin squinted, as he sometimes did when he was angry. This performance was close to the best they could do, and it still wasn't enough for these Western judges. He couldn't raise his pair's technical merit marks any higher—the kids were already at 5.9. It was time to go to work on the second mark. It pained him to do it, but next year he would hire a Western choreographer.

∞

Within a few hours of the Russians' victory in Helsinki, everyone backstage had heard the news: During the pairs final, Canadian television cameras had caught two judges colluding on videotape. There it was, plain as day—the Chinese took their bows, the Ukrainian judge looked over at the Russian judge and tapped his foot to communicate his vote. Two taps—second place. The Russian nodded. Then both judges punched in second place marks for the Chinese.

The videotape caused a stir not because two judges had cheated, but because finally there was *proof* that two judges had cheated. For an ISU judge moves in a shadowy world of atmosphere and implications; proof is a rarity. In a shuttle van, say, a judge overhears snatches of conversation, gossip that three judges will vote together, and wonders if the rumor is true. A group of judges sits together at practices, eats dinner together, and who can say if they are accomplices in a scheme—or merely friends? At the endless cocktail parties in hotels, a judge listens to a steady stream of innuendos, trying to gauge what is true and, ultimately, who can be trusted.

It's hard to tell; it seems everybody's working an angle. Some judges are tightly controlled by the presidents of their national federations—that's clear. They know that if they don't follow orders their federation president will never throw them a good judging assignment again. The judges from poor countries are easy to spot; you can pick them out by their dowdy clothes and beat-up handbags. They take all their meals in the judges' dining room so they can save their honorarium to take home. To them, a hundred dollars a day is a lot of money, and they try not to do anything to put their future assignments in jeopardy. The question is how far a judge might go to keep on judging.

Some judges spend their lives in workaday jobs—teacher, office worker—and only feel important when they stay at a four-star hotel in Tokyo or Paris and decide competitions with their learned opinions. One can imagine that they would be willing to do a federation president a favor to protect their position.

Some judges are simply power-mongers. They like the feeling of manipulating a panel, of working a deal. In secret, they broker complicated vote-trading schemes, participate in fixes that are in clear violation of the rules. Other judges lobby using the old-fashioned method—by giving their opinion loudly in the hopes that it will influence their colleagues. "Her death spiral has improved," an esteemed judge says, or "Their program is the most difficult this year," or "That lift is illegal," and by tiny increments, the general consensus shifts. This method has the advantage of being legal.

Of course, a decent percentage of judges are scrupulously honest, and these judges were invigorated by the emergence of the videotape evidence in Helsinki, especially since it was discovered at the biggest event of the year, with the full force of the world's media to keep pressure on the issue. *Finally,* these judges said, *finally* Ottavio will have to do something. Ottavio was Ottavio Cinquanta, the ISU president, and he promptly announced he wasn't going to do a thing. The ISU would wait until after the World Championships to investigate whether the pairs result had been tainted by cheating, so as not to "distract the athletes." Someone pointed out that the athletes involved had already finished competing, and that the Chinese pair, for one, might like to know immediately whether or not they had been cheated out of a gold medal. But Cinquanta was not susceptible to such arguments. He was savvy enough to know that it was better to expose any potential corruption after the reporters had gone home.

So a month later the ISU convened a closed hearing on the matter, and the two colluding judges got a slap on the wrist: a three-year suspension. By now the story had cooled and only a few papers ran it, and after several months had passed the two judges felt emboldened to quietly appeal. Without comment, Cinquanta's ISU reduced both suspensions. And so within two years, both of the judges were back working two of the biggest events of the year, the Worlds and Junior Worlds. By this time, however, there was no danger of being caught cheating, for the ISU had by now restricted television cameras from focusing on the judges' stand.

Though the story hit few newspapers, every judge in the world knew about it. It was that kind of world: small, interconnected, gossipy. Reaction was mixed. Some of the more earnest judges declared that cheaters should be kicked out of judging for life. On the other side were the cynical types who shrugged and said that everyone was doing it, and if you didn't do the same, you only hurt your own country's skaters.

In any case, after Helsinki, all judges knew that the worst penalty you could get for open collusion was a two- or three-year suspension, and they knew from experience that whistle-blowers were few and far between. Nobody wanted to turn another judge in. The risk was too great. The last time a judge had tried to turn in another judge, after the 1998 Olympics, she had been smart enough to tape-record his voice on the phone when he called to ask her to trade votes. The ISU suspended the cheating judge—but they also suspended the whistle-blower. After that, most judges who overheard something just didn't want to get involved.

The other problem with catching crooked judges was that the system itself was so subjective. It was easy for any judge to manipulate the placements. When two teams were as closely matched as the Chinese and the Russians, you could justify putting either one of them in first place. You could vote for the Russians because your federation president had told you to, and no one could ever prove it. All you had to do was say that you thought the Russians were slightly better that night and justify it using the second mark. And if your federation president asked you to put the Russians first, you'd better do it, because quite often the only way for a judge to get international assignments was to keep the federation president happy.

It was one thing to cross your federation president in America or Canada, where there was a tradition of cantankerous, independent judging, and quite another in, say, France, where the federation president, Didier Gailhaguet, was alleged to have dismissed judges who disobeyed his orders. At least three of the dismissed French judges went public with their claims. One produced a letter Gailhaguet had written asking judges to do "important political work." The dismissed judges gave specific instances of being asked by Gailhaguet to rank skaters higher or lower than they deserved. But there were no negative consequences for Gailhaguet, and in fact he was known to be on quite familiar terms with the ISU president, Ottavio Cinquanta. When Gailhaguet took over the bankrupt French federation, the ISU somehow arranged for France to host two of the biggest moneymaking events of 2000: the Grand Prix Final and the World Championships. It was unheard of for a single country to get both events in a single year, but France managed it, and Gailhaguet was able to generate revenue for his strapped federation.

If such stories were repugnant to the honest judges, they were no longer shocking. What the videotape scandal in Helsinki demonstrated was that the reality was actually grimmer than most people had imagined. When a judge got caught on videotape fixing the World Championships and was back in the same chair two years later—well, the ISU was sending a pretty definite signal.

∞

David Pelletier was not in Helsinki, because three weeks before Worlds, he woke up one morning and literally couldn't get out of bed. It was a severe back strain, the doctor said, and his season was over. Pelletier was so frustrated he didn't know what to do with himself. Finally, after four years, he had gotten himself back to the world level. And here was Richard Gauthier, this touchy-feely mystic of a guy, telling him that everything happened for a reason.

"It's all in the way you look at life," Gauthier told him. "Look, let's say there are two boys standing in the ocean. And suddenly this big wave takes them out to sea. Everybody thinks, Oh, my God, they're gonna drown! Then suddenly the boys come back out. They both had exactly the same experience. And one of the kids is crying his head off, and the other guy is like: *Yeah, yeah! I beat the wave!*"

For a year now, Gauthier had been trying to get Pelletier to look on the bright side. It was a part of a larger strategy to get Pelletier to work well with his partner. Gauthier knew that in pairs, talent was worthless if a guy couldn't learn to control his temper. "When he came to me, David was a perfectionist and did not allow himself to miss anything. He had a very short fuse. It's Monday morning, seven o'clock, and if David would miss a spin side by side, he would totally lose it. But unfortunately," Gauthier sighs, "these are the people that become world champion."

To Jamie Salé, this was her new partner—the guy berating himself in the corner and letting out a big exasperated sigh whenever she missed her double Axel. "I had heard that when he was at Boucherville he was very aggressive and loud, and sometimes mean," Jamie says. "But he knew when he started skating with me he couldn't get away with that. If he didn't treat me well I'd be on the first plane home. Because I won't take that. To me, it just makes the girls get pushed down even more. And they start to lose their confidence."

Gauthier saw Jamie Salé standing up to Pelletier and smiled. He knew from long experience that you couldn't get the guy to treat the girl well if the girl acted like a doormat. "The girls David skated with before were in awe of him and put up with the crap he made them go through. But Jamie had a strong personality," Gauthier says. "She really put her foot down as soon as his mouth went funny, right from the start. She said, 'Listen. I will not tolerate any of that crap.' And he understood that she meant it. If he wasn't going to change, she would leave. So he started to change."

Whenever Pelletier lost his temper, Richard Gauthier made him do exercises to control his anger. This was Gauthier's school, Gauthier's environment, and Pelletier wasn't going to mess it up for everyone. Gauthier had many lectures to this effect, including a few classics. "Bad energy is like a fart on the ice," Gauthier would say. "When someone farts on the ice and you go around once, it stinks everywhere. Wherever you are on the ice, people say: Someone must have farted. Energy is the same thing. If you have one couple on the ice that has this negative energy, in no time you move around, and suddenly these other couples start fighting and getting in a bad mood. It's stressful. Here's someone screaming at someone else, right next to you. It's not pleasant. And then suddenly you get that tension. I think it's contagious." Therefore Gauthier would not tolerate any cursing or kicking the boards. Any time Pelletier had an outburst, Gauthier kicked him off the ice. He took no pleasure in it, but he would do it every time.

Once that fall David Pelletier's parents traveled the six hours from Sayabec to visit and come to practice. His father remembers that "David was kind of stressed out when we were there, because he wanted to show us what he could do. He was putting too much effort into it, trying to be perfect, and he was falling. He lost control and started yelling and cursing. So Richard said, 'Out!' Even though we were there to watch, his practice was over. Richard said, 'You're not going to do that with me. No way.' Of course," his father concludes, "David's skating improved a lot. But more importantly, his temper improved a lot with Richard."

Watching Jamie Salé on the ice for the first time, Jacques Pelletier and Murielle Bouchard exchanged knowing glances. Finally, David had met his match. "Jamie was the first partner who wasn't impressed by David Pelletier," Murielle Bouchard explains. "She had already been to the Olympics, the Canadians, the Worlds, on her own steam. So okay, she was happy to be his partner. But it wasn't like she was in total admiration of him. She treated him like an equal. And we were so happy that finally, here was a woman who would show some spirit and put him in his place."

When Pelletier noticed his coach and his partner staring coolly at him when he lost his temper, or found himself kicked off the ice while the rest of the group practiced, he realized he was in a distinct minority. "When he noticed that nobody else on the ice was acting that way, he got better," Gauthier says. But what really got him to take control of his temper was one simple fact. "Richard made me understand—because he's a very positive guy—that if I want the best out of Jamie, this is what I gotta do. He was right to do it, and he was the perfect person to do it. But it took me about a year to understand that."

That was a long year for Jamie Salé. She moved to Montreal "with basically nothing. I came with three bags and my skates. I didn't have any family, I didn't have really a place to live or anything really yet." In French, she could say hello and good-bye; she stuck to the Anglo part of town. On the ice there were some good days, "when Dave could be himself and we had fun," she says. "But that wasn't very often. Because the first year and a half with his wife and everything—there's just too many things that made everybody feel uncomfortable."

"The summer that Jamie arrived in Montreal, David got married," Gauthier says. "In the first year that was something that was hard for me in coaching them. Because David's wife would come to practices. And every time she would come in the arena, his attitude would totally change. He was mean to Jamie, he would swear. I would go, 'What is this? You weren't like this before.' So finally I had to tell him, 'Your wife can't come in the building anymore. Because whenever she comes, you act differently.' "

In their first year of their partnership, Jamie Salé and David Pelletier were strictly coworkers. After they skated, he sat aloof in the kiss-and-cry, staring at the scoreboard, as if he had forgotten she was there. If he got good results he would whoop and high-five Gauthier, maybe speak quickly to him in French, then remember Jamie and give her an obligatory hug. The feeling was mutual. "In the first year, I wasn't really enjoying his company very much, because of how he was acting," Salé says. "So at competitions we'd skate, and then he'd go his way and I'd go mine. And everyone told us, You can't do that. You have to look like a professional team. And when Jamie comes out of her dressing room, you take her, and you guys go sit together and watch the other skaters. Look professional." But Pelletier was married, so when he came out into the stands, he sat with his wife. "I would have to sit by myself somewhere, you know? But Richard helped me. I think he felt bad for me."

In spite of all the tension, there was one thing in the partnership that was really, really good: the skating. That fall they scored two international assignments and surprised even themselves by winning two bronze medals. They earned a little prize money, and finally David Pelletier could quit his job at the Molson Centre. He was a real skater now.

Gauthier wasn't surprised by the instant success. He knew what he had. "Jamie would go around twice, and every single person in the audience would feel like she was looking them right in the eye. Like that connection straight to the public. This has to come from inside. And usually those athletes, they've had it since they were this high. At little juvenile competitions, they wanted to steal the show. In the case of David and Jamie, they both had it."

There was also an uncanny match in their natural body rhythms. Things that took other pairs years to perfect came to them in two weeks. Pelletier remembers that when they started working on the throw triple loop, "we did the throw double loops for maybe three days. Then she said to me, 'Do you want to try a triple?' The first one we did, she landed. And the second one, she landed. And the third and fourth one, she landed. Since that day, we never had a problem with that throw triple loop. And I see people just working and working and working on throws. We were very lucky."

Everything had been running ahead of schedule—until that morning before the World Championships when Pelletier woke up and couldn't get out of bed. But Gauthier wasn't going to let them spend the summer sulking. They stayed home, forgotten by the other skaters and judges and coaches. Nobody called, but Gauthier didn't mind at all. What a new pair needs most is training time, and now, like it or not, they had it. "That's all they were missing," Gauthier says. "Like side-by-side spins, for example. There's no trick. You need to spend time on it. It's just mileage. Same with lifts."

Gauthier wanted them to start the choreography even before the summer began. While David was resting his back, they could work on things like stroking and choreography. The Canadian federation offered to help find the choreographer and the music. They wanted to give this pair something special. Lori Nichol arrived with music from the movie *Love Story,* and by the time she finished, the program was a masterpiece. Gauthier knew that *Love Story* was going to be big right away, because when they trained it at seven o'clock in the morning, and Jamie Salé came around the corner perfectly in character, even he was moved.

They were going to a fall tune-up called Skate America in October, and Gauthier really thought they had a shot of winning it. All the other top pairs had been touring; nobody else was going to be as ready as these two. They were fit, they were rested, they had an unbeatable program. They could beat the whole damn field, eight of the top ten teams in the world, including Berezhnaya and Sikharulidze. The event was in Colorado Springs, at altitude, and half the field would be destroyed by the oxygen debt. Gauthier called the Canadian federation and proposed that they help sponsor his pair to go to Colorado early, so they could acclimatize. Then he packed them off to Colorado Springs without him. Gauthier would join them just before they competed.

Training on the ice without Gauthier for the first time, Salé and Pelletier finally had to deal directly with each other. By the time Gauthier arrived they were behaving more like a proper team. Pelletier and his wife had separated recently, after just a year of marriage, and although he was going through a rough time, the separation had lifted some pressure off the situation on the ice. Watching *Love Story* unfold, there were people in the crowd who wondered if the attractive young couple had their own romance. Gauthier wondered the same thing himself.

Jamie Salé says that after Pelletier and his wife separated, "It took a long time before we really wanted to be a couple. And we wanted to be good together earlier but it just wasn't good at all, because obviously he got married for love. He was healing. And I had been dating a guy and we broke up. I was healing. We needed to support each other, but we still weren't really good to be together. Now," she continues, with real conviction in her voice, "we really love each other for the right reasons. But in the beginning it was just . . . it was fun. And we were skating well, so it just took off. That's another thing, we did have chemistry. But I think it really was for the skating in the beginning. I'm not saying that I didn't care for him, but obviously skating had a big part in it. And it didn't make our skating better, but it made me happy."

From where Gauthier sat, the romance eventually did make the skating better. "In *Love Story,* people say, '*Ohhh,* they're great actors in it,' " he says, laughing. "That was no acting. The whole thing was real. And looking into your girlfriend's eyes is one of those situations where pretending and not pretending makes a difference." That was the good part of it. The bad side was that if the relationship ended, it could mean the end of the pair.

Like every pair coach, Gauthier would take two coworkers over a boyfriend-girlfriend pair any day, but since Gauthier thought he had the two best performers in the world on his team, he wasn't going to quibble. In the short program, Salé and Pelletier stepped on the ice glowing with health and performing to the back row, and when Berezhnaya and Sikharulidze had a fall on the side-by-side jumps, the unknown Canadians were first in the short. People were clapping for them at *practice.* David Pelletier felt himself riding a wave of—dare he say it—positive energy.

"When I got to Richard I had a lot of frustration inside me from all of the bad years," Pelletier says. "And his biggest work with me was to show me how to control my emotions and make them work for me, not against me." In Colorado Springs, Pelletier followed Gauthier's mantra: Always think positive. He had heard the stories of skaters coming off the ice at altitude and needing an oxygen tank, but he made a pact not to talk about it. They felt it, obviously, but they would act like it was nothing. "And every time I would hear a skater talk about the altitude, in my head I would put a check mark, because I knew that they would be out of contention. Because already there they were not thinking the right way." Salé and Pelletier had been in Colorado Springs for a week; they had already done a full run-through of their program at this altitude. "And I remember having this feeling before the long program that it's going to be easy," Pelletier recalls. "I saw everybody getting off the ice coughing, but I knew that a few days before I had done my full program."

After so much longing, it happened so quickly. It was the biggest upset in pair skating in years: Unknown Canadians Beat Russian World Champions. To David Pelletier, who had never done better than fifteenth at Worlds, that gold medal "was like fifty pounds off my shoulders. All those expectations I had put on myself were lifted at that time. And I could just skate." That fall, everywhere he competed, he felt that skating well was normal. "I didn't have to prove to myself that yes, I can be at the top of the world. Not prove to anybody else—prove to *myself*. It was a tremendous weight off my shoulders. Because I actually got where I always wanted to be."

∞

Throughout most of her career Moskvina had insisted that the inferior conditions in Russia actually produced better skaters. For years she and the rest of the Russian team had loaded up their suitcases with hotel soaps and shampoos to take back to a country where the basic necessities were sometimes unavailable, all the while proclaiming the superiority of the Russian way of life. Moskvina famously told reporters that Yubileiny's bad ice gave her skaters a competitive advantage, because when they finally got to a championship they found the skating so much easier on good ice. For Moskvina, people who skated in nice rinks were of weak character, whereas in Russia, "bad ice and we skate. Dirt around and we don't pay attention. Music is not loud, we skate. Food is not appropriate, we don't pay attention. We don't notice what is worse because we have something better in our country: opportunity for any child to be educated in what they want for free."

By 1999, Russia still had bad ice and dirty rinks, but the free education was quickly slipping away. It was clear that if the athletes were to be educated for free, the coaches would have to live on a pittance. With the collapse of the Soviet Union a coach's salary became something like two hundred dollars a month, and often there was no money to heat the rink or buy gas for the Zamboni. The Zamboni driver took to washing cars at five dollars a pop out in the parking lot. Moskvina had begun to question whether an Olympic champion could still be made under local conditions. Yubileiny itself was owned by a trade union, and like everyone in the new Russia, the trade union leaders were open to any deal for ready money. For a few weeks Yubileiny was rented out to a traveling equestrian show, and there was no ice. Then the city of St. Petersburg decided to renovate Yubileiny and host part of the world hockey championships there. Between the renovations and the games, there would be no ice for figure skating for a few months, and finally Moskvina had to consider a spell in America.

It was getting harder and harder to live in Russia unless you had some guaranteed way to make money. The new Russia was a country where people stuffed cash under the mattress and credit cards were a novelty. The whole country was being run on a cash basis since the banks had collapsed. One morning, Moskvina's connections called her to tell her she'd better get over to the bank and collect what she could of her money before it was too late. She woke Lena and Anton, and helped them save a fraction of what they had. Moskvina had her own money worries. Besides supporting her own family, Moskvina was trying to find work for relatives who had lost their jobs. Moskvina's deal with Yelena and Anton dated back to contracts she had signed long ago; she received a percentage of their earnings and acted as both coach and manager. That stream of income was intact. But they could all make a lot more, she thought, if they knew how to work the American system.

Once she wrapped her mind around it, she even found the idea appealing. Skating had changed radically in the past ten years. Now even "amateurs" earned prize money and got paid to tour. But with her quick mind Moskvina rapidly understood that getting paid to skate was nothing in comparison with getting paid to endorse products. She thought it would be good for Yelena and Anton to spend some time around the American media, learn English better. They were going to need the exposure in America, because the popularity of figure skating had plummeted in Russia. In the seventies and eighties figure skating events had always sold out, and skating stars were prominently featured in Soviet magazines. But now skating events drew pitiful crowds, and Russian television aired the national championships at two in the morning. If they were to make any money from skating, it would have to be in America.

There was a rink with four sheets of ice in Hackensack, New Jersey, that wanted Moskvina to come on board as coach. Free ice for her pupils, easy access to three airports, and a short trip to the fabric stores and costume designers of New York City—what else could one need? Plus, Moskvina thought, I can promote them. It will be convenient for the New York television crews to film Yelena and Anton in the years leading up to Salt Lake City, and the Americans can adopt them.

Moskvina arrived in Hackensack in the summer of 1999 determined to work every angle. She called up a public relations firm in New York and became their first sixty-year-old Russian intern. She wanted to learn show business. She told everyone she had a "Hollywood story" about Yelena's accident and invited producers to call her. "We'll learn the business approach in United States for figure skating," she said. "Promote our skaters better, make them more known in the United States. Then our skaters will not be known as 'Russian couple.' They will be known as Yelena Berezhnaya and Anton Sikharulidze—not just as girl who is famous for having the skate in her head. Not just: Russians who, say, won the Olympics, but their *name*."

It seemed simple enough to bring the two skaters to Hackensack, to find an apartment for herself and her husband on a hill overlooking the city, and install Lena and Anton in two different apartments in the building across the street. But in truth there was a big problem: There was no way for Moskvina to control Anton. In the old system, back in Russia, she had relied on the older boys in the group to help her bend him in the right direction. Back in Soviet times, she could rely on the state, which would cut his scholarship or even kick him out if he got too many bad reports. In the past, she could count on Anton's father to lay down the law. But this was America. Anton was twenty-one years old, and he wanted to go out to bars with Russian friends in New York City until three in the morning. Then he would skip the next day's practice, and there wasn't much Moskvina could do except stand at the boards so Yelena wouldn't feel lonely. A month before the season started, Anton got in a bar fight in Brooklyn and had to get stitches over one eye. They lost ten days of training for that alone.

If Anton was overstimulated, Moskvina could see that Yelena felt depressed. Anton's parents came to visit, and his father regaled them with stories and prepared Georgian dishes, but Yelena's mother couldn't get a visa. In Hackensack Lena had a few friends at the rink, all Russians who had come over with the Moskvina camp, but most nights she went home to an empty apartment. She passed the time buying nice furniture, decorating her house, and doing some painting and needlepoint. She gained weight, grew listless. Anton was always going out without her; then the next morning, according to their arrangement, it was Berezhnaya's job to give him a wake-up call so he could make it to practice. Moskvina urged her to take up a hobby, so she signed up for karate class and painting lessons. But this lonely independent life was not the life she liked.

Berezhnaya missed the rhythm of her life in Russia, where things happened of their own accord. "In Russia it's easier just to get along in life," she says. "Even though you may not do anything special, there is always a commotion around you, that you meet with people, talk with people. And of course, everyone speaks Russian!" In St. Petersburg in the afternoon, she might drop in at a friend's flat to drink tea for an hour or two; now, after the afternoon practice, she found herself thinking, " 'Hmmm, what should I do now?' It's all of us Russians. After practice—so, what now? What do you think? I don't know, maybe this . . . oh. No, too much traffic. Maybe this. Really? No, we did that yesterday." What she most wanted was to go home.

That summer Moskvina was teaching Yelena and Anton the throw quadruple Salchow. They were close, but every time they missed, Yelena fell hard. Moskvina was being criticized from all sides for trying such a dangerous maneuver with Yelena. People were calling from Russia wanting to know why on earth she was trying it. There was only one possible reason: to hold off the challenge from the Chinese. And in the meantime, they went to Skate America and got beaten by a couple of Canadians. Nobody saw that coming.

Sikharulidze didn't know how many more years of hard training he had left in him. Apart from his natural laziness, he enjoyed having a life, "and to put it bluntly," he said, "you don't see the light of day when you train seriously." In America he was sporting a longer hairstyle. He had just seen the Austin Powers movie and was going around saying "Yeah, baby" to everyone. He told his father he thought he might stay in America for good. He drove a Lexus and wore designer sunglasses. He liked skating tours and shows; the skating was easy and the partying was fun. When he lost a few early competitions that fall, he wasn't destroyed. There was more to life than skating. Besides, he still had three or four months to get himself together for the World Championships.

And Moskvina had to take what she could get. She would let him drop his level and raise it again in time for the World Championships in March. "I understand the young people's desires," Moskvina says. "They want to do skating and at the same time, life. If I would make scandals, it won't help. For example, Anton didn't come to practice. So what? Can I kill him, can I write to the federation, can I talk to him, can I talk to his parents, blah, blah—will it change something? I doubt it. So I wait, and when he comes back, I will say something like, 'If I would be you, I would probably try to come to the practice.' "

It was an imperfect system, but Moskvina was dependent on Sikharulidze. In the past Olympic cycles she had always had her group—a few Russian pairs. If one slipped, she had another ready. This had also helped her keep the skaters on their toes. But now, in Hackensack, she trained just one Russian pair. She had two other teams, the American champions and a Japanese team, but this group was not as cohesive as those groups at Yubileiny who grew up together, traveled all over Russia together, ate meals at each other's houses. She missed the camaraderie, and sometimes her husband would cook *solyanka* and invite the skaters to come to the apartment for lunch. But in America this gesture was a gesture, not a natural part of everyday life. In America it was not so easy for the Russians to feel part of the collective, and deep in their nature, they missed that.

When Anton did come to practice he was increasingly irritable. He shouted, cursed, smacked the hockey glass with his hand. "When the boys start to mature," Moskvina sighs, "they take too much on themselves. Then they think they know everything." His temper was flaring up more often. At a competition that fall, after skating a bad short program, he ripped off the top half of his costume and threw it in a trash can. He stormed out, and the next day, when he showed up for the final practice, Yelena didn't come. They arrived separately at the rink that night; backstage, they barely spoke to each other before they stepped out to compete.

When a Russian reporter asked if he was "emotional," Sikharulidze replied, "I think you can tell my character is not sugar. Everything happens in training. I curse, she can cry, and so can I. But as far as bad words during practice, you'd better go to the training of hockey players. You'll hear some nice words there! I never heard such words in my life." When Berezhnaya was asked about the situation, she said, with characteristic simplicity, "His temper couldn't be nastier." Moskvina called him "hot-blooded" and tried to stem the tide by always talking calmly about the task at hand, no matter what curse words he yelled. But it was embarrassing at times, now that they were not at home. There were days when a bunch of kids from New Jersey would be waiting for an autograph, and their eyes would widen as they saw the world champion yell and smack the hockey glass.

But what could Moskvina do? Yelena needed a partner; Moskvina needed a pair; everyone's livelihood was intertwined. And Anton was getting things together in time for the World Championship, if just barely. In March they arrived in Nice for the 2000 World Championships looking well trained and sharp. Yelena had lost those few extra pounds; their jumps were solid again. They were peaking at the right moment. The Chinese and Canadians had been gunning for them all year, but now that everyone stood on the same ice at the World Championships, it was clear which pair were the world champions and which pairs were the challengers.

Then, on the night of the opening draw, Moskvina came to Sikharulidze and told him the news: The ISU was about to announce that Berezhnaya had failed a doping test a month ago at the Europeans. Moskvina maintained that the stimulant came from a bronchitis medication; their doctor in New Jersey backed her up. But it didn't matter to the doping officials. The pair was out of the championship. Berezhnaya felt so humiliated she couldn't even show her face at the arena.

In Soviet times they had always had the team doctors at their disposal. The team doctors never gave you cold medicine with a banned stimulant—they knew better. Now, in America, Berezhnaya walked into a doctor's office and nobody was looking out for her. It might not be possible to train a pair of world champions in St. Petersburg, but it wasn't that easy in America, either.

∞

When Berezhnaya and Sikharulidze withdrew, people started telling David Pelletier he was going to win the World Championships. Even Gauthier was telling people they could win. Pelletier didn't want to jinx himself by talking about it. "But if it happens," he told the press room, "I'll buy everybody a beer."

The real favorites were the Chinese, because to their unbeatable elements they had added Western music and choreography to boost the second mark. They still looked like Chinese skaters performing a program made by a Westerner, but many judges preferred that look to Yao's all-Chinese parts and assembly. Shen and Zhao came out looking sharp and confident—and then a very uncharacteristic thing happened. They started to unravel technically. They made sloppy mistakes that they never made. It was as if the prospect of winning had undone them. Shen Xue seldom cried, but when she reached the backstage corridor and realized that she had failed to win the world championship again, she leaned against the wall and sobbed.

By the time Jamie Salé and David Pelletier skated as the last pair of the evening, the situation was clear. If they skated their long program cleanly, the pair would win the first World Championship they had ever entered. Salé skated out to the middle of the ice. It was her first Worlds in six years. The arena in Nice was beautiful, with potted lemon trees all around the barrier, and outside the rink the air was balmy and the sea smelled wonderful. She would remember this place all her life. She took a deep breath. Her mother was up in the stands, along with the Pelletiers. She visualized herself already done, with the medal around her neck. She knew better, but she couldn't resist the image. It was beckoning to her. She was loose, absolutely confident, relaxed. A month earlier, at Canadians, she had gotten perfect sixes for this program on the second mark.

The *Love Story* music filled the arena, and they went right up into the side-by-side triple toes—

She popped it, Gauthier said to himself. Instead of doing a triple, Salé had done a double. There are two ways to foul up a jump. You can fail to execute it—or fail to even try it. In this case, Salé hadn't even tried. And now she was spooked. Gauthier could see that she was afraid to jump again. Here came a double Axel—and she singled. Gauthier sighed. At this point, there was probably no hope for the last double Axel, but still, it would be great to see her get her head together and fight for the last one. *Come on, Jamie.* But she popped that one too. Gauthier already knew how inconsolable David Pelletier was going to be. To get all the way to the World Championships and have a chance of winning, and then the girl is missing her jumps beside you, just like old times.

As she got off the ice Jamie Salé was already crying. She cried quietly until the marks came up, and then she let go and really sobbed. The marks were devastating. They fell all the way to fourth place. People had cried before in the kiss-and-cry, but few people had ever cried as bitterly as Jamie Salé was crying now. She looked inconsolable. "I remember her saying: 'I just kept thinking what it was like for Dave,' " her mother says. "He wasn't angry, but he was pretty disappointed and he was sitting beside her. And she's thinking, 'How horrible, I let him down totally.' And that's why she's crying so hard. She knew that he did everything he was supposed to do. And she didn't."

Later that night, the Canadian contingent went back to the hotel to celebrate the end of the competition. Jamie was randomly chosen to pass through doping control, so Patti Salé sat in the hotel room with the others and waited for her. It was three hours before she walked into the room and sat down beside her mother on the bed. Patti Salé put her arm around her while she cried, and murmured, "You know what? You're still the most beautiful girl I've ever seen." There was nothing to say, really. And then, from the other side, David Pelletier put his arm around those shaking shoulders, and Patti Salé quietly got up and moved away. "It wasn't that she pushed me away," Patti Salé says. "I just knew that it was time for me to sort of not worry about it anymore. Dave and she would get through this together. It was *their* thing to get through."

∞

After the Worlds Moskvina gave her pair a month off and considered her options. Anton's nerves had been strained by the latest developments. He had always ignited easily, but now he had a legitimate complaint. Because of Lena's mistake he had missed a World Championship, one which he probably would have won. Moskvina weighed the situation. If there was a way to bring him willingly back to the rigors of daily training, the path led through the romantic part of his temperament. She thought he would like the idea of being an artist. So after long thought Moskvina came to two decisions: Anton would play Chaplin, and she would hire Igor Bobrin to make the program.

Igor Bobrin, then in his early forties, had been a pupil of Igor Moskvin. As a skater Bobrin was a good technician, but he was a one-in-a-million artist. Bobrin was destined to work in ice theaters, and somehow he always managed to keep one afloat. He had a show that toured Russia, often playing in the small towns, where he put on everything from operas to rock-and-roll fantasies. Bobrin was really a vaudevillian born too late, and he loved Chaplin. Bobrin agreed; now they had to convince Anton.

Sikharulidze recalls the scene this way. "They came to me and said, 'Okay, we're going to make a free program with Chaplin music,' " he says. "And I said, 'Hey, stupid, it's not a theater, it's a sport.' And they said to me, 'Well, get ready. It's going to happen.' "

"The most difficult thing," Bobrin says more diplomatically, "was to make Anton and Yelena believe in the theme. They had done a lot of great programs. They were famous for their lines. But this was the first program with a theme, where Anton was Charlie Chaplin and Lena was the blind girl selling flowers. And the biggest thing Anton had to do was to kind of step over his shyness. Because this is not some funny clown joke," Bobrin insists. "This is serious actor's work."

Bobrin started off gently. He gave them Chaplin's autobiography and some coffee table books, and when they returned them he was pleased to see that they had taken small notes on different pages. They had actually done the preparation. Bobrin next gave them a small book designed in such a way that if you flipped the pages very fast, it looked like the Little Tramp was moving. With that book they could go frame by frame and see the different stages between one movement and the next. Then he assigned them some Chaplin films to watch, and they brought their own ideas into practice the next day. For the first time, the two skaters became collaborators in the creation of the program they had to rehearse nine hundred times a year.

Bobrin had one inviolable principle for Anton: "Under no conditions should you play Charlie Chaplin. You can try to touch the spirit, the internal life, what is inside Charlie Chaplin. But don't imitate him." At first Anton hated the work. He felt stupid; he swore he could not do it. But when he saw that people passing through the rink liked what he was doing, his attitude began to change. "In Russia we have a saying," Bobrin says. " 'Sometimes you feel with your brain, sometimes you feel with your skin.' When he felt that people were impressed by him, he became impressed with what we were doing. Only then." And when Sikharulidze let go and began to make an effort, he was really extraordinarily good at it.

Chaplin is a painfully hard role for any experienced actor, yet with Bobrin's help, Sikharulidze's Chaplin came to life. It was not Chaplin, nor yet was it Sikharulidze; it was some character in between that possessed some of Chaplin's humor and body language and some of the handsome, romantic quality of Anton Sikharulidze's skating. When he finally "stepped over his shyness" and into the world of performing a character, Sikharulidze was startled to find that he loved skating Chaplin. Moskvina had guessed right: He was tired of the grind of training, but he was extremely interested in being an artist.

"I needed this," Sikharulidze confesses. "And it came at the right time. Igor Bobrin opened something in me with Chaplin. All of us have something inside, and Bobrin knew how to take that. Because usually these choreographers say to you, smile, and you smile, and you look stupid. And in this situation Bobrin told me, 'Never smile. You understand me? If you do something, and you just feel it's cool for yourself, just laugh, and I'm sure anyway that somebody out there will be laughing with you, because they know you're really laughing.' " And, to Moskvina's delight, Sikharulidze found that he now enjoyed being on the ice.

What neither Moskvina nor Bobrin had expected was how much the Chaplin program would move Yelena. At the Russian Championships, just a few months before the 2001 Worlds, Yelena and Anton performed the program with passion and delight. Yelena's eyes were shining with pleasure. "A lot of people put their soul into this, a part of their life, and here is the result," she said afterwards. The program seemed to pass quickly for both of them; they knew they were tired at the end, but somehow, with this program, they never felt it. "This program never skates the same way twice," Berezhnaya said, smiling still. "It's impossible to skate such a thing according to a plan. You live this program each time, and as your soul flies, that's the way you skate it, according to your feeling at each moment."

That fall and winter the program was adored all over Russia and Europe, and Moskvina thought that Chaplin might even be able to do what she had intended for it all along: to beat the Canadians at the World Championships—in Canada.

∞

"Losing a jump," as it is known in skating, is every skater's terror. Losing a jump means that a jump that you have mastered technically suddenly leaves you, and you are left to determine whether the problem is in your boots, in your blades, in your body, or in your head. After Nice, when Jamie Salé attempted none of her planned jumps, it was safe to say that the problem was in her head, but that didn't make it any less of a problem. Gauthier got her working with the sports psychologist. But the complicated situation on the ice was that when Jamie missed jumps, David got frustrated and Jamie felt worse, which in turn made the jumps worse. This situation had become more acute because, depending on the week, the two of them might or might not be a couple.

"It was on one week, off the next week. So I could sort of know by the way they acted on the ice whether this week they were a couple or not," Gauthier says. "But you have to work with the relationship. You can't keep it out of what happens on the ice. For example, the week before Worlds in Vancouver, David calls me and says, 'Jamie left me.' I said, 'Where is she?' He said, 'I don't know. She left. She packed her things. She probably came home and got mad.' So I called her on the cell and she's in a hotel nearby. She said, 'I can't put up with him anymore.' I said, 'We're leaving next Wednesday for Worlds. Is there any way you could focus back on the operational plan now?'"

Jamie Salé came to the rink, and the two of them skated their free program, but they wouldn't look at each other. "So she says, 'I'm going home. If he can't look at me when I'm skating, I'm not skating. I'm not a secretary that's going to come in, punch in, do my stuff, and leave,'" Gauthier recalls. "And David turns around and says to me, 'You get her back on the ice, or I'm leaving, and you'll never see me in this building again.' That was three days before Worlds."

They were passionate people, and Gauthier had known right away that nothing would be simple with them. The pressure on these World Championships was enormous. If Jamie landed her jumps, they had a good enough program to win and go into the Olympics next year as the reigning world champions. If not—well, they were looking at third place. The Chinese looked great, and the Russians had Chaplin.

Gauthier got them back on the ice in time for Worlds, but God only knew what they were going to skate like. In the short program, sure enough, Jamie fell on her side-by-side jump, and eighteen thousand Canadian fans simultaneously went "Ohhhhhh." The Russians won, the Chinese were second; they barely held on for third. But third was enough, because among the top three, whoever won the long program would win the world title.

The Russians skated first, and Chaplin was as good as it had ever been. There was a small collision on the twist, but it was a minor thing. Berezhnaya and Sikharulidze were spectacular, they had done all they could. They went backstage to wait.

Then Jamie Salé and David Pelletier took the ice, and the building erupted. Canadian skating fans are the world's most ardent, and in Vancouver even the practices had been packed. Now the home team had a chance to win the World Championships. It was like a soccer team playing for the World Cup at home in South America—a once-in-a-lifetime opportunity. But Jamie Salé did not consider that now. While she could be friendly and chatty right up until a few minutes before her skate, she could also narrow her focus remarkably quickly. She narrowed it now. They struck their first pose and waited for the music. As he did whenever they competed, Pelletier said to her, "Have fun. Just like home."

She got by the first side-by-side jump, and Gauthier felt it might happen. Then she got by the second side-by-side jump, and he was very excited. When she reached the third one he was sure she had it—but she popped it. It was a good single, done in good unison; some people might not have even noticed that she singled. But all the judges definitely saw it, and the mistake left things open-ended. That single Axel could be the difference between gold and silver.

In the final minute the Canadian crowd became so deafening that the skaters couldn't hear the music. They were going by memory now. Jamie Salé flung her arms around David Pelletier's neck for the last spin and began sobbing twenty seconds before the end of her program. "Oh, my God, oh, my God!" she repeated, and six inches away from her, holding her around the waist and executing a strenuous spin, David Pelletier was hissing through his teeth, "Concentrate! It's not over yet!" Then the entire building stood and thundered with applause. Standing by the barrier, awaiting their turn, the Chinese lost some hope.

Gauthier sat beside them, crying himself, and the crowd still did not stop cheering. Jamie Salé sat with a huge pink stuffed bunny in her lap, tears slipping down her cheeks. Beside her, Pelletier cried too. The second marks flashed—too close to call—and then the scoreboard changed to show the results, and they were first, they were first! The Chinese still had to skate, but probably, they had won! With a full-bodied scream, Jamie Salé jumped out of her seat and heaved the pink bunny over her head, back into the stands.

Half an hour later it was real. All eighteen thousand fans stayed for the medal ceremony, and together everyone sang a round of "O Canada." On the medal stand Pelletier kept his composure. It was only later that he broke down. He was skating around the ice, posing for photographers, and suddenly he saw his parents. He went straight to the place where they waited. And when he saw his mother's face, he buried his face in her shoulder and cried.

∞

The day after her pair skated a brilliant Chaplin and lost the World Championships, Tamara Moskvina was in the backstage hallways of the arena, complaining. "Well, of course, we were in Canada," she shrugged. "What we can do? What?" In terms of the great Chaplin program, which Europe had hailed as a masterpiece, Moskvina was acting very mysterious and wise. "Here, we make the first pancake," she said cryptically. When pressed, she explained, "First pancake, a little too hot. It cooks too much. It's not good yet for company. Second pancake is better." Having tested Chaplin out on North America in the year before the Olympics and gotten burned once, she wasn't going to bring the program back to Salt Lake City.

Moskvina was feeling a little glum. North America clearly did not appreciate them. She had hauled her team over here to be appreciated, so that people would learn to call them Yelena and Anton, and here again they were just "the Russians." She did not grasp the American public relations system yet; she still did not have the tools to promote them properly.

That summer they spent two and a half months in Russia. "After two years in U.S.," Moskvina told a Russian paper, "Lena and Anton have understood that 'home walls help.' Lena visited her native Nevinnomyssk, where she is a *personage,* and everyone admires her. Anton stayed at home in St. Petersburg." Moskvina spent time at her dacha, tending the raspberry bushes with her granddaughter. By the time they came back to Hackensack, Anton was adamant: He wanted to go home. As soon as Lena heard that, she started packing her suitcases.

"They came to me," Moskvina says, "and said, 'Tamara, we're having problems here financially, and psychologically we feel like, more at peace at home.'" Moskvina considered. Politically it could be good to go back to Russia. It would make the federation happier, the Russian judges, too. It was true: Walls did help, and she could use some help in getting them ready for the Olympics. God knows it would help to have the two choreographers, Bobrin and Matveyev, at arm's length; besides all the work they would do on polishing the program, they would help keep Anton interested in the work.

In the end it was Sikharulidze who really decided. In his view, they needed to be in Russia to win the Olympics. So Moskvina packed up and left her husband behind to carry on the Hackensack school, and they settled in again at Yubileiny. They walked through those stale hallways and changed in the dingy locker rooms, made do with two sessions a day and no weight room. But they were home, with family and friends, in a city that spoke their language and knew their thoughts, and none of them missed the lonely apartments and the four pristine rinks they had left behind in America.

Now the Olympics loomed, and they needed a program. All autumn, they quarreled about it. Lena and Anton wanted to keep the Chaplin program, or maybe make a new variant of it. But Moskvina wouldn't hear of it. "I heard many remarks from judges who considered Chaplin program too showy," Moskvina says. "And I was afraid that at the Olympics this principle can be used to judge the program low. So I thought, Okay, I will better take this classical program, that nobody can make any criticism."

So Moskvina went back to the Protopopov files and brought out one of their trademark pieces, Massenet's "Meditation" from *Thaïs.* She brought Bobrin in to choreograph, hoping that his presence would make Anton respect the program more. At the Olympics they would embody two Rodin statues come to life; Moskvina called it "The Eternal Kiss."

Anton hated it. He hated the concept, he hated the difficult steps, and he despised the music. Lena too loathed the music, which she accurately described as a "monotonous, monotonous melody" that became almost unbearable when played ten times in one practice session. In the months that they were supposed to be polishing it, they didn't practice it enough. Whenever they could Berezhnaya and Sikharulidze put in the Chaplin CD instead. As often as she could get away with it, Moskvina popped it out and put in "Meditation."

One day at the end of October, Moskvina was looking through the lens of her ancient camcorder, following her pair into a lift. It was a lift that hadn't been in their program for a couple of years, and as Anton put Lena up and started turning, he stumbled. He fell backwards; Lena went flying. Moskvina saw her drop and heard her yell as her back smacked the ice and her neck snapped backwards. *Oh, God, her head!*

Picking himself up off the ice, Anton saw the blood and thought, *She hit her head. Ohhh—it will begin now . . .* and moving towards her he said breathlessly, "How are you? How are you?"

"I'm fine," she laughed, "but look at yourself." He raised his left arm and saw a long, nasty gash where her skate had ripped into the back of his arm. Instantly he felt better. She was okay. A few hours later, he had three inches' worth of stitches in his arm, and they were looking at at least a week off from hard training.

Now Moskvina was getting anxious, because they were supposed to unveil the new program at the Grand Prix Final in just six weeks. It was to be the only time during the whole pre-Olympic season that they would compete against the Canadians, and the event was in Toronto. "Meditation" was not ready, and time was running out. Moskvina made a final plea: They couldn't afford to take a gamble on Chaplin. The judges might find fault, and they could lose the Olympic gold medal—again. Their entire future earnings depended on winning. Here she reached Anton.

"How much you earn depends on the results of the Olympics," he told a Russian paper that fall. "Nobody gives you big contracts merely for the sake of your innovative ideas." He didn't want to skate the "Meditation" program. But he trusted Moskvina's political instincts, and now, finally, he committed and put himself into high training gear. He gave up most of his extracurriculars and focused on the hardest program he had ever skated. In this program he had to skate fast, without any significant breaks, through the entire four and a half minutes; there were no little places to catch his breath. You needed energy to perform it, because the music was all the same, so the interest for the judges, for the audience, had to come from the performer. It was up to him to create the highs and lows, the tension. Anton still complained, but he did it. The nearness of the Olympics was finally hitting him. He worried that he didn't have enough time, that he needed another month or two before the Olympics. He was finally scared.

Berezhnaya, too, resigned herself to going back to the old romantic style. "In the Olympic season," she said snidely, "all judges want to be fed these 'love carrots.' They don't understand interesting ideas like our beloved Charlie Chaplin. That was considered too theatrical, and they carped about every little thing." She heard what Moskvina was saying; she knew that "to the judges who mark our performances, who are fifty to seventy years old, their ideal is those lyrical programs that were skated in their era. All of us understand it, and in an Olympic season everybody prefers not to take a risk. Still," Berezhnaya went on, "I would like to see those judges when they fall asleep behind their little tables, when all the pairs will show the same 'sniveling.' I would tell them honestly: to skate like this is already boring."

Moskvina still loved the pair she had seen in her imagination and made the impossibly romantic couple. But she could also see that in reality these were two people in their mid-twenties who drove fast cars and listened to rock music. To try to make the work interesting, she told them to think not of love but of passion. "Don't restrain your temperament," she advised. Anton got his stitches out in November, and the program steadily improved. Bobrin came back to polish it, and then Moskvina took her team back to Hackensack for two weeks. They had one last piece of business before the Olympics—to try to beat the Canadians at the Grand Prix Final in Toronto.

And so on a cold winter afternoon in Toronto they came out for the last practice. Yelena wore the dress she would wear for the performance, diaphanous, very pale pink, almost flesh-colored material. The subtlety was quite beautiful. She did look like a statue come to life. It was only practice, but when the music began to play, people all over the building paused. Officials standing in the doorway put down their clipboards, other skaters and coaches stopped talking, volunteers hanging banners paused. In every corner of the small arena, the emotion caught in people's throats. It was so pure, and the music was so gentle. It was romance, but overlaid with sadness. By the time they came around into their last lingering spiral, and one high, sweet violin note carried through the whole building while she arched her back and leaned in to him, people had tears in their eyes, just from the beauty of it.

They didn't skate the "Meditation" perfectly in competition. Berezhnaya fell on a throw. But Moskvina was not worried, because even with their fall and the Canadians' clean program, they still came close. And besides, there was that practice—that practice!—when the world melted away.

∞

At the 2001 Worlds in Vancouver, while Moskvina was making her first pancake, Yao Bin was watching his second pancake in a row go up in flames. In 2000 he had hired Westerners to make their programs, and they had finished second. (He had managed to finish second on his own the year before, without any high-priced Western choreography.) This year he had hired Westerners again. Then, sitting in the kiss-and-cry, he saw a 5.4 go up on the second mark. Yao was livid. Even with the last made-in-China program they'd gotten nothing lower than a 5.5! "Is it our facial expressions?" he fumed. "Is it our speed? Is it our interpretation of the music? No!" he roared. "It's none of these. The only reason is that they want to keep us behind."

So in Vancouver they were *third,* and now their results in the past three World Championships were silver, silver, bronze. "We can't command the judges," Yao snapped. "We can't manipulate them. So our only way out is to prove ourselves through performance. Tonight the judges were almost all from the West. We have to do what they like. Otherwise, we'll never win the gold medal."

Back home in Beijing, Yao walked over to the administration building for a master planning session. It came down to the choreography. The judges still didn't give full credit to Shen and Zhao's artistic impression. After some discussion, Chinese officials hired the American sports marketing company, IMG, to pull together a team of the choreographers, costume designers—the whole package. The federation would pay whatever it cost to develop a more Western image. But—and this was crucial—the program must have "Chinese characteristics." They must step on the Olympic stage with something the sports officials could promote as homegrown. Yao already had that angle covered. They would use the music from *Turandot,* a Puccini opera set in Beijing, and Shen Xue would play a

Chinese princess. They would have their patented Chinese pair skating technique, and with luck, Yao thought they might even be able to develop a quadruple throw in time for the Olympics.

For some time now Yao had believed that Shen Xue had enough height in the jump, and quick enough rotation, to be able to land the first-ever quad throw in competition. During the spring and summer, they could probably learn it. "I thought, if it's possible, why not do it?" Yao says. "But, since it's dangerous, I asked Shen Xue and Zhao Hongbo what they thought."

Zhao Hongbo agreed with him. The only way they would ever break down these judges was to blow them away with their technical merit. He was tired of being marked down. All those second and third places, being told he was inferior—he wanted to do the quad. Shen Xue agreed. She really thought they needed the quad to win the Olympics. She knew that learning a quad would be extraordinarily painful. That was all right. She would do what was needed.

They started directly on the ice—no movement on the floor, no trampoline. Shen Xue put on her spaceman outfit—helmet, pads over pads—and went out to try the first one. "There are different ways of learning it," says Tong Jian, one of the pair skaters in their group. "They chose to do it very high and fast in the air. When it's faster and higher, if the girl falls, she suffers more. Shen Xue would fall on her hip, again and again, but she can endure more than any other female pair skater. So when we saw them first try it, we thought, That really is not easy. We respected them very much."

In the practice rink on the Beijing campus, a set of Roman characters are affixed to the dingy wall, proclaiming *Citius, altius, fortius*—the Olympic motto. Most of the skaters have only a grade-school education, but they all know what the Latin words on the wall mean, and when they saw Shen Xue taking those dreadful falls, they were deeply moved. She was trying to go faster, higher, stronger than anyone before her.

Zhao Hongbo too admired her courage, but there were times when he dreaded throwing her. So many times she went up, and in the air he could already see she was off-kilter, and all he could do was wait for her to crash into the ice or the barrier. They tried three, four, sometimes five a day. Sometimes her hip hurt so much afterwards that they couldn't even practice the other elements.

Whenever Shen Xue called home that spring, she didn't tell her parents about trying the quad, because there was no point in making them worry. Then one day, on the phone with Yao Bin, her father was astonished to hear him say, "Hey, the two kids are doing pretty well with the quadruple." Shen Jie sat there holding the receiver, feeling very strange.

"Later on," Shen Jie says, "some coaches from Harbin went to Beijing for a training. And when they came back, they said to us, 'Shen Xue was badly bruised from trying all these quadruple jumps. We just couldn't even stand to watch what was happening, we had to turn our eyes away.' And her mother was so worried that she just wanted to go immediately to Beijing and see her. But we decided to call first. And Shen Xue did not agree to our proposal to come to Beijing and visit. Because she knew that we would be more worried if we were actually in Beijing, and she would be distracted by this."

"I was hospitalized because my blood pressure was rising like crazy," her mother says. "You know, some coaches actually called me, actually begging me to ask Shen Xue not to do the quadruple jump, because it was so very dangerous. They said to me, 'If you can do without this jump, please, do anything else. We are worried that Shen Xue cannot stand this for long.'" At this point in her story, her mother breaks down in tears. "We heard that the other kids on the ice became so scared from watching this that they were afraid to even try their triple throws. I later learned that the Beijing television was following the story of this quad. But they decided not to air the video on the television, because they feared that it would cause the girl's parents to be too upset."

Her father continues, "The officials later told me, 'We have taken all possible measures to protect her.' The team doctors, the coaches, and the sports administration officials—they would all be there when they were trying this quadruple jump. The sports research institute was there too. Also an ambulance."

On the forty-fourth try Shen Xue dropped down to earth, landed precariously on one foot, and held the edge. The whole practice group cheered for her, and Zhao Hongbo felt enormous relief. He had begun to worry about her, truly, for however careful he was to behave properly and avoid calling her his girlfriend, she held a special place in his life.

It was common knowledge among the people on the campus that wherever Zhao Hongbo was, there you would find Shen Xue too. "They are like figure and shadow," people said, and sure enough, there they were: walking together, carrying their bowls and chopsticks over to the dining hall; playing cards; going to the park on their day off. When Zhao Hongbo got a new computer, Shen Xue was angry because he played on it all day, practicing English and playing video games "to the point that he didn't want to sleep. But as an athlete, how will you do training the next day if you don't sleep well? So I moved his computer to my room. I told him, yes, you can play with the computer, but at bedtime, you must go back to your room. Teacher Yao praised me for this. He said that it is right for me to discipline him." And she didn't mind having him in her room all the time, either.

Over the years, Shen had picked up hundreds of stuffed toys from the ice, but it was the teddy bear that Zhao had given her that held the place of honor on her bed. Her room was decorated with photos of the two of them, mostly off the ice; she especially liked glamorous shots of the two of them dressed up. She was still, in many ways, very young; she liked to collect toys and dolls, and although she was twenty-four years old, her nickname was "Baby." She was an artless girl; once, when a Chinese journalist asked about a burglary in the Shens' home, in which her first skating medals were stolen, she turned to the reporter and said, "I hope that the person who took my medals away can send them back to me after reading this article, because those gold and silver medals are not really pure gold or silver, they are just gold and silver plated. Even if you melt them, you cannot sell them for much."

Zhao Hongbo liked her girlish qualities. In the team meetings, they always sat together, and sometimes Shen Xue would draw a funny figure on her hand and show it to him. After practice, she wiped down his blades with an old cloth and wrapped them in protective cloth. The other boys wiped their own skates, but Shen Xue seemed to consider this almost her wifely duty.

In what Zhao called his "three-point life"—dorm, rink, dining hall—Shen Xue provided the light and sparkle to an endless string of identical days. On the bus rides, she had picked up the Western habit of leaning her head against Hongbo's shoulder or lap. The parents were scandalized at first. But Yao, who had some sympathy for a twenty-nine-year-old who had never been allowed to date, merely shrugged and said, "What can you do? It's the Western influence." The two were close, and sometimes, after a performance, Zhao would even kiss her forehead, but that was as far as anything went openly. They refused to talk about a romance, their parents strictly avoided the subject, and everyone said that one mustn't speak about love now—they were career partners, they had so much work yet to do in sport and for China. Besides, love was against the rules.

"Actually I feel that this is not the time for talking about love, because to us, the priority is our career," Zhao said. But the problem was that part of their career was showing chemistry on the ice. As one Chinese article put it, "In these years, the international pair skating competition trend is that you have to show the passion of love on the ice, and show it like a very hot and spicy Szechuan dish. And now it's really difficult for Shen and Zhao. Although showing the passion is the basic understanding of athletes in this sport, the Western understanding and our way of life are two different worlds. Although Shen Xue and Zhao Hongbo can be called 'two kids who grew up together,' it's still very difficult to show the motions of love in front of thousands of people. It's harder than doing the hardest athletic maneuvers. But one of the reasons Shen and Zhao's scores are lower is because they are still more shy about showing their passion than European and American pairs. So for the honor of the country, and to fulfill their dreams, they have to move closer in this direction."

Therefore, for the good of the country, Shen Xue and Zhao Hongbo, forbidden to show love in the dorm or the dining hall, were now working frantically with their Western choreographers to show love on the ice. "Western judges like romantic elements," Yao told the federation, and now the three choreographers were supposed to give Shen and Zhao some romantic elements. One afternoon, when Renee Roca, Lea Ann Miller, and Gorsha Sur were on the ice working on *Turandot,* Roca was showing Zhao how to feign a caress of Shen Xue's face. His hand was to follow the line of her jaw, and as she moved her head, his hand should follow, never touching her face. "I showed him many times, and at first he would grab at her head," Roca says. "And I'd say no, no, no. He worked hard on it, and then he got it. And that was the exact moment when he said, 'This is exactly what we want, we want more of this. I like this. We want to look at each other.' "

Back in May, when the Chinese federation had hired IMG to make the Olympic package, the officials had requested an entire "emergency makeover"—costumes, image, everything. Shen and Zhao went to the United States with Yao Bin in the late summer to be fitted for costumes costing twenty thousand dollars, and while they were there, Lea Ann Miller sat down with Shen Xue and showed her how to apply her makeup. Someone videotaped the session, and back in China, Shen studied the video. The sports officials had told her to be prepared to change everything, maybe even her eyebrows and her teeth. In fact they had looked into braces. There was not enough time before the Olympics, but Shen was told that after the Olympics, she would need to straighten her teeth in order to maximize their chances with the judges.

By autumn Shen and Zhao were landing the quad forty to fifty percent of the time. They went to a fall tune-up in Germany, and there they easily landed three or four quads in practice. In the competition, they didn't attempt the quad, but their new romantic choreography was a huge success. The second mark was higher than it had been in three years, and they looked forward to taking on the Russians and Canadians at the last competition before the Olympics: the Grand Prix Final.

They arrived in Toronto well trained, with beautiful programs, and they finished third again. A Chinese reporter asked Zhao Hongbo whether the fates were against him. "I don't believe in fate," he said sharply. "We must believe in ourselves. Didn't Beethoven say that we should grab the fates by the throat? We'll also do this."

They hadn't tried the quad in Toronto, not wanting to risk it yet. But when they walked out of the arena in third place, Shen and Zhao committed in their hearts to the Olympic plan. Plucked eyebrows and romantic gestures were not going to be enough to move them up to gold. For that, they needed the quad.

∞

In March of 2001, Richard Gauthier was sitting with his team in the kiss-and-cry when they won the World Championships. By June his team had cleared out of Montreal and moved to Edmonton to train with Jan Ullmark. It was a shocking development. Why, people asked, would they leave the coach who had brought them to the World Championships, and just eight months before the Olympics? Jamie Salé and David Pelletier held a press conference and said simply, "We have our reasons."

Jan Ullmark was as surprised as anyone. One day his phone rang, and it was Jamie, telling him that she might be leaving Montreal. Astonished, he said, "Where are you going?" There was a long pause, and finally she said, "Well, we kind of thought we might come to you."

So they came back to Edmonton. Right away, they hired a conditioning coach. They would be as fit as they had ever been in their lives by the time the Olympics arrived. Ullmark started working with Salé on her singles technique again, and her solo jumps became more consistent. And David Pelletier's temper was now Jan Ullmark's concern.

As much as Pelletier feels he owes Richard Gauthier, it was only with

Jan Ullmark that he finally felt that a coach understood him. "Richard would just say, 'You *can't* act like that, you can't act like that,' and that sometimes made things worse. With Jan, it would be, 'I understand why you're feeling like this.' And as soon as he would say that"—he snaps his fingers—"it would be gone. Because all I needed was to be understood. 'I would get frustrated too,' Jan says, 'because I'm the same as you. I know exactly how you feel.' And he would tell me that, and I would say, 'Oh, thank you.' And it would be gone. You don't have to fight it. It's like a kid. A kid wants to know he's understood. You can't tell him, 'No, you can't feel like that.' That's the worst thing. And that's what I learned."

The on-ice relationship was stabilizing, finding a happy balance. Off ice, they had moved in together. Things were going well. They had won their fall competitions with a new free program they called "The Orchid." It was based on a simple concept—a stem supporting a flower—but it had great difficulty in the transitions and edges, and Lori Nichol thought it would carry weight with European judges. All fall, they stayed in North America. They did no competitions in Asia or Europe. They stayed on their continent and prepared for the Grand Prix Final, the only time before the Olympics that they would go up against the Russians and the Chinese.

The Grand Prix Final is an odd duck among competitions, requiring a pair to perform two different long programs. For the first program, the Canadians chose "Orchid"; for the second, they had resuscitated *Love Story*. There were some people who didn't support "Orchid" fully, so they figured they would use the Grand Prix Final to help them decide which program to skate at the Olympics.

Salé and Pelletier stepped out to skate the Orchid program in front of a home crowd. Then a very strange thing happened. David Pelletier was having an off night. For the whole program, his skates felt sticky, like he couldn't get the flow he needed. He recovered in time for *Love Story,* which they performed as well as they ever had. They got two sixes from judges who were going to be at the Olympics, and they beat the Russians and the Chinese. Now they were heading into the Olympics with a nine-competition winning streak.

It seemed clear that they should take the *Love Story* program to the Olympics, but all the same Salé and Pelletier decided to give "Orchid" one more chance. They brought it to the Canadian Championships in January, which were just a formality on the way to the Olympics. Backstage, waiting to come out and win one more Canadian title, Jamie Salé looked over at the monitor. Normally she never watched another competitor skate, but now she couldn't resist. Some of her younger teammates were trying to make the Olympic team, and she watched them on a backstage monitor, cheering for them. Pelletier passed by this scene and darkened like a storm cloud. She'd better concentrate. But he also knew that she could narrow her focus fast when she needed to. She'd be ready.

They stepped onto the ice—and Jamie was ridiculous. She wasn't focused at all. On the first side-by-side jump, the triple toe, she went down in a heap. She hadn't missed that jump in a year. She flubbed the next jump. She even doubled a throw. They hadn't skated this badly since Nice! They finished, took the bow, and as they skated off the ice, the camera caught David's face contorted with anger. Anyone with an ounce of imagination could easily make out the expletive he was mouthing. Ullmark sat between them in the kiss-and-cry, keeping Salé on one side and Pelletier on the other. As soon as he could, Pelletier stormed out, walking off into a corner by himself and yanking off the top of his costume. It took him more than an hour to compose himself enough to come to the postcompetition press conference.

For Jamie Salé, watching her boyfriend turn on her "was painful, because we'd worked so hard at being able to be there for each other when we don't skate our best," she says. "So I needed him to support me and tell me, 'You know what? It's okay. We're gonna go home and fix this. Don't worry. You just had a bad night.' But I felt that he was basically tearing me apart. And I tried to grab his hand to say I'm sorry and he just pulled it away. And if he wasn't my boyfriend? I would've went, 'Screw you.' You know? But I was like, my heart just shattered. I mean, I was already in pain because I felt like such a loser out on that ice. And the fact that he was like against me, that was it. Like I thought we were breaking up."

Within a few days Pelletier had apologized, and they were training again, but things weren't going well. There were three weeks until the Olympics, and Pelletier was so nervous he sometimes said he wouldn't even go to Salt Lake City. Salé's mood was low. "We had three weeks, I think, to the Olympics. It took me two weeks to get over it. And Dave was trying to be supportive but he was getting frustrated. He said, 'Jan, I can't take this. I mean, she won't let it go.' And I could not do a double Axel for two weeks. I mean, I'd do one and then I'd miss five. I just kinda lost my confidence.

"And then I got sick, the week before the Olympics. Deathly ill. On the couch. I couldn't even sleep in my bed. I had to sleep on the couch for five days. I couldn't really eat much. I was trying to eat, to keep my energy. Dave couldn't touch me. I remember laying there and I was crying and in so much pain. They had me on antibiotics, and I was so scared."

That Tuesday, they had to be in Calgary for a team training day, and from there they would leave for Salt Lake City. Salé tried to skate over the weekend, but it was Monday before she could skate a full practice. She didn't know how she was going to pull off an Olympic performance. She had been laid up on the couch for the past week, and even before that, she hadn't been landing her jumps.

But she was Jamie Salé, and somehow she always found a way. Her partner was so nervous he could barely drag himself to Salt Lake City, and she was frail and her confidence was shot. But now she rallied. On Tuesday she landed her first triple toe, and on Wednesday, they left for Salt Lake City.

∞

The Olympic village lay in a valley encircled by mountains. There were four inches of snow on the ground, and the air was bracingly cold. Everyone went out in big hats and scarves and gloves. Underfoot the snow crunched, and overhead a brilliant sun shone. Beginning at twilight, they turned on the lights on the mountainside, and the athletes could look up from the valley and see five perfect Olympic rings twinkling on the side of a mountain.

Only at the Olympics are the practice sessions closed to the public, and David Pelletier, who was already shaking with nerves, was made even more nervous by the stillness in the arena when he practiced. He and his partner were not jumping well at first—a fact made all the more painful by the knowledge that the Russians had been stunning in practice, and that the Chinese were landing the quad. Ullmark stood at the boards and watched, and he also noticed that Tamara Moskvina was up to her usual publicity campaign. She was up in the stands, openly talking to judges. Ullmark didn't care; he didn't go in for that. Never had, never would.

In the short program the results were predictable: Russia, Canada, China. But now those placements didn't matter. Once you landed in the top three in the short program, you could win the gold simply by winning the long program. They were all still in it for the gold. All three now had a clean slate. Whoever won the final would win the Olympics.

On the afternoon of the long program, Anton Sikharulidze sat in the hallway of his dorm in the Olympic village, shooting the breeze with the

Russian hockey players. Yelena, as usual, went for a short walk alone, drank a single cup of coffee. She read a little bit—Pushkin. She started to stretch, packed the costumes and the skates. She had done this once before, four years ago, though it seemed much more distant than that. She knew so much more now. By the end of this night, as on that night four years ago, her life would be changed. It was nearly time to leave.

In their room in the Canadian dorm, Jamie Salé and David Pelletier awoke from an afternoon nap. Pelletier was excruciatingly nervous. The bus ride to the arena was the part he dreaded more than anything else. They would take the van soon, and he would be so nervous he would almost forget his own name. But Jamie felt calm. From the moment she had woken up that morning, she couldn't wait to skate. She had an almost indescribable feeling about this particular rink, this sheet of ice. For some reason, she kept feeling a little rush of energy, and then a phrase would pop into her head: This is my building.

The Chinese boarded a bus for the arena, and Yao spoke to them soberly about the quad. They agreed that they would do it, with the stipulation that they would make the final determination after the warm-up. Shen Xue had packed the new costumes, never worn before—the expensive American ones. In her new dress she felt pretty. She had done everything to prepare. Now let it happen.

Jacques Pelletier and Murielle Bouchard left early for the arena. They passed through a security checkpoint, emptied their pockets, and were patted down by the National Guard. Then they hurried down a closed-off pedestrian street to the arena. Two dozen languages were being spoken on the little street; there was a buoyant feeling of excitement and goodwill. Strangers were trading pins; Olympic hats and coats were everywhere. It was really happening; it was really the Olympics.

When they got to the arena they climbed into an upper deck and took their seats for the early groups of pairs. The tickets were four hundred dollars each, and since athletes' parents were not entitled to any free tickets, the Pelletiers hadn't known if they would even have seats until a few days ago. It seemed that the Olympics were being staged primarily for the entertainment of the top brass of American corporations, who had the lion's share of the tickets. But fortunately Jamie and David had a contract with Cheerios, and the Cheerios people had helped both families out with some corporate tickets. Jamie's mom and grandmother took their seats beside the Pelletiers, and the two families made small talk: There was a big group watching in the bar of the Royal Glenora Club, and another at the Sayabec community center. Around them the arena crackled with the murmur of thousands of voices. The ice was very bright.

Triumphant music poured from the loudspeakers. An emcee opened the evening. Nine judges, plus a substitute and a head referee, were announced and applauded; they looked tiny from the stands. Nine countries had been randomly selected months ago by the ISU, and now each had a seat at the long table. Nine federations had hand-picked the judge who filled their country's seat. Now the judges took out various tools—pencils, paper, eyeglasses, erasers—and laid them on the table, like draftsmen preparing to work. Soft music played; the atmosphere still felt a bit slack. And then, for the first of many times that night, it felt to the Canadian parents up in the stands as if someone pulled a cord, and the entire atmosphere tightened one notch. Because down at ice level someone opened a gate, the first blade touched the ice, and the night was set in motion.

Chapter Five

*P*ASSING THROUGH THE BACKSTAGE TUNNEL, Anton Sikharulidze feels the muffled vibrations of the crowd above him. When he steps out into the open, the deafening noise breaks over his head. Out here the brightness is dazzling. With that thirty-foot wall rising up from the ice on three sides and seventeen thousand unseen spectators roaring high above him, he feels like a gladiator striding into the pit.

At one end of the rink is a high blue wall dominated by an enormous set of glowing white Olympic rings. Opposite Sikharulidze is a bank of photographers. There must be a hundred of them, training their long lenses on him and snapping off rounds like machine-gun fire. Three feet from his head are two television cameras. The image of his face goes live to the Jumbotron, where seventeen thousand people can see him chewing his lip.

Eight minutes ago Sikharulidze was feeling calm, moving down the ice with Berezhnaya, heading into a throw. Then the crash. The moment his body struck Jamie Salé's his pulse jumped sky-high. Sikharulidze left the ice in a daze. Backstage, he felt as if he were sitting in a ditch after a car crash: nerves shot, heart racing from retroactive fear—*that was a close call back there!* The calm feeling he'd had in the warm-up had exploded; however, fragments of calm remained in him, and he had to grab hold of them, fast.

Backstage, he had eight minutes. Eight minutes before he had to step through the tunnel into this brightly lit world. Now he is here under the strong lights. His nerves are still frayed and there is a dull ache in his arm from the impact. He brushes it off with a quick shake of his head. What's to be done? He skates next.

Berezhnaya doesn't think; she just wants to get on the ice. Quickly she pulls off her skate guards, hands them to Tamara Moskvina, and takes off. With every step there is a surge of relief. The energy is pushed out of her jangling nerves down into her legs and out through her toes. *Okay,* she tells herself. *Now you're like a fish in the water.* As long as she can move, the panic is bearable. She does a few turns on one foot, a simple jump. She looks neither at Sikharulidze nor at Moskvina, though both are within twelve feet of her. She rehearses her own motions, aloof. She is a professional, preparing to do dangerous work.

Standing on tiptoe to see over the boards, Moskvina steals looks at Anton. She knows the collision rattled him; the question is, how much? Backstage, Moskvina decided against asking the referee for a delay. Better not to disrupt things any more. Moskvina is cross. She thinks: *That crash was entirely Jamie's fault. She was not paying attention.* Moskvina recalls how Anton, behaving as a gentleman, rushed to help Jamie. And because of *that,* Moskvina concludes, they didn't get to warm up the throw.

They had saved the throw till the end of the warm-up. It's their weakest element, so naturally they like to do it when they are warm and loose. They were skating into the throw at the moment of impact. After the crash, they just ran out of time. Now, in the program, they will have to do it cold—twice. The throw is their riskiest element. They have to land two throw jumps in the next five minutes, and Berezhnaya doesn't have the feeling fresh in her skates. The last time Berezhnaya did a throw was hours ago. It should have been ten minutes ago—however, Moskvina thinks, Jamie Salé collided with them.

Moskvina knows that ever since the spectators saw Jamie Salé get knocked down they have been firmly on her side. When the Canadians emerge again the Americans will cheer for them like crazy and the pressure on the judges will begin. Moskvina came to America hoping to teach the public to think of her pair not as "the Russians," but as Berezhnaya and Sikharulidze. What she has since learned in America is that they will always be the Russians. Moskvina believes that the North American fans are here to see the Russians get beat by the Canadians. They want to see the Russians knocked down a peg after forty-two years and ten Russian gold medals in a row.

Irina Rodnina, who won three of those golds, is sitting in the Russian television booth above the ice. "Can Russia continue the long-running march, which began in the former times?" she shouts into the microphone. It is dawn in St. Petersburg; the Sikharulidzes are listening to Rodnina in their pajamas. "It will not be easy!" Rodnina declares. "Perhaps this is the first Olympics where we come as just one country among the hopefuls, where our team is not assured of winning. Because there was a joke in the past that the guy who managed the record player had only to learn where they kept the Soviet anthem. Whereas this time, Tamara Moskvina thinks her team is a little bit in the shadow of the Canadians."

After a split-decision loss to the Canadians six weeks ago, in Canada, Moskvina went to some judges for advice. "I talked to different judges directly, indirectly. I want to find out impression of the judges. So we talk, and I am getting like the *feeling*." The feeling was that the "Meditation" program was too subtle. So Moskvina hired a digital composer to add more instruments to the music. She brought the choreographers back to fire up every small gesture, and hastily commissioned new costumes in bolder colors. She ordered billowy fabrics that fluttered in the wind, to show off their speed: gray and black for Anton, a rose-colored dress for Yelena.

Berezhnaya, her blonde hair a striking contrast to that rose-colored dress, skates in a circle near the barrier. Suddenly she slouches and muscles her shoulders roughly. For a moment she looks like a soccer player trapped in a prom dress. It's a small thing, but it's a lapse in the illusion. On Olympic ice one should always look divine, and this defeated posture is vaguely troubling; she is not yet in the state of mind to command the audience. Still less is Anton, who is still trying to calm himself twenty seconds before his name is called. Moskvina is tied in knots. After all her scientific preparations, the three-hundred-day plan! Then along comes this stupid collision, and now Moskvina looks at her pair and *they are not completely ready!*

Yelena Berezhnaya hears the last of the marks for the previous pair. "Five point six, five point five, five point five . . ." That's her cue. She zigzags towards the spot by the barrier where she will meet Anton. She has done precisely this at least fifty times in her life. He snaps his elbow and extends his hand; she drops her palm into his. Finally, their eyes meet. She presses his hand once, hard. There is nothing tender in the gesture. They are no longer lovers or even warm friends, just coworkers in the same enterprise. But just the same they swiftly close ranks and shut out everyone else—even Moskvina.

In three seconds they have already covered enough ice to leave Moskvina far behind. She expected this. Six years ago, when they first came to her, she foresaw this moment: "At the end, when I will teach them what I know, I will stay alone. I will stay at the side, and they will have to do what they need to do. My help won't help them anymore." Anton's palms are sweating. He blows on them to dry them and rubs them on his pants again, then takes his position. Berezhnaya skids to a stop and stretches her body into the starting pose. Anton mirrors her. It is a beautiful shape from the pages of the Moskvina scrapbooks, and all nine judges lean forward, gripping their pencils, willing themselves not to blink. Berezhnaya makes her mind a blank and waits for the music.

Of Berezhnaya, Moskvina has said: "She has been on the border between life and death. The pressure of competition does not compare to being on the border between life and death." And watching Berezhnaya at this moment, one wonders if underneath all the pressure—this deafening crowd, the Olympic rings in the corner, the scared look on Anton's face, and the pounding of her own fast-beating heart—perhaps Berezhnaya possesses some inner spring of endurance, created during her ordeal, that is sustaining her even now. Moskvina thinks: *She won't falter. Watch Anton.*

To the audience they look impossibly romantic; to Moskvina they still look tentative. The first pose is not *fully done,* not extended to its limit as Moskvina would like to see it; the first few dance steps are a little wobbly. But now they begin to glide and all is well. The gliding is as beautiful as the very beautiful music and the very beautiful pair. They look perfect together—their bodies, their lines, their handsome faces. They are the only pair in the world that can command a crowd's attention just by stroking over the ice. The audience thrills to their speed without realizing that they are heading for the hardest side-by-side jump. Up they go, light and airy, perfectly matched—done. Applause like thunder; Moskvina exhales. Okay. They are skating normally.

They turn now and approach the corner for the side-by-side double Axels. Moskvina's pulse is pounding again. They rise in unison; it looks good in the air. But as Anton comes down, Irina Rodnina screams "Ai yai yai!" into her mike. Somehow he stumbled on his landing, touched his other foot down. He grits his teeth and steps right back in sync with his partner. The whole mishap lasted two seconds, no more.

He's overexcited, Moskvina thinks. *Come on, Anton. You have the whole program ahead of you.* At the same instant Berezhnaya tells herself sharply, *Do now, think later!* and shoves his mistake from her mind. Here comes the triple twist. It goes up spectacularly. St. Petersburg and Moscow techniques cooperate this time, and she gets good height, quick rotation, and a decent catch—a little bumpy, but the sloppiness is masked by speed. All in all a pretty good twist. *Take it easy,* Moskvina thinks. *One thing at a time.* Next is the throw.

The last time Berezhnaya did a throw triple Salchow—that is, launched into the air, pulled off three turns, and landed backwards on one foot—was many hours ago. In theory, this shouldn't matter. She has done thousands of throws in her life and should be able to do one without a warm-up. But of all the elements in this program, the throw is the one that gives them fits.

On the way to the throw they pass by the judges' table in a striking movement that as yet has no name. All evening, the judges have watched pairs tick off the standard list of skills; but here is a movement that only one pair in the world can do. Sikharulidze stretches one leg behind him in a perfect spiral and Berezhnaya leans towards him in a spread eagle with a pure arch in her back, resting one arm lightly on his back. The masterpiece. It is a move of such concentrated beauty that it transforms the atmosphere in the building. Up until now this has been an evening of acrobatic stunts. But this couple is poetic. They radiate romance, and for a moment it is possible to forget that this is a contest at all. Moskvina has done it again; she has made the arena into a theater. The music soars; something big is coming. The something big is the throw.

Sikharulidze places one hand on his partner's waist; the other grips her hand. Gliding backwards in front of him, Berezhnaya leans back into the sharp edge of her blade and rakes it against the ice to hoist herself off the ground. And at the precise instant that she rises, Anton Sikharulidze boosts her and sends her flying three times as high and far as she could go on her own strength. The crowd gasps at the height. Berezhnaya's blades are a good three feet above the ice at the top of the jump.

The woman's blade returning to earth after a throw can be thought of as an airplane coming in for landing. The blade, like the airplane, must continue its motion even as it touches down, and a perfect landing should be velvet smooth. This time Berezhnaya's blade comes in for a bumpy landing and bounces once before it grips the runway. She hangs on for dear life. From Moskvina, the landing gets a curt nod. Not perfect, but technically, it still counts as clean.

The hardest section of the program is over, and now Anton Sikharulidze is performing for all he is worth. Berezhnaya too is pouring energy into every one of her elegant fingertips, reaching for every extension of her free leg, her arm, her back. There is ardor in their faces to match the drama in the music. Moskvina, alone at the boards, knows in her gut that with this number of wobbles, her pair will probably lose on the first mark for technical merit. To win, they need at least 5.9 on the second mark. Intuitively Yelena and Anton realize this, and now they are skating with an urgent passion they have seldom shown in their lives. A month ago Anton hated this program; a month ago Lena sarcastically spoke of feeding the judges "love carrots," but now they are performing it as if their lives depended on it. Moskvina's design is pouring it on from all sides: gorgeous movement, two beautiful dancers with perfect bodies, incredible speed, and music to make you sigh. And it is working.

Just one danger remains: the second throw. All week long in practice, their throws sang. Now they need one more. In a flash she is airborne. The height and distance are glorious; she spins three times. But she is racing to get her free leg back in time for the landing. The free leg is still in motion when the other foot touches the ice. With a powerful jerk of her shoulder blades, Berezhnaya checks the landing and stays upright. Her knee is soft, the landing foot holds—and Moskvina can breathe again. Not perfect, but clean.

There are ninety seconds left in the program. At the boards stands Moskvina's first Olympic champion, Oleg Vasiliev. Now, as Vasiliev watches what may be Moskvina's last great pair, he sees the end of the Soviet tradition. "In Soviet Union, the system made the skater," Vasiliev says. "I was normal person. But they put me in the system, they taught me the right way, and they *made* me Olympic champion. And this will never be again. Because I tell you, in Soviet system, old days, it took at least one year, repeat, *one year,* to learn how to do *crossovers.*"

Berezhnaya and Sikharulidze are now doing a simple crossover as well as anyone has ever done one. They move over the ice with a quiet, glorious power that will probably never be seen in pair skating again. This pure glide is the gift of the old Soviet coaches who drilled them as youngsters, thirty minutes a day of basic stroking. In their bodies is a training that triumphs over everything: bad ice conditions, laziness, even lack of desire. Neither Berezhnaya nor Sikharulidze ever wanted to become a figure skater, but this system made them great. In contrast, in North America, Vasiliev sees raw talent emerging at the top. "Salé and Pelletier—those two, that matching is luck! They naturally have absolutely the same body rhythms. They changed seven partners before they found each other. Then when they found each other—snap fingers! It's right away." Vasiliev shakes his head at such luck. "That's talent," he says simply. "That's not *system.*"

On the ice now is the last great pair ever to grow up in the Soviet system. In every elegant raised arm, every flexible motion of a leg, in the softly splayed fingers and the marvelous posture, they reap the rewards of a lifetime at the ballet barre. (There was a special ballet-for-skaters program at the provincial rink in Nevinnomyssk where Berezhnaya grew up, and one at the church on Vasilyevsky Island where Sikharulidze started skating.) Watching them, one can even see the influence of the Soviet culture of their childhoods. They feel this music; they grew up in a world where classical concerts sold out, where the ballet was a national treasure. Anton Sikharulidze belongs to the culture that produced Baryshnikov, a society where men are proud to dance beautifully.

On the ice, Anton Sikharulidze tells himself, *Go ahead, go ahead. Open everything from inside—go ahead.* He is already tired, they are skating at altitude, and he seldom rehearses his full program, but now he reaches deep and gives everything he has left. His face is animated by the feeling of the music, and there is no separation between what his body does and what his face shows. He is passionate, his partner is passionate; and yet a curious thing is happening. The music is romantic, the movement tender, yet between them there is a wall. There is a chill at the heart of the romance. Somewhere along the way, they seem to have become estranged from each other.

A long time ago he loved her. He rescued her from Riga, agreed to skate with her when she was still an invalid. For a time she loved him too. But now they are tied together by work, not love. Recently, when asked if he planned to marry Yelena, Anton retorted: "We're friends and that's it. As for me, I'd much rather sleep with my wife than jump triples with her." In Yelena's cool demeanor, some read shyness, some read nerves, but some see a woman who has been shouted at too many times and has finally averted her eyes for good.

On the ice, this tension between them is strangely moving. Berezhnaya comes down from the final lift with one arm draped around his neck, her breast leaning on his. The moment cries out for a tender look, but they cannot look at each other with love, even feigned love. Each turns to the audience with a passionate look, but they avoid looking deeply at each other. This program is called "The Eternal Kiss." Now they reach the final pose, he holds her in his arms and bends over her face, his nose resting inches from hers, and the crowd is thinking, *Go on, kiss her!* Tamara Moskvina has arranged a kiss, but the kiss doesn't happen. Applause breaks out overhead; they step away from each other. "This program was kind of crying," the Russian television host says finally. "There were tears in it."

As Yelena Berezhnaya finally looks up into the stands, she has the sensation that her mind is floating somewhere far away, looking down on this moment. She is swimming in strange feelings. She thinks: *Maybe this was our last free program.* When they were very young, in those first years after the accident, each time they stepped out to compete, they would calm each other by saying, "After all, it's not the last competition of our lives." But maybe this was the last one.

It is all so strange and surreal. Berezhnaya comes off the ice panting hard; Tamara Moskvina is waiting with the skate guards. She handed those guards to Moskvina so long ago, but by the clock it was only six minutes. She collapses on the bench next to Tamara Moskvina. Anton sits beside her, completely drained. He gave everything for the second mark. He feels emptied out, hollow. Everything he has been preparing to do for four years is over. All that is left is to see what the judges will do.

"They really skated brilliantly!" Irina Rodnina yells over the noise of the crowd. "It was like a piece of art. One of the most beautiful programs I have ever seen. There was just one small mistake. But let's hope the Canadians will make more mistakes."

High up in the stands, the Canadian parents are straining for any sign of their kids. Ever since the crash, Patti Salé has been listening anxiously to every crackle of the loudspeaker, dreading the announcement that they have withdrawn. During the program her eyes darted back and forth from the Russians' performance to the skaters' entrance. Usually the next pair emerges from the tunnel during the last two minutes of the previous skaters' program, but Jamie and David were not there. Murielle Bouchard exchanges a worried look with Patti Salé, who is sitting beside her, clutching her arm. Then, just as the Russians finish, the Canadians arrive at the skaters' entrance, and Murielle Bouchard is astonished to see that Jamie is actually smiling. She nudges Patti Salé and says, in her limited English, "She's all right."

Patti Salé looks down and there she is! Oh, there she is! And there's the old breezy confidence, she's smiling that big smile, and she's going to skate. No problem! David, on the other hand, is white as a sheet. Patti Salé leans back in her seat. She's not thinking about the medals. She just wants to see them skate *Love Story* again. She takes some deep breaths and leans back in her seat. She reaches over and presses Murielle Bouchard's arm.

Murielle Bouchard is astonished at how calm she feels. It's really very strange, because in the weeks leading up to this night, just the thought of the Olympics was enough to make her cry. "Rivers were flowing from my eyes, literally," she says. "All the time I kept imagining all possible scenarios. They'll win, they'll be last, they'll trip, they'll mess everything up." She was expecting her heart to all but come out of her chest tonight, but now she stares at the ice, intense but controlled. Jacques Pelletier, who has seen the parking lots of many lesser arenas, wills himself to stay in his seat.

Jan Ullmark stands at the barrier, thirty feet from where the Russians sit waiting for their marks. Fifteen minutes ago, after Jamie Salé took a sharp elbow to the ribs at fifteen miles an hour and came off the ice hyperventilating, it was Ullmark who took control of the situation. As soon as they stepped backstage, Ullmark could see the people lining up to fuss over Salé, but he wasn't going to have any of that. "Leave her alone!" Ullmark barked, and he and Pelletier took her to a curtained area where the three of them could be alone.

She was still gulping for air, but already she could feel the adrenaline kicking in, numbing the ache in her side and in her arm. She took one look at David and thought: *I'm not giving up. No way.* So she slowed her breathing, started stretching. She turned her focus inward. And she set about the task of convincing David that she was fine. For if she didn't convince him that she was really all right, he would unconsciously try to help her, make the moves easier on her, and those tiny changes in his effort would throw her off. She had to make him feel secure. *Come on, Jamie,* she told herself. *You've worked your whole life for this moment. Think of your jump, think about doing your throw.* And in the midst of all this, backstage, she heard the crowd gasp at the Russians' mistake, and with a rush of confidence, she felt it: *Okay. Okay. It's our night.*

Now the announcer intones, "And now the marks for Yelena Berezhnaya and Anton Sikharulidze, for technical merit," and Sikharulidze puts his hands together in prayer. He was raised an atheist in the Soviet Union, but now he prays, *Okay, okay. God help me, please. Please, one time. I never ask you again about this—just this one time.* He sits there praying, knowing that he's the one who bobbled; if they lose, the mistake was his.

"Five point seven, five point eight, five point eight, five point seven," the announcer begins. Salé, Pelletier, and Ullmark are all thinking the same thing: *If we skate clean, we win.* Jamie Salé bursts into a full-on grin and high-fives her coach. She looks absolutely juiced now; that's probably exactly how she looked when she walked into those provincial locker rooms and said, "I'm gonna beat you, you know?" So assured is Jamie Salé that she barely registers that seven of the nine judges give the Russians 5.9's on the second mark. She's not worried about the Russians anymore. She is unbelievably loose. She's glowing. Ullmark takes one look at her and he can tell she's on. She's focused, she's in the best condition of her life, and she is dying to get out there and show off.

From her seat high up in the arena, Lori Nichol can't make out Jamie Salé's face, but as a choreographer she reads body language expertly, and Jamie's body language is better than she ever dared to dream. "Oh, my God," Nichol says. "They're really going to do it." She can see that David is still really uptight, but that's typical. He's always a nervous wreck before he skates, and he never makes a mistake. She's not worried about him.

From where Ullmark stands he can see that Pelletier's face is drained of all color. It was only two weeks ago that Pelletier flat-out refused to come to the Olympics—he was that nervous. Ullmark gives him a kindly look—not too kindly, still with some firmness in it—and shows with his eyes that he, for one, believes in him.

All day long Jamie Salé has been repeating to herself, "This is my rink." Now her name is announced and the crowd stamps and roars, confirming her hypothesis. She grabs Dave's hand and surges forwards. She can't wait to get out there. "I felt," she will later say, "like a shining star." Waiting for the music, she can barely suppress her smile. Her eyes glow with supreme confidence. She doesn't blink. She is trained, in the moment, completely unafraid. *This is my moment,* she tells herself. Meanwhile, behind her, David Pelletier is battling for control over his nerves. He sets his feet in the start position. One gray pant leg is shaking like a leaf.

He leans in close to his girlfriend's ear and says, as he always does, "Have fun. Just like home." The "have fun" is for her. The "just like home" is for himself. When she hears him say "just like home," she knows what it means. In all the years they have skated, he has always been "just like home." He always skates perfectly at home, just about every day, and he always skates perfectly in competitions. Pelletier has a time-tested method for skating perfectly. Before any difficult element, he thinks purely about his technique. And before each element, he says his one key word for that element at exactly the same time, every time. His method works. At home, he misses a jump maybe once a week. Now he tells himself, *Take it one item at a time.* First up: side-by-side triple toe.

The music starts. The live American audience recognizes *Love Story* and the atmosphere in the stands changes—*Finally, our music!* The first flurry of piano notes rings out in the Royal Glenora Club bar and the Sayabec community center, and all conversation abruptly dies. In Sayabec they are listening to the French-Canadian broadcast, led by a rotund Frenchman named Alain Goldberg. Goldberg is beloved in Quebec, because he narrates with the breathless melodrama of a Mexican soccer announcer. Now Alain Goldberg says, in a heavy stage whisper, *"Silence!"*

Fifteen seconds in are the triple toes. Right now Pelletier is doing the two things he usually does during a program. In the back of his mind he is worrying about Jamie landing her triple toe. At a conscious level, he is all technical. *Now!* Right on time, he thinks of his one key word and goes.

Jan Ullmark sees them heading for the triple toes and his pulse skyrockets. The triple toe has always been Jamie's nemesis. She only got the damn jump back on Tuesday, *Tuesday,* after it went missing for a month. She didn't do it in the warm-up. At this point, Ullmark knows, the triple toe has nothing to do with her body. She's well trained, and her muscles know how to do it. It comes down to guts and confidence. If she hits this, they skate well. If not, the whole ball game is over in the first fifteen seconds.

Up in the parents' section no one is speaking. Patti Salé has Murielle Bouchard's arm in a death grip and her heart is pounding. Jamie speeds into the jump and for once she's not smiling at all. *"Attention!"* whispers Alain Goldberg. The jumps go up, the jumps come down, and Patti Salé leaps out of her seat, cheering and carrying on. Already she's crying. *Thank you God! Thank you so much!* She knows how hard they've worked. *Please, just let them do it.*

There is a minute between the triple toes and the side-by-side double Axels, and it's a terrific minute: a crisp twist, a stunning lift, a beauty of a throw. The Canadians are not as blazingly fast as the Russians; they glide smoothly but not with the same awesome power and deep edges. But where the Russians put the crowd on the edge of their seats, the Canadians put people marvelously at ease. He is so strong, and she is so secure, that when they go up into a twist or a throw, the audience feels that it will happen as a matter of course. They make everything look easy.

At the same time the crowd is falling hard for Jamie Salé. She's no ballerina like that Russian girl, but she looks more real, more sincere. She goes around twice and the whole audience feels she is looking them right in the eye. It's that same performing ability and charm that brought down the house in small rinks all over Alberta when she was still in elementary school, and now she holds the entire Olympic arena in thrall to her every motion. And she loves it.

All of this is lost on the nervous parents, who barely register the minute between the triple toes and the double Axels. All three of them are thinking: *Oh, God, the double Axels!* In the month before the Olympics the double Axel was falling apart. David lost his; Jamie lost hers; both of them were frantic. Jamie would do one and miss five. It was only a few days ago that they started landing them consistently again. David Pelletier is so worried about the jump that he can't relax at all. He's in full robot mode, ticking off the elements one by one.

In singles a skater waits to jump until the moment that he feels ready, but in pairs a skater has to take off at precisely the same time as his partner, ready or not. Pelletier concentrates, comes around the curve, says his one key word. And at the same instant, the two skaters gouge their blades into the ice and lift off.

As soon as he lands Pelletier breaks into a wide smile. Alain Goldberg is going nuts, and so is the Sayabec community center. Up in the stands Patti Salé is jumping up and down; Pelletier's own parents are cheering with all their might. Down on the ice Pelletier flicks an internal switch and goes into performance mode. Salé playfully taps him on the shoulder; he turns around and she's not there; he laughs as she comes around his back in front of him. The audience adores them now. The crowd is clapping in time with the music, and David Pelletier effortlessly puts his partner up in a spinning lift that covers the length of the ice. The crowd is clamoring for more. Now they mimic a snowball fight, and David Pelletier's face is euphoric. They come around into a footwork sequence and move with uncanny unison, each person echoing the other, down to the tiniest motion of the foot or hand, the slightest tilt of the head. Jamie Salé is really showing off now.

The crowd is so hyped up now that people are looking for reasons to cheer, and when the two skaters go to center ice and propel themselves into side-by-side spins, the audience roars. What the crowd doesn't realize is that David Pelletier is counting out the turns so that Jamie Salé can match him; every time he says a number, her head should be in the same position. This is the only way they can match the spin, and now she can barely hear him. But on experience and luck, they make it through.

The music swells; the sad part of the program is beginning. At this point, Jamie Salé, as the Ali MacGraw character, is supposed to be telling

Ryan O'Neal that she is dying of cancer. That's a pretty tall order for figure skating, and only the most sincere performer could hope to pull it off. It helps enormously that Jamie Salé is not a cynical girl, not *at all,* and that from the time she was very small, she has been unabashedly putting her heart and soul into everything she skates, from "Deep in the Heart of Texas" right up through *Love Story.* They come to a dead stop at center ice and face each other, clasping hands. Slowly, they drop their arms to their sides. Their shoulders collapse inward. When they made this program, Lori Nichol built the sadness into the movement. She didn't want them to have to put the sadness on; it should be in the muscles. Right now all of that is working. They face each other hand in hand, he drops her to the ice in a death spiral, and they stop again at center ice. The mood is established. The crowd understands that something tragic is going on; *don't clap too much now.*

Pelletier stands behind his girlfriend and holds her in his arms, and in this position, they glide around in a circle. It is a poignant, beautiful movement, but with a typically Canadian lack of fuss Jamie Salé calls it "our snuggle." The movement was made in this way, with the man standing behind the woman, because on the day when they choreographed it, Nichol was pregnant and couldn't face David Pelletier. A few months later, when David Pelletier skated in from behind Jamie Salé and held her in this way, her pulse quickened, and she realized she was falling in love with him. She began to look forward to that snuggle every time it had to be performed. This program is layered over in many ways with their own story, and perhaps for that reason the emotion in her face seems real. They come around a corner and he caresses her neck, and by now the whole picture is working. The unison of the bodies, the gestures and looks of love, even the two gray costumes reinforce the image: two people skating as one.

Only the throw triple loop remains. Four years ago, the first time they ever tried it, Jamie Salé landed the throw triple loop, and she has rarely missed one since. David Pelletier follows her into the throw, knowing that he must keep his shoulders square. At the crucial moment, he thinks, *Shoulders!* and the throw happens. In the air he knows. He sees her perfectly aligned and then her blade comes down soft and smooth, the long running edge carrying her towards the judges' table, for these two have the confidence to stage their throws right under the judges' noses.

The applause is so loud it hurts the ears, and at the same time the music is building. Pelletier comes up behind Salé and they go into a pair spiral; she clutches his wrists, and the photographers click away. Now there is a moment in the choreography where she reaches back and he hugs her, and into his neck she whispers, "We did it!" He hisses back: "We're not done yet!" She can tell he's mad at her. Two days before, in the short program, he fell on their ending position, and he was furious with himself for losing his concentration. His anger sobers her. She thinks, *Control yourself. Focus till the end.*

Near the end of the program, skating at altitude, they still have plenty of energy, and Ullmark thanks God for the full run-throughs they do every day in practice. Pelletier presses his partner up into the last lift. She rises above his head, holding her body aloft in a seemingly impossible position, and underneath the lift David Pelletier's feet are so quiet that the people at rinkside can't even hear them. He puts her down ever so gently. Jamie Salé wants to burst into a smile, but she forces herself to stay in character. She's supposed to be dying here. To the last strains of the music, she leans down into a perfect death spiral, her ponytail brushing the ice, and finishes in a pair spin. At this point she remembers Lori Nichol's last words to her: "Whatever you guys do, just hold that ending position! Let us savor it." The building is already going crazy, but Jamie Salé pushes away from David Pelletier, lets her hand fall slowly, and, still in the character of the dying girl, counts: one, two, three, four, five. Then her jaw drops and she mouths, plain as day: *Oh, my God!*

The choreography calls for Pelletier to finish in a crouch, and as soon as he breaks character he drops to his knees, bends over, and kisses the ice. He throws his head back and literally roars. Jamie Salé is looking up at the crowd, pumping her fists, and shouting, "Yes!" They are a team, and they are in love—but for the moment they celebrate separately, and one is reminded that on their journeys to this place they spent far more time alone than together. One thinks of Jamie Salé plodding away at singles all those years, and David Pelletier's room at the boarding house in Rimouski. Each turns to the crowd and soaks in the applause to his or her solitary core.

But now Jamie Salé skates into her partner's arms, and he lifts her off her feet and swings her around. "You're number one, buddy!" she yells over the crowd. It's a standing ovation; people are stomping, screaming, ringing cowbells. Up in the stands Patti Salé is screaming, crying, and kissing everyone around her. She turns to the ice and starts blowing kisses to Jamie, who cannot possibly see her. Murielle Bouchard looks like she's in shock. She still can barely speak.

The crowd is stomping, and in the Anglo-Canadian television booth Barb Underhill, herself a world champion in pairs, is overjoyed. "There wasn't a wobble, a waver, anything! They were so sure from the minute they stepped on the ice. Look at her face!" Underhill shouts. "I just can't get over the level of comfort that they had!" The host declares, "And now, forty-two years Canada's waited—and we have to wait for the judges, and one more pair." As the Canadians come off the ice to wait for their marks, the audience stops cheering and takes up a chant: "Six! Six! Six!"

Not far from Underhill's booth, at the Russian desk, the host says gruffly, "I think the pressure of the audience on the judges will be high." Rodnina says sadly, "I hope I'm mistaken, but it looks like yes, the Canadians did it. They did the program very cleanly, very easily. You basically cannot complain." "At least," the host puts in sharply, "they already *behave* as the Olympic champions."

And the Russian host has a point. From the moment David Pelletier kissed the ice, it's been obvious that he expects to take home a gold medal. Now he and Jamie Salé sit in the kiss-and-cry with Ullmark, looking absolutely thrilled. Into the television cameras, Pelletier shouts a greeting to Sayabec in French; in the community center the people break into cheers. Salé says hello to Red Deer and starts to rattle off her greetings to friends. Ullmark pats her on the back and she leans her head on his shoulder. The crowd still chants for sixes as the first mark hits the scoreboard.

Murielle Bouchard sees the marks go up and suddenly fear grips her. *There shouldn't be any 5.8's there, because the Russians had some 5.8's.* She counts—six of the nine scores are 5.8's. And she thinks: *Something's wrong. We might not be first.*

The second mark comes up, and Murielle Bouchard says to herself, *There should only be 5.9's and 6.0's, but here there are 5.8's and 5.9's.* She remembers that the Russians had a lot of 5.9's. Her son got only four 5.9's on the second mark. There should have been more. And again she thinks: *We might not be first.* And just then the scoreboard flashes: second place. The crowd erupts in boos.

David Pelletier's face is being broadcast live to the world as he learns he is second. Immediately he buries his face in his hands. Jamie Salé looks dazed. She vaguely recalls hearing somewhere that it's possible for the results to flip-flop in rare cases—say, if the Chinese were to get some first-place votes and knock the Russians down a bit. She turns to Ullmark, sort of half laughing, and says, "It's gonna switch, right?" He shakes his head: no. She leans over to Pelletier and says, "It's gonna switch." He too shakes his head. She thinks: *It's not possible. For us to have that kind of skate, and then for them to make a mistake, and we're second?* She thinks, with a desperate inspiration: *Maybe they're leaving room for the Chinese and later the standings will flip-flop*. But in her heart she knows: It's over. The marks won't switch.

She looks over at Dave sitting beside her with his face in his hands, and suddenly she becomes aware of the cameras. They have to get out of there. They have to go somewhere where they can have a moment to themselves. She feels confused, upset; the audience is still booing. She thinks: *Try to be a good sport*. At the same time another feeling says, *But this isn't fair*—

Backstage, Yelena Berezhnaya had been talking to reporters, so by the time she got to the locker room and saw the television the Canadians were already sitting in the kiss-and-cry. On the first mark she saw Jamie Salé crying with joy. But when the second mark came up it yanked the smile right off Jamie Salé's face. Berezhnaya registers that the Canadians must be second. Tamara Moskvina rushes over, kisses her, and says, "Congratulations!" But to Berezhnaya it still doesn't feel real. In the hallway, Sikharulidze's cell phone is ringing—a call from home. "Can you imagine?" he says to his mother. "I am Olympic champion."

"Five judges to four!" the Anglo-Canadian host is yelling. "It could change if the Chinese were to get some first-place votes." Barb Underhill interrupts him. "I'm sorry, but I don't care!" she says angrily. "This is *wrong*!" Canadian television shows Patti Salé with her hands to her face, looking shocked and dismayed. "I'm in shock right now," Underhill says. "I'm in absolute shock."

In the Russian booth Irina Rodnina is screaming at the top of her lungs: *"Great! That's it, that's it!"* "Five judges to four," the host says cheerfully. Over the noise of the boos, Rodnina is talking a mile a minute. "And now we can begin celebrating!" she declares. "I would like to congratulate Tamara Moskvina, and Yelena and Anton, and the judges. They decided to stay on our side." "I think," the host puts in, "that the judges were objective." "The Canadians skated clean," Rodnina says happily. "There was nothing to criticize. But we were so easy, light, and then there's the incredible *quality* of our skating. And I would say that the most important thing is that our pair is just a really beautiful pair. That counted for a lot."

It must have counted for a lot, for it was the second mark that put the Russians ahead. That's all the judges know for the moment. The television monitor shows the five–four split, but all the judges can see is the overall placement: second. For a moment every judge on the panel has the same anxious thought: *Who else went with me?* The Canadian judge, Benoît

Lavoie, slams his fist on the table. He was sure the Canadians had it. Now he is obsessed with one thought: How many judges went with him, for the Canadians? Did he miss something crucial? Was he the only one to rank them first? And if not, how did this happen? But there's no time to think about it. The Chinese are already on the ice.

Overhead the crowd is booing and stamping, amassing its strength against the row of judges. But Shen and Zhao hear nothing, as if underwater. They warm up just in front of Yao Bin, at the barrier. Shen Xue shakes out her legs. She is impeccably trained, although she is alarmingly thin. Two days ago, Yao Bin had to force her to eat some of his Chinese New Year dumplings; she could only force one down. But whatever she has suffered to reach this point, she is now smiling very beautifully; already, she is a different person on ice than on land. The warm-up went well, and they are all agreed: They will attempt the quadruple. It is, to everyone's mind, a grand, courageous gesture, and for that reason all three of them want to do it now, here: *Citius, altius, fortius.*

Earlier today, Yao Bin was summoned to meet with the high-ranking team officials. "I can promise you we will do wonders during the Olympics. We can do something that others haven't done before," he told them. "But I can't promise you that we will win the gold medal. That depends on the judges." The quad is the first element in the program. It has to be—a quad takes so much energy that it can't be delayed. The odds are low. At home, they were landing it forty percent of the time. Here in Salt Lake City their success rate has been about the same. The adrenaline should help. They probably have a fifty-fifty chance of pulling it off.

Without the quad, Yao knows, they could be guaranteed third place—a medal at the Olympics. But Yao thinks of how, earlier today, Zhao Hongbo spoke to him with passionate intensity. "Yes," Zhao insisted. "Yes! We want to try this quadruple! Because—third place . . . we have won so many third places. So we'll try the quadruple. And we won't regret it, even if we don't get third place."

At this moment, despite the pressure, Zhao feels really, really good. He stands on Olympic ice for what might be the last time, twenty-nine years old. He and Shen Xue are wearing part of the twenty thousand dollars' worth of costumes that the Chinese federation commissioned from the American experts. They look stunning, he in black, she in a red dress with gold embroidery. The deep red and bright gold are reminiscent of the Chinese good luck banners her parents have always hung on the front door of their apartment. What her father would love most in life is to watch her at the Olympic Games, but her parents cannot afford to be here. In China the performance will be broadcast on a tape delay, so Shen Jie is at the computer his daughter bought for him, checking the Internet every few minutes for news of her. Beside him, Lu Manli feels so proud she almost cannot bear it. Shen Xue's great-grandmother had bound feet; she walked haltingly and could barely carry a bucket of water. Now Lu Manli's daughter is at the Olympic Games in America, about to land the first quadruple throw in history.

Shen Xue has applied her makeup exactly as the Westerners showed her, and from her face you can see that she senses that she looks beautiful. She is radiant tonight. She takes Zhao's hand with a look of absolute trust and happiness, and as she glides into place for the start of her program, she is already in the character of the cold princess. She is determined to do everything right, from the quad down to the smallest character detail. She will give the judges nothing to criticize her for on the second mark.

The violins begin. In her new red dress, at center ice, Shen Xue is acting her role brilliantly, but for once no one is interested in the question of her artistry. Everyone is waiting for the quad. She needs tremendous speed to be able to get enough air time to do four rotations, and they pick up the pace going by the Olympic rings and barrel into the corner. *Hold on,* Yao thinks. *Concentrate!*

It happens in literally one second, but later, Yao thinks of it in frames. Zhao sees the back of her neck. His left hand is on her waist, right hand holding her right hand. He lifts her up and away from his body, and as she rises his view changes. He sees her back, her hips, her knees—and when he sees her knees, he heaves as hard as he can and lets go. His face is contorted by the exertion.

In the stillness of the frames, Shen Xue is climbing on the first rotation. By the second one she reaches the top of the jump, and now she is falling fast to earth. Each rotation drops her by more than a foot, and as the fourth rotation comes around she snaps her body to stop the turning. Zhao, who is facing her from a few feet away, feels his heart burst with joy. *She's got it!* At the barrier, Yao Bin leaps into the air, yelling. Shen Xue herself thinks, *Yes, it's certain, one hundred percent.* She comes down on one foot, but her free leg is not all the way back yet; she has to make an adjustment on the landing. She starts to adjust, careful not to upset her balance over the blade on the ice—

And at that instant her blade rolls over, and she falls.

"Aiiiii!" screams Irina Rodnina. "Ohhhh!" cries Barb Underhill.

Alain Goldberg abandons the stage whisper and gives a full-bodied yell. "She had it!" Underhill cries. "Oh, she had it." And everyone feels a jolt of disappointment, because Shen Xue came so close, and she was not just doing it for herself but for all of them—for the sport. Yao Bin's heart sinks.

Later, in Harbin, Zhao's mother will say, "Actually, the little girl succeeded with the quadruple. The thing is, she got so happy that she fell to the ground afterwards." Zhao Hongbo's final analysis will be more scientific. "The jump was perfect in the air, perfect height and rotation. She actually landed and glided some distance before she fell. Maybe her landing leg was just a little too stiff."

But right now Zhao thinks of nothing. He is relieved to feel his heart start beating again, and now he sees Shen Xue clamber up, wet ice on her stockings. As she turns and skates in close to him, he murmurs to her, "Take it easy, take it easy." Because next up is the hardest side-by-side jump combination of the competition.

Only Yao Bin would be demanding enough to follow up a quad throw with this combination. The Canadians and Russians fretted over having to do a triple toe and, later, a double Axel. Shen and Zhao are now doing double Axels immediately followed by triple toes, within a few seconds. Shen Xue is that kind of girl who likes to do everything perfectly, and she is not about to give up. Double Axel, triple toe—she's flawless. It's Zhao who has a bobble on the second landing. *Shen Xue is fine,* Yao Bin thinks. *But Zhao Hongbo is really rattled.* And sure enough, on the next lift, Zhao can't manage to fully extend his arms and has to put her down early.

At the barrier, Yao Bin is seriously worried, but here comes a slow section, where they can catch their breath. And now something unexpected happens. Puccini's slow, irresistible melody is wafting over the crowd, and down on the ice, Shen and Zhao are deep in character, completely absorbed by the feeling of performing. The Chinese are skating with the open passion of the best Western couples. *Turandot*'s cold princess is warming to the prince, and in every motion, every glance, Shen Xue, perfectly in character, is melting just a little more. Next to her, Zhao Hongbo feels the music stirring him. Each glance at Shen Xue urges him on, and inside now he is performing wholeheartedly. And with a rush of feeling he realizes that he is enjoying himself.

To the Western audience there is nothing surprising in two young people showing love on the ice, but to a Chinese person of Yao's generation, it's a radical act. Twenty-four years ago, when Yao started pair skating, people sent him angry letters. "They said, 'You hug, you hold hands, you embrace. This is a manifestation of bourgeois revisionism and feudalism.' But that's what it was like in the sixties and seventies, because China was pretty closed. When pair skating first started in China, people couldn't bear the sight of men and women embracing and hugging in public. Today, it's not an embarrassment anymore, but Chinese people are still not so open-minded as Westerners."

Now the Chinese skate face to face, and Zhao's hand moves as if to caress Shen's face but instead follows the curve of her cheek without touching it. Her face leans in toward his hand. On the ice in Beijing, when the Westerners taught him this movement, Zhao first understood and loved performing in the Western style. And now this simple motion commands the attention of seventeen thousand people, and the most unlikely thing of all is happening. The Chinese are moving the audience, not with Yao Bin's patented Chinese technique, but with the beauty of their dancing. Now, with a gentle motion, Zhao takes his partner's hand.

In Chinese, pair skating is called "skating hand in hand." The Chinese vocabulary for figure skating developed in isolation from the West, and the pioneers gave things literal names. And truly, watching Shen and Zhao now, everything they do is illuminated by looking only at their hands. Now the hands are clasped simply, relaxed; they are skating side by side. Now the clasp tightens, the fingers stiffen and the knuckles whiten, and all the strength in the arm seems to be joined at the seam of the hands. Press the hands together just so and swing both arms skyward, and the woman's entire body miraculously rises above the man's head in a lift. Clasp the palms together in a certain way, and she descends to the ice for a death spiral, prone, her hair brushing the ice as she spins around his feet. One can understand the essence of pair skating simply by watching the fingers—the joints clasping and unclasping, the pressure changing the knuckles from red to white, the fingers resting when the balance point is achieved and then sustained by the palms, just like the palms of an acrobat. Shen and Zhao's fingers are dexterous, magnificent, and entirely familiar. "Holding hands," says a Chinese writer, "is the thread that holds these incredible movements together, like the pearls in a necklace."

Now the Chinese gain speed and reel off the most spectacular triple throw of the competition. No one has done one better tonight. But as they near the end of the program, Zhao is exhausted. Another lift comes down early, and on the last lift his feet score the ice with loud scraping sounds. It is not the performance they dreamed of, but as Zhao pulls Shen Xue into the final embrace, he is strangely elated. He hugs her with great excitement, and against his shoulder, her face is satisfied. "Don't worry, don't worry," Zhao says into her neck. "It's a pity we didn't succeed, but it's nothing serious." Shen Xue just says sadly, "We were almost there."

Last summer, she took forty-three hard, painful falls before she landed a single quad. Zhao Hongbo feels relief, even joy that it is over, but he also feels the weight of it. He thinks, *We have paid so much for this in the past. It has been so hard. It's even like undergoing torture.* Shen Xue, freshly bruised and far too thin, takes his hand and curtsies beside him. They are weary, but at last, it is over.

At his own Olympics, Yao came off the ice looking miserable. But now he stands in the kiss-and-cry and allows himself to crack a smile. At the moment that Shen Xue flew into the quadruple, Yao Bin felt the greatest thrill of his life. A second later, her ankle turned over, and his spirit sank. But still, Yao feels satisfaction, for he won one battle tonight. Tonight Yao's team tried what no one else dared, and every coach in the world knows it.

From her perch in the Canadian booth, Barb Underhill is expressing the Western perspective. "I think it was a big mistake for them to go for that quad Salchow, because it really affected the rest of the program," she says. "And, had they landed it, I really don't think it would have made a difference."

Yao Bin cares little for that opinion. "Nobody ever dared to try the quadruple at the Olympic Games until us," he snaps. "The meaning doesn't lie in whether they succeeded or not. It lies in their spirit of daring." Faster, higher, stronger—their performance moved Yao immensely, and backstage, Shen and Zhao's younger teammates have tears in their eyes. Now the Chinese stand proudly in the kiss-and-cry, waving and smiling broadly, and when the marks come up, all nine judges put them third.

At this moment Alain Goldberg is apologizing to the Chinese on Quebec television. "I am sorry," he says, "very sorry, but I could not watch the performance of the Chinese. I really apologize to the Chinese. But I can't help it. I cannot stop thinking that our pair should be first. Something is very, very wrong." He rips into the judges, he speculates about corruption. He says: "I am hearing that it may involve the French judge, Marie-Reine Le Gougne."

Le Gougne at this moment is still sitting at the judges' table in her fur-collared coat. Like the other eight judges she is trapped in a force field of tension and animosity that went up as soon as the scoreboard showed the Canadians in second place. Like the others, Le Gougne is still wondering, *Who else went with me?* And now the judges sit, rooted to their seats, and the only thing each person wants is a certain piece of paper that should be arriving at the table within a few minutes.

It is the piece of paper that shows the individual judges' rankings, and as soon as it comes everyone is going to be looking at the same two teams: first and second. Right now, no one on the panel knows that it went five–four, and no one is sure who went for the Russians and who went for the Canadians. But they heard the boos of the crowd and they feel the anger in the building. They know this is going to blow up in the media, and they all want to see who will be on their side tomorrow.

Backstage, Jamie Salé cries. She doesn't let go and sob, the way she wants to, because the cameras are never more than five feet away. But when she leans on David's shoulder, a few tears escape. She carries Kleenex and presses one to her eyes gingerly, careful not to smear her eye makeup. She has to stay presentable. In the ten minutes that she has been backstage, other Canadian skaters have made their way down from the stands and into the corridor to find her. As they hugged her, each one said the same thing: "I don't know what to say, I'm so sorry . . ." And gradually it dawned on her that most of the people upstairs believe she should have won the gold medal. That's when she started to feel queasy.

In her mind it seems that something has gone terribly wrong, but the world around her doesn't seem to acknowledge that fact. The Olympics are racing forwards: surreal, unstoppable. The doping control people conduct their random draw, the media arrive backstage in the mixed zone to ask questions. "Sometimes," she tells a reporter, holding back tears, "skating your best program and coming second is hard to take, and we're not going to lie about it." A volunteer with a badge rounds the skaters up for the medal ceremony. Jamie Salé is about to get a silver medal, and that's that.

Out by the ice the marking sheet, still warm from the copier, hits the judges' table, and the judges grab it and see what they all expected: a five–four split. The four judges who went with the Canadians are still in shock. To them, it was such an open-and-shut case that they still can't believe the result. The Russians won on the second mark. Tomorrow morning at nine o'clock they will all file into the standard event review meeting and have to justify that second mark to the referee. And the whole time, the half of the room that voted for the Canadians will be thinking that the other half flat-out cheated. And what difference will any of it make? In the end, the Canadian pair will still have a silver medal.

Now the trumpets are blaring over the loudspeaker, and Shen and Zhao skate out to receive the bronze medal. Zhao Hongbo smiles warmly at Little Xue to cheer her up. She still feels bad about the quadruple. He tells her, "Now, you tried your best, so that's all." And when she sees his look, she smiles through her disappointment.

Eighteen years after finishing last at the Olympics, Yao Bin stands in a place of honor near the skaters' entrance, the coach of the first pair from China ever to win an Olympic medal. He feels pretty good, in fact. But he is already thinking about how to win the World Championships next month.

Shen Xue and Zhao Hongbo are now on the podium, and the crowd suddenly triples its volume. Yao Bin looks up. The Canadians are coming. If the crowd can't give them the gold medal, they'll give them a gold medal ovation. Hearing the roar, Jamie Salé almost starts to cry right there. She has to crinkle up her eyes and purse her lips to dam up the tears. She's putting up a good fight. David Pelletier is drained and weary. After six months of mounting pressure and the night he's had, it wouldn't take much to make him lose control. But he too is playing the part of the good sport. One thinks of Eric Gillies: "Canadians like the idea of having to have heart to do things, but then they want people to be diplomatic . . ." What is going through Jamie Salé's head right now is, *I'm angry at my sport, I'm angry at everything, and thank you for your support, but I really don't want to be standing here right now.* But with one last burst of energy, she hides it.

Jan Ullmark feels uneasy as he watches this transpire. Earlier this week he was hearing rumors that deals had been struck, that his team wasn't going to win, no matter what. He wrote them off as rumors and kept them away from the kids' ears, but now he thinks the rumors were probably true. At this moment, Lori Nichol cannot believe what she has just seen. "There wasn't even a question. It was as clear as it possibly could be. For Jamie and David to work that hard, to be bashed in two during the warm-up, come back, perform their guts out, and be clean, and then have that happen—it's just too shocking to comprehend."

Up in the stands, Patti Salé isn't angry, though she might be the only person in her entire section who isn't. She aches for Jamie, but as her daughter raises a bouquet, the audience around Patti cheers with such abandon that she thinks: *This is the consolation. At least the people recognize her.* Next to Patti Salé, Murielle Bouchard feels numb. All she wants is to see her son. The way this rink is designed, there is no way to even get close to the ice. It will be hours before she can see him. She wants to give her kid a hug, and he needs it—but she just can't. Jacques Pelletier comforts her, feeling drained and baffled. Questionable results are nothing new in figure skating. No one at David's level has any illusions left. But this is the Olympics. How could this happen?

Now the Russians are announced. The applause is less, but it is friendly. Berezhnaya still feels that she is floating somewhere far away from all of this. Four years ago they won the silver medal. And here, four years later, was the big exam. It's over. She is an Olympic champion. In her lifetime, only eleven pair skaters in the whole world have been Olympic champions. All eleven are Russian. Seven of them trained with Tamara Moskvina at Yubileiny. And one of them is the man next to her.

Anton is breathing in a strange way, exhaling like a blowfish, as if to say *whew* with every breath. Four years. It's so long. Now he has an indescribable feeling. Moskvina is standing just behind the boards and her chin is tilted up so she can see over the barrier. For once in her hectic life, she is still, she does nothing. For a handful of minutes, the one who is never satisfied, is satisfied.

The podium is now assembled, the flags are at the ready. Russia, Canada, China: the world's three most vast countries, all of them stretching into the far, icy north. Figure skating is a sport of civilization. In Europe in the nineteenth century, aristocrats in St. Petersburg sent away for leather boots and steel blades, and hired an orchestra to play for them. Wealthy North Americans, wintering at alpine resorts, fell in love with figure skating and transplanted it to clubs like the Royal Glenora.

China had figure skating even in the eighteenth century, in the Qing emperor's court. "In front of the Five-Dragon Pavilions," the court poet wrote, "the water froze into ice in winter. There were iron teeth on the soles of the shoes worn by the ones on the ice, and they made them slide on the ice as quickly as lightning. The skillful players were like dragonflies skimming the surface of the water, or like purple swallows flying over the waves. It was called skating." But when the courtly life vanished, so did the skates, and only when the Communists reached a certain level of prosperity could they afford to revive an aristocrats' sport.

Figure skating asks for a great deal: ice and tools for smoothing it, leather boots with wooden soles, and smooth steel blades to screw into the wood. And it demands expertise, for while every three-year-old knows how to run, no one is born knowing how to do a double Axel. Behind every skater is another skater, the coach who passes down the knowledge. And often, the coach goes even further, teaching the student to perform feats that the coach himself could never do.

Behind Yelena Berezhnaya and Anton Sikharulidze stand the coaches of the Soviet Union: Nina Ruchkina of Nevinnomyssk, who with pitiless ambition put Berezhnaya on a train to Moscow when she was thirteen years old. There she was passed on to Zakharov of the legendary Red Army Club, the man who taught Gordeyeva and Grinkov to skate pairs, and further to Mikhail Drey, who told her she would be great, and finally to the most successful pair coach in the world by far, Tamara Moskvina. Behind Sikharulidze is the perfectly coordinated work of the St. Petersburg school, from the talent spotters up to the junior coaches up to the world-class Velikovs, and finally by lateral transfer to Moskvina. Neither Berezhnaya nor Sikharulidze even wanted to skate, but all the resources of that astonishing system flowed into them, and they have just won the gold medal.

Behind Shen Xue and Zhao Hongbo, in contrast, stand Yao Bin, the only pairs coach in China, and the indefatigable coaches of Harbin, who passed years of their lives in the bitter outdoor cold, teaching little kids their first jumps. This month, Shen or Zhao's first coaches will be getting an Olympic bonus from the Chinese government as a token of the nation's appreciation.

Jan Ullmark now leans against the barrier, the last of the nine coaches hired by the Salés and the Pelletiers to make their children into champions. Canadian pairs are made by a series of individuals—and, to a large extent, by what they teach themselves through hours of unsupervised work, on and off the ice. The fifteen-minute lesson is a fixture of North American skating; you pay the coach for part of the hour, and the rest of the time you work on what the coach just taught you. Yao Bin has a maximum of four pairs at a time; he plus an assistant coach devote their entire day, every day, to four pairs. Moskvina has roughly the same setup. But never in their entire lives could either Salé or Pelletier have afforded so much of an elite coach's time. For the vast majority of the hours they have practiced, they have skated on their own. At certain points, the Canadians have had the advantage of having a major training center behind them—Boucherville, the Royal Glenora Club. But often they have worked in out-of-the-way rinks with spirited entrepreneurs. They had Richard Gauthier, sometime stained-glass-maker and musician, who took two stubborn individuals and made them a pair. He is at home in Montreal, finding it hard to watch them complete the journey without him. But this is the Canadian system.

In her youth, Jamie Salé had Debbie Wilson to rely on; good old Deb, who drove the kids to Lacombe to get ice and got her husband to sharpen the blades. Wilson has just switched off her television in disgust. David Pelletier had Roland Paquet, the traveling coach who traveled even tonight to the Sayabec Community Center, where people drank beers and waited for the first gold medal in the history of the Gaspésie. They all had goose bumps watching him. They celebrated, and then the marks came up and there was vicious booing, and a lot of French Catholic obscenities. People said: The medal was stolen. Right now Paquet, like everyone else in the place, is livid.

An official drapes the medals over their necks: first bronze, then silver, then gold. As the silver medal bumps against her chest, Jamie Salé feels the finality of it and has to scrunch up her eyes again to stave off the tears. She is trying hard. For the past nine competitions in a row, she has always finished with a gold medal around her neck. But, as David says, number ten is the only one that counts. And now she is wearing silver. Out of the corner of her eye she sees the gold medal, the one she visualized for herself, going over the head of Yelena Berezhnaya.

The old Soviet anthem, reappropriated by Russia, begins with a resolute chord. In general Russians smile less than North Americans, and they express annoyance with the American habit of smiling all the time for no good reason. Berezhnaya and Sikharulidze are not smiling now. Their faces are filled with emotion, but its source, its meaning is not easily understood. Anton Sikharulidze fights not to cry, his mouth quavering. Again he puffs out air like a blowfish. He blinks, licks his lips, licks his lips again. The music touches him to the quick, and though he tries to hold the tears, they run by themselves. When he cries, he looks like an old man— so, so tired.

A head shorter than Sikharulidze, standing in front of him, Berezhnaya starts to sing. She blinks, stops singing. She squints as if something hurts. In her lovely face, pain and happiness are fighting, until finally she seems to surrender to a moment of joy. Unlike the others, she somehow stands apart from this moment. For her alone, this medal ceremony is not the largest experience of her life. What Moskvina said was true: The pressure of competition does not compare.

Of the three—Berezhnaya, Sikharulidze, and Moskvina—it is only

Moskvina who smiles. Standing a few feet from a television camera, she turns her face up like a buttercup to the sun and smiles and smiles. "In America," Moskvina has said, "everyone is like *this*"—and here a smile showing all her teeth—"and I learn a lot from that. Because in Russia we are more normal. In America, everything is like advertisement, everything is like showing off. I thought: Here, when you behave like normal, nobody notice you. So sometimes it's enough to win without smile. But if not, we have to add smile." At this moment Moskvina, inches from the lens, is smiling an awful lot, and one has to wonder if she is adding the smile. Backstage, she has already felt the mood turning against her team. She knows a bad situation is brewing. So maybe her smile is meant to show that she feels untroubled by any controversy. Only one thing is certain: Behind her smile, Moskvina is very, very happy.

"Long life of . . . trying to do what is not possible," she says. "*Challenge,* as probably you say. Trying to make what has been rejected. People think it will never happen." All the pleading with Anton, all the last-minute changes to the programs, the costumes. She relocated to America and went back to Russia for them. Or go back farther—to when Moskvina came to the hospital in Riga. Of all the *challenges,* this Olympics was the hardest. "We did it as a team, but still in every team there is a manager or brain force. I turned them in proper direction. I forced them to do that, I persuaded, fooled them to do what I had planned inside my mind." She sighs. "And slowly you succeed and that is satisfaction. That is relief. Because *in spite of,* you did." And the Olympic gold medal hangs from their necks.

A few feet to the Russians' right, the silver medalists stand, looking solemn. Jamie Salé is giving her mouth strict orders to smile, and it is obeying, but above the forced smile her eyes look wounded. She wipes away tears with a practiced hand. Behind her, David Pelletier leans in to kiss the top of her head, whisper consolation into her ear. But his eyes look hollow and sad. Both are thinking: *We worked our whole lives for this.* "Sweat and tears," Jamie Salé says. "All that money. Twenty years I've been working towards this moment. And they can just take our hearts away like that." She thinks she should have won.

The question of who should have won is thick in the air. Everyone in the world who knows pair skating is either in this building or watching on television, and these experts fall into two distinct camps. For this was a classic judging dilemma, of the type that not infrequently produces a five–four split on a panel. Part of the confusion arises from the fact that the judges don't agree on what pair skating ideally should be, and the rule book leaves plenty of room for interpretation. For instance, Moskvina's trademark asymmetrical choreography is unpopular with many of the North American and Western European judges, who believe that the Canadians' incredible unison in their side-by-side skating is the essence of good pair skating. This view could not be further from the one held by many Russian and Eastern European judges, who, like Igor Bobrin, consider shadow skating to be hopelessly passé. "Pair skating must illuminate a relationship between two *different* people," Bobrin insists. "It's horrible to be like a mirror of your partner. Maybe in this case you ought to just skate with a mirror and just forget about the partner."

But the largest source of the confusion by far is the fact that both teams were simply so very good. "The Canadians sang better on that night," one choreographer says. "But the Russians have better voices." A year from tonight, some of the most outspoken advocates for both sides will soften their stances and say that intelligent people could disagree about who should have won. Some will even argue that it should have been a tie for first place. Because it came down to the second mark, and the second mark is about culture.

But on this night, in this building, the accusation hangs in the air: The Russians didn't deserve it; some judges must have cheated. A corresponding wave of emotion is crystallizing around the idea that the Canadians were robbed, and this wave is sweeping through the Canadian delegation backstage, who are hugging and crying like people at a wake. In response to this the Russian delegation is already formulating rebuttals. The atmosphere prickles the skin.

The skaters descend from the podium and skate around the rink, waving and pausing for photographs. There is awkwardness between the gold and silver medalists, particularly since the Chinese depart quickly, leaving the two rivals alone. The two pairs avoid turning to the same section of the crowd at the same time; there is a feeling that perhaps the Canadians are stealing some of the gold medalists' thunder. And when the Canadians skate over to the judges' table to receive hugs from the Canadian and German judges, the Russians hang back awkwardly and avoid the table altogether. And in all of their eyes there is that strange, stunned look, and the same question flickers across every face: *What just happened?*

Chapter Six

*W*HEN THE SECOND MARK WENT UP for the Canadians and Benoît Lavoie slammed his fist on the judges' table, he felt it in his gut: It was stolen. How on earth could they be second? How? It made no sense. And then a wave of panic came over him. Had he looked away for two seconds and missed some crucial mistake? Was he alone in ranking the Canadians first? His mind was racing, his heart was pounding, but there was no time to think. The Chinese were right in front of him, already on the ice; he had to concentrate *now*. So Lavoie pushed his anger down and focused on his work.

But now the medal ceremony is over, and Lavoie has nothing but time. He has seen the final scoring sheet, and everything is clear to him. There was no mistake in that program. His first instinct was right—the gold medal was stolen.

The whole thing is infuriating to him. *They made me doubt myself,* he thinks. But now he knows he was right all along. His eyes were never sharper than tonight. After all, this was his Olympics, too. He worked for almost twenty years to reach this moment. He attended dozens of seminars, passed all the judges' exams, marked thousands of programs. He spent his weekends and vacation days judging uninspiring local competitions, working his way up to the regionals, the sectionals, the Canadians, the international circuit—and, finally, the Worlds and the Olympics. Judging the Olympics is an awesome responsibility, and Lavoie took it especially seriously, for tonight he was the Canadian judge in an event where Canada had a chance to win a gold medal.

Benoît Lavoie may be Canada's judge, but to Jamie Salé and David

Pelletier, he's also a trusted adviser and a good friend. A thirty-nine-year-old guidance counselor from Quebec City, quietly handsome, Lavoie exudes gentleness. Years ago, when Jamie was a talented little skater making a splash at Canadians, Lavoie made a point of going and finding Patti Salé in the stands and urging her to keep her daughter at home, no matter how many coaches came calling. He'd seen too many kids' lives destroyed by moving away from home too young. Patti Salé had always been grateful to him for that. Years later, Lavoie's good friend Richard Gauthier called and said, "You've got to come down to Montreal right away." That weekend Gauthier ushered Lavoie into his living room, opened him a beer, and showed him the videotape of the Edmonton tryout. Gauthier could barely contain his excitement. "You know, Benoît," Gauthier said at the time, "I think I have the Olympic champions here."

It was Lavoie who suggested to the Canadian federation that Salé and Pelletier deserved a shot at going to Grand Prix competitions in their first year as a pair. Because of that they were able to win some prize money, and David Pelletier was finally able to quit his job and skate full-time. Three years later, after Lavoie got the call from the Canadian federation to judge the Olympic pairs, he told Salé and Pelletier, "If you want someone other than me, I understand." But they didn't want anyone else. Now Lavoie is standing by the judges' table, watching the skaters climb down from the podium and skate a lap around the rink together, waving to the crowd. Jamie skates up to him at the judges' table. She is crying hard, which breaks his heart. "I'm so sorry," she says over and over, tears rolling down her exhausted face. Lavoie pats her cheek as she cries. "You're going to make history because of this performance tonight," he tells her. "Don't give up."

And this kind of special relationship is common in the judges' world. The Canadian federation encourages Lavoie to monitor Salé and Pelletier's progress, to drop in on their practices and give them his advice before they put a new program out in front of international judges. Communication between judges and their skaters is taken for granted. After the event the referee will often ask a judge to carry a message to his country's pair: *We marked them lower because that's an illegal lift—could you let them know?* It's understood that judges are close with their country's skaters. Nevertheless, to most people outside of skating the situation is odd, for it seems an obvious conflict of interest to have Olympic athletes being judged by their mentors and friends.

Lavoie's relationship to his pair is far from unique. The Chinese judge mentors Shen and Zhao, and the Russian judge monitors Berezhnaya and Sikharulidze; moreover, the Ukrainian judge really lives in Moscow and could be assumed to favor the Russians, and so on and so on. If one interrogates the various connections of the judges on the panel for even ten minutes it becomes clear that *all* judges—East or West, honest or crooked—have their favorites. The important thing, as people often say, is to vote based on what you see on the ice on this very night, and not merely based on who was your favorite going in.

And that is why Lavoie was so keyed up when he took his place at the judges' table earlier tonight. He was determined to judge what he saw, no matter how painful the result might be for him personally. To judge well Lavoie needed to remain in a state of hyperalertness for more than two hours. If he could have done so, he would have glued his eyelids open. He watched the final group with unwavering concentration, and when the Canadians finished he was absolutely sure that they had won—until the results were posted. Then he slammed his fist on the table.

But it wasn't until the marking sheet came down the table, hot off the copier, that he felt sure of what had happened. Lavoie grabbed the piece of paper and noted the five-to-four split. Then he traced his finger along the column of judges to judge number four, France. And there he saw what in his heart of hearts he must have been looking for: She had voted for the Russians. *Oh, my God*—Lavoie said to himself—*Marie-Reine.*

Now the skaters have left the ice and the arena is nearly empty. Lavoie grabs his bag, strides out through the backstage corridor, and gets on a bus for the judges' hotel. On the bus he doesn't talk to anyone. *Tonight,* he thinks, *my eyes were so sharp. I know what I saw.* The lights of Salt Lake City twinkle outside the bus window. The city has pasted giant photos of athletes on the downtown skyscrapers, twenty or thirty stories high, and the photos are lit up at night. This valley is encircled by snow-capped mountains, and on one of them, the Olympic rings will glow all night. It is late. Another Olympic event is over. And in Lavoie's opinion, the result was wrong, and it was completely unfair.

By the time he reaches the restaurant at the judges' hotel, everyone is already talking scandal, trading rumors. Lavoie can't take it. He goes upstairs to his room and sits down at his desk. He debates. It is a risk. He looks at a rule book, guidelines for reporting improper influence. The language is so dry in comparison with the situation, which makes your head throb.

It's a risk. Maybe someone is trying to trap him. Let's say that he does speak up. Will anyone even believe him? The people involved are sure to deny everything. Then it will be his word against theirs. In such cases, people often attack the whistle-blower and try to destroy his credibility. To be honest, he wishes he could just walk away.

But he can't. There was that intense moment tonight, when the crowd noise blurred in his ears as if in a dream, and Jamie Salé skated up to him, crying and saying, "I'm sorry, I'm sorry. . . ." And now Lavoie thinks: *I have to come forward. I have to tell what I know.* And he begins to write a letter.

Lavoie sits at his desk and calls up from memory an incident from four months ago, in Saskatoon, Saskatchewan, at a fall competition. Marie-Reine Le Gougne was the referee of the ladies' event; he was a judge for pairs. At first it was just one in a series of forgettable social evenings at competitions. Then something happened that stopped him cold. They were conversing in French, and Marie-Reine was enjoying his wit. Laughing, she turned to him and said, "Oh, Benoît, you're so funny. I like you very much. But I've already promised my good friend, the Russian judge for the Olympics, Marina Sanaya, that I will support the Russian team. But now I got to know you, and you're very nice, and I don't know what to do, really."

Lavoie puts down the incident on paper, as precisely as he can recall it. And then he describes an officials' dinner he attended in Salt Lake City, just twenty-four hours ago. It was the night between the short program and the free program. Lavoie writes that he was standing at the bar having a cocktail when Didier Gailhaguet came up to him and said: "You know, Benoît, it's going to be very hard for your team to win the competition to-morrow."

That really angered Lavoie. Gailhaguet isn't just the French federation president but also a member of the ISU Council, and Lavoie knew that it was against the rules for council members to talk to judges like that. Besides, based on what Marie-Reine had already told him in Saskatoon, Lavoie had a strong feeling that Gailhaguet might be trying to manipulate the results. So Lavoie let him have it. "You know," he said to Gailhaguet, "even if the Canadians deserve to win they might not; your judge will probably not put them first anyway." To which Gailhaguet replied, "Maybe tomorrow I will try to talk to Marie-Reine." At that point, Lavoie walked away.

As far as Lavoie can remember no one else witnessed this exchange with Gailhaguet, but he recalls that when Marie-Reine first told him about her agreement with the Russian judge, a Swiss judge was standing there with them. But God knows if the Swiss judge will be willing to corroborate his testimony. In this self-interested world of judging, nobody willingly talks about such things. Too often, telling the truth just boomerangs at you. But now Lavoie is clear about what he must do. He writes steadily, late into the night.

∞

Watching Benoît Lavoie console her son down by the ice, Murielle Bouchard aches to be able to do the same, but it will be hours yet. The Pelletiers gather their coats and ask Patti Salé if she's ready. They might as well walk over to Canada House, the athletes' lodge in the heart of the city. All that's left is to wait for the kids.

At this same moment, somewhere in Bosnia, Mathieu Pelletier, former figure skater and corporal in the Canadian army, is supposed to be doing an interview for Canadian television via satellite. Watching his brother skate a few minutes earlier, tears were streaming down the corporal's face. "I was so happy for him to be there at the Olympics. I get shivers all over when I watch him." Then the marks came up. Mathieu Pelletier said to the interviewer, "Just give me two minutes." He stepped outside, broke two hockey sticks against the wall, then walked back into the room. "Okay," he said. "Let's do it."

Mathieu Pelletier now steps up to the microphone and says: "They got screwed. They got screwed. They got"—and here a few choice obscenities—"screwed." The crew looks at him dubiously. "Okay," the interviewer sighs. "We're gonna send it to the CBC. But that's not gonna make it past the censors for sure." Mathieu Pelletier doesn't care. "So I was trash-talking big time," he says defiantly. "I know he won. I know what a deduction is." Back at the barracks, the other guys try to calm him down. "It's done," they say. "He's got the silver. That's it." But Mathieu Pelletier won't listen. "It's not over," he insists. "Someone will complain about it. Canada will do something."

And in fact at this moment in Salt Lake City, Canadian sports officials are formulating a strategy for their assault on the ISU. Everyone in skating knows that the ISU is basically Ottavio Cinquanta's dictatorship. Tomorrow, they are confident, Cinquanta will stall, obstruct the process, try to drag things out until after the Olympics. A key part of the plan, therefore, is what they call "keeping Ottavio on the spit." They will keep the pressure on Cinquanta by holding press conferences; they will use the outraged media to keep fanning the flames. Dick Pound, the Canadian IOC member, will flood the in-box of IOC president Jacques Rogge with e-mails from incensed fans around the world. Meanwhile Canada will fire off a formal appeal demanding immediate action. Through the night, Canadians in Salt Lake City and at federation headquarters in Toronto will collect evidence for the appeal. The Canadians' own investigation is already under way.

The Canadians know what they are up against. Olympic appeals have a pathetic rate of success. Even in clear-cut cases, justice usually takes years, not days. But the Canadian strategy is designed to cut through the morass. They want immediate results. By the end of the week Canada wants an admission of guilt from the ISU—and a second gold medal for its skaters.

∞

Backstage at the arena after the medal ceremony, Moskvina's antennae pick up the resentment right away. She knows what will happen now. At the press conference the media will try to make her pair into villains, and she is determined not to let them. "Behave properly," she says to Anton in Russian, as they wait backstage. "Don't make scandals."

They've just won the Olympics, for God's sake. They deserve to celebrate. But Moskvina can see already it isn't going to be that kind of night. American television wants an interview. The reporter says: "Yelena, was this what you wanted? To win *this way*?" Berezhnaya blinks. Even with her bad English, she gets the insinuation. "Which way?" she counters. "What do you mean, *this way*?"

In a backstage room, the exhausted medalists sit on a dais before a standing-room-only crowd of journalists. Microphones and cameras are everywhere. Anton Sikharulidze is emotionally spent. He just wants to be with his own people at Russia House, drinking vodka and celebrating his country's first gold medal of these Olympics. But that's at least another four hours away. He slouches at the table and lets out a hacking cough. He won't "make scandals," fine. But neither does he have the strength to put on an act for the journalists. A reporter takes the microphone and asks him: "Do you feel you deserve the gold medal?" And now the avalanche begins.

∞

Everywhere Jamie Salé and David Pelletier go, cameras are recording their faces. Through the haze of her heartbreak and complete exhaustion, now layered over with a false bravado, Jamie Salé is thinking, *Oh, we just need some privacy.* In the press conference just now, Dave, who is always so steady, actually broke down and cried. Jamie Salé doesn't like to show their private relationship in front of reporters; she tends not to kiss him in the skating rink or even hold his hand except to skate. But when he cried in the press conference, she reached over and squeezed his hand, and held on.

They have a long night ahead of them. At one-thirty in the morning they finally walk through the door of Canada House. Three hundred people are waiting for them and at least as many flags. When they walk in, everyone starts to sing "O Canada." "There was no taped music, you know, just everyone singing from their hearts," Patti Salé says. "It was *really* emotional. Then they gave us a moment to hug them." Jamie goes to her mom, then to her father and grandmother. David goes to his parents.

Murielle Bouchard is relieved to see her son, but she still finds the whole thing hard. She sees Jamie crying in the arms of her father, whom the girl doesn't get to see often, in front of everyone. The kids have no privacy whatsoever. After the first two minutes other people squeeze in front of the parents, who find themselves alone again. There are television cameras, crews, probably a dozen big microphones piled up on a table. Even here, during their break, someone now ushers them over to a table to give a press conference. And now the Pelletiers are proud of their son, because he takes the microphone and says, with remarkable good humor, "Hey guys, put the Kleenex away. Don't ever forget that this is an Olympic medal. A lot of people would like to have it. We have it, we're proud of what we've done. So there'll be no talk of getting ripped off. We're here to celebrate."

It is after two in the morning when they leave Canada House, and now they are passed from TV crew to TV crew. They are doing all these interviews because someone tells them they should; they are too tired, too dazed to worry about why they are doing it. Tomorrow morning, North America will wake up and hear Jamie talking about how her stomach was hurting but she wasn't going to give up. Sipping their coffee, people will hear David Pelletier say: "When the second mark came up, it was like a punch in the stomach." Pelletier will also say: "Figure skating is like that. If I didn't want this to happen to me, I would've gone down the hill on skis." Both of them will say they are proud of the silver medals hanging around their necks, and while they don't understand the judging, "That's their job. We do our job, they do theirs." When pressed, the nice-looking

Canadians say politely that they didn't see the Russians skate. When pressed further, they admit that it's strange that a month ago, at the Grand Prix Final, they got sixes on the second mark for the same program, whereas tonight, they "barely had" 5.9's, but they politely decline to speculate as to why.

Those low second marks are something that Jan Ullmark wonders about, too. The first time he saw the list of countries drawn for the Olympic judging panel, he knew it would be tough for his skaters to win. He just knew by looking. Because Ullmark understood that the former Eastern bloc was linked not just by politics but also by taste. And traditionally the North Americans stuck with Western Europe and Japan for the same reasons. Anyone looking at the lineup could've predicted a four–four split with the unpredictable French as a swing vote. But now Ullmark is thinking more and more about the rumors he heard when he arrived in Salt Lake—that his pair couldn't win no matter what happened on the ice. Ullmark is a reasonable man, and he doubts that. If the Russians had fallen outright he doesn't believe they would have automatically won. But when all that separates the top teams is a little mistake here or there, politics can make the difference. He's seen it a hundred times, if not more.

Ullmark doesn't say this to his skaters, though. To them he says, "You can only control what you can control. The part you can control, you did beautifully. The rest is beyond your control." They nod, they try to accept his wisdom. But the strain of not just this night but also the past nine months is written on their faces. They look drained and exhausted. Between takes, Jamie cries a lot. They don't fall into bed until seven the next morning.

$$\infty$$

After tossing and turning for hours, Marie-Reine Le Gougne finally gives up on sleep. All night her mind was racing, because last night, when she got back to the judges' hotel after the pairs' event, something extremely upsetting happened.

Last night, when Le Gougne walked into the hotel, the British chair of the prestigious ISU Technical Committee, Sally Stapleford, was standing there in the lobby. Stapleford gave her an angry look, and this unnerved Le Gougne, because she wants very badly to be elected to the ISU Technical Committee. For some time now Le Gougne has been planning to run for a spot on the Technical Committee at the next ISU Congress in two months' time. Being on the Technical Committee is the most important position a judge can hold, and Le Gougne has been building up to this for years. So to have the committee's chairwoman glaring at her in the lobby last night disturbed her considerably.

Sally Stapleford started speaking to her about integrity and honesty, implying, quite strongly, that she was lacking in such qualities because she had placed the Russian pair first. Le Gougne is a nervous type anyway, and with no less than Sally Stapleford giving her a dressing-down in front of all the judges passing through the lobby, she began to cry. Then two other members of the Technical Committee joined them, Walburga Grimm of Germany and Britta Lindgren of Sweden. At which point Sally Stapleford said to her, "Okay, tell them what you told me: Why did you do it?" After which all three committee members left convinced that the French federation had forced her to vote as she did as part of a deal with the Russians, to help their pair and—in exchange—get help for the French dance team, which had a shot at a gold medal later next week.

Then Sally Stapleford said, "But, Marie-Reine, how can you expect to be elected to the Technical Committee with judging like that?" And here Le Gougne completely broke down, because skating is her life. She lives with her parents and works as a skating administrator for her region; she spends most of her free time judging and going to skating seminars. And now here stood three members of the ISU Technical Committee, telling her that her whole career was about to be derailed just because she put the Russian pair first.

Then it really got bad, because Sally Stapleford told her that she had to write a letter confessing that she voted under pressure. Through her tears, Le Gougne refused to write any such letter. Very well, then, Stapleford said, she would write the letter herself. Le Gougne felt as if her head was about to explode. She had to get out of that lobby.

That was yesterday, and now, after a sleepless night, Marie-Reine Le Gougne is getting ready to go to the judges' event review meeting at nine o'clock this morning. Casually she flicks on CNN. The image on the screen slams into her consciousness. It is her own photograph. An announcer says that she is alleged to have colluded with the Russians in a deal for the Russians to win pairs, so the French could win the dance event. Le Gougne's nerves were already shot, but now she's overcome by the sensation that a nightmare is pressing in around her. But there's no time to deal with anything now; she has to board a shuttle van for the arena.

The backstage arena corridors are always full of cameras, but now, with a panicky feeling, Le Gougne realizes: *They're here for me.* She turns on her heel and walks briskly away from a television cameraman. Sure enough, he follows her. She ducks into the meeting room like a fugitive and sinks into a chair. The nine judges, two referees, and substitute judge wait in silence. No one says a word. Just before nine, she sees Sally Stapleford enter and hand a letter to the head referee. It's one more jolt to her nerves. An ISU official comes in to put tape over the cracks in the doorframe, explaining that reporters are hovering outside the door, trying to listen in.

They begin by discussing the short program, but everyone knows that's just a formality. All the tension in the room has a single object: the five–four split on the free program. When the referee, Ron Pfenning, an American, moves on to the free program, everyone's pulse quickens. Now Marina Sanaya of Russia is explaining why she put the Russians first. Now Benoît Lavoie justifies his placement of the Canadians. It's all very dignified. Everything is explained crisply, in the expert language of the judge. People are making an effort to drain all emotion from their words. Consequently the room is electric with unspoken feelings. Pfenning looks over at Marie-Reine Le Gougne. She looks teary-eyed. He decides not to ask her any direct questions; she volunteers nothing.

Pfenning declares that the meeting is officially over. But he now takes the unusual step of distributing copies of a personal letter he has written to the judges. He calls it a "private and confidential" statement of his own feelings about the event. He tells the judges that he had the Canadians first on his own marking sheet, which did not count towards the results, and that the judges who voted for the Russians made a serious mistake in judging.

Eleven heads bend over the letter, nine judges plus a substitute and Pfenning's assistant referee, a powerful Russian judge. Pfenning's letter is a high-handed guilt trip. "This was a very sad day for all judges and for our sport of figure skating. . . . Last night's judging was the greatest miscarriage of justice I have experienced in all my years of judging and refereeing. I am personally saddened. . . . You must now live with your decisions." In conclusion, Pfenning states that "the judging of the minority of the panel, plus the substitute, was fair and honest."

The letter has a profound effect on the room, especially the part where Pfenning implies that the judges who voted for the Russians were dishonest. Some judges start to cry, but Marie-Reine Le Gougne has a complete emotional outburst.

Later, Le Gougne will say, "That one word, 'dishonest,' destroyed me." She begins to shriek. She rambles on about the enormous pressure she is under, shouting and sobbing. She says that her federation president, Didier Gailhaguet, pressured her to vote for the Russians, that it was not her own choice. Turning to Pfenning, she makes an impassioned plea. "You must help us!" she cries. The ISU, she insists, must help judges to break free from the pressure of their federations.

The other judges are in a state of disbelief. No one has ever heard anybody confess like this in a judges' meeting. Although what Le Gougne is saying is pretty damning, the other judges mainly feel sorry for her, and not just because she's clearly a very emotional woman. Most of them have judged with her before. She has the reputation of being an otherwise excellent judge who has a tendency to overmark French skaters. For example, at the last Olympics, she gave the French skater, who won only the bronze medal, the only perfect six of the night. But everybody knows the stories of the French federation pressuring judges. And what judge hasn't felt some pressure, subtle or sledgehammer-like, from his or her federation?

Marie-Reine Le Gougne must be at least the thousandth judge to ever vote under pressure from her federation. But she might be the first one to ever admit it in a judges' meeting; and for this there is a mixture of sympathy and even some admiration, because if she didn't open her mouth and say these words, no one would ever be the wiser. Perhaps the same emotional susceptibility that made her vulnerable to pressure from Gailhaguet also makes her vulnerable to pressure from Pfenning's guilt-trip letter— who knows? A lot of people in the room actually like her at this moment, and almost all of them feel sorry for her.

Pfenning collects the copies of his letter. The judges leave through a back door, to avoid the cameras lying in wait for them outside the main entrance to the room. Marie-Reine Le Gougne, still overwrought, manages to escape that way. The media chase has begun.

By the time she reaches the judges' hotel and tells the front desk to refuse all reporters' calls, the ISU president is live on television. Ottavio Cinquanta is fielding hostile questions from the Olympic press conference venue. Reporters, mostly American and Canadian, are attacking from all sides. Cinquanta refuses to hold an ISU Council meeting on the subject until next week. It could be months, he admits, before any action is taken.

Then, boxed into a corner by a reporter, Cinquanta admits that the referee of the pairs event has been presented with an allegation of misconduct. The reporters grab the misconduct revelation and won't let go. The Canadian strategy kicks into high gear: Ottavio is on the spit. Now Canadian officials step into the press room just vacated by Cinquanta to announce that Canada is appealing the pairs decision and demanding immediate action.

Hiding in her hotel room, Le Gougne watches Cinquanta and realizes that sooner or later, the ISU president will be asking for her. And by the very next morning Le Gougne is sitting with Cinquanta behind closed doors. Cinquanta is in a hurry. He has a press conference in an hour. So the two of them discuss the matter in private, and then he calls in the ISU general secretary to witness a statement. The statement gives Le Gougne the greatest possible wiggle room. She admits that, during the event review meeting, she said that Gailhaguet asked her to place the Russians first— but she adds that "my emotional condition at that moment was not such . . . to give a proper response." She denies that she really thought the Canadians were the better team, and she denies any deal with the Russians. Le Gougne signs the statement, and Cinquanta goes off to tell the reporters that he now has both "an allegation and a denial." But Marie-Reine Le Gougne is already fleeing. She leaves her meeting with Cinquanta by a series of back entrances, discreetly picks up her luggage, and goes into hiding.

∞

Bruce Edwards, a college student in Salt Lake City, learned French on his Mormon mission. He was so thrilled when he found out he would be an Olympic volunteer that, in his words, "I decided to keep a diary of my Olympic experience, for myself and my posterity." Edwards didn't keep a written diary but spoke into a tape recorder every night after he got off work.

Bruce Edwards's assignment was working as a chauffeur for the head of the whole French delegation, Didier Gailhaguet. Gailhaguet was also the head of the French skating federation, but Edwards knew almost nothing about skating, so they didn't talk much about it. Bruce Edwards thought Didier Gailhaguet was a nice guy, and he really enjoyed driving him around to all his different appointments. That's why Edwards was so surprised when, a day or two after the pair skating event ended, he started hearing all this stuff on the radio about the French skating federation making a deal with the Russians. Every time he opened a newspaper, there was another story about the French judge and how she had been pressured. That troubled Bruce Edwards, so he went back and listened to his tapes. And then he really became alarmed.

It turned out that on Saturday, February 9, the day of the pairs short program, Edwards had overheard Gailhaguet speaking in English on his cell phone. "He had a phone conversation that seemed strange to me," Edwards later testified. "Because I was not familiar with the figure skating world at that time, I did not want to ask him questions or dig into what was going on. But it sounded to me like Didier was talking to another nation and arranging the results. That was what I thought at the time. He gave, I think, two scenarios, saying, 'If this happens we want to do this, but if this happens we want to do this.'" On his tape recorder, Edwards said it "was about who would win in one area and who would win in another." At the time, Edwards didn't understand the technical jargon, but after he started reading about this swap between dance and pairs, it started to make more sense.

Later on that same day, Edwards overheard Gailhaguet speaking in English to someone named Natalya. "He said the meeting had gone as well as he had hoped, and he was glad that he did not give the 'gift' that day, that they would wait until the following day which was Sunday." Sunday was also the day between the pairs short and the pairs free program.

Later on, more things seemed strange to Bruce Edwards. Why was Gailhaguet's secretary, the lady who kept his schedule, sitting in the French delegation office, frantically copying down all the judges' marks off the television during the pairs short program? And why had Gailhaguet gone to the judges' hotel on Monday, the day of the pairs final?

So Edwards talked it over with his supervisor, an IOC official named Michel Filliau, and Filliau told him he thought he should take his evidence to the ISU. Filliau had been hearing the same things from another of Gailhaguet's chauffeurs, Marie-Odile Devillers. Devillers was a volunteer, but in her professional life she was a judge in the French Ministry of Justice, and Filliau was inclined to take her seriously as a witness. She had told him with absolute certainty that Gailhaguet was calling judges on his cell phone. "She gave me a couple names, saying, 'You know, this is the Russian judge,'" Filliau later testified. "But I am unable to repeat the names." When pressed, the best Filliau could do in terms of a judge's name was vague. He remembered Devillers asking him, "'Do you know Mrs. Sheet, or Seev?'"

Filliau was a careful man, so he asked Devillers some questions. "I checked with her very precisely, saying, 'Marie Devillers, you are a judge in France. You are in front of this kind of case in the civil courts. Are you sure about what you say?' She told me, 'I know perfectly how to call this in my job. This is purely influence.' She was very clear about this."

But how, Filliau asked her, could Gailhaguet have been so careless as to speak in front of her? "And she told me, 'Because I think that this gentleman is such in the system—for him it's so normal—that that's it.'"

According to Bruce Edwards, Didier Gailhaguet called him at ten-thirty on the night before he was slated to testify. Edwards says that Gailhaguet "wanted to know why I was going to speak to the ISU" and offered to let Edwards "ask him anything, and he would explain." So Edwards asked him about the "gift," and Gailhaguet told him that Natalya's husband manufactured gifts that the French Olympic committee gave out to various people. Then Edwards asked Gailhaguet about his meeting at the judges' hotel on the day of the pairs free program. Though Gailhaguet kept a detailed schedule, somehow he "could not remember what it was for."

Gailhaguet's explanations didn't satisfy Bruce Edwards, so he came to the ISU as scheduled and gave his testimony. And that pretty much erased the possibility that the whole scandal could be pinned on Marie-Reine Le Gougne.

∞

In the hidden judges' world in Salt Lake City, in the shuttle vans and the hotel restaurant and the hospitality suite, Marie-Reine Le Gougne's confession has produced nothing less than an earthquake. Finally, someone has confessed to wrongdoing at an important moment. Finally, there is something concrete to back up all the suspicions and rumors. And to most of the judges who move in this shadowy world, the story fits.

Le Gougne would be the type to break down under pressure and confess, that part makes sense. She is known for being passionate about skating, almost to a fault. More than once, she has cried on the job. And Le Gougne could easily have been susceptible to pressure from Gailhaguet. Most obviously, there is that lonely six she gave to France's Philippe Candeloro at the 1998 Olympics. Forever afterwards, Le Gougne has defended that six. But Candeloro's own take, published this week in a French paper, is illuminating. "If she hadn't helped me, I wouldn't have won a medal," Candeloro says bluntly. "All the countries do the same. There are schemes, there is collusion. And if France did not scheme, it wouldn't win any medals. It's easy to attack Marie-Reine Le Gougne, although she only did what she was told to do."

The story fits, too, because Gailhaguet is well known for leaning on his judges. Even here in Salt Lake City, the first vice president of the ISU, Katsuichiro Hisanaga, openly told a reporter that "it's not the first time for Didier to make such pressure. There were other cases in the past." Former French judges have made allegations in the newspapers that Didier had told them to overmark certain skaters and undermark others. "In France," one judge, Alain Miquel, told *The Washington Post,* "people cannot judge the way they want to judge. If they don't report [the pressure] to the ISU, it is because they are scared of Didier. It is a kind of monarchy. It's like a Mafia, and he's the boss. He's got the power. He can decide on anything. The judges are people who are very fond of figure skating. It's very important for them to go on being involved in figure skating, and he has the power to say you won't be involved anymore."

Gailhaguet's own letters to his judges have done nothing for his reputation. In one of them, Gailhaguet, then the French team leader, asks judges to meet with him on the eve of the 1994 Olympics to develop a "conquering strategy" to give France "political influence" at upcoming events. Another judge, Francis Betsch, told a reporter that Gailhaguet used to gather judges together at meetings to talk about "countries that would help and others that wouldn't . . . it was like going to a war, where you have enemies and partners."

On top of all the allegations there are the ISU statistics, which in 1999 showed that Gailhaguet's judges had the worst percentage of "national bias" of any country in the ISU: fifteen percent compared with the overall average of five percent. That year the ISU briefly considered a proposal to ban all French judges from judging for one year. However, France was not banned, and its record dramatically improved over the next few years. People speculated that perhaps the situation in France had improved.

Then Marie-Reine Le Gougne broke down in front of eleven eyewitnesses at the Olympics and said that she had voted under pressure from Gailhaguet.

∞

Didier Gailhaguet is not a man to take such accusations lightly. He is, after all, a member of the ISU Council. Now he is unceremoniously suspended from that post while the council meets to discuss the pairs event.

A beleaguered-looking Ottavio Cinquanta convenes the council. He doesn't want to be here, but the president of the IOC has just released an open letter telling the ISU to act quickly and resolve the situation. So now Cinquanta convenes the council, minus Gailhaguet, to formulate a plan of action. The ISU investigators have been collecting letters and taking sworn statements for a week. Now the council reviews the evidence.

So far, Benoît Lavoie has testified that Le Gougne told him she planned to put the Russians first months ago. Sally Stapleford and the other Technical Committee members have testified that Marie-Reine Le Gougne confessed to collusion in the hotel lobby. Eight judges have testified that Le Gougne confessed to voting under pressure at the judges' meeting, and Le Gougne herself has signed a statement confirming it. Bruce Edwards and Michel Filliau have testified that Gailhaguet spoke to judges before the pairs event, and Benoît Lavoie says that Gailhaguet approached him improperly before the pairs event. Le Gougne and Gailhaguet insist that they've done nothing wrong.

In the Canadians' formal appeal, which is somewhere in each council member's stack of paperwork, Canada has put forward its own solution: a dual gold medal. Cinquanta knows that without a second gold medal, the Canadians are going to go forward with their appeal to the Court for Arbitration of Sport (CAS). CAS is the only legal institution with authority over the ISU. If the appeal goes forward, that means a full-on investigation of the ISU by an independent body. Within twenty-four hours, CAS's lawyers will be expertly deposing the entire judging panel from the pairs event. That seems like the last thing Cinquanta would want. He's trying to keep the scope of this disaster as narrow as possible.

So the ISU Council members vote to void Le Gougne's vote. They will declare the pairs event a tie, and give a second gold medal to Salé and Pelletier. Le Gougne and Gailhaguet are suspended, pending further hearings in the spring. The ISU kicks the matter up to the IOC Council members, who are only too happy to put the thing to bed. One week after the competition, it's official: The Canadians are going to get their gold medal in a second awards ceremony at the Olympic venue.

Jamie Salé and David Pelletier, exhausted from a solid week of media frenzy, are still asleep when the phone rings. "You guys better get over to the press center," their agent says cheerfully, "because you're going to get a gold medal."

Jamie Salé feels elated, exhausted—and cheated out of her Olympic moment. All those years, she visualized herself standing on the top step, seeing her flag go up, hearing her anthem. She was cheated out of that.

David Pelletier feels relief. At least they're out of that interminable limbo, that horrible false position of being celebrated for being the Canadians who got robbed. Salé and Pelletier tell the press that they hope that the investigation will keep going.

Pelletier is weary. He is happy for himself, of course, but his great hope is that the truth will come out and the system will improve. No other skater should ever have to go through this. Pelletier doesn't yet realize that at the very moment that he was awarded the gold, the Canadian Olympic Association dropped its CAS appeal, and at that instant, all hope of an independent investigation vanished. The investigation is now in the hands of Ottavio Cinquanta.

∞

Within the hour, Sayabec is celebrating wildly, although there are still some people who can't get over the fact that the *French* judge is the one who cheated Quebec. The Pelletiers are packing their bags to fly back to Salt Lake City. Patti Salé gets a call from the Canadian federation. "They said they'd like to take me down there," she recalls. "And I remember thinking, Boy, I hope they're paying for it all, 'cause I sure as heck can't afford it!"

The next evening Patti Salé is up in the crowded stands of the Salt Lake Ice Center again, watching her daughter step out for the gold medal ceremony. She's so high up that she can only see "little tiny pieces of them," so she watches on the Jumbotron screen. Jumbotron or not, to Patti Salé the whole thing is "kind of anticlimactic." Don't get her wrong: She's thrilled that her daughter is going to be a gold medalist for the rest of her life. But this ceremony is just painfully awkward for the athletes.

Yelena Berezhnaya and Anton Sikharulidze are standing by the skaters' entrance in their warm-up suits. To them, the whole spectacle is ridiculous. Berezhnaya sums it up in her broken English: "Everybody watching monkey show." The Russian press is eating them alive for even coming to the ceremony, but others argue that if they hadn't come, it would have looked as if the Canadians were the only gold medalists.

Both Berezhnaya and Sikharulidze have lost a lot of weight over the past week. When they are not on camera, Sikharulidze's face is anxious and drawn. "From many sides," he says vehemently, "we are the best pair in the world, and it means we *deserve* this gold medal." Now the Americans have made them look like cheaters. Anton particularly despises how the American TV people, the very ones for whom they moved to Hackensack three years ago to build relationships for this Olympics, "show only one side." Reporters quote Internet polls where ninety-five percent of Americans say the Canadians should have won. All week long, on every channel, they are called "the Russians." And now the Russians just want to get the hell out of here and go back to Russia, where ninety-five percent of the population considers *them* the hands-down winners.

The Chinese are not here. The American media reports that they are missing the ceremony "to observe traditional Chinese New Year celebrations." Zhao Hongbo finds that pretty hilarious. Like most Chinese people, he found the idea of two gold medals too unorthodox for his tastes. Results should stand. But mainly he didn't go to the ceremony because it had nothing to do with him. "Now," he says slyly, "if they had wanted to give me a silver medal, I would have gone."

On this night the people inside skating fall into two camps. One, largely North American, celebrates the victory as a triumph of fairness, a victory over the typical apathy and pessimism that allow bad results to stand. Finally, somebody got Ottavio Cinquanta to act against the collusion that everybody knows is endemic to the sport. To this camp, the second gold medal represents hard-won progress.

The other camp, largely from Communist and former Communist countries, feels that it is wrong to subvert the idea of one gold medal, one Olympic champion. Results shouldn't change. The Russians in particular are bitter. "For two years," Moskvina says, "we considered that Yelena and Anton won." She thinks of the Chaplin program that she believed won the 2001 World Championships outright, but which lost on a six–three decision. "However, it went to the other couple. We didn't accuse the North American bloc, we just accepted." Sikharulidze goes further. If roles were reversed, he says, and the Russians were the ones who had just lost a close five–four decision, "not one person" in North America would make a fuss.

Le Gougne has already admitted to pressure, but nobody thinks this scandal stops there. Who else was in on it? Why would the French federation want to push the Russians? Nobody knows, and it's doubtful that the ISU will make more than a superficial effort to find out.

The double gold medal ceremony is to be packaged as a heartwarming story of Olympic sportsmanship. What no one in the crowd can guess is that the foremost emotion of all four athletes is exhaustion. Sikharulidze is just really happy this thing is finally over. He too feels cheated of his gold medal experience; he is on a continent that has considered him an impostor from the moment they hung the medal around his neck. On that night, the American television commentators said outright he should not have won. The first time he was announced as Olympic champion, the applause distinctly dropped down from the level where it had been for the Canadians. That didn't feel too good.

This manufactured moment is pretty meager consolation for both pairs. Television cameras are inches from their faces. There might as well be a director with a bullhorn yelling "Act natural! This is fun! Now, show us *friendship*!" Waiting to go on, the four skaters rack their brains to find something, anything to talk about. They laugh unnaturally. All of them feel awkward. It's the fakest moment imaginable.

The strange thing about the ceremony is how little it has to do with the athletes, or with the Olympics, or with anything that matters to the four people now on the podium. David Pelletier knows that justice has been done only because of the North American media; if it weren't for them, he wouldn't be getting this medal. The medal didn't come, as it ought to have, from his skating. This whole display is phony, and if you want proof of it, you need look no further than Ottavio Cinquanta, the man now hanging a gold medal around Pelletier's neck, who in future months will effectively block Pelletier's one wish—that the full truth come out.

∞

Two months later, in April, the ISU Council called witnesses to Lausanne for the hearing of Marie-Reine Le Gougne and Didier Gailhaguet. The purpose of the hearing, as its transcripts reveal, was to find both parties guilty—but only precisely guilty enough to warrant suspension, not expulsion. Cinquanta marched the hearing down a very narrow path. The ISU paid the travel expenses of only its own hand-picked witnesses, and Cinquanta ruled the hearing with a firm hand. He kept the hearing on a tight schedule, which effectively prevented the kind of second-tier questions that might have ferreted out accomplices and new evidence. Whenever new evidence of wrongdoing by judges or officials leaked into the hearing—say, allegations of misconduct at another event—Cinquanta would interrupt and say, "Please concentrate on the events of Salt Lake City."

Cinquanta gave the ISU's lawyers only enough time to establish that Le Gougne had confessed to voting under pressure from Gailhaguet and that Gailhaguet had made phone calls to judges. The ISU lawyers did not seek to establish the identity of any Russians who might have colluded with the French.

Benoît Lavoie appeared; and the Swiss judge who had been present for his fateful November conversation with Le Gougne, Christine Blanc, backed him up. Bruce Edwards testified. So did the three judges other than Lavoie who had voted for the Canadians. But with the exception of Le Gougne, none of the judges who had voted for the Russians was present. The ISU had not invited them.

The hearing had certain irregularities. Since Le Gougne and Gailhaguet had been most basically accused of making a deal with the Russians, one would have expected the Russian judge and the president of the Russian federation to be there, but the ISU had not invited them. Marie-Odile Devillers, who, according to Filliau, knew the names of judges that Gailhaguet had spoken to on his cell phone, was not there; nor did the ISU introduce any evidence that might have been in her sworn statement. One might have expected the ISU to call the Chinese judge from the panel as a witness. He had abruptly left Salt Lake City on the day after the pairs event, despite the fact that he was scheduled to judge another event later in the week. And though his federation's press release had claimed he was ill, *The New York Times* had reported that the judge privately told friends he was not ill at all. But the Chinese judge wasn't invited to the hearing, either.

So Cinquanta and his legal team marched everyone down the path, and the witnesses repeated the basic story: Le Gougne had confessed to voting under pressure from Gailhaguet, and Gailhaguet had been talking to judges improperly before the event. Le Gougne's defense (and by extension, Gailhaguet's) was that her confession in the judges' meeting was merely nonsense, which she had uttered while in an overwrought emotional condition.

This emotional state, she claimed, was brought on by the extraordinary pressure of the Olympic Games and the harassment of a "pro-Canadian" lobby. She asserted that one man had temporarily barred her from leaving the judges' stand, that people in the corridor after the event had pushed her, that the three women from the Technical Committee had verbally harassed her and put words in her mouth, and that Pfenning's letter itself was a form of harassment. She denied ever telling Pfenning, Stapleford, Lindgren, Grimm, Blanc, or Lavoie that the French federation had a deal with the Russians, and she further accused Lavoie of trying to get her to "help" his pair. This was Le Gougne's defense: that she had ac-cused Gailhaguet, but falsely.

For his part, Didier Gailhaguet vehemently denied any wrongdoing. He confirmed that he had spoken with Le Gougne by telephone in Salt Lake City before the pairs event—but only, he insisted, about getting her French team uniform delivered, and about the pressure she felt because other camps were "lobbying" for the Canadian couple. Gailhaguet admit-ted that he had spoken to Benoît Lavoie on the eve of the pairs final and told him that it was "going to be a hard competition." But according to Gailhaguet, it was Lavoie who approached *him* and asked about "the posi-tion of Marie-Reine on the pairs event." Gailhaguet admitted speaking about judging on his cell phone in front of his chauffeurs, but insisted that he had merely been speaking about the judging and results of the French National Championships that had already taken place. "If I had special things to say," he declared, "I would not take a car with my chauffeur." Gailhaguet further asserted that the former French judges who had spo-ken out against him had done so simply because they had lost internal po-litical battles in the French federation. And Gailhaguet produced letters from other judges stating that he had never pressured them.

To those assembled in Lausanne, it was clear what motive Le Gougne and Gailhaguet would have to deny the allegations. What was difficult to imagine was what possible motive fifteen judges from various countries, a Mormon college kid, and a French magistrate would have for planning an elaborate conspiracy against them. In the end, the hearing led to its intended result. Le Gougne and Gailhaguet were found guilty of pre-judging the Olympic pairs event in favor of the Russians. But their motive was not determined, and their accomplices were not identified.

Le Gougne and Gailhaguet, who had caused the greatest embarrass-ment to the ISU and the sport in decades, each received a three-year sus-pension, plus a special prohibition from taking part in the 2006 Olympics, to be held in Cinquanta's native Italy. The verdict was a crushing blow to reform-minded judges and skaters, who had hoped for a lifetime ban for Le Gougne and Gailhaguet. The ISU had spoken: even if a judge pro-voked a huge scandal at the Olympic Games, the worst the judge would face was a three-year suspension.

Meanwhile, in Lausanne, Marie-Reine Le Gougne vowed to appeal her suspension all the way up to the independent Court for Arbitration of Sport. She would take Cinquanta and the ISU before a third-party judge and reveal damaging truths about the ISU. "I will explain how it functions," she declared. "It is a system that is extremely slanted, dictatorial, and even corrupt."

Gailhaguet, still fuming, threatened to drag Cinquanta through the mud with them. "If Mr. Cinquanta thinks he's protected his small, personal position, and that he's stopped this infernal machine he's set in motion, he is completely wrong," Gailhaguet warned. "This story is only at its beginning."

So once again, the unlucky band of reformers around the world felt hopeful, for what if Gailhaguet and Le Gougne were mad enough to start talking, to tell what they implied they knew? But within two months it was all gone. By May Gailhaguet issued a statement saying that his decision not to appeal "served as a gesture of appeasement and shows the trust Monsieur Gailhaguet places in the ISU." By June Le Gougne had dropped her appeal for "financial reasons," namely that the ISU would force her to pay its court costs if she lost.

In May Didier Gailhaguet easily won reelection to the presidency of the French federation. He might be banned from the ISU, but for the next four years Gailhaguet had the right to hand-pick every French judge who got an ISU assignment, the right to cross people off the judges' list who displeased him. That summer, in a gesture of open defiance, Gailhaguet ignored his suspension and went to the ISU Congress. That fall, when the ISU Grand Prix series came to Paris, he, like Marie-Reine Le Gougne, mingled freely in the stands. How this could be consistent with their suspensions was hard to understand, but the ISU took no action against them.

∞

By coincidence, on the same April day that Le Gougne and Gailhaguet received their suspensions, Jamie Salé and David Pelletier held their own press conference to announce their retirement from ISU competition. They would turn pro and skate with an ice show. No one missed the subtext: They weren't going to skate in any more competitions controlled by the ISU.

The Canadians sat on the dais, fielding questions, just as they had at a press conference two months before. On that February day Salé and Pelletier had spoken in front of the Olympic rings, thanking the powerful people who had awarded them a second gold medal. In their voices was a depth of understanding and common sense that no one else in the whole mess seemed to possess.

"Justice was done," David Pelletier said then. "And it doesn't take anything away from the Russians. This was not something against them. It was something against the system." Pelletier hadn't slept in a week. He was weary and sick to death of the whole thing, and he just wanted his old life back. But somehow he could see beyond the moment; he could see that he was going to be fine, but that younger skaters were still going to have to live under an unjust system. So he made a plea for them. "We hope," Pelletier said, "that the inquiries won't stop here, and that it will keep on going." Beside him, Jamie Salé added, "We sure hope the truth comes out."

In light of the fact that the ISU hearing in Lausanne seemed designed to prevent the truth from coming out, the Canadians' request now appeared hopelessly naive. In Lausanne there was a collection of people assembled who knew enough to put a hundred big holes in the ISU's leaky ship. But all of them kept their heads down.

By now David Pelletier surely realized that the inquiries wouldn't be pursued. The ISU "investigation" absolutely refused to follow the leads that cried out to be followed: Who was Didier Gailhaguet talking to on his cell phone? What "gift" did he give on the day before the pairs final? Who did Gailhaguet meet at the judges' hotel on that day? Who was on the Russian side of the deal?

The ISU apparently wasn't interested. No, the truth would not come out, because the people at the top of the sport wouldn't seek it.

∞

From February until July it was a little-known fact that, while still in Salt Lake City, both Marie-Reine Le Gougne and Didier Gailhaguet had been approached for questioning by the FBI. The FBI wanted to know what two French skating officials knew about a reputed mobster from Uzbekistan named Alimzhan Tokhtakhounov. The FBI believed that Tokhtakhounov, in addition to being involved in drug distribution and the sale of illegal firearms, had also engineered a Russian-French fix of the Olympic pairs and dance events, and the FBI said it had the wiretap evidence to prove it.

Le Gougne refused to talk to the FBI, but an agent did manage to question Gailhaguet in Salt Lake City, and according to the FBI, Gailhaguet admitted that he had met with Tokhtakhounov in his office in Paris. Tokhtakhounov, who apparently had a lot of money, enjoyed socializing with Russian sports stars and living the good life in France and

Italy. He came to see Gailhaguet to offer a gift of "large amounts of money" to the French federation to "organize a professional hockey team." After several conversations, Tokhtakhounov told Gailhaguet he needed a favor: He wanted Gailhaguet's help in extending his French visa. Gailhaguet told Tokhtakhounov that he would see what could be done and contacted a sports official in the French government. This official warned Gailhaguet not to get involved with Tokhtakhounov. At this point, Gailhaguet told the FBI, he told Tokhtakhounov that the French federation wasn't interested in his proposal, and didn't speak to Tokhtakhounov again.

The FBI's case, outlined in a complaint unsealed in July, went farther. Apparently Tokhtakhounov was a close associate of the skater Marina Anissina, a Russian who skated for France and had just won the Olympic gold in ice dance. Tokhtakhounov had vacationed with her, dined with her, and talked to both Anissina and her mother on the telephone from his villa in Italy. Some of those calls had been taped by the Italian police, and now the FBI's complaint produced wiretap evidence of Tokhtakhounov talking to several people about fixing the Olympics so that the Russians could win the pairs and his friend Marina Anissina, skating for France, could win the dance.

When the story first broke, it sounded like a joke. Now the FBI was investigating *figure skating*? That a reputed gangster could be involved with an Olympic fix was so sordid, so beyond what anyone had imagined, that surely now the ISU would *have* to act.

The U.S. government went public with its complaint against Tokhtakhounov. The next day the story was splashed all over newspapers around the Northern Hemisphere. The FBI had wiretap evidence showing that a week before the Olympics, Tokhtakhounov had called a Russian mobster for the phone number of a contact inside the Russian skating federation. He wanted to help Anissina, and his mobster friend assured him that the Russian skating federation contact "is a good guy, he will do it . . . because there is a lot for him there."

According to tapes, the day after the pairs final, Tokhtakhounov talked with a Russian coconspirator, who told him, "Our French have amazed me in a good way . . . because now the French with their vote pulled out that pair . . . made them champions. . . . Our Sikharulidze fell, the Canadians were ten times better, and in spite of that, the French with their vote gave us first place." In subsequent calls, Tokhtakhounov and his accomplices outlined a plan to get enough judges to give the French the ice dance medal and bragged about how well the pairs fix had gone. The wiretapped conversation echoed the remark attributed to Le Gougne by two women from the Technical Committee who had spoken to her in the lobby of the judges' hotel: "I had to do it. . . . It was a deal with the Russians, first place for first place."

According to the FBI and the wiretap transcripts, two weeks after the Olympics, Marina Anissina, now the Olympic gold medalist, called Tokhtakhounov from France. She apologized for not calling sooner, but she said that Didier Gailhaguet had come to her room in the Olympic village and taken her "to the car," where, in privacy, he warned her that the FBI was questioning him and she shouldn't call Tokhtakhounov from the States. She told Tokhtakhounov that his Russian coconspirator "came up to me and started yelling at me, 'call Alik,' but [Didier] forbid me to call, so I could not call." Tokhtakhounov accepted her apology and assured her that he had done a good job for her: Even had she stumbled, Tokhtakhounov bragged, she still would have won the Olympics.

In July Tokhtakhounov was arrested and taken to an Italian jail. Through his lawyer, Tokhtakhounov asserted his innocence and vowed to fight extradition; meanwhile the U.S. Attorney's office prepared to prosecute him as soon as he could be extradited. And the ISU remained silent. This was too much for the American and Canadian skating federations, who issued press releases pressuring the ISU to acknowledge the charges. Finally, after a few days of criticism in the papers, the ISU released a statement. "If and when the ISU receives from Italian or U.S. authorities evidence establishing . . . improper conduct to influence the results at the Salt Lake City Olympic Winter Games," the press release said, "the ISU will immediately commence further disciplinary actions." The ISU already had the text of the FBI complaint, as well as the wiretap transcripts provided to the Associated Press by the Italian police. Those documents alone would appear to justify further investigation. But incredibly, the ISU didn't act—except to send a letter asking federation presidents to come forward if they knew anything about Tokhtakhounov. That such allegations of corruption could be all but ignored by a federation controlling an Olympic sport was unbelievable, but the ISU had already found two culprits, and, apparently, two was enough.

∞

Marie-Reine Le Gougne went home to Strasbourg and was not heard from for many months. A year after the scandal, she published a book in

France about her life and experiences. Few people read it, but for those who did, there were interesting clues.

Who was Marie-Reine Le Gougne? She was a skating fanatic who had grown up skating on the small lakes of the French High Alps. It was in her alpine village, at the age of six, that she first felt the irresistible pull of the Olympic Games. She had skated in a celebration to mark the passage of the Olympic torch through the town on its way to Grenoble for the 1968 Winter Games, an experience that moved her profoundly. The ideal took hold deep inside her, and the Olympics became her lifelong passion.

She might have gotten to the Olympics as a skater, but when Le Gougne was thirteen her older brother died in a tragic diving accident, and after that, skating was never the same. She drifted away from competing, eventually, she quit. And yet, like many former skaters, she found it hard to give up the sport altogether. By the time she was twenty she had decided to become a judge. She was determined "to give skaters what the French federation had never given me: fairness and respect." She found French skating to be an old boys' club, where a woman had to work twice as hard to get ahead. So she judged any competition, anywhere, even on a moment's notice. And with this strategy she progressed rapidly up the ladder and made important friends at the top. At twenty-five she was already judging international competitions. By the incredibly young age of thirty-six, she had reached the ultimate goal: judging at the 1998 Olympics. She was honored by the ISU with a promotion to referee, and then she got the coveted assignment to judge the 2002 Olympics—two Olympics in a row! It was quite a coup. But still, Le Gougne wanted more.

Specifically, she wanted to be elected to the ISU Technical Committee—the most prestigious position an ISU judge can hold. She wanted desperately to be on that committee. And this very spring, at the ISU Congress, the French federation—that is to say, Didier Gailhaguet—had planned to put Le Gougne forward as a candidate for the ISU Technical Committee. She was *that close*. But then came Salt Lake City. And by the time Le Gougne came home to Strasbourg she knew she would never be a candidate for anything in the ISU again. She had become a pariah.

So Le Gougne stayed home in Strasbourg, cut off from her former world. But as time passed, a strange thing began to happen. The ISU judges who rode in the shuttle vans and ate in the dining rooms began to speak of her differently. People became more sympathetic to her. They began to say, "I wonder why she spoke." People said, "You know, if Marie-Reine hadn't spoken, nobody could have argued. It was a five–four decision. It came up *because* of her, *because* she confessed." And some people said, "She wasn't the first to vote under pressure—she was the first to admit it." And that put her in a different light.

She was not a hero, surely. In the aftermath she had denied it all, gone straight back to Didier Gailhaguet and made amends. But for one moment, which was enough, she had spoken the truth that all of them knew but didn't dare to utter—and in the cushy world these judges lived in, this was mildly heroic. She had spoken up, she had named names. Admittedly, she was emotional, and she had later called her own words untrustworthy. A terrible witness. But in combination with the raft of witnesses coming in to shore—a motley group that included a Mormon college kid, a French magistrate, the Italian police, and the FBI—it began to add up. Something bad had gone on, but the truth would not come out, because the ISU frankly didn't want to pursue it. But Marie-Reine Le Gougne had spoken, and she had said one thing that was unforgettable. She had said: "You must help us."

"You must help us," Marie-Reine Le Gougne had said to the powerful people she confessed to: American, British, German, and Swedish judges—judges from countries where judges were allowed to be relatively independent minded. But the American referee, the British chairwoman of the Technical Committee—these people did not help her. They did not intercede on her behalf, they did not offer to join forces with her and help her take down Gailhaguet. Instead they left her to fend for herself. And as she was not in any condition to stand alone, she fell into the arms of the French federation.

"You must help us!" she had cried. "The ISU must help the judges to be free from pressure from their federations." But no one did help. And a few months after the Olympics, Cinquanta pushed his own ingenious reform through the ISU Congress. For the first time in the hundred-year history of the sport, judges became anonymous. The scoreboard would now hide their identities: You could no longer link a judge with his or her marks. And in one fell swoop, Cinquanta guaranteed that nothing like the Salt Lake City scandal would ever happen again. Because in future Olympics, no one would ever know how an individual judge had voted. It would be impossible for a spectator to look up at a scoreboard and catch a cheating judge.

For a time some people still held out hope that the FBI's investigation of Tokhtakhounov would accomplish what the ISU leadership never would. When the case came to trial, the FBI would name names and hold all the guilty parties accountable. But in July 2003, one year after Tokhtakhounov's arrest, the Italian Supreme Court surprised the FBI by blocking the extradition of Tokhtakhounov. It was a crushing setback for the FBI. Tokhtakhounov was set free and immediately flew to Russia, where the United States had no power to extradite him, and the last hope of discovering the truth disappeared with him.

Epilogue

∞

*O*N LATE MAY IN THE GASPÉSIE, the ice on the lake breaks into pieces and floats a little while longer. Sunset finds the floating shards and illuminates them, as if from within; they glow pink on the dark blue water. Driving through the countryside there is the strong smell of the fields spread with manure. Pockets of snow still nestle in the hollows of the green hills. A rabbit sits in the road, unconcerned. Above the rapids of the Rivière au Saumon, the mountains are covered in pine. Here and there, a small perfect church stands next to the pines, its slender steeple the only white spire among so many green ones.

Murielle Bouchard's grandfather built some of these churches, and later, her father drove past them as he crisscrossed the peninsula on Route 132, delivering lumber. In the winters, Jacques Pelletier's father used to cut down trees in these very forests, and Jacques himself used to be that teenage boy standing in a field, bringing the cows in for the night. Approaching Sayabec, coming over the crest of the last hill, there's a view of its pretty white steeple rising up from the valley. And then, on the right, the red barn of a building with big letters proclaiming, "Centre Sportif David Pelletier."

They renamed the rink after David won the World Championships in 2001, and he and Jamie went through the town in a motorcade. Sayabec is tiny, but somehow they stretched the parade out for twenty minutes. Pelletier's modesty, a subbranch of his Québécois self-deprecating humor, could hardly endure such a fuss. He lay awake the whole night before the parade, too nervous to sleep. He managed to get through it, though, and now, from Murielle Bouchard's back porch, she can look across Route 132 and see the Centre Sportif David Pelletier.

When the arena was renamed, Murielle Bouchard took it upon herself to go over to the front hallway and put up some nicely framed photos documenting David's career. She gave one of the framed photographs to Roland Paquet, who was very pleased. She also redecorated the house with pictures of Jamie and David, and even hung up some framed editorial cartoons about the scandal. In her basement rec room there is a big-screen TV and a collection of videotapes spanning all three boys' entire figure skating careers. In David's old room, she has a display of his medals. She saves all the press clippings, checks the Internet for postings about her son. And she still volunteers with the local figure skating club.

"The real museum is at our parents' place," Mathieu Pelletier says. "My mom has everything classified perfectly in chronological order. I think we've even got a picture of David and Jamie in the bathroom. As for Sayabec," Mathieu says with a laugh, "he's a god. They almost renamed the church for him." On his parents' kitchen counter, David and Jamie smile up from the cover of the regional telephone directory.

After breaking his hockey sticks in Bosnia, Mathieu didn't really feel better until he heard about the second gold medal. But he liked the second gold medal. "It was fair for everyone," he says. "You can't take the gold back once you give it to them. That wouldn't be fair. It was something that was really done in the spirit of sportsmanship, and that's what is nice. I've talked to Anton, and he's a good guy, a very good guy. Seriously, I wouldn't do such things to him."

Since the Olympics ended and Mathieu came home from Bosnia, the brothers Pelletier have been united a few times. "He's really still the same." Martin shrugs. "When we're together, we would never think of talking about figure skating. We just order pizza and hang out."

"I thought it would change him," Mathieu says, "but no. He's still bugging me all the time."

"We still say all the same stupid things to each other," Martin says. "Nothing's changed."

Mathieu considers. "Well," he says, "there was this one thing. I went to Roots, the clothing store, with David. We spent like an hour and a half in there. And they've got these pictures of Jamie and David all over the store. But the girl who was working there—I swear, she never recognized him. He put one of those berets on, you know, the same hat as he was wearing in the big picture on the wall, and he was showing it to the girl. He says, 'Do you think I'd look good in that?'" Mathieu bursts out laughing.

"And she says, 'Yeah, I guess, you'd look good in that.' She never ever recognized him."

In Sayabec, though, everybody recognizes him. Before David Pelletier went to the Olympics, the biggest thing that had ever happened in Sayabec was when the townspeople blocked Route 132 for three days to insist that the region be awarded a big particleboard factory. David Pelletier winning an Olympic gold medal easily surpassed that.

Twice a year, Pelletier makes the twelve-hour trip home and finds that very little has changed. His parents still live in the modest white house with blue trim, right in town. They still spend their summers at the cottage, although in the years since they stopped paying for skating, the cottage has been upgraded from rustic to deluxe. Murielle Bouchard still teaches French; Jacques Pelletier is now a principal in Amqui. They have a dog named Axel.

Jacques Pelletier says they haven't been able to celebrate the Olympic gold medal as a family yet. "After the second gold medal ceremony, in Salt Lake City, we had a champagne celebration in our hotel room. But it was so packed that we had no privacy whatsoever," he recalls. "Jamie and David did stay for a little while, and we had some time alone together—unless you count the bodyguard waiting at the door. Then we had to get back to work, so we came home right away." Since the Olympics, Murielle Bouchard has tried several times to watch her son's performance on videotape. But she can't watch it for ten seconds without crying. "I don't cry because I'm moved," she says. "I cry because I'm angry." And in that moment, she radiates intensity—the kind of rare intensity that is needed to produce, from the resources of Sayabec, Quebec, an Olympic champion in pair skating.

∞

Patti Salé lives in a modest apartment in downtown Edmonton. When reporters come over and ask her, "How has *your life* changed since the Olympics?" she replies cheerfully, "Oh, well, it really hasn't changed a whole lot." In her view, "it's not about the parents. It's never about the parents. It's about the kids. And some people just don't understand that."

Patti Salé plans events for a fancy restaurant downtown, and in her spare time she volunteers to give talks to young athletes. She tells them, "You might not believe this, but Jamie and David still go to the rink at six in the morning. It never went to their heads. Those two never let up."

It is true that Jamie Salé still shows up at the rink at six in the morning in the summers. As she has for much of her life, she walks into the Royal Glenora Club and finds Jan Ullmark waiting for her. "I think it's partly because of him that I kept going all those years," she says. "I liked being on the ice with him, his stories. He's a little bit too much of a socialite on the ice. He likes to tell stories. Dave calls it memory lane. He'll go, 'Okay, memory lane is closed, Jan.' 'Cause I've heard all his stories about forty times. But it's fun now. He's like, 'Do you remember when you landed three triples in one day?' I'm like: 'Yes, Jan, I do.' It's fun."

On the ice now, their outbursts are far fewer, but "we still have our moments," she says. "We'll have these full-fledged arguments on the ice, but we take a break and we come back and it's like, 'Let's talk about it, and we'll go skate again.' But I think, with everything we've been through, with Richard and after, we've become really good communicators, good listeners. It's still work, though. Like every day, it's work. But we've become really strong, and we really love each other for the right reasons."

Four months of the year, touring with a professional show, they spend almost every minute of the day together—training, performing, traveling, sleeping. "Everybody says to me: Don't you guys get sick of each other?" Jamie Salé laughs. "But we actually feel weird when we're not together. And now it's really neat, because we're a couple as people. We have more than skating together. Like if you saw our house, we don't even have any pictures of us skating. We feel like it's bragging. We feel it's too much. I mean—people *know*."

It is late June in Edmonton. Just outside of the city, on the stretch of highway that Patti Salé drove so many times, between Edmonton and Red Deer, signs invite you to board your horse here, pick your own strawberries. The green grass lies smooth under a vast horizon. A band of soft blue sky lies over the saturated summer green.

It is full summer now. The sun sets at eleven at night, Alberta's largest corn maze is now open, and Jamie Salé and David Pelletier are back at their house for a few months. All winter and spring, they zigzagged across North America. They skated shows at night, got on a bus and rode to the next city, falling into bed in a different hotel every night. There were a handful of different buses to choose from, but they opted to share a bus with Yelena Berezhnaya and Anton Sikharulidze, whom they like a great deal. Between shows and practices, the skaters had about four hours of free time a day during which David Pelletier learned to play Ping-Pong from the other skaters on the tour. At the beginning, he was one of the worst players, but after getting beaten several times, he actually began *training* in Ping-Pong. By the end of the season he had beaten all of the guys at least once. Now he's looking into buying a high-end paddle. He wants to consistently beat all the guys on the tour next year.

On Pelletier's rare night off in Edmonton, he may find a pickup hockey game, and when he sees the puck ricochet off the back of the net, he will break into that same irresistible grin he flashed in the best moments of Sayabec street hockey. "That was the fun side about David," Eric Gillies once said. "He was an open book when he was happy. He didn't mind sharing it. And the more he shared it with everyone, the happier he would be."

He can be a tough person at times on the ice, but overall Pelletier is a warm man who gives his friends bear hugs and is always making people laugh. Sometimes, when Jamie Salé misses a jump, he will spontaneously improvise a little song about the triple toe and sing it to her. When skating has called upon him to hurt other people he has been reluctant to do it. He doesn't like to speak ill of other people and shares this with Salé. They may be the only sports celebrities who have ever tried to curb their fans' Internet chat room excesses by a direct appeal to their better impulses. They wrote directly to their fans through their Web site, saying, simply, it isn't right to speculate about our personal lives, you guys, so please don't do it. The approach is charmingly naive, but at the same time it has that Jamie Salé quality—it makes a cynic wonder if perhaps, after all, two celebrities might be able to make their fans behave simply by asking nicely.

Like Jamie Salé, David Pelletier had a so-called normal life before elite skating, and he plans to have a normal life after skating, too. He is thinking of becoming a firefighter after he's done with skating. It's a profession that could satisfy his cravings for both normal life and intermittent adrenaline rushes. He likes to think about the future. He talks about having children with Jamie.

Someday he'd like to get a summer cottage of his own in the woods and take his kids out there to play. The Pelletiers, after all, are one of the first five families of the Gaspésie, and the love of the outdoors is in his blood. On the shores of the lake where he spent his childhood was as splendid a natural world as one could imagine. When David goes home to Sayabec, the cottage is the place he most wants to be. There he sits on the porch with his boyhood friends and drinks his father's beer.

If you ask David Pelletier what on earth people find to do in Sayabec, with its run-down dance hall and its one bar, he will shake his head and reply. "You ask: What do people do in a small town? It's simple. They take the time to live." And this is one of the reasons that he has adjusted so easily to life in Edmonton—it too is a place where people take the time to live. It's a city that feels like a big country town, where the locals wear sweatpants and drive pickup trucks to Home Depot.

The Olympics feel distant to Pelletier, but they have left him disillusioned. "The Olympics can be the complete opposite of what they're supposed to be, what they were made for in the beginning," he says. "But they were beautiful Olympics. You're still dreaming about it. Even though you know how corrupted it is, you still enjoy it."

Even as he was swept along from interview to interview in Salt Lake City, Pelletier kept thinking, *This is not about me.* At a distance, that truth seems even clearer to him. "How many people in the past got screwed by this system? How many?" he demands. "It was probably worse in the old days. No, it was never about me. It's about having a fair chance to compete. Those officials take an oath and they should take it seriously. I take my oath seriously. I don't take dope, I don't cheat."

When he had his chance at the Olympics, Pelletier pleaded for the truth to come out, but when it didn't, he wasn't surprised. "I never believed it would come out," he says with a shrug, "because I know the people that are leading the sport. It's been happening before. It happened at the last Olympics, with the dance. Why would it change now? They had chances to fix it a long time ago.

"But anyway," he says briskly, moving on, "in anything that happens in life you can't lose your sense of humor. I remember doing a TV interview with a guy in Salt Lake. He looks at me and says, 'This is like the Cold War.' " Pelletier arches his eyebrows meaningfully. "I couldn't believe it," he laughs. "First of all, Canada had nothing to do with the Cold War. Second of all, it's figure skating!" He shakes his head, smiling at the recollection. Then he says, like a normal person, "We're talking about *sports* here."

∞

St. Petersburg is a microeconomist's dream. On the sidewalk in August, a long line of babushkas sell their wild apples, puny and insect bitten, and mushrooms gathered from the forest just outside of town. At the corner, under the stoplight, a boy sells flowers just cut from the yard of a dacha, irregular blossoms still wet with dew. A worn-down middle-aged woman sets up a card table near the Metro station and spreads cheap goods across it: tissue packs, ankle socks, razor blades, mini–alarm clocks.

Kiosks are everywhere. The Russian version is a double-wide phone booth in which the occupant is entirely hidden by displays of bananas and pears, chocolate bars, soda bottles, or pirated compact discs. The liquor kiosks do a brisk business day and night; you can spot them easily because they stand in a shiny pool of discarded bottle caps. Near the exit of the subway stations the kiosks multiply until they envelop you in a kind of third-world bazaar of cheap hot sandwiches, toiletries, and batteries.

Everyone is out to make a buck, to run his own small-time outfit and cut out the middleman. Now, at the end of summer, at the corners of the long residential blocks, ripe watermelons collect in special green cages. At night the watermelon sellers lock the cages, leaving the melons in captivity.

St. Petersburg's glorious architecture suffocates in air thick with dust. The palaces and museums, light gold and pale green, rise up from the pavement in their own worlds, unapproachable and preserved in a space all their own by buffers of parks, steps, canals—and the haze of the Petersburg air. The air is said to be especially bad in the center, where the palaces glow through the smog and the parked cars are encrusted in a mixture part construction dust, part factory pollution, part auto exhaust. Superimposed over that is a final layer of unfiltered cigarette smoke that floats on top of all air, outdoors or in.

Along the lovely avenues the houses sit like three-tiered wedding cakes, the layers iced with white frosting with just a pinch of egg dye stirred in. The pastels are somehow rendered otherworldly in the thin northern light. The facades are dusty but proud; the signs of decay come more on the ground, in the small yards in front of the houses, which have gone largely to dust or overgrown weedy grass. If you pass under a house's archway into its hidden back courtyard, you will find the strong smell of kitchen garbage mingled with exhaust.

But from the street they are elegant, the pastel houses side by side— rose, green, gold, rose, blue—each with its own faded elegance or sometimes battered elegance, with the windows broken and covered over with plastic. The trees along the boulevard are slim, even skinny, as if they too had starved during the siege, but their leaves lend a daytime shimmer, a quality of Paris, just as the canals at night lend an air of Venice. By the light of the gas lamps, the gold on a footbridge glitters like a bracelet in the dark.

This is an aristocrat's city. You can take away the aristocrats, but their style, their echoes remain. They cared for elegance, they had panache: fourteen-foot ceilings and ballrooms with inlaid wood floors. They built on a scale of luxury, not efficiency, and these look like the homes of pa-trons of the arts. When Anton Sikharulidze came home to his native city as an Olympic champion, he went back to the grand apartment building that had captivated him in his boyhood. It was still there, near Yubileiny, where he used to go visit it between his practices and imagine that ghosts lived inside it. The building was a masterpiece of the famous architect Benoît, but under communism it had been cut up into tiny, squalid com-munal apartments. Still, the old place was tied up in the fascinations of Sik-harulidze's childhood; somehow, he had always dreamed of living there.

In Soviet times, Olympic champions were issued apartments by the state. In the new Russia, Sikharulidze went to the Benoît building and tried to buy a place with money he had earned abroad. But in post–Soviet Russia, in order to combine seven little communal apartments into one enormous flat, Sikharulidze needed to make deals with all seven fam-ilies, and "one guy's room was empty, because he was in jail." Sikharulidze bought out the other six families, and when the owner of the seventh apartment finally got out of jail, Sikharulidze's offer on the apartment was accepted. Seven families moved out to make room for one wealthy man. It was a sign of the times.

Sikharulidze drives a shiny new-model BMW, black with leather inte-rior, and in the new Russia of haves and have-nots, he is clearly among the haves. Like many young men who find themselves suddenly wealthy, he has bought his parents the things he would want for himself: an apart-ment, a big-screen television, a satellite dish—and another BMW, more sedate, for his father.

Now, six months after the Olympics, Sikharulidze's father is fed up with the media circus that has surrounded his son. "We are so bored by this scandal we can barely talk about it," he says. "I'm just thinking that basically, they should have explained to people that Yelena and Anton had a clean win. And I would say for me that they clearly and absolutely won that night.

"Our newspapers said it's an insult to Russia that they gave the second gold medal," he continues. "I just say that it's a failure of the Olympic Committee and ISU, that they just followed the stream of this publicity. They listened to the press, and under this pressure they just handed out the gold medals to make the scandal quieter."

He is most furious that his son has been linked to Tokhtakhounov in the news. "We don't know this man, we never asked him for any help," Sikharulidze's father says heatedly. "I can speak for Anton, and we know that Tamara Moskvina never did anything wrong. And for the first two days of this scandal, on TV they would just show this mafia guy and our kids. And then in the Russian press, what is really incredibly bad, that they started to show false pictures of Tokhtakhounov and Sikharulidze together. But it was not a real picture—it was like one half of one picture put together with one half of another picture. For three years the FBI were spying on this Tokhtakhounov, and they say he sells guns, he's involved with the money laundering, he deals narcotics. And they're charging him on what? Fixing the Olympics?" He shakes his head. "We don't mind if they want to crack down on the international mafia. Just leave our kids out of it."

In the months since Salt Lake City Anton Sikharulidze has begun to look at the controversy in purely instrumental terms. After all, the scandal made him famous, far more famous than he would have been had he simply won a gold medal at the Olympics. He was all over the television for weeks. He'll take it. He makes good money in the United States on the professional tour, and back in Russia he is starting a business, a chain of restaurants to cater to the emerging middle class in a country where, in the past, only the very wealthy or connected ate in restaurants.

"Russia is really changing now," he says. "We're beginning to have a middle class, and I think it's the most important thing. Because the middle class, it's very important for all countries. Middle class makes the whole life. So what I want to do is open restaurants in St. Petersburg, restaurants for the people. Because Russia is lacking in these kind of places now. It's so that an ordinary family can go and have a bite, and it is possible on their budget. The quality is good, and it's not expensive. And I feel that people will just be grateful for what we do. Plus we will make money, of course, so everyone will be happy."

Moskvina, too, is investing in the new Russia. After the Olympics, she stayed another year in America to finish out her contract. But she knows that home walls help, and now she has closed up her American school, and she and Igor have officially come home to St. Petersburg. "I always have like list when I come home," she says. "Meet people. Meet my relatives and friends. I never take walks because I don't have time. I drive. But when I drive, like when I come from the airport and I drive, it's like, *oh, how beautiful is my city.* You return from the trip—how beautiful! Then you notice at once. And I could be a very good promoter, tourist agent of St. Petersburg."

Financially, it is almost impossible to train pairs in Russia now. "You count: two skaters. For both of them, someone has to find housing, pay for the ice, make their costumes, find skates and boots, feed them, drive to practice and back, buy plane tickets, translate for them at least for the first time." But it is a maxim of Tamara Moskvina's that you can be happy in any system: It depends on you. And she has every intention of being happy.

From Moskvina's kitchen window, she can see Yelena Berezhnaya's new apartment, where she lives when she is not touring in America. Every time Berezhnaya has even a week off, she flies back to Russia. "Home is home," she says with a shrug. "You belong when you're at home."

It does Moskvina's heart good to see Berezhnaya going around as a confident, independent young woman. She drives a fast car, and this summer she has been experimenting with bungee jumping. She stands up to Anton more now. And in her quiet, no-nonsense way, she has become the main support for her family in Nevinnomyssk.

She visits Nevinnomyssk once or twice a year, but the longer she lives in the West and in St. Petersburg, the more distant her childhood home feels. "When I go back," she says, "I feel as if I am traveling back to some-place that remains very, very far away. I feel as if I am traveling to the moon." In this place so distant from her, her family's everyday life unfolds, and she recently opened a café there to give them a foothold in the new economy. "I just want to give some work for my family, you know?" she says. "Because they don't have a good job in our city or anywhere else, and I just want that they should have something of their own."

Tatyana Berezhnaya quit her accounting job at the construction company, and she now manages the Café Axel. "Her older brother Alexei is working there. We have ten people working there," Tatyana Berezhnaya says proudly. "We have been open for a year, and the young people enjoy going there, so it does well. Everything has the theme of figure skating. The food is good, and everybody knows that it is Yelena Berezhnaya who owns it. Right now it's pretty famous."

Berezhnaya wanted to buy her mother a nicer apartment, but "she doesn't want to move anywhere else. She simply can't. She doesn't want to because everything is familiar and dear to her, the people that she knows, and the neighbors. And of course, that bench in front of the apartment building, and the conversation. She can't go anywhere. Everything that she likes and knows is there. My younger brother and my cousin still live with my mother. My mother took in my cousins, you know, because their own mother died from a heart attack, and a year after, their father took poison. So my mom is still taking care of kids and has enough to do even though I'm grown. She has no time to be bored."

Berezhnaya, on the other hand, has plenty of time to be bored, because four months a year she lives out of a suitcase, sitting in a different hotel room every afternoon. Sometimes, when she wakes up, she has to check the hotel directory to recall what city she is in. She eats sparingly and skates every practice. If Anton doesn't feel like practicing, she skates alone. According to her mother, "There's never a time when she doesn't want to be home," and sometimes she does find it hard. But the work is in America, what can you do? On her day off, to pass the time, she often escapes to a movie. "All the time I go to the cinema," she says, "because I like this feeling of being lost in another reality, of removing myself from this reality."

Mostly, she reads. "You see, I look upon our work, this tour we have in America, as if we are sailors that ship out to sea, far from our native land," she says. "So I set some goals in front of myself: I took a bunch of books with me that I could read. For the most part I read about historic figures. For instance, about a Russian general during our civil war. Then I read about Rasputin. All kinds of unusual books. I took Napoleon with me. It's just that I was curious about other people's lives and how they used to live and how they used to survive. And then I look at my life, and I compare it with all these people that I read about, and I am thinking that I am quite lucky; basically, my life is a dream in comparison with those guys. Because you know I always fret that I am so sad because I am so far away from home. But those guys didn't have their families around them any time."

∞

On a bright October day in Harbin, entering the back stairwell of the Zhaos' building is like going into a root cellar. It is one of the ironies of Communist China that nobody takes care of the communal stairwell. When the eyes adjust, you can make out the decrepit cement stairs. Small pieces of trash are lodged between the corner of the step and the wall—a dusty glass bottle, a scrap of plastic wrap. At every landing, the windowpanes are cracked.

It is four flights up to the flat where Zhao Hongbo lived as a child, and since his mother is now almost seventy, she doesn't climb the stairs too often. Most days Jing Yulan sits in the main room of her apartment in an old green felt armchair, wearing a housedress and her slippers. Tacked to the rough white wall above the armchair is an enormous sepia-toned poster that shows a four-year-old Parisian boy flirting with a four-year-old

Parisian girl. Sitting beneath the poster, Mrs. Jing passes the time by pouring out cup after cup of green tea from her electric kettle and rubbing out
one cigarette after another in the plastic ashtray. Sometimes she watches
television. After working hard all her life, she now has just a few chores to
occupy her. She feeds the fish in her aquarium, waters the potted plants,
cooks when her children come to visit.

The best feature of Jing Yulan's main room is its large single-paned
window. Someone has taped over the long crack in the window. Crude
curtains have been cut from thin printed cotton sheeting. If Jing Yulan
leaves the window open, so that her cigarette smoke can drift out, she lets
in an icy October breeze and, worse, the street noise. Urban China is re-
lentlessly loud. Even at five stories up, the street noise is earsplitting. But
Mrs. Jing leaves it open; she is nearly deaf.

A twin bed is flush against the wall underneath the window, and at the
foot of the bed is a full-sized refrigerator. The kitchen is about twenty
paces away, through the doorway, but the refrigerator is here, inches from
the bed. This is because the refrigerator arrived long after the kitchen did,
and had to be squeezed in somewhere. On top of the refrigerator Jing
Yulan has placed a vase of cheap silk flowers and a large stuffed animal,
thrown to the ice by a fan at a skating meet somewhere in the West. At the
Chinese National Championships, stuffed animals are also thrown onto
the ice by excited children. But in China, as soon as the skater scoops up his
toys and steps off the ice, the same children appear, demanding their toys
back. Then they run back up into the stands and throw the same toys on
the ice for the next skater. The stuffed animals are expensive, so after the
competition, the skating club packs them up and takes them home, so they
can be thrown at the next competition.

Mrs. Jing's main room is the kind of room to be found everywhere in
China, tidy but well past its prime. At some point, she lovingly embroi-
dered the homemade cotton covers that are tacked to the bottoms of the
end tables, hiding the items stored underneath. In an earlier time she
stitched together the handmade daytime coverlet that lies on the twin bed,
signaling to visitors that they should treat the bed as a sofa. But now the
linens are worn and faded. The cheap silk flowers look dusty and ragged
in their plastic vases. The single bare fluorescent tube lighting the room
looks as if it came with the building, and the white walls are covered with
scratches. The old parquet floor is yellow and worn, freshly scrubbed, but
even so, the occasional cockroach scuttles over the boards. Zhao Hongbo is
pressuring his mother to move into a new apartment that he will buy for

her, but she feels that she is too old to leave this place. She has been here too long.

By the old television is the framed snapshot of Zhao Hongbo standing in the snow. This is the television on which Mrs. Jing watched the Olympics, with the volume cranked all the way up. Her older son, Zhao Huanzhi, watched with her.

On this blustery October day, Jing Yulan has a lot to say about the Olympics. "Well," she begins, "in the Salt Lake City Olympic Games, they got this idea. They said: 'Well, we didn't win in previous competitions, so we've got to try really hard this time. This time, we're going to try the quadruple throw.' It was a really difficult move. Nobody really did that before. The triple is pretty much the maximum that people usually do. And they tried a quadruple, which they never did before in a big competition."

"We changed to *Turandot*," Zhao Huanzhi says. "Probably the Asian style of performance was not appealing that much to these Western judges. As I can see from the television, if you want to compete with them, you have to adjust to the Western style. If you just use your own style, then the judges just won't appreciate that."

"But even so, if you look at the other teams from Canada and Russia, they did something really funny, some sort of engaging performance, and I think they are sort of better than us in this way," Mrs. Jing says. "But the thing is"—and here Mrs. Jing starts to get really hot under the collar— "the Canadian team, from the first time I watched their performance, they're doing the same program. But the judges give them second and give my son the third! Look at the Canadian team! They are doing the same program again and again. If Zhao Hongbo was doing the same program he was doing all the time, he could do it with his eyes closed—"

Zhao Huanzhi interrupts. "Well, the Canadians were very stable—"

"And still the Canadians are not happy! So they complained, and they got the first place. But the second place was missing!" Jing Yulan says. "In terms of this, I was so angry, the smoke was coming out of my ears. When I saw this, I'm fuming. We were the third, and the second place was empty, there's nobody there. I just couldn't understand why they can make two first places, but we couldn't move from third to second." She gets upset just talking about it. "I just don't know what to say. The Canadians have so much power. But there's nothing we can do. We feel pretty helpless."

Zhao Huanzhi is especially bitter when he thinks of the 1999 World Championships in Helsinki. "There, it was proven on videotape that the judges cheated, and still they could not change our silver medal to the gold medal. But in the Olympic Games, for the Canadians, they did change it back! They changed the judgment and they changed the results." He broods for a minute in silence.

In Harbin, as elsewhere in China, most of the state-run factories are closing. People used to call it "the iron rice bowl," that cradle-to-grave assurance of a job at a state enterprise. But the iron rice bowl is disintegrating. Zhao Huanzhi still has some work at the machinery factory, but his two sisters, who both worked in the textile factories, have been permanently laid off. They have found some work in fledgling private companies, but times are hard. "From this family," Jing Yulan says, "Hongbo is the only one who has some success. The others have no more work." Under the current regulations, if Hongbo wins a competition with a prize of thirty thousand dollars, the state takes half of it, and he, Shen Xue, and Yao Bin get five thousand dollars each. For most Chinese, that is five years' salary. "Hongbo is generous with his money," his mother says approvingly. "Everybody can spend his money."

Judging from her apartment, Jing Yulan has spent none of his money. She lives as she has always lived, except that instead of squeezing into this flat with five other people, she now lives alone. In the next room is a framed photograph of Hongbo's father. Every time he comes home, Hongbo kneels and kowtows to his father's picture. When he leaves, never more than a few days later, he kneels before the picture again. It was his father who shared his skating with him. His father's scrapbooks begin with articles about Zhao Hongbo, kindergarten basketball star, and how he helped win a piano for his classroom. Then there are the childhood competitions, the Chinese Junior Nationals, the Chinese National Championships. Since his death, the family has kept up with the scrapbooks. They have clipped and pasted the articles: Hongbo wins the Asian Games, the silver medal at the World Championships, the Olympic bronze medal. And finally, in 2002, one month after the Olympics at a World Championships without the Russians or Canadians, Hongbo becomes world champion.

He is twenty-nine years old, still living in a tiny dorm room in Beijing. Jing Yulan says she would be happy if he ends up marrying Shen Xue, although it's his own decision. In the not-so-distant past, prospective brides came to the mother-in-law's house and auditioned by cooking with her; the girl might be disqualified if she left an apple peel that was too thick. But Jing Yulan approves of Shen Xue. "Well," she says, "this child is very nice."

Zhao Huanzhi chimes in. "She's very hardworking. She's really that kind of girl that can eat bitterness."

Jing Yulan sits in her chair by the aquarium, smoking, across the room from the framed photo of her youngest boy standing in the snow. "He was taken away when he was still in kindergarten," she says. "I didn't raise him up. He was brought up by the coach. Right? He was selected at the age of seven. It can be said he was raised up by his coaches. And after he went to the school, he had no time to play. As he grew older in the school, he didn't like to talk anymore."

Would she do it again?

Mrs. Jing doesn't understand the question at first. She looks confused. Zhao Huanzhi says gently, "The idea is, if your son was to start all over again from the age of seven, what do you think, do you want him to do it again, the same course of life?"

"No," she says slowly, "I wouldn't choose the same way again. It was too bitter." She shakes her head. "*Tai ku le.* Too bitter, much too bitter. I wouldn't allow him if we can start all over again. My son didn't really live a childhood. He left at the age of seven. He didn't have his childhood at all."

"He lost his childhood happiness," Zhao Huanzhi says.

"No playing, whatever. Nothing. Too bitter. There's no holiday, no weekends. Much too bitter," Jing Yulan repeats. When she scowls, her lined face shows all its creases.

"Besides, you know, if you start all over again, and then he ends up nowhere, then you would regret it," Zhao Huanzhi adds.

"These days they have a lot of newcomers," Jing Yulan cautions. "Those kids could be much, much better than Hongbo."

∞

At home in Harbin, Shen Xue's parents call her "Baby Doll," and in her new bedroom, in the apartment she bought two years ago for her family, she has more than four hundred baby dolls. She keeps them under her bed, which is round like a hatbox and is decorated like a wedding cake. It is a fantasy room, opening onto a wide balcony overlooking the street. With its white bedspread, its elegant floral lamps, its "Hello Kitty" merchandise, and the stuffed panda wearing a gold medal, it looks like a ten-year-old's notion of a bridal suite. Shen Xue sleeps here a few nights a year. The walls are dominated by large studio portraits of Shen, Shen and Zhao (not skating), and Shen and Zhao skating. In the family portraits in the rest of the house, Zhao Hongbo is included. But her parents won't discuss the question of her marriage. "It's still too early to place this matter on the agenda," Shen Jie says in a scolding tone. "Once news about their relationship is out, it will affect the two people's training. We don't want their career to be affected. So their current relationship remains just skating partners."

The apartment is a sixth-floor walk-up in an outwardly unimpressive building, and on the outside door is the same red-and-gold good-luck banner that hung on the Shens' door when they lived in a hundred and sixty square feet in Daowai. But inside it is a first-world luxury apartment in a third-world country. The teak floors are polished to an extremely high gloss, so that you can see your reflection in them. There is beautiful inlaid wood cabinetry along the walls, especially in the trophy room, where glass cases display all her medals. Everything is brand spanking new and perfectly maintained. It is clear that the Shens are tremendously diligent about taking care of what they have. These days, the proof is not in a patched shirt or a five-year-old pair of shoes. Now you see it in the trophy cases, where not so much as a speck of dust rests on any of the medals or plaques.

The living room is enormous, with brand-new furniture and a huge big-screen television. On this magnificent screen they watched the Olympics, half a day after they actually took place. They were not too hopeful of winning. Even if Shen Xue had landed the quad, Lu Manli thought either the Canadians or the Russians would win. The judges had shown who they preferred, the teams from the Western countries. Even with their beautiful *Turandot,* her father thought, the other two countries would have more influence. And when he saw what happened with the dual gold medals, he knew he was right. "As far as I know, there has never been a gold medal tie in Olympic figure skating history," Shen Jie says. "And this happened in the back rooms, behind the scenes, with a few powerful countries struggling against each other to get what they want."

Besides the new apartment, Shen Xue recently bought her father a car. He only got his driver's license two months ago. Until he was forty-eight years old, he always rode a bicycle. Now he is one of the millions of middle-aged Chinese trying to adapt to the new consumerist China. He wrestles with the steering wheel, a latecomer to parallel parking; he often sits in the trophy room at the computer his daughter bought for him and checks her results on the Internet. In his jacket pocket, he carries a lightweight plastic cell phone. His daughter now has braces, just like the Westerners. And on this day in October, across from the new shopping arcade, Shen Jie and his wife eat American-style fried chicken at the recently opened KFC in Harbin. "Of course," Lu Manli says, "when Shen Xue is home, we would never eat like this. We always eat at home, and whenever Shen Xue puts down the chopsticks, we both put down the chopsticks, too. Then, when she goes out, we eat more."

For many years, Lu Manli says, the coaches have been advising Shen Xue to try to eat just one decent meal a day, a morning meal. "The rest of the time, when she's not practicing, she just stays in her room and stays quiet, to conserve her energy. Even after many years, she still feels so very hungry." After the Olympics, while the Russians and Canadians reap the benefits of touring, Shen Xue and Zhao Hongbo are still at the dorm, training, forbidden to date, unable to leave campus without permission. Now there is talk among the sports officials that they may stay in for another Olympics, even—three more years. It's such a long time. Shen Xue will be twenty-seven, Zhao Hongbo, thirty-two.

These days the Shens are both unemployed. "The work unit where we used to work doesn't exist anymore," Shen Jie explains. "It was sold from the state to somebody else." The very idea of unemployment was unthinkable during most of his life in China. You were assigned to a work unit, that's it. Now the state, the *state,* is selling off a factory to a private owner? But in the last five years in Harbin, the world has been turned on its head. "They sent us home, giving each of us ten thousand yuan, and that's it. They no longer take care of anything for us." He grimaces. "To them, it's just like shedding baggage. And even under such miserable circumstances, we were not allowed to tell people the story of what happened."

Since 1997, they have lived off their severance and Shen Xue's earnings. Shen Jie is a young, active man, but jobs are hard to come by in Harbin, one of the hardest-hit cities in all of China. In his upside-down world, his child supports him. "When we were young," Shen Jie says, "to be honest, we didn't really have a very ambitious goal." "All I hoped," Lu Manli sighs, "was that my husband will just someday make money, and our living standard would be higher, and our living space would be better." For a woman who hand-washed the clothes, waited in ration coupon lines, cooked in a kitchen without a sink, rode on the back of the family's one bicycle, it was the most natural dream in the world.

"But actually this dream of a better house, of good living standards was not realized by ourselves," Shen Jie says, and the humility is strong in his voice. "Our dream," he says, glancing over at his wife, "was realized by Little Xue."

∞

Six months later, at the end of March, Shen Jie sits in the trophy room, combing the Internet for any word of his daughter. She is in Washington, D.C., for the 2003 World Championships, and he has just learned from the Web that Shen Xue's ankle is badly injured. She was trying that quadruple in the practice—that quadruple again—and she bashed her foot into the barrier. She may not be able to skate.

Shen Jie is heartsick. Honestly, he does not want her to compete. He is sure that his little girl is in agony. And she probably won't tell anyone how bad it really is. If she falls, she could destroy the ankle. He waits for Little Xue to call, but when she does call, she won't discuss the details of the injury. "I told her to weigh this matter carefully before she decides to compete," Shen Jie says. "The child still has a longer way to go in her career, still several years. I told her, if she does not feel up to it, she should give up. Then my daughter said, 'Dad, I know. I know what I am doing.' When she said this, I realized there was no need for me to say more. She is grown up. She thinks independently now."

Shen Xue may have made up her mind that she's going to compete, but Yao Bin isn't so sure. The kids have had a long season—nine competitions between November and March, changing continents almost every other week. Finally, in the two weeks before the World Championships, they had some time at home to try the quadruple. They hadn't been doing it all season, but now, somehow, Shen Xue started landing it. By the time they left Beijing, she was at sixty percent. So as soon as they got to Washington, of course, the two kids wanted to try one on the practice. They had just arrived, the jet lag was still a factor. Standing at the boards, Yao told them to just wait a minute. But the kids went off and tried one, and Shen Xue hit the boards hard. Immediately she limped off the ice; within minutes, the ankle was grossly swollen.

But the very next morning, Shen Xue rose early and knocked on Yao's door. When he opened it, she was standing there in her skates. "See," she said, "I can stand up in my skates." Yao wasn't buying that. He agreed she could try to practice later that day, but when she got to the ice she couldn't even skate around. Her face was contorted with the pain, and after five minutes even Shen Xue couldn't stand it anymore. The huge swelling was pressing against the boot, and she had to unlace it right there on the ice.

Yao took her to the ISU doctors, who X-rayed it and said it was a serious sprain. She had only one option if she wanted to skate: a sanctioned numbing injection. Shen Xue wanted that injection.

So on the morning of the short program she went for the first injection, then stepped onto the ice for practice. The foot felt numb, like a piece of wood, but by using her muscle memory and her experience, she could land on it. That night, with another injection, she skated perfectly in the short program. It was Zhao Hongbo who was unnerved by the whole experience and had a slipup. They finished second in the short program, and the next day she rested her ankle. Zhao Hongbo went to the rink alone and practiced with the other pairs. It was an eerie sight.

And then it was the day of the competition. "There was a morning practice on the day of the final," Zhao Hongbo says. "She had another injection for that practice. Then in the evening, she had another two before the free program. So altogether five injections. After so many injections, the effect was not as strong. Besides, she had more pain, because her ankle was badly used after the short program. It looked like another piece of ligament got torn. Her ankle swelled up really big."

Yao Bin walked out with her from backstage, thinking: *She can't even walk, and now she's doing throws.* It was hard to even comprehend. Yao thought: Doing a triple throw means flying a distance of twenty feet at a height of three feet. And now she's going to land it on a wooden ankle, twice. She'll have to control her body by memory. And if that doesn't work, she'll have to give up in the first minute.

Now, stepping onto the ice, Zhao Hongbo's heart is in his throat. He's the one who has to throw her. There is something miserable about this, and he wonders if they should have withdrawn. But he looks at Shen Xue's face and knows that she will never give in. For now, the injection is working. She steps onto the ice. She thinks: *Rely on all the experience and feeling you gained over these many years. Try to forget about the injury. It is a beautiful program.*

And it *is* a beautiful program—*Turandot* again, one year later, but surprisingly fresh. It feels as if it has deepened, become truer to its purpose. The music starts. Hours later, at home in Harbin, the families can't watch. Jing Yulan averts her eyes; she doesn't dare to look, she is so afraid. Her older son sits beside the aquarium and watches for her. Both of them are in tears. Lu Manli and Shen Jie sit on the brand-new sofa in front of the enormous television, sobbing. "Her dad and I didn't merely come to tears," Lu Manli says. "We literally cried out loud, head to head. Oh, how we felt . . ."

Shen Xue is moving across the ice on two thin blades, depending entirely on her instinct. She gains speed beside Zhao Hongbo, heading for the side-by-side jumps. Yao forces himself to watch. She goes up beautifully, comes down with the full force of her weight on that wooden ankle. But Shen Xue is really that kind of girl who can eat bitterness. And if Yao didn't know she had just had two injections, he would have thought she was perfectly healthy.

"Before," Lu Manli says, "we loved her just because she's our only daughter. She's always been a little girl in my eyes. But now it's different. I hadn't expected my child to be so brave. It's almost like that she is willing to pay her life for this career. She's such a type of person. I admire her. She has an unbreakable spirit, which is not found in just any ordinary person."

"Her perseverance did not come overnight," Shen Jie says philosophically. "She gained it by overcoming so many hardships through all these years, day by day."

"Everyone, everyone admired her, and they were in awe of how she came to have such endurance, to do such a thing," her mother says, adding, "I was told all this by the other coaches."

"She never tells you anything," Shen Jie remarks.

"Right. She would never say, 'Mom, I did great in this competition.' No." Lu Manli sighs. "She wouldn't say such things. She's very introverted and not good at expressing."

But Shen Xue is a different person on land and on ice, and right now she has the audience in the palm of her hand. She is skating as if it is impossible for her to make a mistake. She flies through a glorious, soaring throw and lands on that dead ankle, and the blade sinks sweetly into the ice. In the stands eight thousand people, among them Jamie Salé and David Pelletier, cannot stop applauding, and many of them have tears in their eyes.

Zhao Hongbo is skating with her, hand in hand. He grips her palm hard and lowers her down into a death spiral. Now he releases her hands and, with one of his own, he follows the curve of her radiant face. It was in the moment that he did this caress perfectly for the first time that he began to love *Turandot*. He feels a strange exhilaration he has never known before. "The first half of my life is devoted to figure skating," Zhao says, "and I guess I won't leave figure skating in the last half of my life. There is still so much to explore. We'll skate in one more Olympics; we will try one more time to win the gold medal. Then I'll go abroad, and study the Westerners' artistic presentation. And then I'll come home to China and teach other skaters. I hope to bring our skaters' unique characteristics to the world. I hope to be able to do it. I hope to be as great a coach as Yao Bin."

Hours later, back home in Harbin, Leader Li watches, and his eyes well up with tears. Fifty years of his life he gave to Harbin skating. Li remembers many things: Yao Bin moving the sewing machine into his dorm room; little Luan Bo in her helmet, climbing up on a table to get into the lift. He remembers standing by the ice at that first World Championships, speaking furiously into his tape recorder. He remembers how Zhao's father refused to let him be a pair skater, until he insisted. He wishes Zhao's father were alive to see this. He chuckles, thinking of Shen Xue's father coming to his office to pester him, and he can still recall his words to Yao Bin when he made him choose Shen Xue: *Since I'm the leader, you just take her, like I said. And if you make a great achievement, then it's yours; if not, blame me* . . . He thinks of his generation, the first generation, skating on the ponds of Black River in the terrible cold. And he thinks: *We were the stones who made the road for other people to walk. Our job was to go abroad for them.* Yao Bin skated in front of the Germans using only half the ice. He'd never been on an indoor rink before. The Germans laughed.

Now, as Yao Bin stands at the boards of another World Championship, he sees Shen Xue, but he cannot believe what he sees. Yao has known her since she was a little girl, but he has not really known her. There is more to her, finer stuff in her than even he had guessed. Compared to a year ago, she is swifter, higher, stronger. The last throw is just around the bend. In Chinese the sportswriters call the throw "spinning like wind, throwing and catching, like lightning and thunder." Zhao throws like lightning, and her steady blade answers; the audience adds its own thunder.

Yao's heart is full to overflowing. From where he stands, he senses a motion, and as he looks up the crowd now rises to its feet as one. Yao Bin glances back to the ice to see what has moved eight thousand people to stand up a full forty seconds before the end of the program, which has never happened in skating history. Can it be? It *is*—that it is not Yao's Chinese technique but the power of so much beauty and heart that has moved the Americans to their feet, where they still stand, applauding wildly. It is so: For at the moment that the crowd rose, they were simply skating hand in hand.

"I could see the audience all around me, and I heard them," Shen Xue will say later, "and my spirit rose." Every seat is empty, every person stands. Later on, many people cannot really say why they stood, or why they cried. But live skating is a performance, and intangible things can pass between the people here, now, at this very moment. People who do not know them at all are crying, and people who know about the ankle are crying harder, and as they watch they are filled with wonder. Yao Bin, who never reacts, swats at his tears, getting rid of them as quickly as he can.

Later, some of the great champions who were in the building will call it the greatest pair performance of all time. "We've been watching pair skating for sixty years, some of us," one former Canadian pair champion says, "and we all agree that this was the greatest pair program we've ever seen. Everything they did, they went for broke. It will be years, years before someone surpasses that—unless they do it themselves."

Shen Xue skates to the barrier. She cannot stop smiling, and she is incredibly beautiful. Her eyes are full of light. Zhao Hongbo will not leave her side. Shen Xue is too excited to sit. She leans against him, taking the weight off her aching foot, waving and smiling. Eight thousand people still stand, applauding as hard as they can. On the second mark, there are two sixes.

NOTES

The narrative of this book is based primarily on personal interviews conducted between February 2002 and August 2003. These interviews are the main source for quotes, including those describing individuals' thoughts. Additional sources are noted below.

Information about Russia comes from my interviews with Vladimir Aparin, David Avdish, Yelena Bechke, Tatyana Berezhnaya, Yelena Berezhnaya, Igor Bobrin, Irina Bykhovskaya, Artur Dmitriev, Mikhail Drey, Tatyana Druchinina, Yekaterina Gordeyeva, Oleg Gorshkov, Alexander Issurin, Olga Kazakova, Stanislav Leonovitch, Oleg Makarov, Alexander Matveyev, Tatyana Menshikova, Natalya Mishketunok, Igor Moskvin, Anna Moskvina, Tamara Moskvina, Denis Petrov, Maria Petrova, Irina Rodnina, Yevgeny Rybalov, Larisa Selezhneva, Anton Sikharulidze, Lyudmila Sikharulidze, Tariel Sikharulidze, Alexei Tikhonov, Yelena Valova, Oleg Vasiliev, Nikolai Velikov and Lyudmila Velikova, Irina Vorobieva, Robin Wagner, Arthur Werner, and Vladimir Zakharov.

My research in China included interviews with Jef Billings, Chen Xinping, Gao Jie, Jing Yulan, Naomi Hellman, Don Laws, Li Yaoming, Luan Bo, Lu Manli, Lea Ann Miller, Renee Roca, Lucinda Ruh, Shen Jie, Shen Xue, Tian Wentao, Tong Jian, Yao Bin, Yao Jinchang, Yao Rongli, Zhang Dan, Zhang Yongde, Zhao Hongbo, and Zhao Huanzhi. A few additional sources requested anonymity.

In Canada I interviewed Sandra Bezic, Murielle Bouchard, Isabelle Brasseur, the Desjardins family, Lloyd Eisler, Richard Gauthier, Eric Gillies, Jean-François Hébert, David Howe, Brian Klavano, Elizabeth Manley, Lori Nichol, Roland Paquet, Bob Paul, David Pelletier, Jacques Pelletier, Martin Pelletier, Mathieu Pelletier, Josée Picard, Jamie Salé, Patti Salé, Lana Sherman, Bob Steadward, Angela Steele, Jan Ullmark, Barb Underhill, and Debbie Wilson.

I interviewed several people about pair skating in general, including Tai Babilonia, Peter Carruthers, Robin Cousins, Christopher Dean, Rob Dustin, Peggy Fleming, Randy Gardner, Deborah King, Ron Ludington, Jirina Ribbens, Meg Streeter,

Doug Wilson, Tracy Wilson, David Winner, Susie Wynne, and John Zimmerman. I also interviewed many judges and officials, including Lucy Brennan, Marilyn Chidlow, Pam Coburn, Sissy Krick, Alexander Lakernik, Benoît Lavoie, Ron Pfenning, Vladislav Petukhov, Valentin Piseyev, Ren Hongguo, Marina Sanaya, Sally Stapleford, Hideo Sugita, and Yang Jiasheng.

Videotape was an astonishing resource for me in writing this book. Many passages are based on my screening of competition footage from the NBC Olympic archives, ABC Sports, Lifetime Sports, CBS Sports, CTV Sports (Canada), CBC Sports (Canada), NTV Sports (Russia), ORT Sports (Russia), and CCTV Sports (China). Taped interviews from these networks were also of great value to me. For background on daily life in Russia and China, the Museum of Television and Radio in New York was an important source. The 1985 BBC series *Comrades* and its accompanying book gave me a terrific window on Soviet life. The Russian State Archive at Krasnogorsk was a godsend, providing extraordinary background on the development of skating in the Soviet Union. I benefited greatly from having the chance to view Nikita Orlov's television documentary on the history of Russian figure skating. The 1997 documentary *China: A Century of Revolution* provided a glimpse of how ordinary Chinese people view recent history. CNN, CSPAN, MSNBC, and NBC covered breaking news during the Olympic scandal and produced a video record of events that was invaluable to me.

While following the scandal and the Tokhtakhounov story I learned a great deal by reading, among others, Jere Longman, Selena Roberts, Richard Sandomir, and John Tagliabue of *The New York Times;* Amy Shipley of *The Washington Post;* Christine Brennan and Vicki Michaelis of *USA Today;* Philip Hersh of the *Chicago Tribune;* Beverley Smith at the Toronto *Globe and Mail;* Helene Elliott of the *Los Angeles Times;* and Nancy Armour, Andrew Dampf, and Barry Wilner of the Associated Press. I also benefited from reading various articles run by Agence France Presse, *Le Monde,* and *L'Equipe.* In Salt Lake City, the Olympic News Service was an important source of information.

PROLOGUE

3 *Yelena Berezhnaya places one white skate:* Descriptions of the warm-up and free skate are based on the author's viewing of NBC Sports coverage of the 2002 Olympic pairs free skate from multiple camera angles. The event took place on February 11, 2002.

4 *three of the six best pairs:* The other three being the Protopopovs, Rodnina and Zaitsev, and Gordeyeva and Grinkov.

6 *"I look at them in their eyes":* CBS interview with Tamara Moskvina, February 1998.

7 *"came home as red as a pig":* Quoted in Cam Cole, "Don't Fret About Salé and Pelletier," *The National Post,* February 11, 2002, p. A-1.

9 *If you miss the quad, it disrupts the rest of the program:* Scott Hamilton made this point during NBC's coverage of the 2002 Olympic pairs free skate on February 11, 2002.

10 *has an astonishing three thousand skating rinks:* Estimates for the number of skating rinks in each country provided by the national skating federations of Canada, China, and Russia.

12 *only two coaches in the history of pair skating:* Americans Kitty and Peter Carruthers, coached by Ron Ludington, landed the throw quadruple Salchow in practice in the mid-eighties. Berezhnaya and Sikharulidze, coached by Tamara Moskvina, also landed the throw quadruple Salchow in practice during the 1999–2000 season.

15 *"Should* The Nutcracker *have only one Christmas?":* Quoted in Dave Stubbs, "Love Makes the World Go Round," *Calgary Herald,* February 12, 2002, p. AAO-1; Adam Thompson, "Russians' Gold Is Surrounded by Controversy," *Denver Post,* February 12, 2002, p. D-4; and in Michael Farber, "High Concept: With Passion and Power, Jamie Salé and David Pelletier of Canada Are Lifting Pairs Skating to a New Level," *Sports Illustrated,* February 11, 2002, p. 12.

20 *"Russians feel deeper anyways than Europeans":* Quoted in Igor Popov, "Interview with Anton Sikharulidze," *The Russia Journal,* March 29, 1999.

24 *They are moving at almost twenty miles an hour:* For this and all other biomechanics information, the source is the author's interviews with Dr. Deborah King of Ithaca College, a biomechanist who has conducted extensive research on the physics of figure skating.

PART ONE

27 *Pair skating is the skating of two persons:* The epigraph comes from the International Skating Union's *Special Regulations, Figure Skating.* Lausanne: International Skating Union, 2000.

CHAPTER ONE

For general background on post–Soviet Russia, David Remnick's *Lenin's Tomb* (New York: Random House, 1993) and *Resurrection* (New York: Random House, 1997) were extremely helpful. Charlotte Hobson's *Black Earth City* (New York: Metropolitan Books, 2001) gave me a glimpse of life in Russia in 1991–1992. Another important resource was Alan Bookbinder, Olivia Lichtenstein, and Richard Denton's *Comrades: Portraits of Soviet Life* (New York: New American Library, 1985). For background on the Soviet sports system I relied on James Riordan's substantial body of work; particularly valuable were *Soviet Sport: Background to the Olympics* (New York: NYU Press, 1980) and *Sports in Soviet Society* (Cambridge: Cambridge University Press, 1977). Robert Edelman's *Serious Fun: A History of Spectator Sports in the USSR* (New York: Oxford University Press, 1993), George Feifer's *Red Files: Secrets from the Russian*

Archives (New York: TV Books, 2000), and Henry Morton's *Soviet Sports: Mirror of Soviet Society* (New York: Columbia University Press, 1963) also illuminated the Soviet sports system. Yekaterina Gordeyeva's *My Sergei: A Love Story* (New York: Warner Books, 1996) provided background on the Moscow skating scene in the eighties.

Some descriptions of Berezhnaya's partnership with Shlyakhov come from CBS and ABC television interviews with Berezhnaya, Sikharulidze, Moskvina, and Shlyakhov after the accident, 1997–1998.

38 *Gordeyeva had been miserable here:* See Yekaterina Gordeyeva with E. M. Swift, *My Sergei: A Love Story.* New York: Warner Books, 1996.

43 *The Bolsheviks called ballet a "hothouse flower":* Quoted in Eleanor Randolph, *Waking the Tempests: Ordinary Life in the New Russia.* New York: Simon & Schuster, 1996, p. 265.

44 *"His aggressiveness":* CBS interview with Yelena Berezhnaya, fall 1997.

44 *"I didn't tell her anything":* CBS interview with Yelena Berezhnaya, fall 1997.

47 *the beginning of their romantic relationship:* CBS interview with Shlyakhov, February 1998. The same interview was described by Philip Hersh, "Intrigue Dogs Pair Skaters After Split," *Chicago Tribune,* February 8, 1998, p. C-8. In the interview transcript Shlyakhov, asked to respond to Berezhnaya's claim that he hit and kicked her, replies, "I can only answer in one way—what happened between us was strictly our own business."

47 *"a kind of pretty packaging that could be presented":* CBS interview with Oleg Shlyakhov, February 1998.

50 *"It's only when a person doesn't know how":* Quoted in Igor Logvinov, "It's Easier to Skate Alone," *St. Petersburg Journal,* March 1992.

51 *"We used to hate it":* Quotes from Moskvina's former students come from author's interviews with Yelena Bechke, Artur Dmitriev, Yelena Valova, Oleg Vasiliev, and Irina Vorobieva.

57 *featured in a Soviet propaganda newsreel:* See *Around the Soviet Union,* #55, 1969, Russian State Archive at Krasnogorsk.

64 *"Sometimes I lost control":* CBS interview with Anton Sikharulidze, fall 1997.

64 *"Truthfully speaking":* CBS interview with Tamara Moskvina, fall 1997.

65 *"It was obvious":* CBS interview with Anton Sikharulidze, fall 1997.

65 *"At first it was only this feeling":* CBS interview with Anton Sikharulidze, fall 1997.

66 *"At the beginning":* CBS interview with Tamara Moskvina, fall 1997.

66 *"If I missed a jump":* CBS interview with Yelena Berezhnaya, fall 1997.

67 *"My reaction":* CBS interview with Anton Sikharulidze, fall 1997.

68 *"I said to her, don't be a victim":* CBS interview with Tamara Moskvina, fall 1997.

69 *"So finally I asked him":* CBS interview with Tamara Moskvina, fall 1997.

69   *"his behavior was outrageous"*: Quoted in Igor Antonov, "The Blood of the Skater Which Melted the Ice," in *The World of Science and Figure Skating*. Moscow: Lemontov Foundation, 2002.

69   *"This plan is to let Oleg be relaxed"*: CBS interview with Tamara Moskvina, fall 1997.

70   *"I didn't want to leave"*: CBS interview with Yelena Berezhnaya, fall 1997.

70   *"She said a lot of things that night"*: CBS interview with Anton Sikharulidze, fall 1997.

70   *"We were in Riga"*: ABC interview with Yelena Berezhnaya, December 1996.

71   *"I felt a jolt"*: CBS interview with Oleg Shlyakhov, February 1998.

71   *"They put me under"*: CBS interview with Yelena Berezhnaya, fall 1997; ABC interview with Yelena Berezhnaya, December 1996.

72   *"I was scared to death"*: CBS interview with Tamara Moskvina, fall 1997; also quoted in Jere Longman, "For Berezhnaya, a Total Comeback from a Gruesome Mishap," *The New York Times,* December 22, 1997.

72   *"Oleg would come in"*: ABC interview with Yelena Berezhnaya, fall 1997.

73   *"she needed human care"*: CBS interview with Tamara Moskvina, fall 1997.

73   *"This was brain damage"*: CBS interview with Tamara Moskvina, fall 1997.

73   she *"couldn't think about anything"*: ABC interview with Yelena Berezhnaya, December 1996.

73   *"they didn't give me the mirror"*: Quoted in Igor Antonov, "The Blood of the Skater Which Melted the Ice," in *The World of Science and Figure Skating*. Moscow: Lemontov Foundation, 2002.

74   *"Hold on to your chair"*: Exchange between Moskvina and Sikharulidze from CBS interviews, fall 1997.

75   *"I was going to Riga"*: CBS interview with Anton Sikharulidze, fall 1997.

75   *"Why did I rush to the train station?"*: Quoted in *"Yelena Berezhnaya y Anton Sikharulidze: Ledovyi Roman,"* Gorodskoy Dilizhans, August 22, 2002.

75   *"And the whole time"*: Quoted in *"Yelena Berezhnaya y Anton Sikharulidze: Ledovyi Roman,"* Gorodskoy Dilizhans, August 22, 2002.

76   *"We kept everything secret"*: CBS interview with Anton Sikharulidze, fall 1997.

76   *"It was on the train"*: CBS interview with Anton Sikharulidze, fall 1997.

76   *"I went to the railway station"*: CBS interview with Tamara Moskvina, fall 1997.

77   *"This was like very sad and emotional moment"*: CBS interview with Tamara Moskvina, fall 1997.

77   *"Listen, this is a person"*: CBS interview with Tamara Moskvina, fall 1997.

78   *"I was responsible for the life of a child"*: ABC interview with Tamara Moskvina, December 1996; CBS interview with Tamara Moskvina, fall 1997.

78   *"Why she's so unlucky"*: CBS interview with Tamara Moskvina, fall 1997.

79   *"as if I were returning from somewhere"*: ABC interview with Yelena Berezhnaya, December 1996.

CHAPTER TWO

For general background on China I am indebted to the work of Jasper Becker, especially *The Chinese* (New York: Free Press, 2000) and *Hungry Ghosts: Mao's Secret Famine* (New York: Henry Holt, 1996). Jung Chang's *Wild Swans: Three Daughters of China* (New York: Simon & Schuster, 1991) was a powerful source of information about women's lives. Jan Wong's *Red China Blues* (New York: Anchor Books, 1996) provided a Western perspective on recent Chinese history. Nicolas D. Kristof and Sheryl WuDunn's *China Wakes* (New York: Times Books, 1994) provided important context on contemporary China.

For background on sports in China several books were helpful, including James Riordan and Robin Jones's anthology *Sport and Physical Education in China* (London: E & FN Spon, 1999) and Susan Brownell's *Training the Body for China* (Chicago: University of Chicago Press, 1995). Two books by Jonathan Kolatch were informative: *Sports, Politics, and Ideology in China* (New York: Jonathan David Publishers, 1972) and *Is the Moon in China Just as Round? Sporting Life and Sundry Scenes* (New York: Jonathan David Publishers, 1992).

85   *a Harbin reporter who has known the Shens:* Zhang Yongde of Photo World Harbin.

102 *"At that moment":* Quoted in "Zhao Hongbo Through the Eyes of His Mother," *Harbin Radio & TV Weekly,* March 24, 2002.

105 *thirty million starved:* Facts and figures about the famine era come from Jasper Becker, *The Chinese* (New York: Free Press, 2000) and *Hungry Ghosts: Mao's Secret Famine* (New York: Henry Holt, 1996).

106 *In Harbin big character posters:* The history of the Harbin figure skating team during the Cultural Revolution comes from author's interviews with sources who have requested anonymity.

CHAPTER THREE

For general background on Canada I am indebted to Jan Morris's *O Canada* (New York: HarperCollins, 1990) and Robert Bothwell's *A Traveler's History of Canada* (London: Cassell & Co., 2001). Debbi Wilkes's *Ice Time* (Scarborough, Ontario: Prentice Hall Canada, 1994) was an invaluable resource on the past forty years of figure skating in Canada.

157 Information about the building of the memorial rinks and skating's aristocratic heritage comes from Debbi Wilkes's *Ice Time.*

CHAPTER FOUR

169 *"Smile! Show more!":* ABC interview with Tamara Moskvina, January 1999.

173 *"No matter if it's the coach or the athletes":* Quoted in Yu Jing, "Teacher and Students on the Ice," *Radio & Television Weekly,* April 2000.

174 *"Normally athletes try to avoid"*: Quoted in Zhao Haiqing, "The Story of Shen Xue, Zhao Hongbo, and Their Coach Yao Bin, Who Just Won the ISU Grand Prix Final," *Radio and Television Weekly,* March 1999.

175 *"They're no joint venture"*: Quoted in Zhao Haiqing, "The Story of Shen Xue, Zhao Hongbo, and Their Coach Yao Bin, Who Just Won the ISU Grand Prix Final," *Radio and Television Weekly,* March 1999.

176 *"There is a saying"*: Quoted in "Yao Bin's diary of Nagano," *Harbin Daily,* March 1998.

178 *On the morning of the 1998 Olympic final:* The account of Chinese experience in Nagano is based on "Yao Bin's diary of Nagano," *Harbin Daily,* March 1998.

182 *"I can remember going to regionals"*: NBC interview with Jamie Salé, February 2002.

186 *"On the first double Axel"*: Quoted in Zhao Haiqing, "The Story of Shen Xue, Zhao Hongbo, and Their Coach Yao Bin, Who Just Won the ISU Grand Prix Final," *Radio and Television Weekly,* March 1999.

191 *The last time a judge had tried to turn in another judge:* Hours before the finals of the 1998 Olympic ice dancing competition, Canadian judge Jean Senft tape-recorded a phone call made to her hotel room by Ukrainian judge Yuri Balkov. On the tape, Balkov distinctly says: "My opinion: three Canada, four Averbukh [Russian team], five France. You understand me?" Senft replies: "Yes." Balkov continues: "And the same opinion, Lithuanian and Czech [judges]." At an ISU hearing in Geneva in September 1999, an appeals commission heard evidence from Senft and Balkov and played the tape. The commission suspended both for misconduct, stating that Senft had also behaved improperly. Senft was suspended for six months, Balkov for one year. Senft has said of the ruling: "It doesn't make any sense. If I was part of the misconduct, why would I bring it forward?" Balkov again judged the Olympic ice dance event in 2002.

192 *At least three of the dismissed French judges:* Francis Betsch, Alain Miquel, and Gilles Vandenbroeck, all former French judges, have made public claims against Didier Gailhaguet. All three have written letters to the ISU and their allegations have been published in the American and French press. All three say that Gailhaguet told them to overmark certain skaters and undermark others. Francis Betsch forwarded the ISU two letters he had received from Gailhaguet in which Gailhaguet, then the French team leader, had written to top French judges, asking them to meet with him on the eve of the 1994 Olympics to develop a "conquering strategy" to give France "political influence" at upcoming events. See, for instance, Amy Shipley, "Skating Judge Alleges More Misconduct," *The Washington Post,* April 9, 2002, p. D-1; Amy Shipley, "Second Skate Judge Alleges Misconduct; French Federation President Accused," *The Washington Post,* April 17, 2002, p. D-1; Stephen Wilson, "French Judges Speak Out Against Federation Chief," Associated Press, April 18, 2002; Vicki Michaelis,

"Gailhaguet Wields Great Power in France," *USA Today,* April 30, 2002, p. 9C; CBS News, *60 Minutes,* April 28, 2002; CBC News, *The National,* April 26, 2002. In one publicized instance, French ice dancers Marina Anissina and Gwendal Peizerat sent a letter to the French federation a month before the 1998 Olympics, asking Gailhaguet's predecessor to assign a specific judge, Jean-Bernard Hamel, to the ice dance panel as a last-minute replacement. "Unfortunately," the skaters wrote, "the results do not come only from the performance, so the work and courage of Mr. Jean-Bernard Hamel as a judge at the Grand Prix Final was very helpful. . . . Mr. Hamel started a very important political work that all specialists of our sport shall recognize as indispensable to get a medal for France in ice dancing." Hamel was assigned to the event. Gailhaguet, who was assuming the presidency at the time, said that the decision was made (not by him) for reasons other than the letter. After Hamel was sent to the Olympics, Gilles Vandenbroeck sent a letter to French skating officials accusing Gailhaguet of "pressuring the skaters and pressuring the judges." Gailhaguet sued Vandenbroeck for libel in France and won on appeal; he was awarded one franc. See Amy Shipley, "Skating Judge Alleges More Misconduct; Former French Official Accuses Federation Head of Attempting to Manipulate Voting," *The Washington Post,* August 5, 2002.

194   *She moved to Montreal "with basically nothing":* CTV interview with Jamie Salé, January 1999.

197   *"When I got to Richard":* CTV interview with David Pelletier, January 1999.

198   *"bad ice and we skate":* ABC interview with Tamara Moskvina, February 1999.

199   *"We'll learn the business approach":* ABC interview with Tamara Moskvina, February 1999.

202   *"I think you can tell my character":* Quoted in "I Did Not Discuss with Lena About Our Future Marriage," *St. Petersburg Chas Pik,* August 31, 2001.

206   *"A lot of people put their soul into this":* NTV interview with Yelena Berezhnaya, December 2000.

210   *"After two years in U.S.":* Quoted in Edward Dvorkin, "It Will Be Hard on Olympiad," *St. Petersburg Chas Pik,* August 23, 2001.

212   *"In the Olympic season":* Quoted in Alina Ruchinskaya, "For the Sake of the Judges We Should Kiss Each Other," *St. Petersburg Sport-Express,* August 22, 2001.

213   *"Is it our facial expressions?":* Quoted in Wei Ming, "Yao Angry with Judges," *Sports News,* March 21, 2001.

215   *"to the point that he didn't want to sleep":* Quoted in Yu Jing, "Teacher and Students on the Ice," *Sports News,* April 2000.

216   *"I hope that the person who took my medals":* Quoted in Zhao Haiqing, "The Story of Shen Xue, Zhao Hongbo, and Their Coach Yao Bin, Who Just Won the ISU Grand Prix Final," *Radio and Television Weekly,* March 1999.

217 *As one Chinese editorial put it:* See Zhang Shu-zhen and Liu Jing-yan, "The Story of Shen Xue and Zhao Hongbo," *Photo World,* November 2001.

218 *"I don't believe in fate":* Quoted in Li Xiaoman, *"Turandot* on the Ice," *Life Newspaper,* May 20, 2001.

CHAPTER FIVE

Information about the pairs' final comes from American, Canadian, French Canadian, Chinese, and Russian broadcasts of the event. Irina Rodnina's quotes are from the ORT broadcast of the event; Alain Goldberg and Barb Underhill's quotes come from the CBC's two broadcasts of the event.

227 *"She has been on the border":* Tamara Moskvina at a press conference in Minneapolis, April 1, 1998.

230 *"We're friends and that's it":* Quoted in Igor Popov, "Interview with Anton Sikharulidze," *The Russia Journal,* March 29, 1999.

243 *"Holding hands":* Zhang Shu-zhen and Liu Jing-yan, "The Story of Shen Xue and Zhao Hongbo," *Photo World,* November 2001.

244 *"Nobody ever dared to try":* Quoted in "Shen Xue and Zhao Hongbo Did Not Succeed in Capturing the Winter Olympics Pair Skating Gold: The Coach and the Students Talk About the Quadruple Throw Jump," *Radio & Television Weekly,* February 17, 2002.

245 *"Sometimes," she tells a reporter:* CBC interview with Jamie Salé, February 11, 2002.

247 *"In front of the Five-Dragon Pavilions":* Pang Rongsheng recorded this in *Dijing Suishiji* (Seasonal Records of the Capital) during the reign of Ch'ien-Lung. Quoted in Wu Wengchung, *Selections of Historical Literature and Illustrations of Physical Activities in Chinese Culture.* Taiwan, ROC: Hanwen Bookstore, 1975.

250 *"Sweat and tears":* Lifetime interview with Jamie Salé, December 2002.

251 *one choreographer says:* Author's interview with Susie Wynne.

CHAPTER SIX

Quotes in this chapter come primarily from the author's interviews and the following two sources: sworn statements given by witnesses to the ISU's investigators in Salt Lake City in February 2002, and the transcript of the ISU's "Disciplinary Inquiry in the Matter of Marie-Reine Le Gougne and Didier Gailhaguet," April 29–30, 2002, Lausanne, Switzerland.

In addition, see Marie-Reine Le Gougne's *Glissades à Salt Lake City.* Paris: Editions Ramsas, 2002.

255 *"I've already promised my good friend":* Le Gougne, in her statements, has acknowledged having the conversation with Lavoie and repeated many similar phrases, but she denies ever telling him that she had promised Marina Sanaya to

vote with her. However, Christine Blanc of Switzerland, who also was present for the conversation, corroborated Lavoie's version in a letter to the ISU and at the ISU hearing in Lausanne in April 2002.

255 *"it's going to be very hard for your team to win":* In his statements to the ISU Gailhaguet acknowledged having a similar conversation with Lavoie at the same time and place. But according to Gailhaguet the conversation was purely about how close the pairs event would be.

256 *A key part of the plan:* The plan is fully described in Robert Russo, "Backstage Intrigue Helped Canadian Pair Wrench Gold Medal from IOC," *The Canadian Press,* February 17, 2002.

257 *American television wants an interview:* NBC interview with Berezhnaya and Sikharulidze, February 11, 2002.

261 *letter is a high-handed guilt trip:* Pfenning read his letter into the record at the ISU hearing in Lausanne, April 29–30, 2002.

265 *She is known for being passionate about skating:* According to a report published in *The Washington Post,* an ISU official stated that Le Gougne had received three ISU letters of reprimand during her career: one for bias and errors at two events in 1990–1991, another for giving Candeloro a perfect six that was deemed excessive at the 1998 Winter Games, and a third for bias and errors related to the 2000 Europeans and Worlds. See Amy Shipley, "Second Skate Judge Alleges Misconduct; French Federation President Accused," *The Washington Post,* April 17, 2002, p. D-1.

265 *But Candeloro's own take:* Quoted in an interview with *France Soir,* February 15, 2002.

266 *Katsuichiro Hisanaga, openly told a reporter:* Quoted in Steve Wilstein, "French Skate Chief Accused," Associated Press, February 18, 2002.

266 *one judge, Alain Miquel:* Quoted in Amy Shipley, "Second Skate Judge Alleges Misconduct; French Federation President Accused," *The Washington Post,* April 17, 2002, p. D-1.

266 *Another judge, Francis Betsch, told a reporter:* See Vicki Michaelis, "Gailhaguet Wields Great Power in France," *USA Today,* April 30, 2002, p. 9C.

266 *showed that Gailhaguet's judges:* Reported by Alexander Lakernik, presently chair of the ISU Technical Committee, at the ISU hearing in Lausanne, April 29–30, 2002. Lakernik conducts statistical research for the ISU.

271 *Marie-Odile Devillers:* According to documents prepared by Le Gougne's legal team, Devillers gave a statement to the ISU in Salt Lake City on February 17, 2002. Although she was invited, she declined to attend the hearing in Lausanne.

271 *The New York Times had reported:* See Jere Longman, "Scrutiny Has Judges Feeling Unsettled," *The New York Times,* February 15, 2002.

271 *she further accused Lavoie:* Lavoie denied the allegation at the hearing in Lausanne and elsewhere.

273 *"I will explain how it functions"*: Quoted in Christopher Clarey, "Two French Officials Suspended Three Years in Skating Scandal," *The New York Times,* May 1, 2002, p. A1.

273 *"If Mr. Cinquanta thinks he's protected"*: Marie-Reine Le Gougne and Didier Gailhaguet quoted in Christopher Clarey, "Two French Officials Suspended Three Years in Skating Scandal," *The New York Times,* May 1, 2002, p. A1.

273 *"served as a gesture of appeasement"*: Quoted in "Disgraced French Skating Chief Tries to Mend Ties," Associated Press, July 5, 2002.

274 Facts about the Tokhtakhounov case come from the unsealed complaint *United States of America* versus *Alimzhan Tokhtakhounov,* filed by William McCausland of the FBI in the Southern District of New York on July 22, 2002. For Italian wiretap transcripts, see "Excerpts from Alleged Fix," Associated Press, August 2, 2002; Andrew Dampf, "More Wiretap Transcripts of Alleged Olympic Fixer," Associated Press, August 9, 2002.

274 *according to the FBI, Gailhaguet admitted:* In a statement on August 2, 2002, Gailhaguet declared that he and the French federation "had no relation, no contact directly or indirectly, either before, during or after the Olympic Games with Mr. Tokhtakhounov, concerning the events in question." He did, however, acknowledge a meeting in the spring of 2000 with Tokhtakhounov, in which they discussed a donation for a professional ice hockey team in Paris. Gailhaguet also confirmed that Tokhtakhounov requested his help with a visa extension. According to an interview published in the French newspaper *Le Figaro* (August 9, 2002), Gailhaguet directly contradicted the FBI's complaint and stated that the FBI agent in Salt Lake City never asked him about Tokhtakhounov. In the same interview, Gailhaguet said, "To seek [Tokhtakhounov's] extradition, a complaint needed to be lodged on American territory. Today, I wonder if the affair started in Salt Lake wasn't orchestrated for that purpose." The FBI flatly denied the allegation. See "French Skating Chief Thinks FBI May Have Orchestrated Scandal," Associated Press, August 9, 2002.

275 *Marina Anissina . . . the Olympic gold:* On August 5, 2002, Marina Anissina admitted that she knew Tokhtakhounov as a "friend" and that they "spoke on the telephone from time to time. But I never asked him for anything. I never telephoned him (after the Olympics). I am sure that that is not my voice." In regard to the tapes, Anissina said, "It's known what it is to cut up music and to make a montage. So maybe these transcripts are fakes. In any case, that is not my voice." Anissina later admitted that she and her mother vacationed with Tokhtakhounov and his daughter in Italy. She also told a Russian interviewer in August 2002 that "it's true that I did have a conversation about this story with Didier Gailhaguet on the plane, when we were coming back to France. He was called up by the FBI and asked questions where, in particular, the name Tokhtakhounov was mentioned. So he advised me to be more careful about choosing

my friends." See John Tagliabue, "Transcripts Suggest Ice Dancer Knew of Fix," *The New York Times,* August 11, 2002; Samuel Petrequin, "French Skater Admits Contact," Associated Press, August 5, 2002; Lyudmila Garsheri, "Alec and I Were Vacationing in Italy," *Newsworld,* August 27, 2002.

277 See Marie-Reine Le Gougne, *Glissades à Salt Lake City.* Paris: Editions Ramsay, 2002.

279 *the Italian Supreme Court:* On June 16, 2003, Alimzhan Tokhtakhounov appealed his extradition to the Corte Suprema di Cassazione in Rome and won. The court ordered his immediate release, stating that the charges against him were not adequate to warrant extradition. According to the treaty between the United States and Italy, a suspect can be extradited only if his alleged crime is punishable under Italian law by a sentence of "greater than one year." The court ruled that of the FBI's five charges against Tokhtakhounov (conspiracy to commit wire fraud, bribery conspiracy, wire fraud, bribery in sporting contests, and travel act violations), only one could legitimately be prosecuted under the Italian criminal code: bribery in a sporting contest. However, in Italy, the crime of fraud in a sporting competition carries a maximum sentence of one year—thus falling short of the standard necessary for extradition ("greater than one year"). This was the reasoning the Italian court gave for releasing Tokhtakhounov. According to FBI spokesmen, the case remains active, and should Tokhtakhounov be arrested in another country, he could again face extradition to the United States. (For the decision, see the sixth criminal session of the Corte Suprema di Cassazione, Rome, sentence number 1267, general register number 8060/03, document number 28959/03, June 16, 2003.)

ACKNOWLEDGMENTS

This book would not have been possible without the extraordinary contributions of hundreds of people all over the world, who shared their stories, expertise, photographs, and documents with me. It is only because of their generosity that this book exists.

I am especially moved by the courage of several Chinese sources in sharing their memories of the fifties, sixties, and seventies with me. This period in history is still sensitive in China, and I am not at liberty to thank some Chinese sources by name, but I am deeply grateful to them.

The skaters themselves, and their families, were enormously patient and open with me, and I will always be grateful to them for entrusting me with their stories. My deepest thanks go to Yelena and Tatyana Berezhnaya; Anton, Tariel, and Lyudmila Sikharulidze; Shen Jie, Shen Xue, and Lu Manli; Zhao Hongbo, Zhao Huanzhi, and Jing Yulan; David, Jacques, Mathieu, and Martin Pelletier, and Murielle Bouchard; and Jamie and Patti Salé.

My debt to the coaches is also enormous. Many thanks to Tamara Moskvina, Yao Bin, and Jan Ullmark, who welcomed me into their training centers and answered my endless questions.

My interpreters were true collaborators in the writing of this book, especially Bai Ruoyun and Yelena Siyanko. My heartfelt thanks to them and to my other interpreters at home and abroad: Roxana Kandrikina, Nicolas Girard, Zhang Jianhua, Cao Jun, and Liu Chang.

While researching Russia many people were very good to me, namely Tamara Moskvina, Olga and Tatyana Bratus, Tariel and Lyudmila Sikharulidze, and Tatyana Berezhnaya. In China I am grateful to Yin Zhimin of the Chinese Skating Association, who helped to make all the necessary arrangements, and to the families of Shen Xue and Zhao Hongbo, who showed me such warm hospitality. In Canada, Bob Steadward was a great help. My sincere thanks to Murielle Bouchard and Jacques

Pelletier for their generosity and patience, and to Patti Salé and Jan Ullmark for their great kindness to me.

My broadcasting colleagues taught me so much. At ABC, I was so lucky to be able to learn on the job from Terry Gannon, Peter Carruthers, and the inimitable Dick Button. Special thanks to Peggy Fleming and Jean Hall for their tremendous support, and for hosting me during the Olympics. Susie Wynne educated me at countless early-morning practices over the years and shared her expertise so generously. Beyond ABC, Draggan Mihailovich, Barb Strain, and Debbi Wilkes were wonderful to me, and I must especially thank Tracy Wilson for her support of this project.

At ABC Sports, I had the best possible opportunity to learn the sport of figure skating. Thanks to Curt Gowdy, Jr.; Kathy Cook; Victor Vitarelli; Doug Wilson; Lana Sherman; Kimberly Molloy; Stu Hothem; Ben Keeperman; Alyssa Litoff; and especially Lee Ann Gschwind and Laura Leitner.

For patiently explaining the biomechanics of pair skating to me, I must thank Dr. Deborah King of Ithaca College. Peter Carruthers and John Zimmerman gave hours of their time to educate me on the finer points of their sport. For their help in tracking the Tokhtakhounov story, thanks to Andrew Dampf of the Associated Press and Joe Valiquette and Jim Margolin of the FBI.

For their able assistance in finding even the most obscure footage, I am immensely grateful to Glenn Morris and Stacy Adduci of the NBC Olympic Archive; Yelena Kolikova of the Russian State Archive at Krasnogorsk; Varvara Ignatova of NTV; Angela Steele and Barb Strain of CTV; Rosaleen Kaye; Mark Mitchell; Meg Streeter; Dick Buffinton; Joan, Lana, and Keith Sherman; Yin Zhimin; Murielle Bouchard; and Patti Salé. For their brilliant photographs, I am grateful to Dave Black, Jerzy Bukajlo, Andrey Chepakin, Yin Nan, and Graham Maunder.

My agent, Heather Schroder, at ICM immediately embraced this book and put her wonderful energy behind it—no thanks are enough for her. At Simon & Schuster, I am immensely grateful to Jeff Neuman; David Rosenthal; and especially Marysue Rucci, my editor, for their unwavering support. Thanks, too, to Christine Rikkers at ICM and Tara Parsons at Simon & Schuster for all the help along the way.

Many dear friends gave comments on drafts. Thanks to Ann Eddins, Carol Goodwin, Jane Gray, Lee Ann Gschwind, Bonnie Molnar, Lana Sherman, and Jude Stewart; their questions and ideas made this a far better book. I must especially thank Jessica Lissy, who is the most wonderful reader a writer could ask for. Her insights transformed this book, and her love for the story was a great source of inspiration to me.

Tom was the first to believe in this book and the staunchest supporter of it. To him and to my family, who have encouraged me from the beginning, love and gratitude.

INDEX

Index

ABOUT THE AUTHOR

JOY GOODWIN is an Emmy Award–winning writer and producer. Since 1999, she has covered figure skating for ABC Sports. She holds a master's degree in public policy from Harvard University. *The Second Mark* is her first book. She lives in New York City.